THE GENDER DIMENSION OF SOCIAL CHANGE

The contribution of dynamic research to the study of women's life courses

Edited by Elisabetta Ruspini and Angela Dale

The POLICY

PRESS

First published in Great Britain in May 2002 by

The Policy Press
34 Tyndall's Park Road
Bristol BS8 1PY
UK

Tel +44 (0)117 954 6800
Fax +44 (0)117 973 7308
e-mail tpp@bristol.ac.uk
www.policypress.org.uk

British Library Cataloguing in Publication Data
A catalogue record for this book is available from the British Library

ISBN 1 86134 332 9

Elisabetta Ruspini is Lecturer in Social Research at the University of Milano-Bicocca, Italy and **Angela Dale** is Professor of Quantitative Social Research at the University of Manchester, UK.

Cover design by Qube Design Associates, Bristol.
Front cover: photograph kindly provided by Mark Simmons Photography, Bristol.

Printed and bound in Great Britain by Bell & Bain Ltd, Glasgow

Contents

List of tables and figures

Tables

Figures

Notes on contributors

Angela Dale is Professor of Quantitative Social Research at the University of Manchester and Director of the Cathie Marsh Centre for Census and Survey Research.

Hugh Davies died, of lung cancer, in October 2000, aged 52, shortly after the paper that the contribution to this volume is based on was presented in Cologne. He contributed to its drafting up to his final week. He was a Senior Lecturer in Economics, Birkbeck College, University of London, where he had worked for 25 years. His interests included family economics, income distribution and pensions. He produced a number of publications based on simulations of lifetime incomes, pensions and divorce, gender and income distribution, income distribution within couples, the domestic division of labour, the economics of childcare, and the estimation of wage, hours and participation functions in data from the British Household Panel Study. Most of this work was done jointly with Heather Joshi, who had been one of his many students. He is sadly missed.

Caroline Dewilde is a PhD student at UFSIA, Research Group on Poverty, Social Exclusion and the City (OASeS), University of Antwerp. She is also associated with the Panel Study on Belgian Households (PSBH) at UIA, University of Antwerp. The main topic of her PhD is the study of poverty dynamics within a life course framework, with special attention for cross-national variations concerning cultural patterns, family structures and institutional arrangements.

Shirley Dex is currently a Principal Research Fellow at the Judge Institute of Management, University of Cambridge. She is the author of many books and learned articles on women's employment, flexible work and other labour market analyses.

Jane Elliott is a Lecturer in Sociology in the Department of Sociology, Social Policy and Social Work Studies at the University of Liverpool. Previously she worked as a Research Fellow at the Cathie Marsh Centre for Census and Survey Research at the University of Manchester.

Siv Gustafsson is Professor of Economics at the University of Amsterdam. She is a Fellow of the Tinbergen Institute. Her research interest is in population and gender economics. Recently she edited, with Daniele Meulders (Macmillan, 2000), *Gender and the labour market: Econometric evidence of obstacles to achieving gender equality*.

Heather Joshi is Professor of Economic Demography at the Institute of Education, London University, where she is Deputy Director of the Centre for Longitudinal Studies and the Lead Investigator in the ESRC Millennium Cohort Study. Many of her publications are analyses of longitudinal data on issues of gender, the family and health inequalities. Previous employment includes the Government Economic Service, London School of Hygiene, Birkbeck College and City University.

Eiko Kenjoh is doing her PhD research at the Department of Economics at the University of Amsterdam. Her current research focuses on fertility decisions, labour force transitions by new mothers and employment of women and men in non-standard work arrangements, using a country comparative perspective.

Karin Kurz is Assistant Professor at the University of Bielefeld, Germany. She studied Sociology at the Universities of Mannheim, Germany and Madison, WI, US. Her research and teaching interests are social inequality and the life course, quantitative methods and statistics. She is currently working on her habilitation on labour market insecurities and their effects on long-term commitments.

Elisabetta Ruspini has a PhD in Sociology and Social Research, and is a lecturer and researcher based in the Department of Sociology and Social Research at the University of Milano-Bicocca, Italy. Her research interests include the process of gender role developments; the gender dimension of poverty and the study of living conditions; the acquisition, allocation and expenditure of resources within the family; lone motherhood. Methodologically, her current research focuses on longitudinal research, the analysis of social change and gender issues in social research.

Colin Smith currently works in the British Government Economic Service. He was formerly a Research Fellow in the ESRC Centre for Business Research and the Geography Department at the University of Cambridge. He has carried out research on lone parents in the labour markets, television workers, flexible employment and business services.

Yayoi Sugihashi is a PhD student in the Cathie Marsh Centre for Census and Survey Research, University of Manchester. Her main fields of interest are the gender wage gap and gender statistics.

Cécile Wetzels is Senior Researcher at the TNO Institute for Applied Scientific Research in Delft, the Netherlands. In 2001 a revised version of her dissertation *Squeezing birth into working life* was published by Ashgate Publishing. Since 1994 her work has focused on the economics of fertility. She has recently analysed the position of Dutch women re-entering the labour market after a long career break, and has looked at how (potential) re-entrants in the labour market may be informed of labour market issues using new Information and Communication Technologies.

Acknowledgements

Many thanks to the Office of Official Publications of the European Community for permission to reproduce the Eurostat figures in the appendix. The editors would like to acknowledge the help provided by the participants at the session 'Engendering longitudinal data analysis: the contribution of dynamic research to the study of women's life courses', at the Fifth International Conference on Logic and Methodology: Social Science Methodology in the New Millennium. Their comments and hard work made this volume possible.

Glossary

Attrition
The measure of the degree of success in interviewing the same set of units (individuals, households, firms, etc) over time. Some units participate in the initial assessments but then drop out of the study: this poses the question of whether they are different in some important way from the ones who stayed with the study throughout.

Cohort
A group, or set of persons, who have experienced the same event-origin within a given interval of time: birth, first marriage, reaching the age-of-consent. If the distinguishing event is birth, one speaks of a birth cohort (or of a marriage, work, graduation, cohort, as the case may be). Thus, a cohort is closed against new entries because such entries are, by definition, impossible.

Cross-sectional data
Data recorded at one point in time only. Should be distinguished from cross-sectional surveys which may also collect retrospective data (Davies and Dale, 1994).

Diachronic relationship
A relationship which evolves over the course of time; the opposite of *synchronic*.

Episode
The period between two changes of state (for instance, from 'being employed' to 'being unemployed') is called an *episode*, *waiting time*, or *spell*. The change from one spell to another is commonly termed a *transition* or (terminal) *event* (Taris, 2000, p 95).

Event
A *transition*, from one discrete state to another, a passage which takes place at a specific point in time and which constitutes a radical departure from what came before the 'catalysing' event: for example, marriage, the birth of a child, starting work, divorce (Allison, 1984). Thus, an event can be defined as a change that gives an individual new status, that is different from the previous status the individual was in before the change took place. This definition of an event enables us to visualise events as transitions between statuses (Rajulton, 1999). The most important transitions (for example, the transition to adulthood) usually introduces a multiplicity of changes into individuals' lives (Billari, 1998). Also worklife, marriage and parenthood represent multiple, interlocking *trajectories*: each trajectory is marked by a sequence of states in which people move from one state to another (Elder, 1985). However, apparently similar transitions may assume a different significance depending

on the point at which they take place within a particular trajectory: going to university straight from school or after taking a few years out to work; having a child at the age of 20 or 40; being made redundant as a young adult and losing a job when middle-aged, with adolescent children to support (Olagnero and Saraceno, 1993).

Event history analysis (EHA)

The study of duration data – or rather of the time that elapsed before an event (which could be, for example, bereavement, a new marriage, the birth of a child, divorce). More precisely, EHA is the name given to a wide variety of statistical techniques for the analysis of longitudinal data (event history data) and for studying the movement over time (transitions) of subjects through successive states or conditions, including the length of the time intervals between entry to and exit from specific states (Blossfeld and Rohwer, 1995, p 33).

Event history or duration data

Data that offer a record of the events that have punctuated the life course of a group of subjects. Typically, this is done beginning with the current situation and taking respondents backwards in time, in order to retrospectively investigate the life of the subjects studied. Duration data are typically gathered using retrospective cross-sectional studies in which respondents are asked to remember events and aspects of their own life courses. Also, prospective studies can gather retrospective pieces of information through the use of calendars and/or suitable batteries of question.

Generation

Membership of a generation is usually defined as follows: being born within the same time period, undergoing certain, more or less similar, social, cultural and psychological experiences; being exposed to analogous primary and secondary socialisation processes (Gallino, 1993).

Gross change

Change at the individual level or the description of flows (gross changes) between states (for example, between employed to unemployed). This is essential for any study of mobility between states because it reveals the true extent of change.

Household Panel Studies (HPS)

Studies that involve collecting information on individuals and households on repeated occasions. HPS follow individuals and families over time by, periodically, re-interviewing the same subjects and providing multiple observations on each individual/household in the sample. The basic feature of the HPS design is the possibility of detecting and establishing the nature of individual change (gross change).

Life course

The history of each family or individual and the way this history evolves and changes over time. The life course is determined by interdependent *trajectories* and *transitions* that subjects (individual or collective - woman, man, couple, firm or organisation) undergo during the course of their lives. Trajectories refer to the path taken, as time goes on, within a specific sphere, for example, the family, work, income, which usually continues for a large part of the individual's life span. Transitions are fluctuations/changes within a trajectory; in other words, trajectories are characterised by the transitions, or changes, of social, economic and demographic interests which evolve in response to specific *events*.

Longitudinal data

Data collected during the observation of subjects, on a number of variables over time, and which present information about what happened to a set of units during a series of time points. In contrast, cross-sectional data refer to circumstances of respondents at one particular point in time.

Memory errors

Memory errors are non-deliberate errors in reporting of a behaviour, caused either by forgetting that the event occurred or misremembering some details of the event (Sudman and Bradburn, 1982). These errors occur during the retrieval of information from memory (for example, respondents may be unable to recall a particular item or tend to situate events in the wrong time period).

Net change

Change at the stock level or the *net effect* of all the changes. For example, a comparison between the incidence of poverty and the characteristics of the population below the poverty line at time t and at time $t-1$ or between the pool of employed and unemployed people in two different years.

Prospective studies

Studies that gather information about events even as they are taking place. The subjects are measured repeatedly on a number of variables relevant to the phenomenon of interest.

Reproductive work

All work related to the household and childcare.

Retrospective studies

Studies where subjects are asked to remember and to reconstruct aspects of their life course.

Trend studies

Repeated cross-sectional surveys (conducted at two or more occasions) on different samples or using a largely different sample.

Waves

The number of times a panel study is repeated.

Part I:
Introduction

ONE

Introduction

Elisabetta Ruspini and Angela Dale

This volume was developed from the Fifth International Conference on Logic and Methodology: Social Science Methodology in the New Millennium, Cologne, 3-6 October 2000, at which a session was organised by Elisabetta Ruspini 'Engendering longitudinal data analysis: the contribution of dynamic research to the study of women's life courses'. The session intended to explore the potential of longitudinal research as a powerful tool for appreciating the gender dimension of social life. The papers presented at the conference all used a longitudinal, gender-sensitive and comparative research approach; moreover, they all focused on issues where gender differences are central: employment, family changes, motherhood, poverty, social exclusion, income. Finally, they used a number of different longitudinal data sources: from repeated cross-sectional surveys to household panel studies, from cohort studies to retrospective interviews.

The topic of how to engender longitudinal analysis is of much interest and still largely unexplored: thus the editors collected the papers together in one volume, aimed at making explicit the importance of a longitudinal perspective in understanding gender differences and their evolution over time.

The gender dimension of social change is an innovative book – written for social scientists interested in the systematic empirical investigation of social change – which examines gender transformations from a comparative, international perspective and introduces the reader to dynamic research, demonstrating its contribution to the analysis of women's and men's life courses and public policy formulation. Another aim of the book is to provide new evidence for those interested in gender differences and in the gender dimension of social life, providing also a transparent account of the gender dimension of social inequality. Finally, the book is an invitation for those who wish to carry out their own research to launch their own longitudinal, gender-sensitive research project. While the level of statistical complexity varies between chapters, all authors have included a methods section aimed at giving a clear account of why they adopted a particular method, of its strengths and limitations, of the data requirements and of the statistical assumptions. In order to encourage the use of longitudinal data, we believe there is a strong need to exchange information between researchers and scientists, those who already perform longitudinal research, those who are approaching it, or those who would like to perform it but do not yet know how.

The volume opens with two chapters by Elisabetta Ruspini that set the context for subsequent empirical analyses. Chapter Two provides a discussion of social change, the forces that have shaped social change in the last century; the impact of this on women's lives and the role that women have played as actors in this change. This chapter provides the conceptual framework for the theoretical and policy discussions that are contained in the subsequent chapters that report empirical analyses.

Chapter Three provides a context for the longitudinal analysis that is a hallmark of the book. 'Longitudinal' is indeed a rather imprecise term; there are also many different methods that can be used to collect longitudinal data, which means that there are also many different types of research. Longitudinal data can be defined as data, gathered during the observation of subjects, on a number of variables over time. This definition implies the notion of repeated measurements: the observations are made on a certain number of occasions (van der Kamp and Bijleveld, 1998). In contrast, cross-sectional data refer to the circumstances of respondents at one particular point in time. Thus, the term 'longitudinal' refers to a particular type of relations between phenomena: the type which evolves over the course of time and is termed *diachronic*, the opposite of *synchronic*.

Part II begins by looking first at one important element of social change: *education*. The increase in women's employment is strongly related to a rise in educational attainment so that, in many countries, women have now overtaken men in terms of gaining university-level qualifications (see Figures 1.1 and 1.2). The link between higher qualifications and occupational attainment is well established and leads to a widening differential in women's earnings as well as an increase in the opportunity costs of having children. However, the economic effect of childbearing and childrearing is directly influenced by the presence or absence of a coherent set of policies designed to enable women to maintain their employment while having children and taking care of the family.

Figure 1.1: Percentage of the population that has completed tertiary education, by age group (1999): men

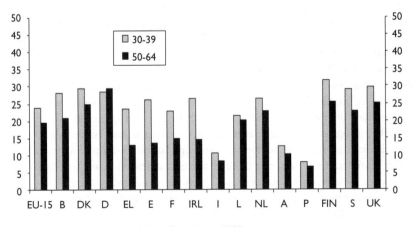

Source: Eurostat: European Union Labour Force Survey (1999)

Figure 1.2: Percentage of the population that has completed tertiary education, by age group (1999): women

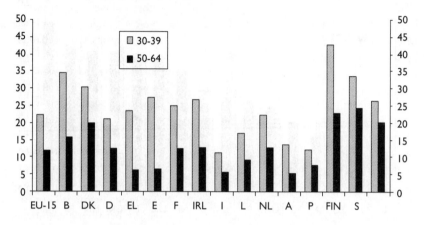

Source: Eurostat: European Union Labour Force Survey (1999)

Siv Gustafsson, Eiko Kenjoh and Cecile Wetzels pose this question in Chapter Four, which examines the role of education on the timing of childbearing in Britain, Germany, the Netherlands and Sweden. They start from the assumption that women will want to minimise the financial consequences of family formation. They find the smallest effects of education on the timing of maternity in Sweden and East Germany – both countries that provide considerable public support for maternal employment. By contrast the UK and the Netherlands showed the strongest effects of education and the greatest likelihood of childlessness – and are countries which have, traditionally, placed the responsibility for childcare firmly within the family and, by default, with mothers.

The narrative then touches on another important element of the gender dimension of change: the *family*. Family formation and dissolution are rapidly changing phenomena: these changes exert an impact on women's life course and life chances. It is evident from Figure 1.3 that in countries where women have great difficulty in reconciling continuity of employment with family formation and caring responsibilities, fertility is low and falling (Italy, Spain). However, for all women there are choices to be made over how and when to have children in relation to the impact that this is likely to have on both career and family living standards.

Heather Joshi and Hugh Davies (Chapter Six) demonstrate the effect, for the UK, of differences in levels of skill, or education, and number of children on the lifetime earnings of women in partnerships. Using simulated data for the earnings of couples, and making assumptions about gender roles, they show that women with higher skill levels are able to maintain levels of lifetime earnings approaching those of men – whether or not they have children – but that, at lower skill levels, women face very considerably lower lifetime earnings than men, particularly if they have children. This has serious implications for women's

Figure 1.3: Total fertility rate (1995-99)

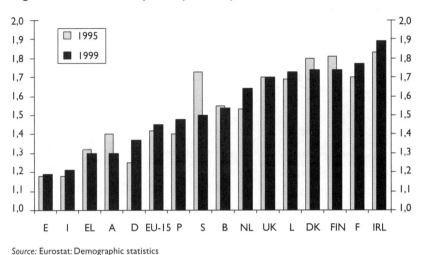

Source: Eurostat: Demographic statistics

financial well-being if they face marital dissolution. Again, figures for the European Union show that divorce rates have increased substantially over time but there remain very marked differences between EU member states (Figure 1.4).

The consequences of divorce on women's incomes are discussed by Caroline Dewilde (Chapter Five) who highlights women's vulnerability to partnership dissolution but also shows the macro-level, country-specific influences on outcomes. Dewilde shows that lone mothers' access to the labour market and the availability of welfare payments are the major factors in minimising the financial consequences of a relationship breakdown.

Figure 1.4: Proportion (%) of marriages dissolved by divorce in the 1980 marriage cohort

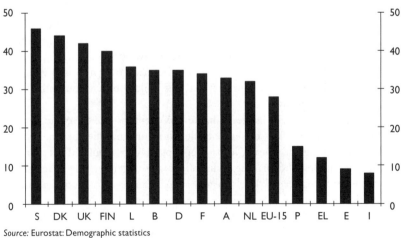

Source: Eurostat: Demographic statistics

Table 1.1: Employment rates (15-64 years) (1999)

	EU-15	B	DK	D	EL	E	F	IRL	I	L	NL	A	P	FIN	S	UK
Females	52.6	50.2	71.6	57.1	40.3	37.3	53.5	51.4	38.1	48.5	61.3	59.7	59.6	64.6	68.9	63.7
Males	71.6	67.5	81.2	72.4	71.6	67.8	67.5	73.6	67.1	74.4	80.3	76.7	75.7	70.2	72.1	76.9

Key: EU-15=European Union Member States/; B=Belgium; DK=Denmark; D=Germany; EL=Greece; E=Spain; F=France; IRL=Republic of Ireland; I=Italy; L=Luxembourg; NL=the Netherlands; A=Austria; P=Portugal; FIN=Finland; S=Sweden; UK=United Kingdom.

Source: Eurostat: European Union Labour Force Survey

Finally, the book looks at the relationship between women, change and *employment structure*. As mentioned earlier, in recent decades there has been an increase in women's employment across most Western industrialised countries. However, there are still differences between countries (see Table 1.1 and Figure 1.5) in the overall level of employment and the form that that employment takes. For example, Scandinavian countries still have considerably higher levels of women's employment than many other EU countries. There are also differences in the composition of employment (that is, the extent of full-time and part-time working). For example, the Netherlands, the UK, Denmark and Sweden have substantially higher levels of part-time working than most other countries (Figure 1.6). There are also differences in levels of temporary or short-term working and self-employment. These differences reflect historical and cultural differences between countries as well as different policies towards employment, the family and different welfare regimes.

In recent decades the changes in employment structure have been a response to increasing competition from global markets and attempts to minimise wage costs. The flexibility sought by employers has often been acquired by offering

Figure 1.5: Female employment rates (15-64 years) (1989 and 1999)

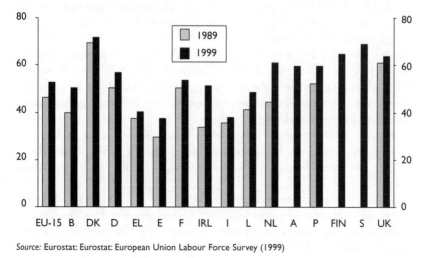

Source: Eurostat: Eurostat: European Union Labour Force Survey (1999)

Figure 1.6: Percentage of persons in employment working part time, by sex (1999)

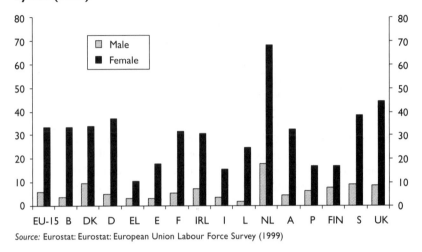

Source: Eurostat: Eurostat: European Union Labour Force Survey (1999)

temporary or short-term contracts to employees, which may lead to unemployment if contracts are not renewed. In Chapter Seven, Karin Kurz asks whether, in Germany, there are gender differences in who bears the costs of these changes. She looks at some of the factors that explain who takes fixed-term or precarious contracts as a first job and then whether men and women in these positions are more likely to face unemployment. She shows that the use of fixed-term contracts has increased for more recent cohorts of young people entering the labour market and that for unskilled and semi-skilled workers insecurity accumulates, with the risk of a fixed-term contract linked to a greater risk of unemployment. She also shows that, among these labour market entrants, who have not, generally, embarked on family formation, there are no marked gender differences. However, education and occupational position do not shield women to the same extent as men: at the same educational level or in the same occupational group women seem to face a higher unemployment risk than men.

Shirley Dex and Colin Smith (Chapter Eight) focus on the very specific restructuring that has occurred in the television industry in the UK, where there has been an abrupt move to self-employment and fierce competition between small production companies. They ask whether women have been disproportionately disadvantaged by these changes. Their analysis highlights the diversity of responses to these changes, with some people finding the increased insecurity very stressful while others actually found it liberating. However, the overriding commitment to working in television cuts across gender differences.

Questions about equality of earnings between men and women are addressed by Yayoi Sugihashi and Angela Dale (Chapter Nine) who compare the earnings of men and women in Japan and Britain. The size of the earnings gap is much greater for Japan than Britain. However, Japanese women in full-time work are disadvantaged in terms of both the characteristics that they bring to the labour market, for example, educational qualifications, and also the amount of remuneration which they receive. By contrast, in Britain the gender pay gap is much smaller; women working full time have slightly better qualifications than men and the pay gap is mainly due to gender discrimination.

In Chapter Ten, Jane Elliott seeks to examine how women's lives are represented in longitudinal surveys. She explores the importance of a dynamic perspective in women's lives and poses an important question: how can empirical analyses be conducted that illuminate gender differences and inequalities without simultaneously reifying the concept of gender. She argues the importance of avoiding assumptions about the category 'woman', for example, by conflating 'woman' with motherhood – a point of particular importance when considering the decreasing fertility levels across Europe. In the final section of her chapter Elliott asks us to look more carefully at how we ask questions, what data we collect and the assumptions which we build into the analysis in order to avoid misrepresenting women's life course trajectories.

A presentation of the most salient features of existing longitudinal files concludes the work in the Appendix.

Reference

van der Kamp, L.J.Th. and Bijleveld, C.C.J.H. (1998) 'Methodological issues in longitudinal research', in C.C.J.H. Bijleveld and L.J.Th. van der Kamp with A. Mooijaart, W.A. van der Kloot, R. van der Leeden and E. van der Burg, *Longitudinal data analysis, designs, models and methods,* London: Sage Publications, pp 1–45.

TWO

Women and social change

Elisabetta Ruspini

> Despite all these radical [social and economic] changes ... there has been
> relatively little change in two important social relationships ... the first is that
> of the continuing social inequality between women and men.

> The second sex is still precisely that: throughout the West, women have a
> lower level of professional education than men, they are paid less, have less
> social power, and are still assumed to have the primary ... responsibility for
> the care of children and dependent relatives. The 'new' woman remains just as
> much a fiction (or no doubt in some quarters a spectre) as the 'new' man....
> (Evans, 1994, pp 1-2)

The problematics of change have always occupied a central position in
sociological thought (Smelser, 1981; Haferkamp and Smelser, 1992), and the
modern social sciences have emerged in response to an era of very rapid social
change and the consequent need for greater understanding of social, economic
and political processes. Indeed, if one begins to study society only when it can
no longer be taken for granted, then change is a feature of social reality that
any social-scientific theory must sooner or later address.

We still live in a time of profound change, such as the transformation to a
knowledge-based society, globalisation, post-industrialisation, post-Fordism,
late-, reflexive-, or post-modernity, among others (see, for example, Bell, 1973;
Touraine, 1974; Giddens, 1990; Bauman, 1992; Beck, 1992). On a more individual
scale are welfare restructuring, the transformation of work patterns, population
ageing and dramatic family structure changes (Rose, 2000).

However, even if the analysis of social change represents the touchstone of
sociology, it remains underdeveloped (Wiswede and Kutsch, 1978). This may
be due to the combination of two elements, one theoretical and one
methodological. First is the difficulty of reconciling theories about social
change – developed at the macro-sociological level – with the results of empirical
analysis of the changing life course patterns of individuals. Second is the lack
of longitudinal information about the social-demographic characteristics of
both individuals and families (prospective longitudinal data on households
became available in the US in the 1970s, but only in the 1980s in Europe) and
of techniques designed to manipulate the diachronic or dynamic dimension of
data.

Of course, change is a highly complex process, involving many factors (including population change, cultural and political change, and changes in technology and material resources), all of which are interwoven and dependent upon each other. Indeed, macro-social and economic changes interact with the life courses of women, men and the family, producing changes at a micro-level. The particular aspects of social and economic change that intersect with individuals and family life courses are briefly reviewed below.

The family sphere

The most dramatic changes in a life course are portrayed in the family sphere. Family life course changes include: increased longevity; an increase in separation, divorce and non-marital unions; an increase in births out of wedlock, in lone parenthood and a decline in nuptiality. Associated with these changes is the weakening of kinship networks (related to both increasing individualism and falling birth-rates), and the erosion of the protective role of the nuclear family and the break-up of the older forms of solidarity upon which the post-war welfare states have depended. All these factors result in new and more complex relationships of obligation and exchange which may have an impact on the caring capacity of women and families (Millar, 1998), such as new and complex ties of love, care, obligation, duty and support across and between generations and households.

There is another – perhaps even more deeply unsettling issue – which relates to changes and conflicts *within* the family. Gender identities, and particularly women's roles, are undergoing tremendous change. The shifts in these identities can be a source of anxiety for both women and men. This relates to 'unwritten contracts between the sexes', in terms of the social construction of a system of exchanges, entitlements, and responsibilities allocated among members (women and men) of a household or family (Rogers, 1990), where households are defined on the basis of residence, while families are defined primarily by kinship. An example of this inter-family change relating to relationships between women and men, is the extent to which lone motherhood reflects a 'rejection' of men (Millar, 1998).

The labour market

Changes in the labour market have created a complex scenario, marked by a reduction in the number of opportunities for obtaining permanent job opportunities and by a parallel increase in flexibility. The various forms of flexibility include unemployment and marginal forms of employment (particularly for social groups such as women, immigrants or young people), a decline in lifetime occupations, and a shrinkage in permanent contract career ladders. Labour demand is shifting from permanent, full-time, male jobs in manufacturing industry to temporary, part-time, very low paid, female jobs in the service industry. Over the past two decades, labour demand has failed to keep pace with labour supply and long-term unemployment has increased among all groups in society but especially among those without relevant skills or with no skills. In addition, the extent of migrant labour has increased internationally.

The economic context

Dramatic changes are also occurring in economic contexts. Capital has become internationalised and industry now competes in a global market (particularly with the emergence of new competitors, notably in the Asian-Pacific region). Due to economic restructuring, the old locations of production are collapsing with increasing speed. There is a growing interdependence of markets and an increase in interactions and networks across national borders.

Welfare provisions

These changes are leading to new demands on welfare provision. They have created serious difficulties for social support systems, which had developed on the basis of different lifestyles, different forms of family organisation, marked and rigid diversity, and division between male and female gender roles. The industrial society was dominated by a process of institutionalisation and standardisation of the life course (Kohli, 1986; Mayer, 1991; Olagnero and Saraceno, 1993). Life course was a fairly persistent temporal pattern of transitions and sequence of activities with a high synchronic role segmentation: it was triangulated into education, work and retirement.

Women were allowed only to assume secondary roles in the labour market: welfare state capitalism was based on the full employment of men, a presumption of a nuclear family as the basis of social policy, social insurance oriented to male 'breadwinners', and state transfers to cover 'temporary interruptions of earning power'. However, the rigid patterns in the social organisation of the Fordist life course are now dissolving. What is here called a Fordist regime is an ideal construction, characterised by: predominance of manufacturing production; stability of employment and social insurance arrangements for the (male) breadwinner; long-term economic growth at high rates; expanding welfare expenditure; standardised life course; central role of nuclear family; average life-expectancy (Mingione, 1996). Fordism was also characterised by inequalities and tensions: as Morris (1996) discussed, the Fordist social regime was based on a very marked gender asymmetry to the disadvantage of women. Instead, we face a process of de-institutionalisation of the life course which favours the growth and transformation of poverty risks, for employment and the family are becoming less stable in protecting individuals from falling into poverty. Transformations in the labour market and within the family, and the relationships between these factors – together with the role of social policies (on work, family and income supplements) – are redesigning the mechanisms of production and reproduction of inequality and of vulnerability. There is, indeed, a growing tension between poverty and social exclusion and the system of citizenship, as it is not possible to rely on sufficiently high rates of economic growth or on stable employment to compensate for social exclusion and poverty.

Growth does not necessarily create new jobs and new investments in manufacturing may actually destroy jobs (Mingione, 1996, p 13).

Impacts on individuals and families

These transformations do not have the same impact either on the diverse groups which make up society or on the individuals within each family: some subjects – such as women – are more vulnerable (or vulnerable in a different way) than others. To give an example, families where the head of the household is a woman, often separated or divorced and with dependent children, are far more vulnerable to economic deprivation than families where the head of the household is a male or where an adult male is present. Indeed, lone motherhood has become one of the key groups for the analysis of gender and poverty. It is also true, however, that men are more affected than women by the deindustrialisation process that destroyed a large number of low qualified manual jobs and, in doing so, raised levels of male unemployment. Why do some individuals benefit from economic integration? How do women (and/or men) face the challenge of post-modernism in terms of opportunities and risks? Who controls the technological developments and infrastructure that underpin much globalising activity? Are men and women involved differently in new technologies? Can we talk about a polarisation process between groups of women, and if yes, why? These are some of the basic questions that must be asked.

If it is true that there are huge differences in levels of well-being between well qualified women and women in routine non-manual and manual work, it is also true that, in the case of women, it is not only educational and occupational qualifications that matters. Women's vulnerability to poverty is a result of a combination of economic and social factors that include the organisation of reproductive work within the household and the costs of being a primary carer (see Kurz, Chapter Seven in this volume). Indeed, the implications of globalisation, economic restructuring, and global structuration at the political, socio-economic and cultural levels vary among individuals. They are linked to the social construction and legitimisation of processes of dependency. That is, the assumption that men maintain the right to appropriate female time for housework, caring and maintenance; that children 'need their mothers'; that family, through the unpaid work of women, is the 'natural' main provider of welfare; that women are 'better carers'; that the female is dependent on the male/family income; that dependence on welfare provisions is 'bad' and therefore stigmatised, while private forms of dependencies are legitimised and socially accepted. As Giullari (2000) argues, the social construction of dependency that stigmatises public dependency, and fetishes private dependencies is embedded in current policy developments.

As a consequence, critical family events – such as lone parenthood, divorce or separation (particularly in the presence of children) – are stronger predictors of poverty transitions for women than for men because of the female economic dependence on a male breadwinner combined with caring responsibilities at home. Data from the Panel Study of Income Dynamics (Corcoran et al, 1984) show that a divorced mother in the US faces the double economic bind of assuming complete responsibility for her children's care while attempting to make up for lost income with small child support payments and poorly-paid wage labour. Burkhauser et al (1991) show that the same is true in Germany, and Jarvis and Jenkins (1998) found that marital splits in Great Britain are associated with substantial declines in real incomes for wives and children, whereas on average the real incomes of husbands changes much less. Fathers are at lower risk of an income decrease as they are more likely to have paid work after their partnership breaks down. As Elder (1985) argued, those not economically active or only partially active would experience these events primarily through change in the family environment, whereas breadwinners are more directly subject to economic, work-related and other social events. These tendencies are particularly relevant if connected with the 'remarriage gender gap'. While remarriage is one of the most important determinants of physical and economic well-being among divorced or widowed women, divorced men of any age usually have a higher likelihood of remarrying than women. While the proportion of remarriages in the total number of marriages is rising steadily in the EU, it is men (either widowed or divorced) who are more likely to remarry (Barbagli, 1990). Moreover, second marriages seem to be very unsteady among women: for example, divorced women who remarry in Great Britain are twice as likely to divorce than women who marry for the first time (Haskey, 1983, 1993).

Impacts on women's poverty

Indeed, the structural causes of women's poverty are to be found in the peculiar interaction between social change, social exclusion[1] and dependency/ interdependency processes within resource systems: family, labour and financial markets and welfare systems (Ruspini, 2000). Social change, social exclusion and dependency first interact in *the private domestic sphere*. The impact of poverty risks varies among women and over women's life courses, as it is linked to their responsibility for caring and domestic work: women draw income from men, the labour market and the welfare state in different proportions, according to the burden of caring responsibilities, time constrains, life chances and choices (Lewis, 1993; Scheiwe, 1994). Power within marriage and the family is directly related to the control of financial resources and to the degree of participation in the labour market. Generally speaking, husbands have more power than wives in the control of family resources (Pahl, 1989) because of their stronger relationship with the labour market and greater earning power. Therefore, women's access to information, economic resources, capacities and opportunities, are still mediated and limited by men, and by women's acceptance of domestic responsibilities. The economic and political invisibility of women caused by the 'inside-outside dichotomy' still exposes the vulnerability of women, as they have much weaker bargaining power than men in the economy and in the home. Studies on families below the poverty line found that women primarily bear the burden of the family's poverty, inasmuch as they have primary responsibility for managing scarce resources and often restrict their own consumption to ensure more for their families. Thus, the decline in the quality of life from poverty affects women more than men (Graham, 1987; Lee, 1999). Moreover, the passage (over the course of the past century) from a fairly standardised industrial society to a picture of instability and heterogeneity of family and work biographies have increased and diversified poverty risks, especially for women. While women have traditionally been dependent on husbands for income as they rear children, increasing trends towards delayed marriage, higher rates of divorce and separation, and more single mothers, mean that men are contributing less than previously to the income of women and children. Increasingly, women depend on their market earnings, which remain lower than those of men, owing to labour market discrimination, the fact that the law has long supported the primacy of the husband in the household – in every historical period, some forms of family, shaped by the economic, social and cultural patterns of the time and place, were more socially 'acceptable' than others – and that women may curtail their employment during childrearing years. Indeed, evidence has shown that different marital histories exert an impact on women's finances (see Joshi and Davies, Chapter Six in this volume). Finally, changing family patterns, and especially population ageing, result in new and more complex relationships of obligation which may have an impact on the caring capacity of women. Women are likely to be disproportionately affected by current welfare restructuring policies which shift a greater responsibility for the care of elderly people onto relatives. Indeed, one of the most relevant reasons for concern about growth in welfare spending is that such spending is particularly focused on older people: public spending on education, health and social security varies with age. For example, in Great Britain both social security and health spending rise rapidly after pension age, reaching more than £7,500 per year for those aged 85 or over (Hills, 1993). There is also evidence of a strong relationship between caring and social class. Arber and Ginn (1993) find that working class women are doubly disadvantaged by being more likely to be called on to provide care to elderly parents at an earlier age, when it conflicts with the demands of employment, and by having less financial resources with which to ease this caring burden. There is also increasing awareness of the number of young people taking on the major responsibility for the care of an adult, usually a parent. Caring at a young age has a significant effect on earnings and risk of poverty in later life as young carers are often absent from school and fail to gain even basic qualifications. Even caring roles at such an early age are gendered: more of these young carers are girls, and although young boys also carry out caring work for parents, gender plays a complex role in expectations of care from each sex (Olsen, 1996; Payne, 2001).

Women's lives, then, are shaped by traditional family responsibilities. These tasks also shape women's *work patterns, the type of occupation they work in, their earnings and their social security benefits*. Firstly, 'moral obligations' create a time conflict between paid and unpaid work, care tasks and employment: such inequalities in the distribution of unpaid work remain even when the man is unemployed. Secondly, women's responsibilities for reproductive labour *limit* the range of paid economic activities they can undertake. Women often take a poorly paid side job in order to meet family needs (Graham, 1987) or find employment which fits in with their domestic chores. Women are also less mobile than men because of their reproductive and caring labour activities and *because of social norms that restrict their roles in public.* If, on the one hand, flexible employment helps in reconciling caring responsibilities and work needs, on the other, it can also become one of the routes that take women into poverty (see for example the UK situation) because these forms of employment are low-paid and insecure. It is hard for such workers to organise themselves for collective action. Thus, it is much harder for women to *transform* their capabilities into incomes, and/or well-being. Finally, the inequalities which women experience in paid work are mirrored in their different access to, and levels of, income replacement benefits (Glendinning and Millar, 1991)[2].

Women are also subject to discrimination in credit and a variety of other markets, and they own less property than men. *Financial institutions,* for example insurance companies, mutual societies as well as employers and the state, provide mechanisms for distributing resources between women and men, as well as between generations. Tax systems subsidise some of these transfers through tax relief on contributions paid by employers and/or employees as well as on the funds generated by the insurance or mutual companies themselves. *Financial markets,* as well as labour markets, have an impact on the distribution of resources between men and women but the assumptions on which they operate – especially with regard to access to credit and to mortgages – have not yet been subject to the detailed scrutiny to which labour markets have been subjected (Land, 2000).

All this is reflected in the private, occupational and public systems of *welfare provisions.* In most welfare states rights to benefits are still linked to occupational welfare and those who are denied entry into the labour market are also denied many welfare rights. The productive worker is still at the centre of the redistribution: consequently, women's right to welfare is often a function of their dependence on a male breadwinner (Lewis and Ostner, 1994; Daly, 1995). More specifically, economic and financial dependency on men has traditionally been assumed to protect women from poverty. This is a wrong and dangerous assumption for two reasons: on the one hand, as we have seen, in most Western countries there are more and more economically independent single women as well as increasing numbers of women who are the breadwinners of their family (for example single mothers). In view of this rise in the female labour participation rate and the growth of female-headed households, it is evident that women's treatment as economic dependants by social security systems contributes to women's poverty (Lee, 1999). Moreover, by ignoring the informal economy of the unpaid labour market where women are massively over-represented, the welfare state creates class divisions.

The challenge for the welfare state

Social change poses a formidable and radical challenge to the state. More particularly, one of the challenges of the modern welfare state is to find a solution to the gender dimension of change: how does the public sector, in providing employment and services, affect the situation of women? Can policy interventions advance women's concern through altering the gender division of labour and reducing inequality between the sexes? While the emancipatory potential of the welfare state has been increasingly emphasised (O'Connor, 1993; Orloff, 1993), there is also an increasing public recognition that the costs of the welfare crisis (in terms of decreases in the 'generosity' of the welfare state due to pressures on welfare spending) are disproportionally borne by women. Indeed, in the case of women, the ability to be independent and autonomous is linked to the degree to which women can uphold a socially acceptable standard of living, *independent of family relationships*, either through paid work or social security provisions (Lister, 1994; Sainsbury, 1996). This would mean restructuring the welfare state through gender equality reforms. For example, it would require legislative and policy frameworks that recognise the wide variety of households and their fluidity, and which grant equal or parallel status to different family types, irrespective of their perceived moral legitimacy. In addition, there would need to be stronger measures to prevent women from falling into poverty in the event of family breakdown or bereavement. It should also be remembered that family breakdown may also leave single men highly vulnerable, particularly where they have limited networks of social support (Baden, 1999).

The welfare state should also respond to the changes in gender expectations, linked to the growth in female education, that have an impact on family formation and dissolution and on women's participation in the labour market. Women do more paid work and, particularly in the absence of help from the welfare state to reconcile work and family, tend to adapt their reproductive decisions (such as fertility rates) to their need to take paid work (Italy is a good example of this). Many policy decisions can affect these choices, for example, the provision of social benefits aimed at promoting women's ability to fully participate in the labour market (and achieving financial independence through their own earnings) and also policies designed to relieve the double burden of care and domestic work.

Changes in women's lives

In the social changes discussed above, the role of women seems to be underdeveloped, and their patterns of life and expectations have changed more fundamentally than those of men, but in contradictory and ambivalent ways. It is important to recognise the role of women as actors of change in two senses. First, in the post-war decades life course changes have been more pronounced for women than for men both in the family and in the labour market: women's employment across most Western industrialised countries has steadily increased; women's educational attainment is rising; their economic independence is increasing; their fertility and family behaviour is rapidly changing. We should also mention the increased motivation of young people to achieve higher levels of education and training, and the greater centrality of these goals, rather than motherhood and family formation, for young women. Social, economic and legislative improvements and scientific advances have allowed women to have greater control of their lives.

However, equality has yet to be achieved in many fields. While some women have been able to take advantage of the new opportunities, many have not. As we have seen, the risk of social exclusion of women has diversified. Even if, from a general point of view, the gap between the two genders has been reducing since the 1970s (increasing equality in educational opportunities has helped a lot, together with a reduction in discrimination and segregation in the labour market), women remain at a higher risk of poverty than men in many countries and gender differences in the causes, extent and experience of deprivation are evident. Even though more jobs are made available when globalisation and economic growth is occurring – including those at managerial level – that does not mean that women are more likely to advance to executive level positions. Elevation to senior executive status requires that women have certain types of contacts, credentials and social networks that do not automatically become available to them as part of the economic integration process. In general, theories of globalisation and its impact on women and work suggest that it significantly expands opportunities for women in the workplace, but it does not remove barriers to advancement, cushion the impact of recessions, or ameliorate the predominance of low-paying, insecure jobs held by women[3].

This book discusses many of these issues. It uses empirical evidence that has significant implications for both social science and public policy, and suggests methods of analysis suitable to understand and follow the dynamic nature of women's lives, embedded in a scenario that combines increased diversity of life courses and life chances, as well as increased insecurities. It is important to underline that the issues discussed do not affect all countries in the same way and, in fact, the book is designed to highlight differences *between* countries. Concerning the data used, there will have been marked cohort changes in women's behaviour in all countries during the time period covered in the discussion. Therefore, research that uses data from the 1970s or 1980s will show a different picture from that based on data from the 1990s.

This book touches on different elements of the gender dimension of social change, in terms of the consequences of social change on women's (and men's) life courses, and of the role of women and men as actors of change. More specifically, the discussion focuses on the relationship between women, modernity and social inequality with regard to demographic models, divorce, labour market participation, education and social exclusion. The gender dimension of poverty and inequality is clearly shaped by social change.

While the empirical analyses are carried out using microdata (Table 2.1), the various chapters link the micro- with the macro- perspective: each analysis is contextualised with both a national and institutional dimension. Many relevant

Table 2.1: Description of the studies used in the book

Germany
Socio-Economic Panel (SOEP)

Type:	panel study launched in 1984
Original sample:	5,921 households
Purpose:	to monitor household change; occupational and family biographies; employment and professional mobility; earnings; health; personal satisfaction

Great Britain
National Child Development Study (NCDS)

Type:	cohort study started in 1958
Original sample:	17,414 individuals
Purpose:	to improve understanding of the factors affecting human development over the whole lifespan

Labour Force Survey (LFS)

Type:	repeated cross-sectional survey launched in 1973. In 1992 the LFS adopted a rotating quarterly panel design (QLFS)
Original sample:	60,000 households. From 1992: every quarter is made up of five 'waves', each of which contains about 12,000 selected households
Purpose:	to provide information on the UK labour market for international comparisons

Women and Employment Survey (WES)

Type:	retrospective study carried out in 1988
Original sample:	5,588 women in Great Britain aged 16-59 and the husbands of 799 of the married women
Purpose:	to establish what factors determine whether or not women are in paid work and to identify the degree to which domestic factors shape women's lifetime labour market involvement

British Household Panel Study (BHPS)

Type:	panel study launched in 1991
Original sample:	5,511 households
Purpose:	to further the understanding of social and economic change at the individual and household level in Britain

British Film Institute Television Industry Tracking Study

Type:	panel study launched in 1994
Original sample:	questionnaires were sent to 533 individuals aged between 21 and 65 who were employed in all sectors of the television industry
Purpose:	to examine the impact of structural changes in the television industry on individual production workers

(continued)

Table 2.1: Description of the studies used in the book (continued)

Sweden

Household Market and Non-market Activities (HUS)

Type:	panel Study started in 1984
Original sample:	2,600 households
Purpose:	study of labour market experiences, earnings, schooling, socio-economic background, housing, childcare, incomes and taxes, wealth and time-use

The Netherlands

OSA Labour Supply Panel

Type:	panel study launched in 1985
Original sample:	4,020 households
Purpose:	the survey aims to find out about respondents' employment situation, and about their behaviour in the labour market

European Community

European Community Household Panel (ECHP)

Type:	panel study started in 1994
Original sample:	60,819 households
Purpose:	to investigate both poverty and social exclusion at the level of the European Community

questions, such as unemployment, poverty, social exclusion, can be disentangled only by linking social change to the changing life course patterns of women and men and by analysing the interaction between individual action and social structures. As Elder (1985) and Mayer (1991) argue, life courses are shaped by a large number of inputs: specific structures offering political and economic opportunities; ideas shaped by the culture; norms that stipulate legal age for certain activities; sequence of positions and institutional passages; socialisation processes and selection mechanisms.

This volume underlines the relevance of longitudinal research in the study of women's life courses. An interest in what unites poverty with macro- and micro- social processes, and the consequent need to follow up the biographies of subjects in difficulty, has encouraged a move towards more systematic gathering of data and the development of techniques that permit dynamic interpretation of the processes of social exclusion and poverty. Particularly in the case of women, the diachronic perspective may offer a fruitful starting point. The importance of a longitudinal perspective is very strongly related to the fact that, for women, there are major life course influences as well as big differences between cohorts. Therefore longitudinal data are essential. For men such differences are much less marked.

This book also offers guidelines to anyone who needs to carry out research based on longitudinal data and tries to promote a better understanding of the type of information that longitudinal data provide, and of the appropriate techniques needed to analyse such data – always in a gender perspective. The obvious advantages of longitudinal designs over cross-sectional ones have been underlined by many authors (see, among others, Menard, 1991; Duncan, 1992; Davies and Dale, 1994; Trivellato, 1999; Rose, 2000; Ruspini, 2002: forthcoming). Because they do not use the same sample, trend studies only enable change to be analysed at the macro-level (for example, comparisons of the proportion of the population that is below the poverty line at time t and at time $t-1$). Given that the same individuals are not followed over a period of time (that is, subjects are not re-interviewed), such studies are not suitable if one is seeking to identify the causal mechanisms that govern social change. Furthermore, it is very hard to distinguish between the effects of age and cohort: the principal limitations of repeated cross-sectional design are indeed its inappropriateness for studying developmental patterns within cohorts and its inability to resolve issues of causal order. Thus, cross-sectional type data cannot be a suitable source of information for identifying changes in behaviour that are the result of growing older. Consequently, it should come as no surprise that conclusions drawn on the basis of cross-sectional data have often been challenged by analyses based on longitudinal data.

However, even if there is a growing recognition that longitudinal data provide the most appropriate empirical information for understanding social processes, it is also extremely important to consider the implications of understanding this type of analysis. In order to 'go beyond marking the female box on a questionnaire', a suitable, gender-sensitive research paradigm is also required. The final aim is to develop an understanding of why and how gender is such an important factor on an individual's experiences (see Elliott, Chapter Ten in this volume). Thus the need is to 'contextualise' women within longitudinal research by adopting a more reflexive, gender-sensitive paradigm, that is, to separate the language of data, and of variables into male and female, in order to study, in depth, the changes in the position of women in society, in the relationship between the sexes and in social inequalities that still exist between women and men.

Notes

[1] Many authors have tried to distinguish between poverty and social exclusion by pointing to the wider meaning of the latter concept. The concept has the potential to combine different dimensions: impoverishment, labour market exclusion, service exclusion and exclusion from social relations. For details see, among others, Levitas, 1999; Gordon, 2000.

[2] The tension between tradition and modernity also influences women's patterns of sociability. Previous research findings show that women who face the double burden of full-time work, housework and caring find it particularly difficult to find time to socialise outside work (Martin and Wallace, 1984; Russell, 1999). Women's pattern of labour market participation is critical in building up a social network which is resistant to unemployment: it is unlikely that women who work full time will have the same

supportive local networks as housewives or part-time workers. This happens because women's social networks are more home-centered and because their responsibility for caring provides the opportunity to build up supportive social networks in the community. However, a social network that is external to the labour market may also have some negative implications. If women's social networks are dominated by housewives or unemployed women they may become even more cut off from the world of work. Indeed, women's social networks are usually less useful in providing help to find a job: while women have fewer but more intimate social contacts, men usually have a wider range of friendships based on joint activities rather than intimacy (Russell, 1999).

[3] For details see http://www.haynesboone.com/briefing/mears1.htm

References

Arber, S. and Ginn, J. (1993) 'Class, caring and the life course', in A. Arber and M. Evandrou (eds) *Ageing, independence and the life course*, London: Jessica Kingsley.

Baden, S. (1999) *Gender, governance and the 'feminisation of poverty'*, Background Paper No 2, Meeting on Women and Political Participation: 21st Century Challenges, United Nations Development Programme, 24-26 March, New Delhi, India.

Barbagli, M. (1990) *Provando e Riprovando. Matrimonio, famiglia e divorzio in Italia e in altri paesi occidentali*, Bologna: Il Mulino.

Bauman, Z. (1992) *Intimations of postmodernity*, London: Routledge.

Beck, U. (1992) *Risk society: Towards a new modernity*, London: Sage Publications.

Bell, D. (1973) *The coming of post-industrial society: A venture in social forecasting*, London: Heinemann.

Brannen, J. (1992) 'Combining qualitative and quantitative approaches: an overview', in J. Brannen (ed) *Mixing methods: Qualitative and quantitative research*, Aldershot: Avebury, pp 3-37.

Burkhauser, R.V., Duncan, G.J., Hauser, R. and Berntsen, R. (1991) 'Wife or Frau, women do worse: a comparison of men and women in the United States and Germany after marital dissolution', *Demography*, vol 28, no 3, pp 353-60.

Corcoran, M., Duncan, G.J. and Hill, M. (1984) 'The economic fortunes of women and children: lessons from the Panel Study of Income Dynamics', *Signs-Journal of Women in Culture and Society*, vol 10, no 2, pp 232-48.

Daly, M. (1995) 'Sex, gender and poverty in the British and (West) German welfare states', Paper presented at the Conference 'The Cost of Being a Mother, the Cost of Being a Father', European Forum, Florence, European University Institute, 24-25 March.

Davies, R.B. and Dale, A. (1994) 'Introduction', in A. Dale and R.B. Davies (eds) *Analysing social and political change. A casebook of methods*, London: Sage Publications.

Duncan, G.J. (1992) 'Household Panel Studies: Prospects and problems', Working Papers of the European Scientific Network on Household Panel Studies, Paper 54, Colchester: University of Essex.

Elder Jr, G.H. (1985) 'Perspectives on the life course', in G.H. Elder Jr (ed) *Life course dynamics. Trajectories and transitions, 1968-1980*, Ithaca, NY and London: Cornell University Press, pp 23-49.

Evans, M. (ed) (1994) *The woman question*, London: Sage Publications.

Giddens, A. (1990) *The consequences of modernity*, Cambridge: Polity Press.

Giullari, S. (2000) 'Sostegno o (in)dipendenza? Reti di parentela e madri sole', in F. Bimbi and E. Ruspini (eds) *Povertà delle donne e trasformazione dei rapporti di genere*, 'Inchiesta', no 128, April-June, pp 91-8.

Glendinning, C. and Millar, J. (1991) 'Poverty: the forgotten Englishwoman', in M. MacLean and D. Groves (eds) *Women's issues in social policy*, London: Routledge.

Gordon, D., Adelman, L., Ashworth K., Bradshaw, J., Levitas, R., Middleton, S., Pantazis, C., Patsios, D., Payne, S., Townsend, P. and Williams, J. (2000) *Poverty and social exclusion in Britain*, York: Joseph Rowntree Foundation.

Graham, H. (1987) 'Women's poverty and caring', in C. Glendinning and J. Millar (eds) *Women and poverty in Britain*, Hemel Hempstead: Harvester Wheatsheaf.

Haferkamp, H. and Smelser, N.J. (eds) (1982) *Social change and modernity*, Berkeley, CA and Los Angeles, CA: University of California Press.

Haskey, J. (1983): 'Marital status before divorce and age at divorce: their influence on the chance of divorce', *Population Trends*, no 32, pp 4-14.

Haskey, J. (1993) 'First marriage, divorce and remarriage: birth cohort analysis', *Population Trends*, no 72, pp 24-33.

Hills, J. (1993) *The future of welfare: A guide to the debate*, York: Joseph Rowntree Foundation.

Jarvis, S. and Jenkins, S. (1998) 'Marital dissolution and income change: evidence for Britain', in R. Ford and J. Millar (eds) *Private lives and public responses: Lone parenthood and future policy*, London: Policy Studies Institute.

Kohli, M. (1986) 'The world we forgot: a historical review of the life course', in V. Marshall (ed) *Later life: The social psychology of aging*, Beverly Hills, CA: Sage Publications.

Land, H. (2000) 'La ricostruzione della dipendenza delle donne', in F. Bimbi and E. Ruspini (eds) *Povertà delle donne e trasformazione dei rapporti di genere*, Inchiesta, 128, aprile-giugno, pp 85-90.

Lee, A. (1999) 'Income distribution within household and women's poverty', Paper prepared for APEC Study Centre Consortium 1999 Conference: 'Towards APEC's Second Decade: Challenges, Opportunities and Priorities', Auckland, New Zealand, 31 May-2 June.

Levitas, R. (1999) *The inclusive society*, London: Macmillan.

Lewis, J. (1993) 'Introduction: women, work, family and social policies in Europe', in J. Lewis (ed) *Women and social policies in Europe: Work, family and the state*, Aldershot: Edward Elgar, pp 1-24.

Lewis, J. and Ostner, I. (1994) *Gender and the evolution of European social policies*, ZeS-Arbeitspapier No 4, Zentrum für Sozialpolitik (ZES) (Centre for Social Policy Research), University of Bremen.

Lister, R. (1994) 'She has other duties – women, citizenship and social security', in S. Baldwin and J. Falkingham (eds) *Social security and social change: New challenges to the Beveridge model*, New York, NY: Harvester Wheatsheaf.

Martin, R. and Wallace, J. (1984) *Working women in recession: Employment, redundancy and unemployment*, Oxford: Oxford University Press.

Mayer, K.U. (1991) 'Life courses in the welfare state', in W.R. Heinz (ed) *Theoretical advances in life course research*, vol I, Weinheim: Deutscher Studien Verlag.

Menard, S. (1991) *Longitudinal research*, Sage University Paper Series on Quantitative Applications in the Social Sciences, London: Sage Publications.

Millar, J. (1998) 'Policy and changing family forms: placing lone parenthood in context', Paper presented at the Seminar: 'Current European Research on Lone Mothers', Gothenburg University, Sweden, April.

Mingione, E. (1996) 'Urban poverty in the advanced industrial world: concepts, analysis and debates', in E. Mingione (ed) *Urban poverty and the underclass*, Oxford: Basil Blackwell, pp 3-40.

Morris, L. (1996) 'Dangerous classes: neglected aspects of the underclass debate', in E. Mingione (ed) *Urban poverty and the underclass*, Oxford: Basil Blackwell, pp 160-75.

O'Connor, J.S. (1993) 'Gender, class and citizenship in the comparative analysis of welfare state regimes: theoretical and methodological issues', *British Journal of Sociology*, vol 44, no 3, pp 501-18.

Olagnero, M. and Saraceno, C. (1993) *Che vita è. L'uso dei materiali biografici nell'analisi sociologica*, Roma: La Nuova Italia Scientifica.

Olsen, R. (1996) 'Young carers: challenging the facts and politics of research into children and caring', *Disability and Society*, vol 11, no 1, pp 41-54.

Orloff, A.S. (1993) 'Gender and the social rights of citizenship: the comparative analysis of gender relations and welfare states', *American Sociological Review*, vol 58, no 3, pp 303-28.

Pahl, J. (1989) *Money and marriage*, London: Macmillan.

Payne, S. (2001) 'Malattia e ruoli femminili: la relazione tra dipendenza economica, responsabilità di cura e povertà', in C. Facchini and E. Ruspini (eds) *Salute e disuguaglianze: Genere, condizioni sociali e corso di vita*, Collana Transizioni e Politiche pubbliche, Milano: Franco Angeli.

Rogers, B.L. (1990) 'The internal dynamics of households: a critical factor in development policy', in B.L. Rogers and N.P. Schlossman (eds) *Intrahousehold resource allocation: Issues and methods for development policy and planning*, Food and Nutrition Bulletin, Supplement No 15, Tokyo: United Nations University Press, pp 1-19.

Rose, D. (2000) 'Household Panel Studies: an overview', in D. Rose (ed) *Researching social and economic change. The uses of Household Panel Studies*, Social Research Today Series, London: Routledge, pp 3-35.

Ruspini, E. (2000) 'Poverty and the gendered distribution of resources within households', *Issue of Radical Statistics on Money and Finance*, no 75, Autumn.

Ruspini, E. (2002: forthcoming) *Introduction to longitudinal research*, London: Routledge.

Russell, H. (1999) 'Friends in low places: gender, unemployment and sociability', *Work, Employment and Society*, vol 13, no 2, pp 205-24.

Sainsbury, D. (1996) *Gender, equality and welfare states*, Cambridge: Cambridge University Press.

Scheiwe, K. (1994) 'Labour market, welfare state and family institutions: the links to mothers poverty risks: a comparison between Belgium, Germany and the United Kingdom', *Journal of European Social Policy*, vol 4, no 3, pp 201-24.

Smelser, N.J. (1981) *Sociology*, Englewood Cliffs, NJ: Prentice Hall.

Touraine, A. (1974) *The post-industrial society*, London: Wildwood.

Trivellato, U. (1999) 'Issues in the design and analysis of Panel Studies: a cursory review', in E. Ruspini (ed) *Longitudinal analysis: A bridge between quantitative and qualitative social research*, Special Issue of Quality and Quantity, vol 33, no 3, July-August.

van der Kamp, L.J.T. and Bijleveld, C.J.H. (1998) 'Methodological issues in longitudinal research', in C.J.H. Bijleveld et al, *Longitudinal data analysis. Designs, models and methods*, London: Sage Publications, pp 1-45.

Wiswede, G. and Kutsch, T. (1978) *Sozialer Wandel*, Darmstadt: Wissenschaftliche Buchgesellschaft.

THREE

Survey designs for longitudinal research

Elisabetta Ruspini

What is longitudinal research?

'Longitudinal' is a rather imprecise term. It implies the notion of repeated measurements: the observations are made on a certain number of occasions (van der Kamp and Bijleveld, 1998, p 1; Taris, 2000). Thus, the term longitudinal refers to a particular type of relation between phenomena: the type which evolves over the course of time and is termed *diachronic*, and the opposite of *synchronic*. With longitudinal research, time regains its rightful place within the explanatory model (Menard, 1991):

- data are gathered over two, or more, successive periods (in the case of retrospective studies, data are collected through asking questions about the past – 'retrospective questions');
- either the same cases as before are analysed, or cases which can be directly compared with those from the previous period are studied;
- data are analysed by comparing the different periods: the linkage of data records for different time periods creates a longitudinal record for each observational unit.

Essentially, longitudinal research elicits data from the future for each observational unit. Moreover, where individuals are surveyed at successive time points or retrospectively, taken backwards in time, then it is possible to investigate how particular outcomes are related to the earlier circumstances of the same individuals. Therefore, longitudinal data recognise the temporal nature of individual behaviour. If we are to understand temporal tendencies in micro-level behaviour, then longitudinal research is essential (Davies and Dale, 1994).

There are many different methods that can be used to collect longitudinal data, resulting in many different types of research designs. The most commonly used longitudinal designs are:

- *repeated cross-sectional studies* (trend), which are carried out regularly, using a very different, or completely new, sample each time;
- *prospective longitudinal studies* (panel), that repeatedly interview the sane subjects

over a period of time. This means surveying a given sample of individuals and/or households and following them over time with a sequence of rounds of data collection (or 'waves', as they are often termed);

- *retrospective studies* (duration data), in which interviewees are asked to remember, and reconstruct, events and aspects of their own life courses.

Of these three, prospective studies are considered the most 'truly longitudinal' (and are consequently preferred when analysing micro-social change), since they gather information about the same individuals who are asked an identical sequence of questions at regular intervals (Janson, 1990; Magnusson et al, 1991). In particular, prospective longitudinal surveys provide the most reliable data on change in behaviour or attitudes, because the data are collected while the subjective states actually exist. Indeed, some consider retrospective surveys to be 'quasi-longitudinal', because they offer only an incomplete contribution to the study of causal processes and, above all, because of distortions due to memory errors (Hakim, 1987, p 97; Draper and Marcos, 1990; Dex, 1991; Taris, 2000).

Longitudinal research is rarely based on one investigative method alone. Rather, longitudinal data can be obtained:

- through repeated cross-sectional surveys which seek retrospective information about a relatively long period of time;
- through panel surveys, which gather information from the same subjects who are interviewed, periodically, over a period of time;
- by putting administrative records together and adding in any further information that can be drawn from census surveys (record linkages);
- through a combination of all the three methods above (Trivellato, 1999).

Some examples of longitudinal mixed designs are:

- repeated cross-sectional studies, one part of which are done in the form of panel studies. For example, the British Social Attitudes Survey (BSA) and the Labour Force Survey (LFS) in the UK, or the Bank of Italy Survey of Household Income and Wealth (SHIW) in Italy, are repeated regularly on a largely different sample but with a small part as a panel study. The LFS is a repeated cross-sectional survey of households living at private addresses in the UK. The main purpose of the LFS is to produce a set of national and regional employment and unemployment statistics for use by government departments and for comparison with other European Union countries, based on internationally standardised definitions. It is carried out by the Social Survey Division of the Office for National Statistics in Great Britain and by the Central Survey Unit of the Department of Finance and Personnel in Northern Ireland, on behalf of the Department of Economic Development. The LFS was conducted biennially from 1973 to 1983 (in Great Britain and Northern Ireland), and annually from 1984 to 1991 for Great Britain, and from 1984 to 1994 for Northern Ireland. The Quarterly Labour Force Survey (QLFS), designed on a rotating quarterly panel, has been conducted since the spring of 1992 for Britain, and from the winter of 1994/95 for Northern Ireland. Every quarter is made up of five 'waves', each of which contains about 12,000 selected households. The households are interviewed in five successive waves. Accordingly, at any one time, each quarter will contain one wave receiving the first interview, one wave the second interview, and so on, until the fifth interview. (Further information can be found at http://www.mimas.ac.uk/surveys/lfs/, and http://www.mimas.ac.uk/surveys/qlfs/);

- prospective studies that gather information systematically through the use of calendars and/or suitable questionnaires, which aim to investigate retrospectively the life of the interviewee, but not necessarily enquire about the same subject each time. Typical examples are Household Panel Studies (HPSs), the most important being the Panel Study of Income Dynamics (PSID) in the United States, the German Socio-Economic Panel (GSOEP), and the British Household Panel Study (BHPS);

- cohort studies that are also prospective and/or retrospective (two British examples of this being the *National Child Development Study* and the *Birth Cohort Study*). Typically, in a cohort study one or more generations are followed over time, that is, over their life course. A cohort has been identified as "the aggregate of individuals who experienced the same life event within the same time interval" (Ryder, 1965, p 845): birth, marriage, moment of entry in the labour market, moment of diagnosis of a particular disease, and so on. One particularly important type of cohort is the 'birth cohort', that is, the set of people who were born in the same period of time year (for example, everyone born in 1970). A more restricted conception of cohort – which is better suited to a life course approach – is that a cohort is a group of individuals who began their life course during the same interval of time (Billari, 1998). Thus, cohort studies may begin at birth, but may also begin at a much later age (Davies and Dale, 1994; Bynner, 1996; Taris, 2000).

To sum up, longitudinal research collects information about the temporal evolution of individual behaviour and ensures that the same individual will be involved each time. Although it may make no difference whether the events experienced by this individual are recorded over a period of time, or whether his/her biography is reconstructed *a posteriori* up to the moment when the information is being gathered, there may be differences in accuracy (Duncan and Kalton, 1987). Consequently, the term 'longitudinal', as it is used here, describes what can be defined as the minimum common denominator of those methods which aim to reveal the flux of social change (Zazzo, 1967; Menard, 1991).

The following designs of longitudinal research are discussed in this chapter:

- Repeated cross-sectional surveys
- Panel design
- Consumer panels
- Prospective panels
- Rotating and split panels
- Cohort panels
- Linked or administrative panels

- Event oriented design
- 'Qualitative' longitudinal sources.

Repeated cross-sectional surveys

The most common distinction made between cross-sectional and longitudinal studies (Ruspini, 1999; Ruspini, 2002: forthcoming) is the different way in which they take time into account. A cross-sectional survey, as the name makes clear, studies a cross-section of the population from a wide sample of people of different ages, education, religion, and so on – at a specific point in time. Thus, details about an event/phenomenon are gathered once (and once only) for each subject or case studied. Therefore, cross-sectional studies provide an instant, but static, 'photograph' of the process being studied. Social scientists should be very careful when attempting to extrapolate longitudinal inferences on the basis of analyses of cross-sectional data as they have to assume, implicitly, that the process being studied is in some sort of equilibrium[1]. This is the reason why cross-sectional studies are not the most suitable tools for the study of social change. However, their one-off nature makes such studies both cheaper and easier to organise, as well as giving them the advantage of immediacy, by offering instant results. Unsurprisingly, these studies have always been the mainstay of both academic and market researchers.

To compensate for this disadvantage, cross-sectional surveys are usually repeated twice or more, at different points in time, and use a completely new sample each time. In other words, any overlaps that may occur are so rare that they cannot be considered significant. The term 'trend studies' is used for these repeated cross-sectional surveys (conducted at two or more occasions) on different samples. In order to ensure the compatibility of the measurements across time, the same questionnaire should be used in all cross-sectional surveys.

As Hagenaars and Taris (2000) argue, trend studies have some advantages over panel and cohort studies, in that trend data are more readily available and allow the detection of change at the *aggregate* level. More specifically, the investigation of long-term social change has to rely on trend rather than panel data. Firstly, long-term panel data are scarce and, moreover, suffer from attrition problems (subsequent loss of membership due to non-contact, refusal to answer, failure to follow-up sample cases for other reasons, death, emigration), while cross-sectional surveys can be arranged into a long-term trend design.

Cross-sectional data can indeed be organised in two alternative ways (Davies and Dale, 1994):

- *data gathered at the individual level* (micro). Line-vectors (relative to cases) contain the same variables which are studied at different points in time. These can then be joined in order to create a single data file (or pooled data file). This increases the size of the sample and makes it possible to insert a time dimension into the analysis;
- *data at the aggregate level* (macro), where information is compiled into tables in which time is the main independent variable. These aggregate data

effectively bring together information about the same population, but are gathered on a series of different occasions.

However, because these surveys are not based on the same sample, they only offer a means for analysing net changes at the aggregate level – the net effect of all the changes (Firebaugh, 1997). For example, a net effect may be a comparison between instances of poverty and the characteristics of the population below the poverty line at time t and at time $t-1$, or between the pool of employed and unemployed in two different years. Thus, cross-sections can tell us about populations either at one or at a series of points in time.

Examples of repeated cross-sectional surveys

The General Household Survey (GHS) is conducted by the Social Survey Division of the Office for National Statistics (ONS). This annual, multipurpose survey began in 1971 and data is available from 1973 onwards. Based on a sample of around 10,000 private households in Great Britain, interviews are conducted with each member of the household aged 16 and over (around 18,000 adults). The GHS offers unparalleled opportunities to explore the relationships between income, housing, economic activity, family composition, fertility, education, leisure activities, drinking, smoking, and health. Topics covered to date are listed each year in the annual report, *Living in Britain: Results from the GHS*. In addition to regular 'core' questions, certain subjects are covered periodically, such as family and household formation, health and related topics, use of social services by the elderly, and participation in sports and leisure activities. In addition, new topics have been introduced at various times. (Details are available at http://www.mimas.ac.uk/surveys/ghs/ghs_info.html.)

The Family Expenditure Survey (FES) studies how families spend their money. It is a continuous and comprehensive household survey carried out by the ONS from a sample of around 7,000 households in the UK. Each individual spender over 16 is asked to complete an expenditure diary, listing every item bought over a period of two weeks and noting if a credit card was used to make the purchase (ONS, 1996). Thus, the FES provides detailed information about income (including details about the sources of income), possession of consumer durables and cars; plus basic information on housing, and many demographic and socio-economic variables which are mainly used for classification purposes. (See www.mimas.ac.uk/surveys/fes/, and www.data-archive.ac.uk/findingData/fesAbstract.asp for more information.)

Panel design

'True' longitudinal surveys can be of two types: prospective and retrospective. The former gather information about events even as they are taking place, whereas the latter are based on historical accounts: subjects are asked to remember and reconstruct aspects of their life course. More precisely, prospective longitudinal studies, especially Household Panel Studies (HPS), follow individuals and families over time by periodically re-interviewing the same subjects and providing multiple observations on each individual/household in the sample. Such studies involve not only a random sample of households, but also all those members and subsequent co-residents, partners and descendants who are repeatedly re-interviewed. Thus, these studies accumulate records of employment, income, family status and attitudes over extended periods. This makes it possible to study change at the individual, that is, the micro-level (Hakim 1987; Rose and Sullivan, 1996; Gershuny, 1998, 2000). In other words, it is possible to analyse changes within the institutional, cultural and social environments that surround the individual and shape the course of his/her life course. This also permits the analysis of gross change, that is, the analysis of flows between states. Thus, they offer a basis for further study of the dynamics of social phenomena.

The term 'panel data' covers a variety of data collection designs, but generally refers to the repeated observation of a set of fixed entities (people, firms, nation states) at fixed intervals (usually, but not necessarily, annual). Thus, there are various basic types of panel.

Firstly, those which seek to ascertain the degree of stability or fluctuation of opinions and attitudes (usually surveys on political opinions or consumption), for example, consumer panels, which are used in market research in order to keep track, over time, of changes in purchasing and consumption patterns in relation to a particular product (Sudman and Ferber, 1979). The participants in such panels provide the researcher with information on a regular basis about their level of consumption of particular brands of products (van de Pol, 1989), and data collection is at frequent intervals.

The most representative prospective surveys, Household Panel Studies (HPS), are based on a probability sample of individuals/households, and seek to discover what happens/has happened to the same subjects over a certain period of time. The population from which the sample is drawn is made up of all the individuals resident/present in a given area, or a subset of these. As already noted, HPS are conducted using repeated interviews carried out at fixed intervals which could be anything from every 2-3 months to once a year (with some significant exceptions) (see Appendix for details). The shorter the time interval, the easier it is for a relationship to develop with the interviewees, ensuring a high and constant percentage of response over time. Usually, the composition of the population is dynamic in two ways: on the one hand, it changes over time, in terms both of entrants (through births and immigration) and leavers (through deaths and emigration). On the other, its basic aggregate units (households) – which are also the sampling units of the HPS – also change continually, in the wake of events affecting family formation and dissolution (Trivellato, 1999). It is individuals, not households, who are followed over time: individuals are much more stable in a longitudinal context and so are easier to track and follow. Thus, if HPS tell us about the dynamics of households, the data come from individuals who are related to their changing households and family contexts (Rose, 2000, p 9). The most important advantage these surveys offer is that they make it possible to study micro-social change. When individuals are studied over time it becomes possible to investigate the dynamics of both individual and family behaviours in the socio-economic field and, also, the personal responses and adaptation strategies adopted in the face of previous circumstances and events. But proof of the growing importance attributed to HPS can be found in the multiplicity of studies, set up in recent years, in order to examine and make comparisons, both ex ante and ex post, between longitudinal data. For example, in 1994, Eurostat launched a panel study (the European Community Household Panel (ECHP), which extends over all the member countries of the EU. Four projects have been set up which seek to increase the ex post comparability of prospective panel studies:

- The Panel Comparability Project (PACO) aims to build up an archive of longitudinal data that can be compared at the supra-national level by drawing on various prospective longitudinal surveys currently underway in some European countries and in the US.
- The PSID–GSOEP *Equivalent Data File* attempts to compare GSOEP and PSID data. This is now being replaced by the *Cross-National Equivalent Files* (CNEF) that contain harmonised panal data from Canada, Germany, the US and the UK.
- The European Panel Analysis Group data set (EPAG).
- The Consortium of Household Panels for European Socio-Economic Research (CHER) aims to develop a comparative database for longitudinal household studies by harmonising and integrating micro-datasets from a large variety of panels.

Rotating and split panels

It is important to distinguish between rotating panels and split panels (Kish, 1986, 1987). The former are surveys in which a new group of probabilistically chosen individuals is added to the sample at each successive wave in order to correct distortions which may have arisen within the sample between time t and time $t-1$ (for example, one sixth of the sample retire and are replaced by an equal number of employed persons). The idea is to keep samples of changing populations up to date. Sample size is controlled by stipulating the period of time any subject will be included in the survey; that is, there is a limit on the time each subject will participate in the panel (for example, two years). Such rotation serves both as a good method of maintaining the original characteristics of the sample and reduces the distortion which would otherwise be created by natural loss of subjects. This 'refreshing' of the sample has the advantage that subjects will less easily develop 'survey boredom', that there will be fewer testing and learning effects, and that there will be less panel mortality, that is, attrition. As already said, attrition occurs when respondents leave the panel – because of refusal to answer, physical incapacity of the respondent to provide information and/or failure to follow up sample cases – after having participated in one or more consecutive waves, including the first wave of the study. Thus, rotating panel surveys combine the features of both panel and repeated cross-section studies. Two important examples of longitudinal studies which use rotation are the Survey of Labour and Income Dynamics (SLID) in Canada, and the Survey of Income and Program Participation (SIPP) in the US (Kalton and Lepkowski, 1985; Citro and Kalton, 1993).

Split panels are also referred to as 'classic' panels which include a rotating sample that is interviewed alongside another sample of the long-term panel members. The rotating sample is interviewed once only, and serves as a control group since they are not exposed to the potential effects of participating in the survey (attrition and conditioning). In other words, a panel study is combined with a repeated cross-sectional study (van de Pol, 1989), by flanking one-off independent samples with the long-term sample. The British Social Attitudes Survey is an example of a split panel survey.

Longitudinal cohort studies or cohort panels

Cohort analyses are similar to panel studies except that, in cohort studies, only a random sample of the individuals who experienced the same life event within the same time interval is observed over time. Usually a researcher will choose one or more birth cohorts and administer a questionnaire to a sample drawn from within that group; thus, longitudinal analysis is used on groups that are homogeneous with regard to age, and a number of generations are followed throughout their life courses.

A cohort study may not necessarily start with the birth of the interviewees: good examples of this are the National Longitudinal Surveys which, retrospectively, gathered the work histories of two cohorts of men and women aged between 30 and 44 years in 1967 and those between 24 and 37 years in 1978 (Centre for Human Resource Research, 1981). Unlike HPS, where there is a dynamic population (which changes over time because of births, deaths, immigration, and so on, and where family organisation may change because of divorce, remarriage, a new marriage or children leaving home), the main characteristic of this type of research is that a cohort cannot admit new entries because such entries are, by definition, impossible (Ghellini and Trivellato, 1996). Examples of this are panel studies on scholastic career (and/or on the transition from school to an active working life), where the event-origin used to identify the cohort is that of being present in (or entering or leaving) a given class in a given school year. This type of study is used to investigate the particular experiences of specific groups of people, usually re-interviewed only every five years.

Since they are longitudinal studies, cohort studies can be either prospective or retrospective. The former usually study one or more cohorts, at successive intervals, over a period of time, while the latter gather retrospective information about just one cohort at a time and may thus be made up of more than one study. Because of this, retrospective studies may evince, simultaneously, both cross-sectional features (samples are only interviewed once) and prospective panel features (they offer information about the life histories of the interviewees). Examples of the first group are the National Child Development Study (NCDS) and the 1970 British Cohort Study (BCS70), both British, and the series of National Longitudinal Surveys (NLS) carried out in the United States. The German Life History Study (GLHS) is a good example of the second group.

The US played a pioneering role in the development of longitudinal research based on cohort data. By the late 1920s and early 1930s, many longitudinal studies on childhood were already well underway. Many, but not all, of these studies concentrated on the evolution of children's physical characteristics (for details see Wall and Williams, 1970; Mednick and Mednick, 1984). Among the 'classic' longitudinal studies of human development was that begun in 1921 by Terman, which aimed to study the physical, mental and personality development of gifted children (Terman, 1925, 1939; Terman and Oden, 1947, 1959), as well as studies of psycho-physical development which were launched at the Merrill Palmer School in Detroit (1923), the Medical School of Colorado University (1923) and the University of Minnesota (1925). In 1928 the Berkeley Growth Study began, and a year later the Berkeley Guidance Study, the Fels Research Institute Project, and the Harvard Growth Study were launched. The final project of this series was the Oakland Growth Study, initiated in 1932. To give an example, Terman's study maintained a continuing record, at approximately ten-year stages, of physique, health, personal and social adjustment, nature of interests and activities – with detailed educational, vocational and marital histories – of 1,528 children (857 males and 671 females) selected from the State of California. The study began when most of the children were approximately 11 years old and when Terman was in his mid-forties; before Terman died (at the age of 80) the children had been contacted on three later occasions (Wall and Williams, 1970, pp 102-3). The Harvard Growth Study – entitled Longitudinal Study of Child Health and Development – was conducted by the Harvard School of Public Health (1929) on 309 newborn children. An interdisciplinary team of medical, biological and social scientists collected about 200,000 observations over a period of 18 years and, when the subjects were aged between 25 and 34, they launched a follow-up, on themes connected to health and social relations[2]. Finally, the Study on Human Development, launched by the Fels Research Institute, followed between six and eight newborn infants enrolled annually. From 1944 onwards the number increased to ten. In the late 1960s the active sample consisted of about 300 subjects from volunteer middle-class families, ranging from birth to 39 years of age (Wall and Williams, 1970).

The underlying idea behind any cohort study is that long-term social change must be interpreted within the context of generational change. By following one generation throughout its entire life course, the consequences of growth, maturity and ageing are rendered visible. Furthermore, it also becomes possible to investigate the influence of a variety of events that take place over the course of time and, likewise, to understand whether a specific event has influenced an entire generation in the same way (Hagenaars, 1990). Consequently, cohort studies are particularly suitable when studying populations that are subject to radical changes (Olagnero and Saraceno, 1993).

Age, period and cohort effects

There are three types of changes in attitudes or behaviour of cohorts associated with three temporal dimensions and three levels of experience and change (see, for example, Glenn, 1977; de Graaf, 1999). The first type of change may be a product of the age of the individual concerned, that is, is associated with changes in age (age effect). Changes of the second type – called cohort or generation effects – are associated with the time when the individual was born, and concern all events that one generation experienced and other generations did not. Finally, period effects concern those events which affect all generations equally and simultaneously, that is, the period at which the data were collected. The term *generation* is often used to clarify the inter-connection between age, period and cohort effects, indeed, generation expresses the socio-cultural changes which highlight the historical aspects of cohorts. In Mannheim's view (1952), a generation is not merely a birth cohort: historical events (especially if they occured during the 'formative' period at around 15 years of age) may determine a whole generation's capacity for cultural elaboration, stimulate a common world view and, consequently, encourage the development of the consciousness of being a socio-cultural entity.

More specifically:

- *Age effects* concern all events associated with changes in age. Here chronological age is taken as one indicator of levels of maturity and of both physical and psychological skills. Obviously the specific effects of age will vary from one age to another but are the same for all those who are part of a specific age group (Saraceno, 1986).
- *Cohort effects* are associated with year of birth, and concern all those events that one cohort has experienced and others have not. They are often interpreted as a special interaction between age and period effects: they interpret growth within specific historical conditions. Cohort effects are the same for all the individuals born within a specific, pre-defined period of time but will vary from subject to subject. Cohorts not only differ from one another, but are also not internally homogeneous. Given that the members of one cohort will be of different genders, health conditions, social classes and so on, they may not only have different life course models but at the same time may also be influenced differently by the same historical events. Using a sample of people who entered adolescence during the Great Depression in the 1930s, Elder (1974) demonstrated that the same events may even have the opposite effects on the male and female cohorts involved (see also Saraceno, 1986; Hagenaars, 1990).
- *Period effects* concern those events which affect all cohorts equally and simultaneously. In its most limited sense, the period effect refers to the time at which the observation is carried out. In practice, the concept is used as an indicator of the effects of events which affect all generations equally and simultaneously and which will have taken place during the observation period or between two consecutive observations (for example, the long-term

influences of such processes as industrialisation, urbanisation, and so forth). Individuals born in different historical periods will come into contact with social circumstances which will affect and modify the passages connected to age and the phases of life. Although these effects vary over the course of time, they will be the same for all subjects at any one particular point in time.

Linked or administrative panels

Linked or administrative panels are the by-product of data collected as part of public administration processes (census or administrative data). Their value may come from joining disparate data sources; for example, registration data linked to data from the Census. In these cases, data items which are not collected primarily for panel purposes are linked together using unique personal identifiers (the combination of name, birthdate and place of birth is normally enough to identify individuals, and enable linkage of administrative and/or other records). One good example of such panels is the Longitudinal Study (LS), organised by the ONS. It is based on the census and vital events data (births, cancer, deaths) collected for a sample of 1% of the population of England and Wales (approximately 500,000 individuals at any one point in time). Since it was established in the early 1970s, the LS has brought together 1% of the sample used for 1971, 1981 and 1991 censuses. Administrative panels are particularly widespread in the Scandinavian countries; for example, the Finnish Longitudinal Study (launched in 1971) which studies the whole resident population (Bynner, 1996); the Integrated Database for Labour Market Research (IDA) in Denmark; the Longitudinal Individual Data for Sweden database (LINDA) and the Swedish Income Panel (SWIP).

Without doubt, administrative panels offer the least intrusive method of collecting longitudinal data. Moreover, the data sets obtained are large; thus, sampling errors are few even for small population subgroups. They are also inexpensive. However, they do have some clear disadvantages. Above all, they can only offer a very small variety of information, data which have often been collected with long intervals of time elapsing between one collection and the next (as in the case of census data). Consequently, such data often pose problems of comparability. Furthermore, the analytical possibilities such panels offer are limited to those issues which correspond to the bureaucratic concerns of the administrators who collect the data (Gershuny and Buck, 2000). Lastly, these panel studies are frequently impeded by laws concerning data protection, which may make it difficult to obtain access to such data (Buck et al, 1994; Bynner, 1996).

As already discussed (see page 30), these designs can, of course, be fruitfully combined. For example, the BHPS collected complete life and work history records for all its respondents using retrospection. Indeed one of the options now beginning to be discussed for the 'missing' mid-1980s British birth cohort is a combination of administrative and other records with a new interview sample of adolescents (Gershuny and Buck, 2000).

The analytical advantages panel studies offer (when compared with those offered by repeated cross-sectional studies or by a single retrospective study) are often highlighted in the literature[3]. While cross-sectional studies do not reveal whether changes should be attributed to the introduction of new individuals entering or to a real change in behaviour, panel studies provide the opportunity of re-interviewing the same subjects again and again. This makes them an indispensable tool for the analysis of social change, of evolution in behaviours, and of both individual and family change. Longitudinal prospective studies allow the life course of one individual to be followed over time. Thus, statistics are used here to examine the relations between the distribution of one variable (identified at the family or the individual level) which refers to one time and the distribution of the same variable or of other variables at a different point in time.

The prospective approach also makes it possible to discern the dynamics of behaviour that may be discontinuous or difficult to analyse. The results of analyses carried out using panels have shown that changes in the lives of families and/or individuals are considerably greater than would appear from taking single snapshots (Kasprzyk et al, 1989; Dale and Davies, 1994).

Panel studies also offer the opportunity of analysing change in a way which takes into consideration different dimensions of time. The German Socio-Economic Panel, for example, contains questions which measure time in several ways (Frick, 1998). The following are examples:

- Single retrospective questions on certain events in the past (past time): how often have you changed your job during the last ten years?
- Retrospective life event history since the age of 15 (past time): employment or marital history.
- Monthly calendar on income and labour market related issues (past time): employment status January to December last year.
- Questions concerning a period of time (past time): demographic changes since the last interview (such as marriage or death of spouse).
- Questions about a point of time (present time): current employment status or current levels of satisfaction.
- Questions concerning future prospects (future time): satisfaction with life five years from now, or job expectations.

Finally, another major advantage panel studies have over cross-sectional research designs is that they offer the possibility of performing an analysis of causal interrelationships among variables. In other words, panel data offer multiple ways of strengthening the causal inference process (Finkel, 1995). As Engel and Reinecke (1996, p 8) argue, one great virtue of panel data analysis is its ability to subject causal propositions to rigorous empirical examinations. For each unit of analysis, panel data place not only one but at least two or more repeated observations at the researcher's disposal – and this in definite time order; it appears much more reasonable, therefore, to infer ongoing processes than in cross-sectional research. Since these observations are not collected retrospectively, as is often the case in event history analysis (EHA), memory and possible re-evaluation of past experience cannot distort the data.

Event oriented design (event history data)

Event history or duration data offer a record of the events that have punctuated the life course of a group of subjects. Duration data are usually gathered using retrospective cross-sectional studies in which respondents are asked to recall events and aspects of their own life courses. Typically, the study begins with the current situation and taking respondents backwards in time. In panel surveys, data may be collected at the first wave either retrospectively for a fixed initial reference period or as far back as a specific event such as marriage or first employment (Skinner, 2000). While this design is both simple and cheap, these data are typically more complicated than those obtained with trend or panel techniques, because detailed information is given for each episode (that is, the time-span a unit of analysis, for example, a woman/man, spends in a specific state), including the duration and frequency of the event and any other aspects which show marked diachronic variation. However, retrospective surveys do have clear limitations, both in the necessarily simplified form in which they are forced to reconstruct experiences and, above all, because memory often distorts reality when trying to recall past events (Dex, 1991). Hence, retrospective surveys are usually limited to significant but infrequent life events such as births, marriages, divorces and job changes (Rose, 2000, p 12).

However, repeated cross-sectional and longitudinal prospective data do have one important element in common which constitutes an important limitation for both: they are gathered at discrete points in time (for example, every six months or annually). An analysis of the evolution of many types of social phenomena really requires continuous (in time) investigation of discrete events in order to permit study of both the sequence of the events that have taken place, and of the precise intervals which may have elapsed between one event and another. Such information is crucial if one is to understand the development of a life course and the way in which events and processes are interrelated.

Given that events are defined in terms of changes over time, it is usually accepted that the best way to study them together with their causes, is to gather duration data or event history data. In other words, to record what has happened to a sample of individuals, or a collective, together with precise information about the point in time when these events took place. As already described, duration data are typically collected retrospectively through life history studies – which generally cover the whole life course of individuals – or through the use of event histories, gathered using either prospective panels or cohort studies. In the former case, a sample of respondents is interviewed about aspects of their lives; they may be asked about all jobs and spells of unemployment they have experienced since leaving school. In the latter case, members of a sample are tracked over time and questioned every so often about all the important events that have affected family members since the last interview (Gilbert, 1993, p 168).

Detailed information about each episode is collected: the duration of the event, the origin state and the destination state, and so on. Take 'first marriage' as an example: each time an individual marries for the first time (origin state or initial event) an episode begins which will only finish with the transition into the state of 'no-longer married' (destination state or terminal event) (Blossfeld and Rohwer, 1995).

Examples of retrospective questions

The measurement of event histories is generally based on the following types of retrospective questions:

1. Has the initial event ever occurred?
2. When did it occur?
3. Has the terminal event occurred?
4. When did it occur?

Time in (2) and (4) can be measured in several ways, such as, age at occurrence, date of occurrence, or time between occurrence and survey. Any of the measurements may be recorded continuously or grouped into intervals (Skinner, 2000, p 121).

Furthermore, such studies often collect information relating to repeated events (consecutive jobs, unions, separations, births, for example) which take place both during parallel processes (work, matrimonial and family histories) and at different levels (micro-, meso- and macro-: for example, individual work history, history of the firm in which the individual is employed and structural changes in the labour market). The underlying idea, or principle, is that an individual's life course can only be understood if or when it is placed into the context of the trajectory of his/her social life. In Abrams' view (1982, p 360) "certainly, the lives of individuals are unique but their uniqueness does not depend on personal, intangible factors, rather it is based on the diversity of moves that individuals, historically placed within historically determined social worlds, can make". Wright Mills states (1962, p 167): "the biographies of men and women, of the different individuals that they become, cannot be understood if they are not considered in relation to those social structures within which and within whose context their daily lives are organised". Lastly, in Mayer's opinion (1990): "Life courses are shaped by a large number of inputs: specific structures offering political and economic opportunities; ideas shaped by the culture; norms that stipulate legal age for certain activities; sequence of positions and institutional passages; socialisation processes and selection mechanisms"[4]. In other words, these data make it possible to analyse developments within the institutional, cultural and social context in which an individual's life course is unfolding, since by focusing on events and transitions in individual lives, the interaction between action and structures can be closely observed.

Thus, in an event oriented matrix each line vector corresponds to the duration of one state or episode. For example, it could express a job episode (first job, second job, third job). If only one episode is considered for each case (for example, the birth of the first child or the first marriage), then the number of vectors will correspond to the number of cases examined. However, if these are repeated and/or parallel episodes (the number of which may vary greatly from one individual to another), the sum of the episodes that characterise each individual life course represents the total of line-vectors in the data matrix[5].

Since the termination of the entire observation time period is given in event history analysis, an episode may not be closed: indeed, by censoring we mean a state that occurs when information about the duration is incompletely recorded because of the temporal limits of the observation window we take into account. Censoring of a time period may occur from the right (observation stops before the event is observed) or from the left (observation does not begin until after the event has occurred; that is, the correct beginning of a process is unknown). Right censoring affects estimation procedures because the timing of the transition is not observed for one reason or another. One reason for right censoring might be that the event in question never happens to certain individuals: for example, not all people experience first marriages or change jobs. Another reason might be that some individuals have not experienced an event during the period of observation, but may experience the event some time later. In either case, all we know about the event is that it exceeds the time the individuals were last observed. Although the data are missing, the individual's censoring-time still constitutes valuable information when estimating transition rates. Figure 3.1 gives some examples of censoring (left, right censoring).

One good example of a study oriented towards events is the German Life History Study (GLHS). This is made up of a set of retrospective cohort studies that seek to gather detailed information both about events in the lives of the subjects involved, and about their most important activities. The study is made up of diverse studies (12 in all) of cohort samples drawn from the population of Germany. These cohorts were not followed over time, but were contacted just once during the data gathering activities. The groups were chosen in such a way that the transition phase between school and work coincided with periods that were particularly important from the historical point of view: the immediate post-war (Second World War) period; in a period of fast economic growth (boom); in a period of expansion within the welfare state and during a period of contraction in the economy (bust). The fundamental hypothesis underlying this study was that specific historical conditions would have had an equally specific impact on the working lives of those interviewed. As well as information about education and work, the GHLS also offers information about other important aspects of individual life, such as cultural background, family and residential history, etc (Blossfeld et al, 1989, pp 17-25). One further example is the UK 1980 Women and Employment Survey (WES), which collected very detailed work histories from a nationwide sample of more than 5,000 working women aged between 16 and 59 years living in Great Britain (Martin and Roberts, 1984) (see the Appendix for details).

Two good examples of prospective studies that retrospectively investigate the

Figure 3.1: Examples of censoring within an observation window

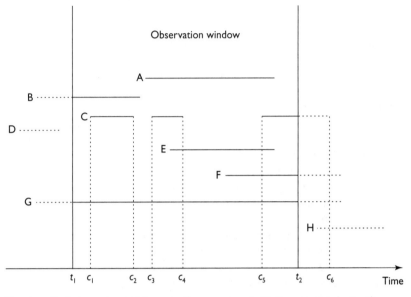

Sources: Re-elaboration from E.So.Po. (1998)

Case A: Beginning and end of the event (for example, cohabitation or unemployment) within observation window, not censored.

Case B: Left censored. Beginning of cohabitation/unemployment, before observation period and end of event within observation window

Case C: Beginning of cohabitation within the observation period, recurrent episode of receipt, end of last episode after the end of observation period, right censored.

Case D: Beginning and end of receipt before observation window.

Case E: Completely within the observation window, not censored.

Case F: Right censored.

Case G: Right and left censored.

Case H: Outside the observation window.

life of the subjects studied are again the BHPS and the GSOEP. The British Household Panel Study has taken the opportunity (over the first three waves) to get a very good picture of respondents' lives by asking for lifetime retrospective work-histories, and marital and fertility histories, hence investigating and illuminating vital areas of the lives of those who make up a representative sample of the households of Britain.

The German Socio-Economic Panel includes two calendars in the core questionnaires:

1. an activity calendar that, on a monthly basis, records participation in schooling, vocational education, military service, full-time and part-time employment, unemployment, homemaking and retirement for the previous year;
2. an income calendar where respondents indicate, also on a monthly basis, whether they have received income from various sources in the past year and the average monthly amount received from each source.

Moreover, the GSOEP provides spell-oriented data on 12 different kinds of labour market involvement, defining the beginning, end, and censoring status of any period of, for example, full-time work, part-time work, or unemployment. Additionally, the database contains spell data on the periods in which a person received different types of income (such as income from employment, pensions, unemployment benefits) (Merz and Rauberger, 1993; Frick, 1998).

'Qualitative' longitudinal sources

Longitudinal research does not only use data gathered through surveys on samples or that derived from mixing data from samples with information from censuses or administrative records. Another important longitudinal source can be found in the collection techniques used in biographical analyses (Walker and Leisering, 1998). This type of analysis, which takes many forms (the analysis of life histories or biographies, study of life courses and study of life events), is increasingly showing both theoretical and epistemological autonomy and developing a considerable repertory of themes: the paths of physical and psychological distress; situations of social exclusion; deviance; mobility and career events; changes in role especially in relation to gender characteristics; and transitions and changes in status, particularly in relation to age (Olagnero and Saraceno, 1993). Indeed, the biographical method aims to unravel the subjective dimension of time, the perceptions, orientations and self-interpretation that people develop during the course of their lives. Thus, this type of research demands a high degree of creativity from its practitioners (Walker and Leisering, 1998, pp 28-9).

Biographical material may be collected either directly, through structured and/or in-depth interviews, or indirectly. Different types of interviews can be used for the direct collection of information:

1. Relatively structured biographical interviews which aim to reconstruct events and behaviours: examples include, marriage and birth, relations with institutions (school or work), moving around the territory, consumption and saving behaviour. Such interviews may reconstruct the events experienced either entirely through retrospective investigation or through repeated interviews over a period of time. The problem with this type of interview, however, lies in the fact that the researcher has to trust entirely in the reliability of the subject's memory in order to discover how, and under what conditions, a previous situation started and then developed. The degree of error will also depend on how well or badly the interviews, and questionnaires, are

structured. There are techniques that can be used in order to minimise distortion; for example, it is better to start an interview with something that is based entirely on memory and then go on to more complex questions which require opinions. A retrospective interview is fairly reliable when it deals with crucial past events or transitions, such as those concerning work, marriage, changes in family composition, maternity, and so on. Results are less trustworthy when one wants to find out about precise and detailed results of short-term life plans, or about more complex matters, such as economic strategies and behaviour.

2. Semi-structured or unstructured interviews are suitable for discerning the cultural/symbolic level of the discourse; that is, defining the situation in terms of perceptions and representations. One could argue that the strength of such an interview (where at the most extreme the interviewer might say one thing only 'start from wherever you wish') is that it allows an individual to elaborate his/her personal history and to give meaning to his/her life (indeed these are called 'narrative' interviews). The strength of a theme-based interview, by contrast, is when seeking to reconstruct specific experiences and relations. However, this type of interviewer-led, focussed questioning may create resistance and block the narrator.

3. Life stories or autobiographical accounts, as told through conversations and interviews, between subject and interviewer. A life history is a story about an individual, his/her experiences, strategies, vicissitudes and emotions. If the individual relates events in which s/he has taken part, that is, if this personal account focuses on society at large and on social events, then it is termed oral history.

Among the indirect techniques are:

• Written, requested/commissioned autobiographies: these are records of subjects who, in the interests of research, are asked to write a first person account of their whole life. Here an autobiography is considered to be written by the subject him/herself over a fairly limited period of time, hence, written from a retrospective standpoint. This account may be oriented or directed through questions, or through the provision of a list of the most useful themes and/or subjects. One problem that should not be ignored is how the subjects may react: any relationship with the institution that collects these autobiographies could influence the account. Furthermore, such autobiographies risk being affected by hindsight, by a posteriori rationalisations of past events[6]. The ideal autobiography is that which is produced spontaneously (a rare find in the Social Sciences today).

• Biogrammes are a particular kind of written autobiography; not only does the researcher commission it, but s/he also controls and checks it. In other words, these autobiographies are fragments, or life events, briefly described by subjects in response to deliberate prompting on the part of the researcher. Like other sources listed above, these methods tend to disappear as the importance of oral testimony increases.

- Personal and day-to-day diaries have both been used considerably in the past, especially during the 1920s and 1930s when the Chicago School dominated social research. The main characteristics of a diary are that they are strictly personal, and that events are written down, simultaneously, as they unfold. These subjects become the archivists of their own day-to-day experiences; indeed, it is often worth telling them what the survey is seeking to achieve and asking them to record personal experiences related to that specific problem. While a great many diaries have been published as literature, very little social research has as yet made use of them: diaries are not only rare but it is also very difficult to generalise from them. Diaries are already widely used in psychotherapy but could also be used effectively in social research in order to keep track of the development of difficult situations or crises (reactions to the news of serious illness, redundancy) and the way in which responses change over time[7].
- Letters. As telephones have spread, so communicating by letter is becoming more and more unusual in today's society, and sociological research based on them has become equally rare. However, letters are still a means of communicating during periods of enforced separation (wars or emigration). Letters were however used in the famous study carried out by Thomas and Znaniecki (1918-20) on Polish emigrants to the US.
- Life history calendars or LHC (also called biographical/life history matrices) collect biographical longitudinal type information on individual charts – usually a large grid – in the form of a matrix. This specifies both the type of events the individual has experienced and when those events took place. One dimension of the matrix concerns the behavioural patterns being investigated; the other is divided into the time units for which these behavioural patterns are to be recorded (usually, the year, or years, in which such events took place and the age of the individual at the time are both recorded). In other words, LHC usually list horizontally the features and events which punctuate an individual's life (birth, end of education, marriage, first child, divorce, for example) (line-vectors), and the temporal meaning of the events vertically (row-vectors). A LHC can have two main advantages for collecting retrospective survey data. First, it can improve recall (and thus the quality of retrospective data) by increasing the respondent's ability (both visual and mental) to place different activities within the same time frame and to cross-check the timing of an event across several different domains. Second, very detailed sequences of events are easier to record within a LHC than with a conventional questionnaire (Freedman et al, 1988).

To sum up, the world of longitudinal research is extremely heterogeneous; moreover, the use of longitudinal data poses crucial theoretical and methodological problems. However, the use of both retrospective and prospective data ensures a more complete approach to social empirical research (Ruspini, 2002: forthcoming). With such data, social investigators have powerful instruments with which to get to the heart of many processes of social change and to craft effective policies for addressing social problems. Longitudinal research collects information about the temporal evolution of behaviour and ensures that the same subjects are involved each time. When individuals are surveyed at successive time points, it is possible to investigate how individual outcomes are related to the earlier circumstances of the same individuals. Thus, longitudinal data not only begins to unravel the nature of change at an individual level but also presents opportunities to explicitly recognise that individual behaviour is characterised by strong temporal tendencies. Longitudinal data then becomes essential if we are to understand these temporal tendencies in micro-level behaviour (Davies and Dale, 1994).

Notes

[1] For critical comparisons of cross-sectional and longitudinal studies data see, among others: Coleman, 1981; Davies, 1994; Dale and Davies 1994; Blossfeld and Rohwer, 1995; Rajulton and Ravanera, 2000.

[2] See also Tanner (1961, 1962, 1963) on adolescence and sexual development.

[3] Cf Duncan and Kalton (1987); Duncan, Juster and Morgan (1987); Solon (1989); Duncan (1992); Ghellini and Trivellato (1996); Trivellato (1999); Rose (2000).

[4] Cf Featherman (1980); Tuma and Hannah (1984); Sandefur and Tuma (1987); Mayer and Huinink (1990). Mayer (1991) identified four categories of mechanisms that 'impose order and limits' on the life history of an individual, all of which differ greatly both in themselves and between one individual and another: (a) institutional careers; (b) public intervention and regulation; (c) cumulative contingencies; (d) the overall conditions under which individuals belonging to diverse birth cohorts may end up (Billari, 1998).

[5] The history of life events might include not only the unit analysed, but also the event itself. In this case the line-vectors concern individual histories relating to that event (the birth of children, hospitalisation, retirement).

[6] As Gobo (1997, pp 39-40) reminds us, the process of remembering/re-evoking information is considered, by Cognitivists, to be a process of construction in which the person remembering will add something of his/her own to the event. Having carried out this type of 'incorporation', the individual is no longer able to distinguish between what s/he saw or heard and what s/he inferred.

[7] As was shown by Negri (1990, pp 184-5), individual strategic autonomy is extremely important: a trajectory of need and/or crisis is characterised by the inextricable bond between the catalysing event and the individual's strategy which, by redefining the event, allows the individual to adapt to it. Consequently the way in which a subject adapts to a problematic event is a process of construction within his/her life course.

References

Abrams, P. (1982) *Historical sociology*, West Compton House: Open Books Publishing Ltd.

Allison, P.D. (1984) *Event history analysis. Regression for longitudinal event data*, London: Sage Publications.

Billari, F. (1998) *Appunti di demografia sociale*, Italy: University of Padova.

Bijleveld, C.J.H., Mooijaart, A., van der Kamp, Leo J.Th. and van der Kloot, W.A. (1998) 'Structural equation models for longitudinal data', in C.J.H. Bijleveld et al, *Longitudinal data analysis. Designs, models and methods*, London: Sage Publications, pp 207-68.

Blossfeld, H.P. and Rohwer, G. (1995) *Techniques of event history modeling. New approaches to causal analysis*, Hillsdale, NJ: Lawrence Erlbaum Associates.

Blossfeld, H.P., Hamerle, A. and Mayer, K.U. (1989) *Event history analysis. Statistical theory and application in the social sciences*, Hillsdale, NJ: Lawrence Erlbaum Associates.

Buck, N., Gershuny, J., Rose, D. and Scott, J. (eds) (1994) *Changing households: The BHPS 1990 to 1992, ESRC Research Centre on Micro-Social Change*, Colchester: University of Essex.

Bynner, J. (1996) *Use of longitudinal data in the study of social exclusion. A report for the Organisation for Economic Co-operation and Development*, Social Statistics Research Unit, London: City University.

Citro, C. and Kalton, G. (eds) (1993) *The future of the Survey of Income and Program Participation*, Washington, DC: National Academy Press.

Coleman, J.S. (1981) *Longitudinal data analysis*, New York, NY: Basic Books.

Davies, R.B. (1994) 'From cross-sectional to longitudinal analysis', in A. Dale and R.B. Davies (eds) *Analysing social and political change. A casebook of methods*, London: Sage Publications, pp 20-40.

Davies, R.B. and Dale, A. (1994) 'Introduction', in A. Dale and R.B. Davies (eds) *Analysing social and political change. A casebook of methods*, London: Sage Publications.

de Graaf, N.D. (1999) 'Event history data and making a history out of a cross-sectional data', in E. Ruspini (ed) *Longitudinal analysis: A bridge between quantitative and qualitative social research, Special Issue of Quality and Quantity*, August, pp 261-76.

Dex, S. (1991) *The reliability of recall data: A literature review*, Occasional Papers of the ESRC Research Centre on Micro-Social Change, Paper 6, Colchester: University of Essex.

Draper, T.W. and Marcos, A.C. (eds) (1990) *Family variables. Conceptualization, measurement, and use*, London: Sage Publications.

Duncan, G.J. (1992) *Household Panel Studies: Prospects and problems*, Working Papers of the European Scientific Network on Household Panel Studies, Paper 54, Colchester: University of Essex.

Duncan, G.J. and Kalton, G. (1987) 'Issues of design and analysis of surveys across time', *International Statistical Review*, vol 55, no 1, pp 97-117.

Duncan, G.J., Juster, F.T. and Morgan, J.N. (1987) 'The role of panel studies in research on economic behavior', *Transportation Research*, vol 21A, no 4/5, pp 249-63.

E.So.Po (1998) *Evaluation of social policies from the local urban level: Income support for the able-bodied*, Final report (Research Team Co-ordinator, Chiara Saraceno).

Elder Jr, G.H. (1974) *Children of the Great Depression. Social change in life experience*, Chicago, IL: University of Chicago Press (1999, reissued as 25th Anniversary Edition, Boulder, CO: Westview Press).

Elder Jr, G.H. (1985) 'Perspectives on the life course', in G.H. Elder Jr (ed) *Life course dynamics. Trajectories and transitions, 1968–1980*, Ithaca, NY and London: Cornell University Press, pp 23-49.

Engel, U. and Reinecke, J.R. (1994) *Panelanalyse*, New York, NY: De Gruyter.

Featherman, D.L. (1980) 'Retrospective longitudinal research: methodological considerations', *Journal of Economics and Business*, vol 32, pp 152-69.

Finkel, S.E. (1995) *Causal analysis with panel data*, Sage University Paper Series on Quantitative Applications in the Social Sciences, No 105, Thousand Oaks, CA: Sage Publications.

Firebaugh, G. (1997) *Analyzing repeated surveys*, Sage University Paper Series on Quantitative Applications in the Social Sciences, No 115, Thousand Oaks, CA: Sage Publications.

Flood, L., Klevmarken, A. and Olovsson, P. (1997) *Household market and non-market activities (HUS), Survey Description*, vol III, Uppsala: Department of Economics, Uppsala University.

Freedman, D., Thornton, A., Camburn, D., Alwin, D. and Young-DeMarco, L. (1988) 'The life history calendar: a technique for collecting retrospective data', in C.C. Clogg (ed) *Sociological methodology*, vol 18, San Fransico, CA: Jossey Bass, pp 37-68.

Frick, J. (1998) Handout prepared for GSOEP summer workshop 29-30 June, Berlin, German Institute for Economic Research (DIW), material distributed to GSOEP users on CD-Rom.

Gallino, L. (1993) *Dizionario di Sociologia*, Milano: Tea.

Gershuny, J. (1998) 'Thinking dynamically: sociology and narrative data' in L. Leisering and R. Walker (eds) *The dynamics of modern society*, Bristol: The Policy Press, pp 34-48.

Gershuny, J. (2000) 'Time budgets, life histories and social position', in E. Ruspini (ed) *Longitudinal analysis: A bridge between quantitative and qualitative social research, Special Issue of Quality and Quantity*, August, pp 277-89.

Gershuny, J. and Buck, N. (2000) *ESRC National Strategy for Longitudinal Studies: Enquiry into social scientists' requirements for longitudinal data*, UK Longitudinal Studies Centre, Colchester: University of Essex [http://www.iser.essex.ac.uk/activities/NSLS-Enquiry.php].

Ghellini, G. and Trivellato, U. (1996) 'Indagini panel sul comportamento socio-economico di individui e famiglie: una selezionata rassegna di problemi ed esperienze', in C. Quintano (ed) *Scritti di Statistica Economica* 2, Napoli: Rocco Curto Editore.

Glenn, N.D. (1977) *Cohort analysis*, Beverly Hills, CA: Sage Publications.

Gilbert, N. (1993) *Analyzing tabular data. Loglinear and logistic models for social researchers*, London: University College London Press.

Gobo, G. (1997) *Le risposte e il loro contesto. Processi cognitivi e comunicativi nelle interviste standardizzate*, vol 8, Collana Metodologia delle Scienze Umane, Milano: Franco Angeli.

Hagenaars, J.A. (1990) *Categorical longitudinal data. Log-linear panel, trend and cohort analysis*, London: Sage Publications.

Hakim, C. (1987) *Research design. Strategies and choices in the design of social research*, London: Allen and Unwin.

Kalton, G. and Lepkowski, J. (1985) 'Following rules in SIPP', *Journal of Social and Economic Measurement*, vol 13, no 3-4, pp 319-29.

Kasprzyk, D., Duncan, G.J., Kalton, G. and Singh, M.P. (eds) (1989) *Panel surveys*, New York, NY: John Wiley.

Kish, L. (1986) 'Timing of surveys for public policy', *Australian Journal of Statistics*, vol 28, pp 1-12.

Kish, L. (1987) *Statistical design for research*, New York, NY: John Wiley.

Klevmarken, A. and Olovsson, P. (1993) *Household market and non-market activities (HUS), Procedures and codes 1984–1991*, Stockholm: Industrial Institute for Economic and Social Research.

Janson, C.G. (1990) 'Retrospective data, undesirable behavior, and the longitudinal perspective', in D. Magnusson and L.R. Bergman (eds) *Data quality in longitudinal research*, Cambridge: Cambridge University Press.

Lazarsfeld, P.F. (1948) 'The use of panels in social research', *Proceedings of the American Philosophical Society*, vol 42, no 5, pp 405-10.

Magnusson, D., Bergman, L.R., Rudinger, G. and Torestad, B. (eds) (1991) *Problems and methods in longitudinal research: Stability and change*, Cambridge: Cambridge University Press.

Mannheim, K. (1952) 'The problem of generations', in P. Kecskemeti (ed) *Essays on the sociology of knowledge*, New York, NY: Oxford University Press, pp 276-322.

Marlier, E. (1999) *The EC Household Panel Newsletter*, Statistics in Focus, Population and Social Conditions, Theme 3, no 2, Luxembourg: Eurostat.

Martin, J. and Roberts, C. (1984a) *Women and employment: A lifetime perspective*, London: HMSO.

Martin, J. and Roberts, C. (1984b) *Women and employment: Technical report*, London: OPCS.

Mayer, K.U. (1990) 'Lebensverlaufe und sozialer Wandel. Anmerkungen zu einem Forschungsprogramm', *Koelner Zeitschrift fuer Soziologie und Sozialpsychologie, Sonderheft* 31, Opladen: Westdeutscher Verlag, pp 7-21.

Mayer, K.U. (1991) 'Life courses in the welfare state', in W.R. Heinz (ed) *Theoretical advances in life course research*, vol I, Weinheim: Deutscher Studien Verlag.

Mayer, K.U. and Huinink, J. (1990) 'Age, period and cohort in the study of the life course: a comparison of classical A-P-C analysis with event history analysis or farewell to lexis?', in S. Magnusson and L.R. Bergman (eds) *Data quality in longitudinal research*, Cambridge: Cambridge University Press, pp 211-32.

Mednick, S.A. and Mednick, B. (1984) 'A brief history of North American longitudinal research', in A.M. Sarnoff, M. Harway and K.M. Finello (eds) *Handbook of longitudinal research, vol 1: Birth and Childhood Cohorts*, New York, NY: Praeger, pp 19-21.

Menard, S. (1991) *Longitudinal research*, London: Sage Publications.

Merz, J. and Rauberger, T.K. (1993) 'Time use questions in a panel design: experiences with the German Socio-Economic Panel', in *Time use methodology: Toward consensus, Proceedings of the 1992 Conference of the International Association for Time Use Research*, Rome, June: Institute Italiano di Statistica, pp 207-18.

Negri, N. (1990) 'Introduzione', in N. Negri (ed) *Povertà in Europa e trasformazione dello Stato sociale*, Milano: Franco Angeli, pp 11-72.

Olagnero, M. and Saraceno, C. (1993) *Che vita è. L'uso dei materiali biografici nell'analisi sociologica*, Roma: La Nuova Italia Scientifica.

Rajulton, F. (1999) 'Lifeheist: analysis of life histories, a state space approach', *Paper presented at the Workshop on Longitudinal Research in Social Science: a Canadian Focus*, Windereme Manor, London Ontario, Canada, 15-27 October.

Rajulton, F. and Ravanera, Z.R. (2000) 'Theoretical and analytical aspects of longitudinal research', *Paper presented at the Annual Meeting of the Canadian Population Association* held in Edmonton, Alberta, 28-30 May.

Rose, D. (2000) 'Household Panel Studies: an overview', in D. Rose (ed) *Researching social and economic change. The uses of Household Panel Studies, Social Research Today Series*, London: Routledge, pp 3-35.

Rose, D. and Sullivan, O. (1996) *Introducing data analysis for social scientists*, Milton Keynes: Open University Press.

Ruspini, E. (1999) 'Longitudinal research and the analysis of social change', in E. Ruspini (ed) *Longitudinal analysis: A bridge between quantitative and qualitative social research, Special Issue of Quality and Quantity*, vol 33, no 3, July–August, pp 219-27.

Ruspini, E. (2002: forthcoming) *Introduction to longitudinal research*, London: Routledge.

Ryder, N.B. (1965) 'The cohort as a concept in the study of social change', *American Sociological Review*, vol 30, no 6, pp 843-61.

Sandefur, G.D. and Tuma, N.B. (1987) 'How data type affects conclusions about individual mobility', *Social Science Research*, vol 16, no 4, pp 301-28.

Saraceno, C. (ed) (1986) *Età e corso della vita*, Bologna: Il Mulino.

Skinner, C. (2000) 'Dealing with measurement error in panel analysis', in D. Rose (ed) *Researching social and economic change. The uses of Household Panel Studies, Social Research Today Series*, London: Routledge, pp 113-25.

Solon, G. (1989) 'The value of panel data in economic research', in D. Kasprzyk, G.J. Duncan, G. Kalton and M.P. Singh (eds) *Panel surveys*, New York, NY: John Wiley, pp 486-96.

Sudman, S. and Bradburn, N.A. (1982) *Asking questions*, Jossey-Bass Series in Social and Behavioral Sciences, San Francisco, CA/London: Jossey-Bass Publishers.

Sudman, S. and Ferber, R. (1979) *Consumer panels*, Chicago, IL: American Marketing Association.

Taris, T.W. (2000) *A primer in longitudinal data analysis*, London: Sage Publications.

Terman, L.M. (1925) *Genetic studies of genius, vol 1: Mental and Physical Traits of a Thousand Gifted Children*, Stanford, CA: Stanford University Press.

Terman, L.M. (1939) 'The vocational success of intellectually gifted individuals', *School and Society*, vol 49, pp 65-73.

Terman, L.M. (1959) *Genetic studies of genius, vol 4: The gifted group at mid-life: Thirty-five years' follow-up of the superior child*, Stanford, CA: Stanford University Press.

Terman, L.M. and Oden, M.H. (1947) *Genetic studies of genius, vol 4: The gifted child grows up: Twenty-five years' follow-up of a superior group*, Stanford, CA: Stanford University Press.

Thomas, W.I. and Znaniecki, F. (1918-20) *The Polish peasant in Europe and America*, Boston, MA: Gorham Press.

Trivellato, U. (1999) 'Issues in the design and analysis of panel studies: a cursory review', in E. Ruspini (ed) *Longitudinal analysis: A bridge between quantitative and qualitative social research, Special Issue of Quality and Quantity*, vol 33, no 3, July-August.

Tuma, N.B. and Hannah, M.T. (1984) *Social dynamics. Models and methods*, Orlando/London: Academic Press.

van de Pol, F.J.R. (1989) *Issues of design and analysis of panels*, Amsterdam: Sociometric Research Foundation.

van der Kamp, Leo J.Th. and Bijleveld, C.J.H. (1998) 'Methodological issues in longitudinal research', in C.J.H. Bijleveld et al, *Longitudinal data analysis. Designs, models and methods*, London: Sage Publications, pp 1-45.

Walker, R. and Leisering, L. (1998) 'New tools: towards a dynamic science of modern society', in L. Leisering and R. Walker (eds) *The dynamics of modern society*, Bristol: The Policy Press, pp 17-33.

Wall, W.D. and Williams, H.L. (1970) *Longitudinal studies and the social sciences*, London: Heinemann.

Wright Mills, C. (1959) *The sociological imagination*, New York, NY: Oxford University Press.

Zazzo, R. (1967) 'Diversité, realité, et mirages de la méthode longitudinale: rapport introducif au symposium des études longitudinales', *Enfance*, vol 2, no 20, pp 131-6.

Part II:
The issues

The role of education on postponement of maternity in Britain, Germany, the Netherlands and Sweden

Siv Gustafsson, Eiko Kenjoh and Cécile Wetzels

Introduction

In most European countries, age of the mother at first birth has reached an all-time high. The number of women who never give birth to a child, the ultimate childlessness rate, has increased to the highest level since the Second World War. In a series of articles[1] we have argued that economic rationality works in favour of postponement of maternity, while presumably biological rationality calls for a halt to this trend, and perhaps a reversal.

Postponement of maternity has not yet received the attention it deserves from economists. In *Population and family economics*, Hotz, Klerman and Willis (1997) devote only one-and-a-half pages to the timing of births, while there is more demographic than economic research on postponement of maternity (see, for example, Bosveld, 1996 and Beets, 1997, 1998). Bongaarts (1999) argues that there is no reason to worry about decreasing fertility rates, because they are caused by an increase in the age at maternity. He points out that if women are 30 instead of 25 when they start families, they can still reach replacement rates (that is, about two children per woman). We argue that there is reason to worry. If the mean age is around 30 it means that many women will be approaching 40 before they have 'organised' their lives to start a family. Many women may therefore be approaching their biological limit when they wish to get pregnant. This results in more demands on medical assistance (such as in vitro fertilisation) and it carries more risks for mother and child (see Wetzels, 2001, ch 7) and more ultimate (including some involuntary) childlessness. This chapter analyses these effects of education on postponement of maternity. We distinguish between level of education completed and time of leaving full-time education as determinants in explaining the timing of first birth.

We use household panel data from four countries: for Britain we use the British Household Panel Survey (BHPS) (see Taylor, 1999); for Germany, the German Socio-Economic Panel (GSOEP) (see Wagner et al, 1991; Haisken-

De New and Frick, 1998); for the Netherlands, the *Organisatie voor Strategisch Arbeidsmarkt-onderzoek* (OSA) (see Allaart et al, 1987); and for Sweden, the *Hushållens ekonomiska levnadsförhållanden* (HUS) (see Flood et al, 1997; Klevmarken and Olovsson, 1993[2]). These countries have been selected for the following reasons:

- They provide interesting cases of different policy approaches to supporting families with children.
- Their household panel surveys have been conducted over long and comparable periods of time.

The main focus of this chapter is constructing comparable educational variables across countries, and constructing two duration (or waiting time) variables: the waiting time of a woman from age 15 until she has her first child, and the waiting time of a woman since finishing education until she has her first child. This we do by distinguishing women's birth cohort (by decade), and first child birth cohort (again, by decade). We link a recent wave of each of the respective household panels to information on birth and education history that had been collected in earlier waves, and follow all women from age 15 until they have their first birth, or are censored at the latest wave because they have not yet given birth to a child. We construct variables on duration of schooling, time at completing full-time education and the duration of time between ending full-time education and time at first birth.

We then develop our hypotheses concerning the role of education in the timing of maternity. It is likely that different patterns of investment in human capital play a decisive role between educational groups within a country. Comparisons between countries are likely to be influenced by public policies on parental leave and childcare. We define three educational groups across our four countries and describe how we translate national definitions from the widely diverging educational systems into comparable groups. We also discuss our measures of waiting time or duration until first birth. We then go on to show that higher educated women are most likely to postpone motherhood. We look at the educational distribution of recent mothers across the consecutive decades when the child was born. We then estimate postponement of maternity in two ways:

- starting to count from age 15;
- starting from the time she left full-time education.

We offer our concluding remarks in the final part of the chapter.

Why do women postpone maternity? A theoretical discussion

There are basically two different economic reasons for the timing of maternity – namely the 'consumption smoothing motive' and the 'career planning motive'

(Hotz et al, 1997). The 'consumption smoothing motive' implies that children should be born when household income is highest so that other consumption needs can also be fitted into the budget. For this motive, therefore, the husband's income profile matters. Generally, the 'career planning motive' also calls for a postponement of maternity. It refers to the need to make time for childbearing and caring. Traditionally, the career planning motive has, to a high degree, had an impact on prospective mothers; there would be no difference between the 'consumption smoothing' and 'career planning' motives for prospective fathers, because of the passive fathering roles predominant in most of Europe. Both economic motives tend to postpone births. The reason for this is that a young person can expect higher earnings later in life when education has been completed and work experience has increased the demand for that person's skills. Economists see education and the accumulation of work experience as investments in human capital that have some costs during an initial phase when people are in education or new in the labour market and searching to find a career that suits them. This chapter concentrates on women's 'career planning motive' by analysing the role of education in the timing of maternity. This means that we disregard the influence of husband's and wife's income profiles which would be the relevant variables for analysing the consumption smoothing motive.

There are reasons to believe that highly-educated women are most likely to postpone motherhood. Firstly, education (being in school) is incompatible with having children, because of lack of adequate income to pay for childcare and other costs, and because the student lifestyle does not fit with family responsibilities. It follows that, since highly-educated women stay longer in school, they will have children later. Secondly, after finishing school highly-educated women are likely to spend time seeking employment and other career planning. Generally age-earning curves of higher educated people rise more quickly than age-earning curves of less educated people, and for all educational groups the first years after finishing school show more steeply rising wages than later on in life. Economists interpret the rising wages as investments in job training that, in addition to schooling, increase a person's human capital. In general, there is a positive correlation between schooling and job investments which results in the steeply rising wages of highly-educated people. It is therefore costly to leave a job and spend time caring for a child – not only in the short run because of income loss, but also in the long run because of foregone investments in job training. The third reason why highly-educated women may postpone maternity longer than less educated women is that the former may have a different attitude to the conflict between caring for children and caring about their career. A woman who discontinues education at an earlier age may make a family plan and fit in labour market work only if there is time left after the needs of the children. By contrast, a highly-educated woman makes a career plan: she thinks carefully about when her career would suffer the least from a career break or part-time employment. This third reason is called the 'attitude parameter'. There is reason to believe that the proportion of 'career aware' women increases in relation to their education and thus the labour force participation of married women and women with children increases over time. To summarise, we have indicated three reasons why highly-educated women have their children later than less educated women:

- Education is finished at a later age.
- The period of finding the optimal job may take longer after finishing school.
- The 'career aware' attitude may be stronger: being concerned with how children will fit a career, rather than how work can fit the time schedule of being a mother.

Economists see the realisation of family formation as a decision based on an evaluation of costs and benefits so that the demand for children is realised when benefits exceed costs (Becker, 1981). The benefits of having children in modern societies are emotional, psychological and of other non-financial kinds. The earlier in life your children are born, the longer you can enjoy them, and more likely you are to have grandchildren when young enough to enjoy them, and so on. In many cases the 'biological clock' strikes earlier in life than is optimum for career-planning. Medical research shows higher risks for first-time mothers approaching the age of 40: fecundity problems may arise after age 30, and will require higher medical costs as couples seek assistance in childbearing.

Public policies can change the costs of children. In general, subsidised childcare, paid parental leave, child benefits, tax credits, maternity job protection periods, and parental leave shared between father and mother are all measures that decrease the cost of children, but to different extents. Policies that help in combining work and family reduce the cost of children, proportionally more for women with a career oriented attitude than for women with a traditional family oriented attitude (Gustafsson, 1984, 1994, 2000; Sainsbury, 1994, 1996; Wetzels, 2001).

Contextual information on countries

Sweden

Although women have, since the 1970s, increasingly invested in a lifetime labour market career, Sweden was the only country of the four analysed here, that, at this time, introduced policies that supported combining work and family to meet the needs of two-earner families. Swedish parents are entitled to 75% of earnings compensation for a maximum of 12 full-time months[3]. The Swedish job protection period expires when the child is 18 months old, when the parents are expected to bring their child to day care for five days a week. One of the parents, however, has the legal right to reduce his/her hours in a regular job to six hours a day until the child is eight years old.

By contrast, policies in the Netherlands until the 1990s and Germany until 1997 have supported single-earner families, mostly by child benefits and tax credits. Britain has had the least public support for families with children (see, among others, Chester, 1994; Bradshaw, 1996). In the Netherlands and Germany (except for former East Germany), the view that a child needed 24 hours a day attendance by its mother made it virtually impossible for mothers in these countries to combine work and family until fairly recently[4].

In contrast to Sweden, paternity and maternity leave corresponded to a type of 'sick leave' and concerned the final period of the pregnancy and the two to three months after the birth of the child. It was not meant to be parental leave. This short pregnancy leave and very little day care for children made it very difficult to continue working after giving birth to a child in the Netherlands[5], former West Germany and Britain. This implies that, until the 1990s, women in these countries implicitly made a decision to give up their careers when they had a child.

Germany[6]

More specifically, in former West Germany from the 1980s onwards maternity leave had been extended from six months in 1979 to 36 months by 1993, by which time Germany was unified. However, leave benefits are low compared to Sweden and, during the period covered by our analyses, most women were only entitled to leave benefits for six months after childbirth. The family policies of former West Germany apply to the reunified Germany. In former East Germany working mothers were encouraged to make use of full day care for children (see Kreyenfeld, 2000b, pp 4-5). Public policies were aimed at keeping women in the labour market when they had children. The decision on timing of the birth of children did not imply a decision to stop a labour market career. There is still a relative abundance of public day care in former East Germany (Kreyenfeld, 2000b). Shared parental leave between father and mother has been introduced since 2001, and part-time work of 30 hours can be taken at the same time as parental leave. In addition, there is freedom to choose one year with a higher benefit rather than two years with a lesser benefit[7].

The Netherlands

Since 1990, the Dutch government has supported an average working week of 29-32 hours for both women and men (Wetzels, 2001). It has implemented policies to encourage both fathers and mothers to work long part-time hours and share caring tasks for children. However, there are still waiting lists for childcare and six-month leave at 75% earnings is only available in the government sector[8]. In the Netherlands the 1990 Childcare Stimulation Act was the first government action which explicitly catered for the needs of the working mother, rather than assigning priority to the educational needs of the children[9]. The percentage of pre-schoolers in childcare was less than 4% in 1990.

Britain

Public policies to support combining work and family is minimal in Britain[10]. It was only when Britain committed to adopt the European Union Parental Leave Directive by 1999, that British parents became entitled to unpaid parental leave of up to three months. The leave is granted on a non-transferable basis, as in the Netherlands, to promote equal opportunities between men and women. It is the first time that British fathers have had any right to paternity leave to care for a child. Although the job protection period in Britain is quite long (40 weeks) compared to the Netherlands, payment of maternity leave is only for 18 weeks of which only six weeks is compensated for at 90% of earnings, and 12 weeks at a flat rate which is quite low − £55.7 per week in 1997, 35% of an average income for a woman working part-time. Until 1997 there was no public policy to provide subsidised day care other than schools. Since 1997 the Labour government has taken major initiatives to supply more childcare spaces, for example, a childcare space for all three-year-olds, and to make childcare spaces affordable to more parents than before[11].

Thus, the cost of children to mothers' careers is lowest in Sweden (during most of the time period that we study, namely the 1980s through the 1990s, until 1998 for Britain and Sweden and 1996 for Germany and the Netherlands).

Later in this chapter we ask whether fertility patterns are affected by dual-earner friendly public policies. If so, Swedish women who have enjoyed career friendly policies since the 1970s might be expected to show less postponement than women in the other three countries.

Data and construction of variables: why panel data?

As stated above, empirical analysis has been carried out using household panel data from four countries: Britain (BHPS), Germany (GSOEP), the Netherlands (OSA) and Sweden (HUS) (see Appendix A1 at the end of this chapter). More specifically, information on women's level of education and their year of birth is obtained from BHPS 1992 and 1998, GSOEP 1996, OSA 1996 and HUS 1984, 1986, 1993, 1996 and 1998.

The crucial variables for this analysis are the education variables and two duration (or waiting time) variables, namely the duration of time since the woman was 15 years old until she has her first child and the duration of time between finishing full-time education and the birth of her first child. These variables can in principle be collected in a cross-sectional survey with retrospective information, but we have retrieved them from the household panel study making use of several waves of data. The strongest case for panel data is when behaviour is analysed before and after a critical event such as labour force transitions of a woman around her first childbirth[11]. Further, panel data allow future extensions where the panel data aspects become crucial.

We created three groups of education: low, medium and high. All education that is shorter than medium education is called low education, and all education that is longer than medium education is called high education. Because of the parallel school systems there is not a single normal study time to achieve medium education. We define medium education as an interval of 12 to 14 years of education. This is the level of the US high school diploma which takes 12 years of schooling. There are corresponding secondary school diplomas in the four countries of our analysis. In Germany this is the Abitur; in Britain the General Certificate of Education A-levels, in the Netherlands *hoger algemeen voortgezet onderwijs* (HAVO) or *voorbereidend wetenschappelijk onderwijs* (VWO), and in Sweden the *studentexamen*. The Swedish system is most similar to the US system, since all secondary school education, since reforms in the 1960s, end up in *studentexamen*. We used variables on highest educational level attained in order to construct variables on years of schooling (technical details on variable construction are given in Appendix A3, at the end of this chapter).

In order to create the two duration variables we need to have information on age at finishing education and age at having the first birth. Details of how age at finishing education or training is calculated is given in Appendix A3. In each country, the age of finishing education is younger among those who are highly-educated in the 1970s cohort than in older cohorts. This is mainly because in this youngest cohort there are many women who are still in education, and these women will be in the highly-educated group in the future. We do not include these women in our sample. Consequently, the mean age of women when finishing education among highly-educated women in the 1970s cohort is rather younger compared to highly-educated women in the other cohorts. Note that our definition of high education includes not only university level but also lower levels like technical schools, or other higher qualifications.

The age of the mother at first birth is calculated from the difference between the birth year of the first child and that of the mother for each observation. The data from the Netherlands differ from the others in that they account for adopted children. Since fewer women in the sample were born before 1930, figures for the 1950s and the 1960s are less representative of the whole population. In the Dutch sample, this problem is rather severe: of all Dutch women who gave birth to their first child between the 1950s and 1990s, only 0.2% were born before 1930. The corresponding proportions were 8.6% for Britain, 8.7% for West Germany, 3.9% for East Germany and 8.8% for Sweden.

Development over time of age at maternity and age at finishing school

Previous research has shown that the mean age of the mother at first childbirth in European countries since around 1950 forms a U-shaped pattern with substantial variation around the mean. Age of the mother at first childbirth began decreasing from the 1950s and reached its lowest level around 1970 or 1975 (Gustafsson et al, 2002a, 2002b), before increasing to the highest level yet observed. For example, in 1950 in the Netherlands mothers' age at first birth averaged 26.5 years; in 1970 it had decreased to 24.7 years, by 1991 had increased to 27.7 years and in 1997 the mean age of the mother at first birth was as high as 29 years. The strongest increase revealed by demographic data in mean age of the mother at first birth is observed in former East Germany, from 22.2 years in 1985 to 27.3 years in 1996 (Bosveld, 1996; Council of Europe, 1998).

Beets (1997, 1998) presents information about variation around the mean by reporting medians and quartiles of women's age at first childbirth for a number of countries. The third quartile, that is, the age at which 75% of women of a birth cohort have had their first child, has risen much more dramatically over time than has the mean age. For women born in 1955 the third quartile for West German women is as high as 34 years. Some of the variation around the mean comes from different behaviour across educational groups. In Table 4.1, based on the household panel data, the pattern of a U-shape is confirmed. Although births that took place in the 1950s occurred at an older age than births in the 1970s, the 1990s mothers are much older than the 1950s mothers. In Table 4.1 we observe the emerging divergence of the mean age at first birth of highly-educated women in comparison to women with lower education. In the 1990s the difference in mean age between high- and low-educated women was 5 years in Britain, 3.4 years in West Germany, 2.7 years in East Germany, 4.1 years in the Netherlands and 4.3 years in Sweden. The corresponding figures for mothers of the 1960s are much smaller for all countries. We hypothesised above that the 'career planning motive' would induce women to postpone births in order to finish education and establish themselves in a job before starting a family (Joshi, 1990; see also the chapter by Kurz in this volume).

The mean age at motherhood of highly-educated women starts to increase more rapidly than less educated women only from the 1970s, resulting in a marked divergence of mother's age at first birth between educational groups, which increases over time. This suggests that the career planning motive has become more important over time. In the 1960s student marriages were not uncommon, but it was also not uncommon for highly-educated mothers to give up their career plans because of lack of support in terms of childcare, parental leaves and the like. Table 4.1 also tells us that there is not much difference between Sweden and West Germany in this regard, although Swedish family-friendly policies have been in effect since the 1970s. We have shown in other work (Gustafsson et al, 2002a, 2002b), that the work patterns of Swedish mothers is very different from those of the other three countries, with a return to work after 12-18 months, and 90% of Swedish mothers in paid work by the time the child is five years old. By contrast in the other three countries half of the mothers have not entered paid work by the time the child is five years old. From Table 4.1 one can conclude that the dual-earner friendly policies in Sweden have not stopped postponement of maternity although they did allow mothers to work and have changed Sweden into a dual-earner society to a much larger extent than in the other three countries. It is rather disappointing that Swedish policies do not seem to have brought a halt to postponement of maternity. East Germany shows a very different fertility pattern from West Germany. Kreyenfeld (2000a, 2000b) has researched the fertility pattern of

Table 4.1: Mean age of mothers at first birth by time period in which first child was born and education in Britain, Germany, the Netherlands and Sweden

	Time period in which first child was born (number of observations)					
	1950s	1960s	1970s	1980s	1990s	Total
Britain						
Low	24.7	23.9	23.8	23.6	24.2	24.0 (2,546)
Medium	26.2	23.5	24.4	25.5	25.5	25.0 (402)
High	26.5	24.8	26.0	27.1	29.2	26.6 (469)
Total	24.9 (590)	23.9 (738)	24.2 (801)	24.5 (931)	25.4 (357)	24.5 (3,417)
West Germany						
Low	25.2	23.9	23.3	24.9	26.4	24.6 (1,387)
Medium	28.0	25.3	25.2	28.2	29.2	27.5 (114)
High	26.2	25.8	27.5	28.0	29.8	28.1 (171)
Total	25.5 (254)	24.0 (379)	23.8 (328)	25.6 (429)	27.3 (282)	25.1 (1,672)
East Germany						
Low	22.5	22.3	22.0	22.2	23.3	22.3 (813)
Medium	23.1	22.0	23.1	23.2	23.8	23.0 (253)
High	*	25.6	23.1	24.8	26.0	24.5 (153)
Total	22.6 (168)	22.7 (234)	22.4 (346)	22.9 (358)	23.8 (113)	22.8 (1,219)
Netherlands						
Low	23.1	24.5	24.7	25.6	26.6	24.9 (1,038)
Medium	a	25.3	25.0	25.7	28.0	26.1 (439)
High	a	25.8	27.3	28.5	30.7	28.3 (178)
Total	23.2 (82)	24.7 (341)	25.0 (575)	26.0 (397)	28.0 (256)	25.5 (1,655)
Sweden						
Low	24.7	23.7	24.2	24.4	25.5	24.3 (1,547)
Medium	25.6	23.6	24.3	25.6	26.1	24.9 (316)
High	24.7	24.6	25.7	28.2	29.8	26.8 (387)
Total	24.8 (402)	23.8 (613)	24.5 (620)	25.7 (405)	27.0 (210)	24.8 (2,250)

ª less than 10 observations.

Source: Authors' own computations based on BHPS 1992 and 1998 for Britain; GSOEP 1996 for Germany (Sample A, that is, Germans in former West Germany and Sample C, that is, Germans in former East Germany); OSA 1996 for the Netherlands; and HUS 1984, 1986, 1993, 1996 and 1998 for Sweden.

Education high: obtained highest qualification requires 15 years or more of schooling. Education medium: obtained highest qualification requires between 12 years and 14 years of schooling. Education low: obtained highest qualification requires less than 12 years of schooling. Women still in education are not included.

what used to be East Germany using GSOEP. She shows that although the total fertility rates have recently decreased sharply, postponement of maternity has not yet reached figures for West Germany.

Increased education, we emphasise, is one possible explanation for the postponement of maternity. Table 4.2 presents duration of education by birth cohort of the women by looking at the age of the woman when finishing education. If we look at the average number of years a woman has studied across educational groups, we can perceive compositional effects, in that high- and medium-educated women make up the greatest part of the overall total. Since the youngest women in the youngest cohort born 1970-79 in Britain are only 19 years old (1998-79), the figures on duration of education are censored to some extent, and influence the mean age at finishing education downwards. However, a comparison of the 1930-39 cohort with the 1960-69 cohort is not affected by this bias: the increase in average education among British mothers rises from age 17.0 to age 18.2, an increase of only 1.2 years in 30 years. In Sweden during the same 30 year period, the increase is 2.6 years, from age 16.9 to age 19.5. In Britain, East Germany and Sweden, age of finishing education peaks at 24 for women born between 1940-49, and then decreases. This may be a compositional effect since high education includes everyone who has a qualification that requires more than 14 years of schooling. Therefore, there are more people with 15 years of education among the younger cohorts, and more people with 17 years of education in the 1940s cohort. The main conclusion from Table 4.2 is that there is an increase at the age when women finish education in all countries.

Duration until first birth: an econometric analysis

One way of illustrating duration of time from age 15 until first birth is by way of the Kaplan-Meier estimator (see Appendix A1). In Figure 4.1, Kaplan-Meier estimates are presented for highly-educated women for each country. The curves show the proportion of women, according to age, who have not yet become a mother. The higher the level of the curve, the more women are childless. We also see that the curve for West Germany is, for most of its extension, on a higher level and more to the right than any of the other curves. This means that West German highly-educated women are the least likely to have children in comparison to highly-educated women in the other countries. By contrast, the curve for East Germany lies more to the left and at a lower level than for any other country, meaning that more East German highly-educated women have children earlier. The curves flatten out at age 35, meaning that few women have their first child after age 35. The almost parallel section of the curves after age 35 shows West Germany on top, with Britain, the Netherlands, Sweden and East Germany below. This parallel section of the Kaplan-Meier estimates is an estimate of the ultimate childlessness of women with high education. Similar Kaplan-Meier estimates for low-educated women and medium-educated women respectively show much smaller differences between countries. Figure 4.1 does not distinguish between women of different birth cohorts who gave birth to their first child at different points of time, as do Tables 4.1 and 4.2, but uses all the data in the 'Total' columns of these tables.

Let us now turn to analysing the duration from age 15 to first childbirth, and the duration from finishing full-time education to first childbirth, using a different duration model for each dependent variable. Appendix A2 explains the

Table 4.2: Mean age of women when finishing education or training by cohort and education in Britain, Germany, the Netherlands and Sweden

	Time period of women's year of birth (number of observations)					
	Born 1930-39	Born 1940-49	Born 1950-59	Born 1960-69	Born 1970-79	Total
Britain						
Low	15.7	16.0	16.5	16.5	16.4	16.2 (2,948)
Medium	20.5	19.9	20.6	18.8	17.6	19.1 (675)
High	24.1	24.2	23.1	21.7	20.4	22.6 (857)
Total	17.0 (672)	17.9 (922)	18.4 (1,000)	18.2 (1,279)	17.4 (607)	17.9 (4,480)
West Germany						
Low	17.4	17.7	17.9	19.4	19.6	18.4 (1,691)
Medium	20.0	20.7	21.6	22.6	21.1	21.7 (162)
High	22.8	23.6	24.5	24.7	22.7	24.2 (274)
Total	17.9 (308)	18.4 (376)	19.3 (543)	20.6 (673)	20.0 (227)	19.4 (2,127)
East Germany						
Low	17.2	17.9	18.3	19.0	19.9	18.4 (944)
Medium	18.9	20.5	20.3	21.1	20.7	20.5 (276)
High	22.6	23.2	22.9	23.7	22.3	23.1 (189)
Total	17.9 (214)	19.0 (264)	19.6 (395)	20.2 (375)	20.2 (161)	19.4 (1,409)
Netherlands						
Low	15.3	15.4	15.8	17.0	17.6	15.9 (1,217)
Medium	18.8	18.4	18.6	19.9	19.7	19.3 (665)
High	23.3	22.7	22.5	23.4	22.2	22.9 (283)
Total	16.3 (282)	16.8 (493)	17.5 (583)	19.5 (562)	19.1 (245)	17.9 (2,165)
Sweden						
Low	15.9	16.8	17.7	17.9	18.5	17.1 (1,742)
Medium	21.2	20.3	20.2	20.2	19.7	20.1 (621)
High	22.7	24.0	22.5	22.4	22.1	22.8 (530)
Total	16.9 (473)	18.5 (750)	19.5 (698)	19.5 (584)	19.5 (388)	18.8 (2,893)

Source: Authors' own computations based on BHPS 1991-98 for Britain; GSOEP 1996 for Germany (Sample A, that is, Germans in former West Germany and Sample C, that is, Germans in former East Germany); OSA 1996 for the Netherlands; and HUS 1984, 1986, 1993, 1996 and 1998 for Sweden.

Education high: obtained highest qualification requires 15 years or more of schooling. Education medium: obtained highest qualification requires between 12 years and 14 years of schooling. Education low: obtained highest qualification requires less than 12 years of schooling. Women still in education are not included.

econometric model used, where the focus is on birth cohort of the woman and her education. One reads the results of Table 4.3 and 4.4 by first looking at the Z-value given in parenthesis below each estimated coefficient. The Z-value corresponds to a T-value in an ordinary least squares regression and therefore a value of about 2 is required for the coefficient to be statistically significant, with

Figure 4.1: The Kaplan-Meier estimates of not giving first birth, high educated

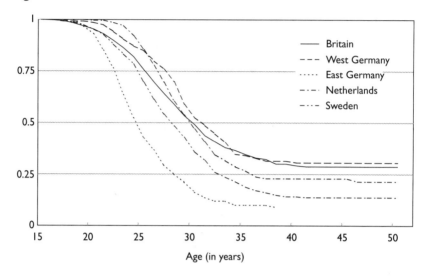

Source: Author's own computations, see note on Table 4.2

a minus sign if the effect is negative and a plus sign if the effect is positive. The value of the base group is set to 1, so that a value of 0.5 means that women with that characteristic are half as likely as the base group to have not given birth to their first child. In Table 4.3 the probability of a woman in full-time education having a child is between 44% and 55% of the probability of women who have finished full-time education for Britain, East Germany and Sweden. For the Netherlands and West Germany, the probability of having a child while a student is smaller: 24-29% of the probability of women who have already finished their studies. This result is to be interpreted holding constant the other variables in the model, so that the education effects are purified from cohort effects and the cohort effects are purified from education effects.

In Table 4.4, we estimated a second model on waiting time since finishing education, because we thought that the large educational effect observed in Table 4.1 might disappear when we looked at time since finishing education. This expectation is also confirmed by a comparison of the results of Tables 4.3 and 4.4. By counting duration since finishing education (Table 4.4), we have no indication that low-educated women have children earlier, whereas by counting the waiting time since age 15 (Table 4.3), the indication is that low-educated women do indeed have children earlier. Highly-educated women are also not slower than medium-educated women when time since finishing education is analysed, except in Britain, Britain being the exception to this rule.

The cohort patterns when comparing waiting time since age 15 to waiting time since finishing education also differ. With the exception of the British 1970 cohort, there is no postponement of maternity after finishing education in the 1960s and 1970s, while there is such postponement after age 15 in Table

Table 4.3: Model 1: Cox-proportional hazard models, duration of time from age 15 to first birth (Z-values are in brackets)

Covariate	Britain Hazard ratio	West Germany Hazard ratio	East Germany Hazard ratio	Netherlands Hazard ratio	Sweden Hazard ratio
In education (time-varying)	0.552 (–7.40)	0.241 (–11.86)	0.473 (–7.91)	0.289 (–7.01)	0.439 (–9.50)
Education completed	–	–	–	–	–
Education = low	1.316 (4.81)	1.254 (2.17)	0.977 (–0.31)	1.307 (4.45)	1.257 (3.39)
Education = medium (base)	–	–	–	–	–
Education = high	0.690 (–5.23)	0.895 (–0.87)	0.868 (–1.33)	0.733 (–3.43)	0.922 (–1.04)
Cohort = born in 1930s (base)	–	–	–	–	–
Cohort = born in 1940s	1.195 (3.28)	1.266 (2.87)	1.063 (0.62)	1.310 (3.45)	1.187 (2.76)
Cohort = born in 1950s	1.058 (1.04)	1.057 (0.71)	1.570 (4.96)	1.364 (4.02)	1.118 (1.69)
Cohort = born in 1960s	0.904 (–1.78)	0.816 (–2.56)	1.323 (3.00)	0.841 (–2.04)	0.875 (–2.76)
Cohort = born in 1970s	0.953 (–0.52)	0.649 (–2.87)	0.594 (–3.30)	0.559 (–3.01)	0.475 (–4.81)
Log likelihood	–23,902	–10,556.47	–7,620.77	–11,303.42	–14,609.12
LR Chi^2 (7)	410.09	368.09	166.45	312.93	305.85
N (number of women)	4,480	2,127	1,409	2,165	2,893

Source: Authors' own computations based on BHPS 1991-98 for Britain; GSOEP 1996 for Germany (Sample A, that is, Germans in former West Germany and Sample C, that is, Germans in former East Germany); OSA 1996 for the Netherlands; and HUS 1984, 1986, 1993, 1996 and 1998 for Sweden.

Education high: obtained highest qualification requires 15 years or more of schooling. Education medium: obtained highest qualification requires between 12 years and 14 years of schooling. Education low: obtained highest qualification requires less than 12 years of schooling. Women still in education at the end of observation period are not included. See Appendix A2 for explanation of our model.

The gender dimension of social change

Table 4.4: Model 2: Cox-proportional hazard models, duration of time from age 15 to first birth since finishing education (Z-values are in brackets)

Covariate	Britain Hazard ratio	West Germany Hazard ratio	East Germany Hazard ratio	Netherlands Hazard ratio	Sweden Hazard ratio
Education = low	1.111 (1.76)	1.184 (1.54)	0.883 (−1.49)	0.889 (−1.95)	0.978 (−0.30)
Education = medium (base)	—	—	—	—	—
Education = high	0.761 (−3.62)	0.952 (−0.36)	0.959 (−0.33)	0.933 (−0.75)	0.925 (−0.91)
Cohort = born in 1930s (base)	—	—	—	—	—
Cohort = born in 1940s	1.223 (3.62)	1.297 (3.10)	1.009 (0.09)	1.335 (3.67)	1.229 (3.20)
Cohort = born in 1950s	1.146 (2.42)	1.060 (0.73)	1.607 (4.95)	1.424 (4.54)	1.215 (2.79)
Cohort = born in 1960s	1.085 (1.41)	0.963 (−0.46)	1.368 (3.15)	1.102 (1.13)	1.142 (1.64)
Cohort = born in 1970s	1.270 (2.49)	0.853 (−0.99)	0.667 (−2.20)	0.855 (−0.77)	0.791 (−1.39)
Log likelihood	−22,180	−9,889.53	−6,089.21	−11,021.33	−12,987.13
LR Chi²(6)	63.63	27.56	60.97	37.57	18.61
N (number of women)	4,256	2,028	1,194	2,089	2,541

Source: Authors' own computations based on BHPS 1991-98 for Britain; GSOEP 1996 for Germany (Sample A, that is, Germans in former East Germany); OSA 1996 for the Netherlands; and HUS 1984, 1986, 1993, 1996 and 1998 for Sweden.

Education high: obtained highest qualification requires 15 years or more of schooling. Education medium: obtained highest qualification requires between 12 years and 14 years of schooling. Education low: obtained highest qualification requires less than 12 years of schooling. Women still in education at the end of observation period are not included. The women who gave birth to the first child during education are not included in this study, since the time origin is the time of completing education for each individual. See Appendix A2 for explanation of our model.

4.3. This comparison of the duration models of Tables 4.3 and 4.4 indicate that the educational expansion explains part of the postponement of maternity over time that we have observed (Dex et al, 1998).

Conclusions

We began by stating that there are two economic motives that impact on the timing of maternity. The first is the 'consumption smoothing motive': couples want to reach an income level where they could afford having a child without having to forego other consumption that they find essential. The second is the 'career planning motive'. For men, the two motives have traditionally coincided because the woman did all the childcare work and did not aspire to professional employment. The traditional social policy model of supporting family income by tax credits for children has an effect on the consumption smoothing motive making it affordable to have children earlier than would otherwise be the case. However, the dual-earner family that cares about the career planning motive needs other kinds of help, such as paid parental leave, right to shorten work hours soon after the birth of a child, affordable, good quality childcare, and an active policy to help parents share care duties, as well as financial provision for the family.

Among the countries analysed Sweden and East Germany paid the most attention to the dual-earner family. But this has not stopped the delay in motherhood in the most recent decades. However, we found the smallest percentage of ultimate childlessness in these two countries as well as the smallest effects of the level of education completed. The strongest educational effects were found in Britain and the Netherlands, where highly-educated women have considerably later maternity and higher rates of ultimate childlessness than less educated women. In all countries analysed, women do not choose to combine motherhood and studies, in spite of the fact that people spend longer periods of their life in education. On finishing education, there are no educational differences in waiting time to the first birth (holding cohort constant). Also the waiting time to first birth since age 15 is considerably larger, holding education constant, whereas the waiting time since finishing education does not show such a pattern. This means that much of the postponement of maternity can be explained by the fact that women spend more time in school and do not combine motherhood with schooling. Therefore, educational expansion is a major reason for postponement of maternity in all the four countries we studied.

Appendices

A1: The Kaplan-Meier estimator of the survivor function

Let $F(t) = \Pr(T \leq t)$ be the cumulative distribution function of the random variable of the duration until first birth T. The survivor function can be defined by $S(t) = 1 - F(t)$. Here, the survivor function $S(t)$ gives the probability that a woman has not given birth to the first child until age $t + 15$ (we define t as the duration till age at first birth since age 15).

The empirical survivor function for a sample of N observations with no censoring is $S(t)$ (# of $T \geq t$)/N. Because some observations are censored (that is, there are some women who have not given birth to the first child by the end of the observation period), we calculate the Kaplan-Meier estimator of the survivor function, allowing for censoring as follows (see Kiefer, 1988).

Let us suppose the completed durations until a woman gives birth to the first child in our sample are ordered from smallest to largest, $t_1 < t_2 < \ldots < t_K$ (because of ties and censoring, $K < N$). Let d_j be the number of completed spells that end at time t_j or the number of women who give birth at time t_j for $j = 1,2,\ldots K$. Let m_j be the number of observations censored between t_j, and t_{j+1}. The number of spells neither completed nor censored before duration t_j, namely, the number 'at risk' at duration t_j can be defined as $n_j = \sum_{i>=j}^{K}(m_j + d_j)$. The hazard $h(t_j)$ is the probability of completing a spell at duration t_j, conditional upon the spell lasting at least to t_j. A natural estimator for $h(t_j)$ is $\hat{h}(t_j) = d_j/n_j$. The corresponding estimator for the survivor function is $\hat{S}(t_j) = \prod_{i=1}^{j}(n_i - d_i)/n_i = \prod_{i=1}^{j}(1 - \hat{h}_i)$, which is the Kaplan-Meier, or product-limit estimator of the survivor function.

A2: Econometric model

In order to look at the effect of being in education on the timing of first birth, and the level of education, we estimate two semi-parametric duration models: one on the duration until giving birth to a first child since the age of 15 (Model 1; see Table 4.3) and the other on the duration until giving birth to a first child since leaving education (Model 2; see Table 4.4).

Let us suppose that the random variable of the duration until first birth, T, has a continuous probability distribution $f(t)$, where t is a realisation of T (see Kiefer, 1988; and Greene, 1997, pp 984-99; for more explanation of duration models). Then the corresponding cumulative distribution function is $F(t) = \int_0^t f(x)dx = \Pr(T \leq t)$ and the survivor function $S(t)$ can be defined by $S(t) = 1 - F(t)$. The hazard (or hazard rate), or the probability of maternity at time t, given that the woman has not given birth to a first child until time t since the age of 15 or the time of completing education is defined by:

$$h(t) = \lim_{dt \to 0} \frac{\Pr(t \leq T < t + dt \mid T \geq t)}{dt} = \lim_{dt \to 0} \frac{F(t + dt) - }{dtS(t)}$$

Since $h(t) = f(t)/S(t) = [dF(t)/dt]S(t) = [-dS(t)/dt]/S(t) = -d/n S(t)/dt$, we can obtain the survivor function:

$$S(t) = \exp\left[-\int_0^t h(x)dx \right]$$

We estimate the proportional hazard function, in which the hazard [RATIO?] depends on a vector of explanatory variables or covariates, $x_- = \{x_1, x_2, \ldots, x_k\}$ with unknown coefficients $b_- = \{b_1, b_2, \ldots, b_k\}$ and $h_0:h(t, x_-, b_-, h_0) = f(x_-, b_-) h_0(t)$. The function $h_0(t)$ is a 'baseline' hazard corresponding to $f(\times) = 1$. Then, $h_0(\times)$ has an interpretation as the hazard function for the mean individual in the sample, which gives the shape of the hazard function for any individual.

The term $\phi(x, \beta)$ indicates the difference in the level of the hazard across individuals. We specify this $\phi(x, \beta) = \exp(x'\beta)$, following the popular specification. We estimate parameters β without specifying the form of the baseline hazard function $h_0(t)$, using maximum likelihood, following Cox (1972), since we have little advance information on the shape of the hazard function. In the likelihood function, right censored spells (the spells of women who have not given birth to the first child at the end of the observation period), contribute only to the survival component, whereas uncensored spells contribute to both the survival component and the conditional probability component. (By 'spell' we mean the duration, on the interval from a point in time until the event or until the last moment of observation.)

The positive coefficient estimates of β indicate that higher levels of the variable increase the hazard rate of giving birth, or equivalently, that the waiting time until giving birth to a first child is shorter. The negative coefficient estimates have the opposite effect. The hazard ratios, which are estimates of $\exp(\beta)$, indicate the effects of one-unit change in the corresponding variable. For example, if the hazard ratio of x_1 is 1.10, it means 1 unit increase in x_1 raises the hazard rate by 10%. If the hazard ratio is smaller than 1, it indicates a negative effect of x_1 on the hazard rate. The proportional hazard model assumes that the ratio of the hazards of any two individuals is constant over time.

We take the age of 15 for each individual as a time origin in Model 1 and the time of completing education for each individual as a time origin in Model 2. We also take the number of years elapsed since the time origin as a time scale in each model. Our covariates x are dummy variables of the level of education obtained, dummy variables whether or not the woman was born in the defined birth cohort (1940s, 1950s, 1960s or 1970s). Model 1 includes also a time-varying dummy variable whether the woman is in education (= 1) or she has finished education (= 0).

A3: Variable construction

Age at finishing education

In order to create the two duration variables we need to have information on age at finishing education and age at having the first birth. Age at finishing education or training is calculated in the following way. For Germany, using Biography Spell Data in GSOEP 1996, which gives the information on yearly-level aggregated monthly job status since age 15, we regard the last time of full-time schooling or training that started before age 25 as the age at finishing education. For the Netherlands, we proceed in the same way, using spell information on education and training history in OSA 1996. For Britain, there are two variables on school leaving age for every survey: one is on the age at leaving school and one is on the age at leaving further education. We use the latter if the women receive further education and we use the former if not, using the latest information from BHPS 1991-98. For Sweden, since HUS does not give information on the age of the woman or the year when she finished education, we use the information of 'years of schooling since elementary school' and add seven to this because school starts at age seven (based on HUS 1984, 1986, 1993, 1996 and 1998), assuming that women go to school without any interruption. Since interviewees are asked to transform their full-time equivalent for this variable into part-time studies, we cannot distinguish if the education they had was full-time or part-time. In each country, the age at finishing education is younger among highly-educated women in the cohort who were born in the 1970s than in older cohorts. This is mainly because there are many women who are still in education in this youngest cohort; these women will be in the group of the highly-educated in the future. These women are not included in our sample. Consequently, the mean age of women when finishing education among highly-educated women in the 1970s cohort is rather younger compared to highly-educated women in the other cohorts. Note that our definition of high education includes not only university level but also technical schools, or other higher qualifications, and so on.

Age of mother at first birth

The age of the mother at first birth is calculated from the difference between the birth year of the first child and that of the mother for each observation. The information of the birth year of first biological child is collected as follows. For Britain we use the lifetime fertility history file of biological children of BHPS 1992 and the file for individual respondents in 1998, in which a respondent was interviewed if not interviewed before, or has turned 16 years of age. For Germany, the birth history file of women in GSOEP 1996 is used. This data consists of several samples: sample A includes people of German ethnicity living in what was once West Germany, and sample C includes people living in the eastern part of Germany, what was once East Germany. We use these two samples. For Sweden information on biological children is collected at entry to the survey and for individual women it can be either of the surveys HUS 1984, 1986, 1993, 1996 and 1998. For the Netherlands, the information on own children from OSA 1996 is used. This study alone makes no distinction between adopted and non-adopted children.

Figures for the 1950s and the 1960s are less representative of the whole population because fewer women in the sample were born before 1930. In the Dutch sample, this problem is rather severe. Of all Dutch women who gave birth to their first child from the 1950s to the 1990s only 0.2% were born before 1930. The corresponding proportions were 8.6% for Britain, 8.7% for West Germany, 3.9% for East Germany and 8.8% for Sweden. However, the quartiles of the birth year of mothers are almost the same across countries such that the first quartile is around 1940, the second quartile is around 1950 and the third quartile is around 1960. In Table A4.1 the number of observations used for the analyses below are presented by country, birth cohort of the woman and from which wave of the household panel data they have been taken.

Table A4.1: The number of observations used in the analyses

	Time period of women's year of birth							
	Born before 1930	Born 1930-39	Born 1940-49	Born 1950-59	Born 1960-69	Born 1970-79	Born 1930-79	Total
Britain								
Fertility information derived from								
1992	1032	548	804	831	971	327	3,481	4,513
1998	219	124	118	169	308	280	999	1,218
Total	1251	672	922	1000	1279	607	4,480	5,731
West Germany								
Fertility information derived from					·			
1996	388	308	376	543	673	227	2,127	2,515
East Germany								
Fertility information derived from								
1996	157	214	264	395	375	161	1,409	1,566
Netherlands								
Fertility information derived from								
1996	5	282	493	583	562	245	2,165	2,170
Sweden								
Fertility information derived from								
1984	298	188	270	212	85	0	755	1,053
1986	74	65	90	80	78	0	313	387
1993	174	141	235	220	275	135	1006	1,180
1996	0	1	6	10	13	84	114	114
1998	47	78	149	176	133	169	705	752
Total	593	473	750	698	584	388	2,893	3,482

Source: data: BHPS 1991-98 for Britain; GSOEP 1996 for Germany (Sample A, that is, Germans in former West Germany and Sample C, that is, Germans in former East Germany); OSA 1996 for the Netherlands; and HUS 1984, 1986, 1993, 1996 and 1998 for Sweden. Women are only included in the samples when they have all the following information: the year of birth, the year of education (or training) completed, the level of education obtained, and the fertility information, that is, the information on whether or not a woman has children and if she has, in which year she gave birth to her first child. We collect the fertility information in principle from the most recent wave of each data set, namely GSOEP 1996 for Germany and OSA 1996 for the Netherlands. For Britain, however, we take the information from the lifetime fertility history file of biological children of BHPS 1992 as well as the most recent wave BHPS 1998, since the wave 1998 do not ask all the respondents on their fertility history. For Sweden, we use the surveys HUS 1984, 1986, 1993, 1996 and 1998 because HUS asks the fertility information at entry to the survey and we cannot obtain enough observations for our analyses only from HUS 1998.

Notes

[1] Gustafsson and Wetzels, 1997, 2000; Gustafsson, 2001; Wetzels, 2001, chapter 7.

[2] We hope in future work to extend the number of countries included, particularly Japan (Kenjoh, 2001). Today, Italy and Spain are experiencing the most rapid decrease in total fertility rates and postponement of maternity (see, among others, Bosveld, 1996; Council of Europe, 1998). We hope to include such work in the future.

[3] These 12 full-time months can be distributed between father and mother as they please. There is a gap between the job protection period and the compensation period, if the mother chooses to be full-time at home. In order to encourage fathers to avail of parental leave, they are obliged to take one of the 12 months with 90% salary compensation, while another month is set aside for mothers with identical salary compensation. Other months are compensated by 75% of earnings of the parent who stays home caring for the child (see Gustafsson, 1984, 1994; Wetzels, 2001, chapter 2; Sundström, 1996).

[4] The Dutch welfare state had a strong influence of the pillarisation, the Catholic principle of subsidiarity and the Protestant doctrine's sphere of sovereignty. It therefore gave central importance to traditional familyhood, determined by the constant presence of the mother in the home with the children. In 1930 employed women were granted 12 weeks of leave with 100% of payment. By international standards, this was rather early: 1939 in Sweden (12 weeks), and 1957 in Germany (14 weeks). However, Dutch women did not have job protection for pregnancy, childbirth or marriage until 1973. Since so few women were active on the labour market and eligible to maternity leave and pay, total public expenditures on maternity benefits (out of sickness benefits) were extremely limited. Feminists, and employers who were in need of female employees demanded more (public) childcare facilities. Between 1960 and 1988, more subsidies for part-day playschools were granted, but the number of facilities remained small (see Wetzels, 2001). Till now, demand for childcare facilities has exceeded supply, resulting in waiting lists for daycare.

Germany is characterised as a Christian Democratic Welfare State, with a strong traditional familial ideology. The German tax system is expected implicitly to support traditional family formation, by giving a 'marriage benefit' to all couples, except those where the husband and wife earn the same incomes. In the period 1950-60, conservative governments strengthened the family as an institution, installing the so-called 'Duales System des Familienlastenausgleichs', with tax deductions for children and child benefits to ease the cost of children. From 1969 to 1982 social liberal governments abolished the tax deductions for children and aimed at more active involvement of women in the labour market by introducing the Maternity Leave Act in 1979. It was in 1976 that German women became legal and equal partners in family decisions on financial issues including her labour force participation. However, after this period conservative liberal governments reintroduced and extended the tax deductions for children. The maternity leave period has been extended several times, but monthly maternity benefits have not increased. The federal government programme for maternity leave is complemented by some of the German states (Länder) with a conservative government. In line with conservative views on the role of the mother, "A basic condition for additional support [by these Länder programmes] is a withdrawal from the labour market" (Zimmermann, 1993, p 210).

Childcare facilities in Germany are mainly provided by local governments and by churches and other welfare organisations. Childcare centres are subsidised, resulting in a low average monthly user's price of about DM 65 in 1987. Daycare and commercial facilities charge higher prices. There are no subsidies for non-institutional childcare, and childcare expenses are not tax deductible. Since childcare facilities are meant to educate the children, not to facilitate the combination of paid work and children for mother, they accept children older than three, part day and not during lunch (two hours). Similarly schools are open five hours a day and assume a parent to help with the home work (see Wetzels, 2001).

[5] The discussion on parental leave started in the Netherlands in the 1990s. Similarly the first act to stimulate childcare facilities dates from 1990.

[6] The data for Germany in this study is separated into East and West Germany before reunification, and eastern and western Germany after. East and West Germany is used throughout to include both before and after reunification.

[7] We are grateful to Heikke Trappe of the Max Planck Institute für Bildungsforschung, Berlin, for making us aware of reforms to German parental leave policies that came into force in 2001 and for giving us the reference www.bmfsfg.de.

[8] The law on parental leave does not deal with the payment during leave, and leaves this to negotiations between employers and employees. In a few collective labour market agreements payment is taken care of, but the payment itself differs between the different agreements in the Dutch *Centrale Arbeids Overeenkomst* (CAO), which cover different sectors of the labour market. However, 90% of CAO do not cover paid parental leave; the CAO of the public sector offers 75% of earnings, and 47% of all eligible parents take leave in this sector. In contrast, only 8% of eligible parents make use of their right to unpaid leave (see Wetzels, 2001, chapter 2).

[9] Public involvement in childcare concerns the quality of childcare, fiscal incentives for employers to create childcare facilities, fiscal incentives for parents who use childcare facilities, and publicly subsidised jobs for the unemployed in the childcare sector. The Dutch government intends to stimulate employers to supply childcare for their personnel by having municipalities give companies subsidies out of state subsidies. Dutch municipalities receive 95% of their income from the national state (see Wetzels, 2001).

[10] The maternity leave period is short with little income compensation. McRae (1991) analyses for the period 1980-1989 the proportion of working mothers in Britain who are entitled to a very small maternity grant, and those working mothers who receive

more benefits. In 1980 all British mothers received a maternity grant, 50% of all mothers received the maternity allowance and 30% of all mothers received the Earnings Related Supplements (ERS). Among employed mothers 90% received the maternity allowance, and 50% received the ERS (18 weeks). In 1989, 40% of all mothers received some type of maternity pay, 20% of all mothers received 90% of earnings for six weeks. Among employed mothers 80% received some benefit, 65% received Statutory Maternity Pay (lower rate means on average 20% earnings of a full-time worker [EOC, 1991, p 25]), 40% received a higher rate. All flat rate benefits like the maternity grant, and allowance, are very low and not indexed for consumer prices.

Apart from pre-primary education which is typically part day, public provision of day care is extremely limited. The state has only been involved in a few day care nurseries and a few nursery schools. There is also no right to parental leave to care for sick children or other home care. Childcare has not been supported through large public expenditures. On the contrary childcare services provided by employers were liable to taxation up to 1990 (OECD, 1990a, p 139). British mothers on state benefits have access to housing and have priority to publicly provided day care, along with lone parents (see Wetzels, 2001).

[11] From 1999 a national childcare strategy has been proposed to target children under three. A 'Childcare Tax Credit' was introduced in October 1999 to increase accessibility of childcare spaces for low- and middle-income families. The Childcare Tax Credit is a maximum £70 per week for one child and up to £105 per week for two or more children to a limit of 70% of the costs of registered and approved childcare. Families can benefit from the maximum Childcare Tax Credit if household earnings are less than £14,000 per year with one child, and £17,000 per year with two or more children. Families with up to £20,000 per year with one child in childcare and £30,000 with two or more children in childcare may also be eligible for some help toward childcare costs (Moss, 1999, p 299).

References

Allaart, P.C., Kunnen, R., van Ours, J.C. and van Stiphout, H.A. (1987) *OSA trendrapport 1987: Actuele informatie over de arbeidsmarkt*, OSA voorstudie nr 18, The Hague.

Becker, G.S. (1981) *A treatise on the family*, Cambridge, MA: Harvard University Press.

Beets, G.C.N. (1997) 'Kinderen worden later geboren: een demografische analyse', in G.C.N. Beets, A. Bouwens and J.J. Schippers (eds) *Uitgesteld ouderschap*, Amsterdam: Thesis Publishers, pp 13-31.

Beets, G.C.N. (1998) 'Onderwijs en de geboorte van het eerste kind in Europa: FFS gegevens', *Bevolking en Gezin*, vol 27, no 2, pp 99-121.

Bongaarts, J. (1999) 'Fertility in the developed world. Where will it end?', *American Economic Review, Papers and Proceedings*, May, pp 256-60.

Bosveld, W. (1996) *The ageing of fertility in Europe: A comparative demographic-analytic study, PDOD*, Amsterdam: Thesis Publishers.

Bradshaw, J. (1996) 'Family policy and family Poverty', *Policy Studies*, vol 17, no 2, pp 93-106.

Chester, R. (1994) 'Flying without instruments or flight plans: family policy in the United Kingdom', in W. Dumon (ed) *Changing family policies in the member states of the European Union*, Commission of the European Communities, European Observatory on National Family Policies.

Council of Europe (1998) *Recent demographic developments in Europe*, Strasbourg: Council of Europe.

Cox, D.R. (1972) 'Regression models and life tables', *Journal of the Royal Statistical Society, Series B*, vol 34, pp 187-220.

Dex, S., Joshi, H., Macran, S. and McCulloch, A. (1998) 'Women's employment transitions around child bearing', *Oxford Bulletin of Economics and Statistics*, vol 60, pp 79-97.

Dielens, D. (ed) (2000) *EISS yearbook 2000: Confidence and changes: Managing social protection in the new millennium*, The Hague/London/New York, NY: Kluwer Law International, pp 119-41.

Flood, L., Klevmarken, A. and Olovsson, P. (1997) *Household market and nonmarket activities (HUS) 1993*, Volumes I – VI, Stockholm: Almqvist & Wiksell International.

Greene, W.H. (1997) *Econometric analysis* (3rd edn), New Jersey, NJ: Prentice Hall.

Gustafsson, S.S. (1984) 'Equal opportunity policies in Sweden', in G. Schmid and R. Wietzel (eds) *Sex discrimination and equal opportunity: The labour market and employment policy*, West Berlin and England: Wissenschaftzentrum and Gower Publishing Company, pp 132-54.

Gustafsson, S.S. (1994) 'Childcare and types of welfare states', in D. Sainsbury (ed) *Gendering welfare states*, London: Sage Publications, pp 45-62.

Gustafsson, S.S. (2001) 'Optimal age at giving birth: theoretical and empirical considerations on postponement of maternity in Europe', *Journal of Population Economics*, vol 14, pp 225-47.

Gustafsson, S., Kenjoh, E. and Wetzels, C.M.M.P. (2002a) *A new crisis in European populations: Do modern family policies help?*, Cheltenham: Edward Elgar.

Gustafsson, S., Kenjoh, E. and Wetzels, C.M.M.P. (2002b) 'The labour force transitions of first-time mothers in Britain, Germany, the Netherlands and Sweden', in H. Mosley, Y. O'Reilly and K. Schömann (eds) *Labour markets and industrialised change: Essays in honour of Günter Schmid*, Cheltenham/ Northampton, MA: Edward Elgar, pp 185-211.

Gustafsson, S.S. and Wetzels, C.M.M.P. (1997) 'Paid careers and the timing and spacing of births in Germany, Great Britain and Sweden', in K. Tijdens, A. van Doorne-Huiskes and T. Willemse (eds) *Time allocations and gender: The relationship between paid labour and household work*, Tilburg: Tilburg University Press, pp 99-122.

Gustafsson, S.S. and Wetzels, C.M.M.P. (2000) 'Optimal age at giving birth: Germany, Great Britain, the Netherlands and Sweden', in S.S. Gustafsson and D.E. Meulders (eds) *Gender and the labour market. Econometric evidence on obstacles in achieving gender equality*, London: Macmillan, pp 188-209.

Gustafsson, S., Wetzels, C.M.M.P. and Kenjoh, E. (2002c) 'Postponement of maternity and the duration of time spent at home after first birth: panel data analyses comparing Germany, Great Britain, the Netherlands and Sweden', *Journal of Finance and Management*.

Gustafsson, S.S., Wetzels, C.M.M.P, Vlasblom, J.D. and Dex, S. (1996) 'Labor force transitions in connection with child birth: a panel data comparison between Germany, Great Britain and Sweden', *Journal of Population Economics*, vol 9, no 3, pp 223-46.

Haisken-De New, J.P. and Frick, J.R. (eds) (1998) *Desktop companion to the German Socio-Economic Panel Study. Version 2.2*, Berlin: German Institute for Economic Research.

Hotz, V.J., Klerman, J.A. and Willis, R.J. (1997) 'The economics of fertility in developed countries', in M.R. Rozenzweig and O. Stark (eds) *Handbook of population and family economics*, Volume 1A, Amsterdam: Elsevier.

Joshi, H.E. (1990) 'The opportunity cost of childbearing: an approach to estimation using British data', *Population Studies*, vol 44, pp 41-60.

Kenjoh, E. (2001) 'Rishoku Kosuto ga Dai-isshi Shussan Taimingu ni Ataeru Eikyo' ('The effect of women's career cost on the timing of first birth in Japan'), *Quarterly Journal of Household Economy*, vol 50, pp 50-5.

Kiefer, N.M. (1988) 'Economic duration data and hazard functions', *Journal of Economic Literature*, vol 26, pp 646-79.

Klevmarken, A. and Olovsson, P. (1993) *Household market and nonmarket activities: Procedures and codes 1984-1991*, Volumes I-II, Stockholm: Almqvist & Wiksell International.

Kreyenfeld, M. (2000a) 'Changes in the timing of first birth in Eastern Germany after German re-unification', *Zeitsschrift für Wirtschaft und Socialwissenschaft*, vol 120, no 2, pp 169-86.

Kreyenfeld, M. (2000b) *Educational attainment and first births: East-Germany before and after unification*, MPIDR Working Paper WP 2000-011, December.

Moss, P. (1999) 'Renewed hopes and lost opportunities: early childhood in the early years of the labour government', *Cambridge Journal of Education*, vol 29, no 2, June, pp 229-38.

OECD (Organisation for Economic Co-operation and Development) (1996) *Education at a glance*, Paris: OECD.

OECD, Bertram, T. and Pascal, C. (2000) *The OECD thematic review of early childhood education and care: Background report for the United Kingdom*, Centre for Research in Early Childhood, University College Worcester.

Sainsbury, D. (ed) (1994) *Gendering welfare states*, London: Sage Publications.

Sainsbury, D. (1996) *Gender, equality and welfare states*, Cambridge: Cambridge University Press.

Sundström, M. (1996) 'Determinants of the use of parental benefits by women in Sweden in the 1990s', *Scandinavian Journal of Social Welfare*, vol 5, pp 76-82.

Taylor, M. (ed) (1999) *British Household Panel Survey user manual*, Colchester: University of Essex.

Wagner, G.G., Schupp, J. and Rendtel, U. (1991) 'The Socio-Economic Panel of Germany, methods of production and management of longitudinal data', *DIW Discussion Paper* 31a, Berlin.

Wetzels, C.M.M.P. (2001) *Squeezing birth into working life: Household panel data analyses comparing Germany, Great Britain, Sweden and the Netherlands*, Aldershot, Hampshire: Ashgate Publishing Ltd.

FIVE

The financial consequences of relationship dissolution for women in Western Europe[1]

Caroline Dewilde

Introduction

The main focus of this chapter is the financial consequences of relationship dissolution for women. We link cross-national variations to the types of welfare regimes in the countries of the EU using data from the European Community Household Panel (ECHP).

The outline of the chapter is as follows. We start with a review of the literature concerning the financial consequences of family breakdown, with special attention to the situation of the women involved. Next, we try to link the financial consequences of relationship dissolution to the sources of economic independence available to women – access to the labour market and the availability of welfare transfers – in the different welfare regimes. The literature suggests the existence of four 'worlds of welfare' in the EU: the social-democratic cluster, the conservative-corporatist countries, the liberal cluster and the Southern European countries. We test the validity of this typology by adding some additional indicators referring to the sources of economic independence available to women experiencing relationship dissolution. We then go on to the actual analysis, limiting ourselves to five countries: Denmark, the UK, Belgium, Germany and Italy. The choice of countries is based on their different position in our welfare regime typology, with Belgium and Germany representing substantial variation within the continental cluster. We conclude the chapter with a discussion of the results.

There are two main advantages of using longitudinal panel data for this analysis. Firstly, panel data provide us with a picture of the actual 'living situation' of the individual respondents and how they change. With the growing number of consensual unions and the rising number of children born out of wedlock, it is clear that the analysis of relationship dissolution needs to take into account the growing number of cohabitation dissolutions. The second advantage of using longitudinal panel data is that we can evaluate the financial implications for all women experiencing the event during the period covered by the study, irrespective of their subsequent relationships, rather than just the subgroup of women who have experienced a family breakdown and are currently single (see Chapter One on longitudinal designs for details).

Theoretical background

The financial consequences of relationship dissolution

At the end of the 1970s Diana Pearce (1978, cited in Daly, 1992) formulated the 'feminisation of poverty' hypothesis: despite growing female labour market participation in the US and the related financial independence, Pearce noticed a shift in the burden of poverty from men to women during the 1950s and the 1960s. Although this trend was not confirmed in the decades that followed – subsequent research indicated a slight decline in the proportion of poor women – the 'feminisation of poverty' hypothesis generated a lot of research into the gender dimension of poverty. The most important critique, however, was that, far from being a new phenomenon, poverty was becoming increasingly visible: "the main reason advanced for this emergence of female poverty is that women's lives no longer fit the conventional assumptions on which both poverty research and social policy are based" (Daly, 1992, p 3). While in previous decades female poverty was mainly hidden in households above the poverty line[2], more and more women now showed up in the poverty statistics. The growing visibility of female poverty can be attributed to the increasing number of lone mothers and elderly women, and to the disadvantaged position of women in the labour market.

Older women, especially lone women, have long been a group at high risk of poverty. According to Daly (1992, p 5), one must consider the social and economic position of women and men prior to retirement: "Throughout their lives women have less access to the labour-market and the assets that flow from it. Hence, they are less likely to have accumulated assets during their lives and also to have built up entitlements to pension and other occupational benefits". Secondly, the disadvantaged position of women in the labour market results in higher unemployment, a higher proportion of part-time jobs, a higher concentration in service-sector jobs and lower wages in comparison with their male colleagues (O'Connor, 1996). A third group of women at risk of poverty are lone mothers. This is the case in most countries, regardless of the route to lone parenthood. Since marital breakdown is the main route taken to lone parenthood, divorce is a key contributor to the high poverty rates among lone mothers (Millar, 1988).

The importance of divorce in creating female poverty is also documented in studies based on longitudinal data. Duncan and Morgan (1984, p 10), using the Panel Study of Income Dynamics (PSID), conclude that "the single most important factor accounting for changes in family well-being was a fundamental change in family structure: divorce, death, marriage, birth or a child leaving home". In particular, the economic status of women and young children turns out to be very sensitive to changes in the composition of the family due to divorce or remarriage. Male poverty on the other hand is more dependent on changes related to the labour market (see, among others, Duncan and Morgan, 1984; Ruspini, 1998). Furthermore, women's poverty trajectories turn out to be longer than those of men. Women are not only more vulnerable to persistent deprivation, but they also run a greater risk of recurrent poverty (Ruspini, 1999b).

The financial impact of relationship dissolution usually falls on the women and children involved: Burkhauser and Duncan (1987) found that income levels drop by about 40% between the years just before and after divorce for women and children, while men experience a more modest decrease of 15%. The disadvantaged position of women after divorce has several causes. First of all, the majority of children stay with their mothers following relationship dissolution. The wife becomes a lone parent, while the husband becomes a single man. Secondly, the introduction of no-fault divorce laws in most European countries has had profound effects on the situation of women after divorce (Weitzman, 1988, cited in Daly, 1992). The interpretation of equality adopted by the courts produces unequal results, since the inequalities created by marriage, for instance the gender division of labour, are ignored. Also, the 'equal' division of property is in fact unequal, since most children stay with their mother. In addition, no-fault divorce laws reduce women's bargaining power, as formerly they were often the innocent party and could therefore be compensated as such. The third reason for the disadvantaged position of women following divorce is linked to the inadequacy of alimony and child support to make up for the lost income. These payments usually do not make a substantial contribution to the resources of women (Millar, 1988), since they are either nothing or low, and not always paid regularly. Furthermore, the interval of time since the separation is important. The longer the period, the less likely it is that the husband will be willing or able to provide financial support. Thus very few lone mothers are able to rely upon maintenance as their main source of income.

The inadequacy of alimony and child support in alleviating the financial consequences of divorce leaves women with two options for achieving economic independence: they can either rely on the labour market or on the transfers provided by the welfare state. Access to these sources of income, however, vary cross-nationally according to the type of welfare regime. The comparative analysis of social phenomena cannot take place in a conceptual void; therefore we aim to link the financial consequences of relationship dissolution with the types of welfare regimes found in the member countries of the EU. In the next section, we discuss the main sources of economic independence for women, and the way they are determined by the interrelationships between the welfare state, the family and the labour market.

Welfare regimes and economic independence for women

We argue that welfare regimes consist of three main systems of resource distribution: the welfare state (social security and taxation), the market, and the family (see, among others, Daly, 1992). These systems are not independent: the interaction between them creates and maintains the economic dependence of women, and the economic independence of men. In other words, the combined position of women in the welfare state, the family and the labour market determines the extent of economic independence they can achieve. The concepts of dependence, independence and interdependence are very complex and vary across countries and within countries over time. The term dependence has various meanings, especially for women: they can be financially dependent on their partner, on the welfare state (public dependency), or on the labour market (wage dependency). On the other hand, many people are dependent on the unpaid labour or care provided by women. One form of independence is usually reliant on another form of dependence. For instance, labour market participation for women with young children is dependent on the provision of childcare by the state or the family. The type of welfare regime determines the way in which the issues of dependence, independence and interdependence are played out (cf Finch, 1989; Ostner, 1993; Bimbi, 1993; O'Connor, 1996; Bimbi and Ruspini, 2000).

Within this conceptual frame, the financial consequences of relationship dissolution are dependent on the sources of economic independence available to women. As already said, this independence can be achieved in two ways: labour market participation, and the availability of welfare payments to single women and, especially, lone mothers.

In assessing welfare availability (Castles and Flood, 1993) we have to consider the availability of transfers, the adequacy of transfers and the basis for claiming them. Many single women and lone mothers are dependent on social assistance. However, the stigma attached to these payments leads to problems of non-collection of payment. Although some welfare states (for example the Netherlands) provide lone mothers with a generous social wage which treats them as the head of a legitimate household, these transfers are, nonetheless, provided via means-tested social assistance. Furthermore, in the 1990s, a public opinion backlash led to questions about the generosity of these transfers and to increased pressure on lone mothers to find a job (Hobson, 1994).

The second source of economic independence is labour market participation. According to Orloff (1993), we need to look at the extent to which the welfare state encourages (or discourages) women to seek paid employment. Two factors determine women's access to paid labour: the taxation system and the socialisation of care responsibilities by the welfare state. However, labour market participation is a limited indicator, since women are over-represented in part-time and service-sector jobs. The quality of labour market participation is dependent on the sector (primary versus secondary), employment patterns over the life course, the social rights attached to part-time work and the general social and economic policy (O'Connor, 1996).

To summarise, two factors determine women's ability to alleviate the financial consequences of relationship dissolution: the transfers and services provided by the welfare state and access to the labour market. As the combined position of women in the three main systems of resource distribution – the family, the welfare state and the labour market – varies cross-nationally according to the welfare regime, we expect to find clusters of countries which are similar on the consequences of family critical events such as divorce/separation. To test these hypotheses, we use a welfare regime typology that takes into account the position of women. This typology is mainly derived from the work by Esping-Andersen (1990, 1999), Siaroff (1994) and Bonoli (1997), and will be discussed in the next section.

Developing a comparative perspective

Three worlds of welfare?

The most influential publication of the last decade concerning welfare state typologies is undoubtedly Esping-Andersen's *The three worlds of welfare capitalism* (1990). Concluding that an approach solely based on social expenditure is unsatisfying, he developed a new welfare state typology. This typology is based on cross-national variations along three dimensions: the relationship between the state and the market in the delivery of welfare, the stratifying effects of the welfare state, and the quality of social rights. Central to this last dimension is the extent of de-commodification: "the degree to which individuals or families can uphold a socially acceptable standard of living independently of market participation" (Esping-Andersen, 1990, p 37). Considering cross-national variations along these dimensions, Esping-Andersen identified his well known 'three worlds of welfare': the social democratic welfare state, which can be found in the Scandinavian countries, the mainly Anglo-Saxon liberal welfare state and the conservative corporatist welfare state, which prevails in continental Europe (cf Esping-Andersen, 1990, 1999).

The 'three worlds' typology of Esping-Andersen was the starting point for a renewed interest in comparative welfare state research, and has engendered an abundance of theoretical criticisms, empirical tests, and alternative typologies. Feminist researches, however, criticised one important feature: the central concepts of the Esping-Andersen typology are based on a male standard (cf Orloff, 1993, 1996; O'Connor, 1993, 1996; Bussemaker and van Kersbergen, 1994; Daly, 1994; Sainsbury, 1994). In the literature, we can find a series of alternative, gender sensitive typologies (cf Lewis and Ostner, 1992; Sainsbury, 1994; Siaroff, 1994). We select two alternative typologies, the combination of which reveals an interesting picture of the variation of welfare regimes in Western Europe.

Siaroff's typology

The gender sensitive welfare regime typology developed by Siaroff (1994) is based on three dimensions, measuring the sources of economic independence available to women: female work desirability[3], family welfare orientation[4], and the parent who actually receives the family benefits.

Based on these three dimensions, Siaroff developed a new typology defined by four clusters of countries. The protestant social democratic welfare states are the only countries where women have a real choice between work and welfare. Family benefits are high, and paid to the mother. We find this model in the Scandinavian countries. The protestant liberal welfare states, dominant in the Anglo-Saxon countries, are characterised by modest transfers and a minimal family welfare orientation. Female labour market participation is encouraged. Family benefits are paid to the mother. The third cluster consists of the advanced Christian Democratic welfare states in continental Europe. The pattern in these countries relates to the catholic notion of encouraging families and discouraging female labour market participation. The mother is usually not the recipient of family benefits. The final cluster of countries is characterised by a minimal family welfare orientation, as well as low female work desirability. Common for these countries is late female mobilisation: women have been late entrants into the political process, and have been, until now, under-represented. We find this model in Ireland, Switzerland, the Mediterranean countries and Japan.

Bonoli's typology

A number of authors, who do not write from a gender perspective, also identify an additional Mediterranean cluster. According to Leibfried (1991), the rudimentary welfare states of southern Europe are underdeveloped and residual. The family, as the cornerstone of society, carries the burden of unprotected risks. Furthermore, the Mediterranean countries are characterised by a deeply rooted tradition of mainly confessional charity. Ferrera (1996) justifies the identification of a fourth world of welfare by pointing out a number of common traits: a highly fragmented and corporatist system of income maintenance, a healthcare system based on universalistic principles, a low degree of state influence on the welfare sector, and a highly collusive mix between public and non-public actors and institutions, and finally the persistence of 'clientelism' and patronage, resulting in the selective distribution of cash benefits.

According to Bonoli (1997), the de-commodification approach of Esping-Andersen fails to reflect substantial differences in the way welfare is delivered. Bonoli makes a distinction between a Bismarckian model of social policy, based on social insurance and mainly concerned with income maintenance for employees, and a Beveridgean model, characterised by universal provision and aimed at the prevention of poverty. However, the distinction between a Bismarckian and a Beveridgean model does not imply any relationship in quantitative terms (see Baldwin, 1990; Chatagner, 1993; Hirsch, 1993; Rosanvallon, 1995). Therefore, Bonoli proposes a two-dimensional classification, based on the dominant model of social policy[5] on the one hand, and the quantity of welfare (social expenditure as a proportion of Gross Domestic Product [GDP]) on the other.

Based on these two dimensions, four ideal types of welfare state can be identified. Beveridgean high spending countries guarantee a high level of coverage for the whole population. This model is dominant in the protestant social democratic welfare states of Scandinavia. Beveridgean low spending countries also cover the whole population, but protection is lower and there is more means testing. We can find this model in the Anglo-Saxon protestant liberal welfare states. Bonoli dichotomises the continental European countries in a similar fashion. The advanced Christian Democratic welfare states are characterised by Bismarckian high spending, while the late female mobilisation welfare states are characterised by Bismarckian low spending.

The similarities with the gender sensitive welfare regime typology developed by Siaroff are striking. Although based on different dimensions, the same countries belong to the corresponding clusters identified by Siaroff on the one hand, and Bonoli on the other. The only difference concerns the classification of Ireland, as a late female mobilisation state by Siaroff, and as a Beveridgean low spending country by Bonoli. With the exception of Ireland, the Beveridgean states are mainly protestant, while the Bismarckian states are characterised by a catholic or a mixed tradition. Obviously, the main differences between the typologies of Siaroff and Bonoli on the one hand, and the three worlds of Esping-Andersen on the other, concern the identification of an additional cluster. This cluster consists of the Mediterranean countries, Switzerland, and arguably, Ireland.

Developing hypotheses in relation to the financial consequences of relationship dissolution

The outline of this section is as follows. Firstly, in order to assess our combined typology of welfare regimes, we evaluate three additional indicators based on the ECHP (for more information about the ECHP, consult the Appendix in this volume). These correspond with the sources of economic independence available to women experiencing events such as divorce and separation. Then we use these results to develop more specific hypotheses concerning the financial consequences of relationship dissolution for women in Western Europe.

Preliminary analyses: welfare regimes and economic independence

The first indicator concerns access to paid labour, and is calculated as the proportion of women aged 18 to 40 in full-time employment (35 hours per week or more), with children between 0 and 6 years. This variable is an indication of the acceptability for women with responsibility for the care of younger children to engage in paid employment, as well as an indication of the available childcare.

The second indicator concerns the availability of welfare payments, and is computed as the main source of income[6] for lone mothers (heads of households) aged 18 to 55.

Our third indicator concerns the generosity, from a comparative perspective, of these welfare payments, and is computed as the median[7] current total monthly net household income (equivalised[8] in purchasing power parities [PPP][9]) for lone mothers (heads of households) aged 18 to 55 whose main source of income

Figure 5.1: Percentage of women in full-time employment, with children between 0 and 6 years (1996), weighted (in relation to all women aged 18-40 years)

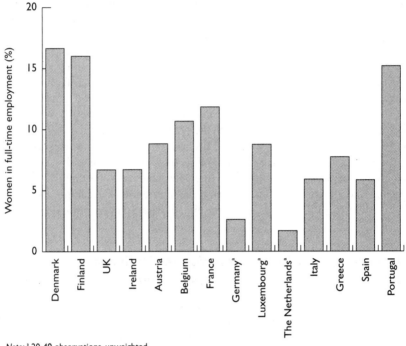

Note: ª 20-49 observations, unweighted

are social transfers (for example, pensions, unemployment/redundancy benefits, and any other social benefits or grants).

As we can see in Figure 5.1, the proportion of full-time working women with young children in 1996 is highest in Denmark and Finland, the two protestant social democratic welfare states in the ECHP. Due to the low provision of public childcare (O'Connor, 1996), the number of full-time working mothers is relatively low in the only protestant liberal welfare state, the UK. The Bismarckian high spending countries can be subdivided into three groups: the proportions of working mothers are relatively high in Belgium and France, medium in Austria and Luxembourg, and very low in Germany and the Netherlands. This variation can partly be explained by the availability of pre-primary education in Belgium and France. Germany and the Netherlands on the other hand are strongly committed to the male breadwinner family model. Germany for instance uses an exceptionally good parental leave system as an alternative to childcare (O'Connor, 1996; Chapter Four in this volume). With the exception of Portugal, the number of full-time working mothers is generally lower in the late female mobilisation welfare states. Nevertheless, the proportions are higher compared to the proportions in Germany and the Netherlands. This might be partly explained by the higher availability of informal childcare

Table 5.1: Women in full-time employment with children between 0 and 12 years, according to type of job (%) (1996), weighted (18-40 years)

	Paid employment	Self-employment or unpaid family labour
Beveridgean high spending		
Denmark	96.9	3.2[a]
Finland	90.4	8.9
Beveridgean low spending		
UK	86.3	13.7[b]
Ireland	91.2	8.8[a]
Bismarckian high spending		
Austria	80.4	19.6
Belgium	85.9	13.5[b]
France	94.3	5.6[b]
Germany	94.3	5.6[a]
Luxembourg	88.1	11.9[a]
The Netherlands	75.7	24.2[a]
Bismarckian low spending		
Italy	84.7	15.4
Greece	69.2	30.8
Spain	82.6	17.1
Portugal	84.4	15.4

Notes:
[a] less than 20 observations, unweighted
[b] 20-49 observations, unweighted

offered by the family. For instance, the number of people living in multi-generation households is generally higher in the late female mobilisation countries, and ranges from 5.0% in Ireland to 11.3% in Spain and Portugal. Another contributing factor is possibly the greater participation of women in self-employment and unpaid family labour (Table 5.1). The proportion of mothers with young children (aged 0 to 11) working full-time in self-employment or unpaid family labour in 1996 ranges from 15.4% in Italy and Portugal to 30.8% in Greece, while it is generally lower in the other countries. However, proportions are also quite high in the UK, Austria, Belgium and the Netherlands.

Let us now look more closely at the situation of the specific subgroup of lone mothers. The main source of income in 1996 for lone mothers is presented in Table 5.2. The initial impression is that, in every country, private transfers are the main source of income for only a minority of lone mothers. Although benefits are universal and high, social transfers are not the main source of income for mothers in Denmark. The contrary is the case in the Beveridgean low spending countries, the UK and Ireland, although transfers are generally lower. The difference between the Beveridgean high spending countries and the Beveridgean low spending countries can be explained by the differential access to the labour market. As we saw in Figure 5.1, full-time employment for

Table 5.2: Main source of income for lone mothers (%) (1996), weighted (18-55 years)

	Income from labour	Social transfers	Private income[a]
Beveridgean high spending			
Denmark	67.0	33.0[d]	0.0[c]
Finland	–	–	–
Beveridgean low spending			
UK	23.8	73.9	2.3[c]
Ireland	20.5[d]	72.7	6.8[c]
Bismarckian high spending			
Austria	65.2	31.0[d]	3.8[c]
Belgium	48.3	51.8	0.0[c]
France	68.9	27.8	3.3[c]
Germany	55.6	42.8	1.6[c]
Luxembourg[b]	–	–	–
The Netherlands	31.5[d]	68.6	0.0[c]
Bismarckian low spending			
Italy	80.5	18.4[d]	1.1[c]
Greece	63.8	23.0[c]	13.1[c]
Spain	70.3	19.8[d]	10.0[c]
Portugal	79.7	14.6[c]	5.6[c]

Notes:

[a] The category 'private income' consists of the following components: capital income, property/rental income, private transfers.

[b] Due to the small number of observations, the results for Luxembourg are not presented.

[c] Less than 20 observations, unweighted.

[d] 20-49 observations, unweighted.

women with care responsibilities is more limited in the Beveridgean low spending countries. The Bismarckian countries again can be subdivided. In Belgium and the Netherlands, the majority of lone mothers (51.8% and 68.6% respectively) can rely on social transfers. This is not the case in Austria, France and Germany, where the main source of income for the majority of lone mothers is labour market participation. Welfare payments are generally less available as a main source of income in the southern European countries. Furthermore, there is no national minimum income guarantee (in Italy, the Reddito Minimo di Inserimento is currently being trialled in certain municipalities and is due to be implemented nationally) which encourages lone parents with children of school age to find employment. Lone mothers have to rely on the labour market, although, as we saw in Figure 5.1, access is limited.

Table 5.3 gives an indication of the generosity, in comparative terms, of welfare payments to lone mothers (1996). Generally, there is a clear divide between the high spending and the low spending welfare states. Transfers are

Table 5.3: Median current total monthly net household income (equivalised, in PPP) for lone mothers with social transfers as the main source of income (1996), weighted (18-55 years)

	Median current total monthly net household income
Beveridgean high spending	
Denmark	564.4[c]
Finland[a]	–
Beveridgean low spending	
UK	374.0
Ireland	401.2
Bismarckian high spending	
Austria	684.0[c]
Belgium	644.4
France	372.9
Germany	592.2
Luxembourg[b]	–
The Netherlands	539.5
Bismarckian low spending	
Italy	353.6[c]
Greece	304.8[d]
Spain	401.5[c]
Portugal	257.7[d]

Notes:

[a]No data for Finland in 1995.

[b]Due to the small number of observations, the results for Luxembourg are not presented.

[c] 20-49 observations, unweighted.

[d] Less than 20 observations, unweighted.

fairly high in Denmark, our social-democratic welfare state, and in the Bismarckian high spending countries of continental Europe, the only exception being France. Transfers are generally lower in the UK and Ireland, our liberal welfare states, and in the Bismarckian low spending countries of southern Europe.

The positions of the European welfare states on our three indicators of economic independence are presented in Figure 5.2 by means of a scatter-plot. Its results conclude that the availability of the sources of economic independence for women is generally in line with our welfare regime typology. In Denmark, women can rely on the labour market as well as on the welfare state. For women with care responsibilities, access to the labour market is limited in the Beveridgean low spending countries (the UK and Ireland), but transfers are widely available, although these are relatively low. On the basis of Figure 5.2, we can conclude that Ireland is a Beveridgean low spending country, rather than a late female mobilisation state. The picture for the Bismarckian high spending cluster is less clear. In the Netherlands, and to a lesser extent in

Figure 5.2: The European welfare states according to the sources of economic independence for women (1996)

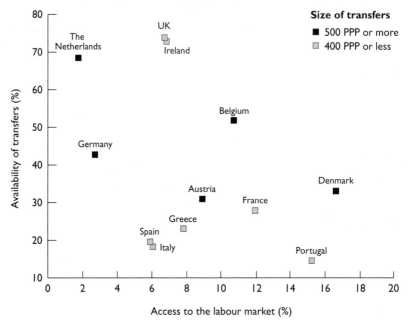

Germany, the welfare state is a more reliable source of economic independence than the labour market. In France, Austria and Belgium, both sources of economic independence seem to be available, although to a lesser extent than in the social democratic welfare states. In the Mediterranean countries, the labour market seems to be the best option. However, with the exception of Portugal, access is limited, especially for women with younger children.

Hypotheses

Based on the cross-national variations in the sources of economic independence for women in the previous section, we can now formulate more specific hypotheses concerning the financial consequences of relationship dissolution:

1. In Denmark, our only social-democratic welfare state, both the labour market and the welfare state are available to women as a source of economic independence. Furthermore, transfers are high and social services extensive. Therefore, we expect the financial consequences of relationship dissolution to be quite limited.

2. Although the welfare state is widely available in the Beveridgean low spending countries (the UK and Ireland), transfers are low and social assistance is means-tested. For mothers with young children, the low provision of public childcare makes it difficult to engage in full-time

employment. Therefore, we expect the financial consequences of relationship dissolution to be moderately adverse

3.   The picture is more complicated in the Bismarckian high spending countries of continental Europe. The financial consequences of relationship dissolution should be more limited to the extent that both sources of economic independence are more widely available. The combined position of women in the three systems of resource distribution – the state, the market and the family – seems to be most favourable in Belgium, characterised by relatively high full-time employment opportunities for women with young children. Furthermore, the majority of lone mothers can rely on social transfers as their main source of income. In Germany on the other hand, the majority of lone mothers has to rely on the labour market, although in general only 2.7% of women with young children are engaged in full-time employment. In both Belgium and Germany, social transfers for lone mothers are relatively high.

4.   In the Mediterranean countries, social transfers are generally not the main source of income for lone mothers and in the cases where they are, transfers are relatively low. Furthermore, with the exception of Portugal, the full-time employment opportunities for women with younger children are quite limited as well. Therefore, we expect the financial consequences of relationship dissolution to be relatively adverse in these countries.

We restrict our analysis of the financial consequences of relationship dissolution to a smaller number of countries, which are representative of the different types of welfare regimes identified by Siaroff (1994) and Bonoli (1997):

• Beveridgean high spending countries – protestant social-democratic welfare states: Denmark.
• Beveridgean low spending countries – protestant liberal welfare states: UK.
• Bismarckian high spending countries – advanced christian democratic welfare states: Belgium and Germany.
• Bismarckian low spending countries – late female mobilisation welfare states: Italy.

Data, methods and results

Data

Introduction to the dataset

As is clear from the illustrative analysis on welfare regimes, we will use data from the ECHP to analyse the financial consequences of relationship dissolution in the five selected countries. The ECHP is a panel study, that is, a standardised questioning of an initial sample at regular time-intervals. A prospective database is thus created, registering changes in the 'living situation' of households and individuals.

The cross-national comparability of (longitudinal) surveys is first of all dependent on the accuracy, reliability and comparability of the sample estimates, which are in turn dependent on the sampling design and the sample size. Comparability in the ECHP is achieved through a standardised design and common technical and implementation procedures, with centralised support and coordination of the national surveys by Eurostat. The first factor limiting comparability within the ECHP is linked to the degree of harmonisation of the questionnaires (Ditch et al, 1998). Although a blueprint questionnaire was designed at the central level, national adaptations were allowed, due to differences in national systems, or to the inclusion in the ECHP of existing national household panels, with slightly different data collection arrangements and procedures. Furthermore, the construction of the *Longitudinal Users' Database* (UDB) resulted in a highly standardised dataset, with seemingly small national differences. However, it is possible that important national differences are masked.

A second factor that influences data quality and limits cross-national comparability concerns the differing cross-sectional and longitudinal response rates for the countries in the ECHP. Although the overall response rate in wave 1 exceeded 70%, there was a large variation among countries, from 85% in Greece, Italy and Portugal to under 50% in Germany and Luxembourg (Eurostat, 1997). Given the rather small sample size in some countries, this could be a problem. Additionally, the estimates are biased given the extent to which this non-response is not random. The problem of selective non-response is especially important in longitudinal studies: every new wave brings about additional attrition. Analysis of the attrition between wave 1 and wave 2 revealed that the pattern of longitudinal non-response rates is fairly uniform across countries and for different types of variables. The largest effects were found in the UK, Ireland and Denmark (Eurostat, 1999). The differential non-response in the ECHP is corrected by the calculation of weighting coefficients.

Why longitudinal panel data?

As mentioned before, a prospective database allows us to register changes in the lives of individuals/households. Moreover, longitudinal studies allow us to take living conditions into account before the event took place, as well as the outcome of the event under consideration. Thus, it becomes possible to map more complex transitions in the respondent's 'living situation', taking the temporal order of events into account[10]. When considering the financial consequences of relationship dissolution, the panel design allows us to compare the financial situation of women before and after the event. In other words, we can evaluate the short-term implications of relationship dissolution for all women experiencing the event. This degree of clarity cannot always be reached with cross-sectional data. For instance, the group of divorced women in a cross-sectional survey consists of women who experienced relationship dissolution over a longer period of time. Some women divorced many years ago, while others only recently experienced relationship dissolution. Furthermore, since most women eventually remarry or enter a consensual union, it is possible that the group of women remaining single and divorced is a quite selective subsample of all women experiencing relationship dissolution.

Furthermore, the ECHP is structured in such a way that it can provide the necessary data to give us a more accurate view on the de facto relationship status and the actual number of relationship dissolutions. Research concerning relationship status often uses the de jure indicator marital status[11]. However, this de jure indicator of relationship status is no longer adequate to describe the de facto relationship status. We define the de facto relationship status of a respondent as his or her 'living situation', that is, whether or not the respondent lives together with a partner in the same household. In principle, all respondents in any of the categories of marital status can be either single or living together with a partner.

Use of a de facto measure of relationship dissolution is important because, while divorce is a formal event for which, in the public sphere, there is a clear set of procedures, in the private sphere the transition from marriage to divorce is a process that can take several months, even years. During this period, the married couple may have started living in different households, with or without a new partner. Secondly, a growing number of people are living in consensual union (Jacobs et al, 2000). Taking this into account, and considering the general finding that the chance of dissolution for couples who cohabit is greater than that of married couples, it becomes clear that the analysis of relationship dissolution needs to take into account cohabitation dissolution.

One of the advantages of a household panel is that we have data on all the members of a household, as well as on the relationships between them. To identify the actual relationship status of each respondent, we combine the information on the presence of a partner in the household with the marital status of both partners. This couple-based approach[12] allows us to determine the type of union in greater detail. The structure of the ECHP allows us to further identify the people who have experienced relationship dissolution between two waves. Based on this actual indicator, it is possible to construct transition tables and to compute all relationship dissolutions[13] occurring between waves 1 and 2, and waves 2 and 3.

Unfortunately, this prospective method is hampered by the small number of dissolutions between two consecutive waves, possibly resulting in less reliable conclusions for some countries. This problem is only partly solved by pooling data over different waves. This means that we join the two separate files, containing the women experiencing relationship dissolution between waves 1 and 2, and between waves 2 and 3, into one bigger file.

Results

The outline of the analysis is as follows. First, we determine the actual relationship status of the female respondents. A comparison between the marital status of the respondent and the actual relationship status shows that the de jure indicator of relationship status does not provide us with a realistic estimation of the de facto situation. In the same way, the number of divorces is inadequate as an indicator of the actual number of relationship dissolutions. Secondly, we assess the financial consequences of relationship dissolution in our example countries, which are representative of the different welfare regimes discussed earlier.

Relationship status and relationship dissolution

We now determine the relationship status of the female respondents in our example countries based on the actual 'living situation', that is, whether or not the respondent lives with a partner in the same household. Firstly, we look for the presence of a partner in the household. Then, by combining the marital status of both partners, we can unambiguously determine the type of union. (The only problem with this approach is that, when both partners are married, we assume that they are married to each other.)

The actual relationship status for the female respondents in the countries analysed is presented in Table 5.4. In line with general findings on this subject, cohabitation is most popular in Denmark, while it is still restricted to a minority of the population in Italy. The proportion of women living in a consensual union in the countries of continental Europe, and in the only protestant liberal welfare state, the UK, is in-between these two extremes.

Our longitudinal indicator of relationship dissolution is presented in Table 5.5. Based on a comparison of the actual relationship status in pairs of consecutive waves, Table 5.4 shows the proportion of women, living with a partner in wave $(t-1)$, who experience relationship dissolution between wave $(t-1)$ and wave (t). The number of transitions computed in this prospective way is very small, even using large national samples. Therefore, further analysis is based on a pooled transition file, as explained earlier. The number of relationship dissolutions is highest in Denmark and the UK. The advanced Christian Democratic welfare states occupy an intermediate position, while the number of relationship dissolutions is lowest in Italy.

To summarise, there seems to be a cluster-specific pattern of relationship dissolution. The number of relationship dissolutions is slightly higher in Denmark than in the UK, possibly reflecting differential employment opportunities for women. As far as the Bismarckian high spending countries are concerned, the number seems to be highest in Belgium, where both paid labour and social transfers are more readily available as sources of economic independence. However, there is little difference with Germany. Furthermore, the number of relationship dissolutions is higher in the Bismarckian high

Table 5.4: Actual relationship status of women (%) (1996), weighted (18 years and older)

	Denmark	UK	Belgium	Germany	Italy
Married	51.6	57.0	56.0	57.5	57.4
Consensual union	14.6	5.6	4.8	4.5	0.9
No partner	33.8	37.4	39.3	38.0	41.7

Table 5.5: Percentage of women with relationship dissolution between waves 1 and 2 (1994-95) and waves 2 and 3 (1995-96), weighted (18 years and older, women with a partner)

	Wave 1 – Wave 2	Wave 2 – Wave 3	Pooled
Denmark	2.8	2.5	2.6
UK	2.0	2.5	2.2
Belgium	1.1[a]	1.6	1.4
Germany	0.9	1.4	1.2
Italy	0.4[a]	0.5[a]	0.5

Note: [a]10-29 observations, unweighted

spending countries than in Italy, which belongs to the Bismarckian low spending cluster.

The financial consequences of relationship dissolution

The impact of family breakdown on the economic well-being of the women involved can be evaluated in several ways. In principle, the choice of the measurement instrument is based on a number of underlying ideas about the nature of poverty. The main issues concern the distinction between absolute or relative measures, direct or indirect measures and uni-dimensional or multi-dimensional measures (cf Dewilde and De Keulenaer, 2001). Furthermore, the decision on the thresholds separating the poor from the non-poor is usually based on some arbitrary criterion. According to Ruspini (1999b, p 329), "poverty rates are very sensitive to the definition of poverty itself. The adoption of either one or another method may heavily influence both the number and the structure of the population in poverty". In this chapter, we focus on the impact of relationship dissolution on the financial situation of the women involved, using a relative income poverty approach.

In order to evaluate the financial consequences of relationship dissolution, we compare the income situation of our respondents before and after the event. This requires a monthly measure of household income. The only way to obtain this is to use the summary question concerning the current total monthly net household income available in the ECHP. This variable is based on estimates provided by the reference person of each household. Previous research has shown that this method usually results in an underestimation of the real household income (Van Dam and Van den Bosch, 1997). Furthermore, this underestimation seems to get more serious with increasing household size, possibly because the reference person forgets to take some income components into account, or does not know the exact personal income of the other household members.

We use a relative income poverty line, and our reference points are 60% and 70% of the median equivalised household income in the respective countries[14]. We also construct an additional 'poverty index'. This index compares the equivalised household income for each respondent – or group of respondents – to the median equivalised household income in the countries under consideration[15]. An index of 1 means that the median income for a particular group of respondents is equal to the median income in the population, while an index higher or lower than 1 refers to a more or less favourable income position, respectively, compared to the typical respondent. In this way, the financial situation of the respondent is compared to the ordinary standard of living in her society. Furthermore, the income statistics are expressed in PPP, so as to facilitate cross-national comparisons.

Our first step is to compare the income situation of all women living with a partner in wave (*t*-1) with the subgroup of women in wave (*t*-1) who experience relationship dissolution between wave (*t*-1) and wave (*t*). As Tables 5.6 and 5.7 show, income poverty is usually higher for the last group, indicating that financial problems are a precursor as well as an outcome of relationship dissolution – except for Italy. In particular, this is the case in the UK, Germany and Belgium.

Our second step is to consider the subgroup of women experiencing relationship dissolution, and to compare the financial situation of each group before and after the event (Tables 5.8 and 5.9). In terms of relative income poverty, as well as in terms of the median income and the poverty-index, the change in financial situation is greatest in Denmark and the UK, followed by Germany. Changes are more limited in Italy, while the effect of relationship dissolution is negligible in Belgium. This surprisingly strong drop in median income for Danish women can be explained by a number of factors. Firstly, female labour market participation in Denmark is very high – 75.9% (OECD, 2001) – so that the majority of women experiencing relationship dissolution make the transition from a dual-earner to a single-earner household. This is also the case in the UK – 68.9% (OECD, 2001). Secondly, the proportion of women establishing an independent household is highest in Denmark – 86.3% (see Table 5.10). Thirdly, income inequality in Denmark is among the lowest

Table 5.6: Income poverty before relationship dissolution between 2 waves (1994-95 and 1995-96, pooled), weighted (18 years and older, women with a partner)

	All women with a partner at (t-1)		Women with dissolution between (t-1) and (t)	
	60% poverty line	70% poverty line	60% poverty line	70% poverty line
Denmark	8.0	14.4	9.2[a]	18.9[b]
UK	14.5	20.5	28.2[b]	31.9[b]
Belgium	16.0	26.1	31.3[b]	34.4[b]
Germany	6.4	14.3	12.7[a]	26.5[b]
Italy	13.0	20.3	12.7[a]	17.9[a]

Notes:

[a] Less than 10 observations, unweighted

[b] 10-29 observations, unweighted

Table 5.7: Median equivalised income in PPP and poverty-index before relationship dissolution between 2 waves (1994-95 and 1995-96, pooled), weighted (18 years and older, women with a partner)

	All women with a partner at (t-1)		Women with dissolution between (t-1) and (t)	
	Median income	Poverty-index	Median income	Poverty-index
Denmark	1,026.7	1.08	1,021.5	1.07
UK	952.3	1.18	836.6	1.02
Belgium	976.4	1.04	891.8	0.96
Germany	1,006.2	1.05	890.6	0.91
Italy	662.8	1.03	709.5	1.10

in the European Union (Maître and Nolan, 1999a), meaning that even a relatively small drop in income can have the effect of pushing the individual below the poverty line.

With reference to the Bismarckian high spending countries, we hypothesised that the financial consequences of relationship dissolution would be more limited in Belgium than in Germany, since women in Belgium occupy a more favourable position vis-à-vis the labour market and the welfare state. As seen before, access to the labour market is less restricted for women with young children, while social transfers for lone mothers are relatively high and widely available. Our hypothesis appears to be confirmed. The financial situation of women following divorce is virtually unchanged in Belgium, while in Germany it is more pronounced.

As far as relative income poverty is concerned, poverty rates are highest in the UK and lowest in Italy. Relative income poverty in Denmark, the social democratic welfare state, is in-between these extremes and comparable to the situation in the Bismarckian high spending countries. However, when we use

Table 5.8: Income poverty before and after relationship dissolution between 2 waves (1994-95 and 1995-96, pooled), weighted (18 years and older, women with a partner)

	Before relationship dissolution		After relationship dissolution	
	60% poverty line	70% poverty line	60% poverty line	70% poverty line
Denmark	9.2[a]	18.9[b]	25.0[b]	40.5
UK	28.2[b]	31.9[b]	46.4	54.4
Belgium	31.3[b]	34.4[b]	29.0[b]	41.7[b]
Germany	12.7[a]	26.5[b]	33.5[b]	40.7[b]
Italy	12.7[a]	17.9[a]	17.3[a]	29.1[b]

Notes:

[a] Less than 10 observations, unweighted.

[b] 10-29 observations, unweighted.

Table 5.9: Median equivalised income in PPP before and after relationship dissolution between 2 waves (1994-95 and 1995-96, pooled), weighted (18 years and older, women with a partner)

	Before relationship dissolution		After relationship dissolution	
	Median income	Poverty-index	Median income	Poverty-index
Denmark	1,021.5	1.07	777.4	0.79
UK	836.6	1.02	607.2	0.68
Belgium	891.8	0.96	950.0	1.00
Germany	890.6	0.91	838.0	0.83
Italy	709.5	1.10	614.7	0.91

Table 5.10: Median equivalised income in PPP after relationship dissolution between 2 waves (1994-95 and 1995-96, pooled), according to household type, weighted (18 years and older, women with a partner)

	Established an independent household			Joined another household		
	%	Median income	Poverty-index	%	Median income	Poverty-index
Denmark	86.3	777.4	0.79	13.7[a]	1095.1[a]	1.14[a]
UK	75.6	535.7	0.64	24.4[a]	1064.7[a]	1.23[a]
Belgium	73.9	906.2	0.91	26.1[a]	1099.5[a]	1.16[a]
Germany	75.2	781.4	0.78	24.8[a]	1027.0[a]	1.01[a]
Italy	68.2	645.9	0.91	31.8[a]	545.4[a]	0.85[a]

Notes: [a] 10-29 observations, unweighted

an absolute standard and compare the median income in PPP, the financial situation of women experiencing relationship dissolution is relatively comfortable in the high spending countries (Denmark, Belgium and Germany) and relatively poor in the low spending countries (the UK and Italy). This is especially true for the UK, where the difference with the financial situation of the typical household is greatest (Table 5.9).

To summarise, our hypotheses concerning a cluster-specific pattern in terms of the financial consequences of relationship dissolution are partly confirmed. Although the changes in income and poverty in Denmark are more adverse than expected, the financial situation of women experiencing relationship dissolution is relatively positive in comparative terms. The financial consequences of relationship dissolution are more limited in the advanced Christian Democratic welfare states. As expected, the change in financial situation is more pronounced in Germany than in Belgium. Although transfers are widely available, women who experience relationship dissolution are worst off in the UK. Contrary to our hypothesis, the financial consequences of relationship dissolution are less strong in Italy.

In Table 5.10, we consider the impact on the financial situation after relationship dissolution of the formation of an independent household (single or as a lone mother) versus the formation of a new union or joining an already existing household, mostly the parental one. As mentioned before, the proportion of women establishing an independent household is highest in Denmark (86.3%). A significant proportion of women (around 25%) in the UK and in the Bismarckian high spending countries has formed a new union or has returned to the parental household. This strategy is even more pronounced in Italy, our Mediterranean welfare state (31.8%). According to Finch (1989), the tendency to return to the parental home after relationship dissolution is strongly influenced by economic considerations, in particular the ability (both financial and in terms of social housing regulations) to acquire decent housing. The same argument is probably valid for the women forming a new union. Furthermore, joining another household probably opens up more labour market opportunities for women with children, since the other household members may provide informal childcare, on a regular basis or in case of emergencies.

Generally, in so far as all household members have equal access to the household resources, joining another household leads to a more favourable income situation compared to establishing an independent household. The poverty-index which, as explained before, compares the financial situation of the respondent to the typical respondent in her country, is higher than 1 in Denmark, the UK, Belgium and Germany, indicating a more favourable income position than the average household. Contrary to the situation in the other countries, joining another household has no significant positive effect on the median income in Italy. This indicates that there might be a selection process at work. When sources of economic independence are available, women opt to establish an independent household. When no sources are available, they have to join another household, and in this process they lower the standard of living of their new household. This hypothesis is in line with the results of Casper, Garfinkel and McLanahan (1994), who state that, where neither the labour market nor the welfare state are available, marriage and, in our case, returning to the parental household, are the key to low female poverty.

Although we found some evidence that the welfare regime – access to the labour market and availability of welfare payments – is related to the financial consequences of relationship dissolution, so far we have only asserted this relationship at an aggregate level. We cannot, therefore, be sure that the relationship is valid at the individual level. Unfortunately, the data do not allow for a full test of our hypotheses at the individual level. Due to the specific income concept used in the ECHP, it is not possible to determine whether the respondent can rely on the welfare state after experiencing relationship dissolution[16]. What we do have, however, is information on the labour market position of the respondent after relationship dissolution.

In Table 5.11 we consider the median income and the poverty-index after relationship dissolution according to the main activity status. The women who

Table 5.11: Median equivalised income in PPP after relationship dissolution between 2 waves (1994-95 and 1995-96, pooled), according to main activity status, weighted (18 years and older)

	Not working		Part-time working		Full-time working	
	Median income	Poverty-index	Median income	Poverty-index	Median income	Poverty-index
Denmark	580.0[b]	0.58[b]	589.3[a]	0.61[a]	870.7	0.90
UK	355.9[b]	0.41[b]	530.3[b]	0.69[b]	834.6[b]	0.99[b]
Belgium	570.4[b]	0.59[b]	971.9[a]	1.00[a]	1,393.6[b]	1.44[b]
Germany	534.2[b]	0.52[b]	744.9[b]	0.75[b]	937.7[b]	0.93[b]
Italy	559.8[a]	0.83[a]	535.6[a]	0.82[a]	774.2[b]	1.18[b]

Notes:

[a] Less than 10 observations, unweighted.

[b] 10-29 observations, unweighted.

formed a new union or returned to the parental household are not considered, since their financial situation is not comparable to the women who established an independent household. Generally, we can conclude that the income position of those women who do not have a job – and probably have to rely on the welfare state – is least favourable. With the exception of Italy, the median income for this group of women is less than 60% of the median income of the population, with the largest discrepancy occurring in the UK. British women are also worst off when we use a more absolute standard, comparing the median income in PPP for the different countries. Next, women with a part-time job are in a better income position than those who are not working. However, the poverty-index is still below 0.7 in Denmark and the UK. The median income in PPP is lowest in the UK, Italy and Denmark while it is highest in Belgium. The financial situation of full-time working women experiencing relationship dissolution is generally comparable to that of the population as a whole. In all countries, the poverty-index is equal to 0.9 or higher. Based on an absolute standard, full-time working women in Italy receive the lowest wages, while the German and especially the Belgian women occupy quite a favourable income position.

We can conclude that the relationship between the position of women in the welfare regime, on the one hand, and the financial consequences of relationship dissolution, on the other hand, is valid at the individual level. The income position of those women who do not have a job and did not join another household is significantly worse than the population in general. Generally, income position improves with increased number of working hours.

Finally, comparing the proportions of women establishing an independent household and joining another household (Table 5.12) and the proportions of women in the different employment statuses (Table 5.11), let us try to link the results at the individual level to the results at the aggregate level. Among social democratic welfare states, we can conclude that the high accessibility of the labour market results in a high proportion (54.9%) of women who experience relationship dissolution being able to work full-time. This can be attributed to the extensive provision of publicly funded childcare arrangements (O'Connor, 1996): 64% of children under three years of age make use of formal (public and private provision) arrangements (OECD, 2001). However, since social transfers are widely available and relatively high, the number of women without a job is also quite high (31.8%). The availability of both the labour market and the welfare state results in a low proportion of women forming a new union or returning to the parental household (13.7%). Although the change in financial situation following relationship dissolution is quite pronounced in Denmark, from a cross-national perspective poverty rates are relatively low and median income is relatively high.

Transfers are widely available in the UK, but rather low. The majority of women experiencing relationship dissolution opt for a part-time or a full-time job (64.2%). However, the limited access to the labour market for women with care responsibilities results in a lower proportion of women working full-time (33.9%) compared to Denmark. In the UK, maximum private responsibility for childcare leaves the majority of working parents dependent on informal care arrangements (O'Connor, 1996). Furthermore, a higher proportion of women experiencing relationship dissolution do not establish independent households (24.4%). Although both the labour market and the welfare state are available to a certain extent, neither is optimal for women establishing an independent household. This results in high poverty rates.

Among the Bismarckian high spending countries, the more favourable position of Belgian women vis-à-vis the welfare state results in a high proportion of women not working (53.5% compared to 35.2% in Germany). Furthermore, the higher accessibility of the labour market in Belgium results in twice as many women having a full-time rather than a part-time job (31.2% compared to 15.4%). Again, this can be linked to the availability of childcare. In Belgium, 30% of children under three years of age use formal childcare, compared to 10% in Germany. The number of part-time working women in Germany on the other hand is relatively high. This is consistent with our finding that the financial consequences of relationship dissolution are more limited in Belgium than in Germany.

It seems that the labour market is the best option for women experiencing relationship dissolution and forming an independent household in Italy: 71.0% are working, the majority in a full-time job (Table 5.12). Although formal childcare arrangements for children aged three and less are scarce, 95% of children aged three to mandatory school age are enrolled in pre-primary education. It should also be remembered that a very important factor in explaining full-time female employment in Italy is the active solidarity of women belonging to different generations: for every young working woman there is at least one older woman (mother or mother-in-law) who may not live in the same household but who plays an active part in taking care of the children (Bimbi, 1998). One of the characteristic features of the Italian welfare model is its 'familistic' nature, that is, the importance given to family and voluntary support.

Table 5.12: Main activity status after relationship dissolution between 2 waves (%) (1994-95 and 1995-96, pooled), weighted (18 years and older, women with relationship dissolution who establish an independent household)

	Not working	Part-time working[a]	Full-time working[b]
Denmark	31.8[d]	13.2[c]	54.9
UK	35.8[d]	30.3[d]	33.9[d]
Belgium	53.5[d]	15.4[c]	31.2[d]
Germany	35.2[d]	34.6[d]	30.3[d]
Italy	29.0[c]	15.4[c]	55.6[d]

Notes:

[a] Less than 35 hours per week.

[b] 35 hours per week or more.

[c] Less than 10 observations, unweighted.

[d] 10-29 observations, unweighted.

The familist tendency of welfare assistance is strongly connected with the fact that the Italian welfare regime is virtually inactive as regards family policies. As a result, the help coming from public or private service facilities is less crucial: for example, our data show that only 29.0% of women establishing an independent household rely on the welfare state. Furthermore, 31.8% of women experiencing relationship dissolution do not establish an independent household (see Table 5.10). Although the change in financial situation following relationship dissolution is limited and poverty rates are generally lower, from a cross-national perspective median household income is quite modest.

Conclusion

This chapter has linked cross-national variations in terms of the financial consequences of relationship dissolution to the types of welfare regimes in the countries of the EU, using the de facto or actual 'living situation' of the respondent.

We have argued that the position of women in the welfare regime – access to the labour market and availability of welfare payments – is related to the financial consequences of relationship dissolution. This relationship holds at the individual as well as the aggregate level. Generally, the consequences of relationship dissolution in terms of income poverty are more limited when both sources of economic independence are widely available.

However, some unresolved issues remain. Firstly, the small number of transitions occurring on a yearly basis, that is, between two consecutive waves, is a handicap in analysing relationship dissolution. More waves will bring about more transitions, but it is clear that the full potential of panel studies can only be realised when the number of waves is considerable. Secondly, the highly standardised and simplified format of the *Longitudinal Users' Database* (UDB) results in a high level of generality, possibly masking important national differences. Furthermore, the specific income concept used in the ECHP, aimed at providing annual estimates, is probably better suited to cross-sectional than longitudinal analysis.

Where the substantive results are concerned, the pronounced changes in the income situation following relationship dissolution in Denmark and the UK point to the fact that the growth of the dual-earner households may 'produce' more poverty for single women and lone mothers, when using conventional poverty measures. Using both a household- and an individual-based income measure might give us more insight when considering income mobility following family composition changes (Ruspini, 1999b).

Additionally, we should also consider economic well-being following relationship dissolution using non-monetary poverty indicators. After all, poverty is an ambiguous concept. Income-based measures fail to address the multi-aspect nature of the poverty phenomenon. According to Ruspini (1999b, p 331), "the non-monetary dimension of deprivation is very important if we wish to capture the gender nature of poverty.... There are less quantifiable aspects of poverty ... which are not only different for women and for men but also differ between diverse groups of women".

Finally, when more waves are available, we should make a distinction between short-term and long-term consequences of relationship dissolution, again within the context of the different welfare regimes in the countries of the EU.

Notes

[1] Initial paper prepared for the Fifth International Conference on Logic and Methodology: Social Science Methodology in the New Millennium, October 3-6, 2000, University of Cologne, Germany. Many thanks to Thérèse Jacobs (CBGS) and Rudy Marijnissen (PSBH).

[2] Most poverty measures are based on the assumption that the distribution and consumption of resources within the household are equally distributed. However, research shows that in reality this assumption is not tenable: within the family, power relationships are reflected in the differential access to family resources (cf Glendinning and Millar, 1992; Daly, 1992; Ruspini, 2000).

[3] The female work desirability score is based on data concerning the labour market participation of women, but it also takes into account the quality of female jobs. It is calculated by averaging the female to male wage ratios in the industry and in desirable, well-paid, high-level jobs. This figure is then multiplied by a weighted average of female to male ratios in the employment population ratio and in official employment.

[4] The family welfare orientation score is calculated by averaging the scores on the following indicators: social security spending, family policy spending, childcare policies, policies concerning maternity and parental leave.

[5] Bonoli (1997) determines the relative size of the Bismarckian component in the different countries on the basis of the proportion of total social expenditure financed by contributions.

[6] Since the variable measuring the main source of income pertains to the calendar year prior to the survey, we only include households who qualify as a lone parent household in the current wave and the previous wave.

[7] The median is the value where 50% of the incomes lie above and 50% of the incomes lie below. Unlike the mean, the median is not influenced by extreme values.

[8] To adjust for differences in the size and the composition of households, we use the modified OECD-equivalence scale: the first adult in a household is given the value 1, each additional adult is given the value 0.5 and each child (younger than 14 years) the value 0.3. The equivalised income of the household is then attributed to each member, assuming a common standard of living within the household (Maître and Nolan, 1999b).

[9] In order to obtain cross-nationally comparable income estimates, taking into account the purchasing power of the different national currencies (influenced by different inflation rates), we applied the PPP provided by Eurostat. Although PPP are designed for currency adjustment of gross domestic product figures, they are superior to exchange rates when applied to (household) income.

[10] However, panel analysis also has a number of disadvantages (Ruspini, 1999a). Blossfeld and Rohwer (1997) point out a number of deficiencies inherently linked to panel data: panel biases, attrition of the sample, missing data, distorted estimation of transition rates, and a number of problems related to the discrete-time character of the measurement. They suggest that a "continuous measurement of qualitative variables seems to be the only adequate method of assessing empirical change" (1997, p 379). Unfortunately, there is no retrospective module on the relationship history of the respondents in the ECHP. Furthermore, calendar data are only collected for the main activity status of the respondent.

[11] Marital status divides the population according to the following categories: unmarried; married; separated; divorced; widowed.

[12] A methodological drawback of this couple-based approach is caused by the fact that the male and female respondents in the dataset stem from the same unions. This means that many characteristics of the respondents are doubled. Furthermore, the household-related variables have the same value by definition. However, since we focus on the women in the ECHP, we do not have to deal with this problem: we select the female respondents, and thus only one possible relationship dissolution.

[13] The situation is more complicated than this, however. We have to take into account the information on both partners since it is possible, for instance, that some respondents are living in the same type of union in two consecutive waves, but with a different

partner. This means that, during the time interval between two waves, these people experienced the dissolution as well as the formation of a partnership. Furthermore, we also have to make the distinction between dissolutions due to the death of a partner, and 'real' dissolutions due to separation or divorce.

[14] Since the median income is quite low in some countries, it makes sense to use the 60% and 70% poverty line (Maitre and Nolan, 1999a). Furthermore, due to the small number of observations, it is feasible to use a slightly higher poverty line.

[15] For each respondent, the equivalised household income is compared to the median equivalised household income in the population (income/median). The summarising income-index for sample subgroups is again based on the median, so as to avoid the influence of extreme values.

[16] This problem can probably be solved when more waves are available: we then could use the income information from the next wave. However, this solution is not feasible with only three waves. For the respondents experiencing relationship dissolution between wave 1 and wave 2, we could use the information from the third wave (wave 3). For the respondents experiencing relationship dissolution between wave 2 and wave 3, we would need the information from a fourth wave (wave 4), which was not yet available at the time this research was carried out.

References

Bimbi, F. (1993) 'Gender, "gift relationship" and welfare state cultures in Italy', in J. Lewis (ed) *Women and social policies in Europe. Work, family and the state*, Aldershot: Edward Elgar, pp 138-65.

Bimbi, F. (1998) 'Family paradigms and women's citizenship in the Italian welfare state 1947-1996', *Contribution to the TMR Workshop 'Family and Family Policies in Southern Europe'*, Turin, 20-21 November.

Bimbi, F. and Ruspini, E. (2000) 'Povertà delle donne e trasformazione dei rapporti di genere', *Inchiesta*, vol 128, April-June.

Blossfeld, H.-P. and Rohwer, G. (1997) 'Causal inference, time and observation plans in the social sciences', *Quality and Quantity*, vol 31, no 4, pp 361-84.

Bonoli, G. (1997) 'Classifying welfare states: a two-dimension approach', *Journal of Social Policy*, vol 26, no 3, pp 351-72.

Burkhauser, R.V. and Duncan, G.J. (1987) 'Life events, public policy and the economic vulnerability of children and the elderly', Paper presented at the Pack Meeting, 7 May.

Bussemaker, J. and van Kersbergen, K. (1994) 'Gender and welfare states: some theoretical reflections', in D. Sainsbury (ed) *Gendering welfare states*, London: Sage Publications, pp 8-25.

Castles, F.G. and Flood, M. (1993) 'Why divorce rates differ: law, religious belief and modernity', in F.G. Castles (ed) *Families of nations. Patterns of public policy in Western democracies*, Dartmouth: Aldershot, pp 293-326.

Casper, L.M., Garfinkel, I. and McLanahan, S.S. (1994) 'The gender-poverty gap: what we can learn from other countries', *American Sociological Review*, vol 59, August, pp 594-605.

Daly, M. (1992) 'Europe's poor women? Gender in research on poverty', *European Sociological Review*, vol 8, no 1, pp 1-12.

Daly, M. (1994) 'Comparing welfare states: towards a gender friendly approach', in D. Sainsbury (ed) *Gendering welfare states*, London: Sage Publications, pp 107-70.

Dewilde, C. and de Keulenaer, F. (2001) 'Developing a European multi-aspectual poverty index?', Paper prepared for the EuroConference on 'European Welfare States and Changing Life Courses', Kerkrade, 6-10 October.

Ditch, J., Barnes, H., Bradshaw J. and Kilkey, M. (1998) *A synthesis of national family policies in 1996, European Observatory on National Family Policies (The University of York)*, European Commission.

Duncan, G.J. and Morgan, J.N. (1984) 'An overview of family economic mobility', in G.J. Duncan (ed) *Years of poverty, years of plenty*, Michigan, MI: Institute for Social Research, pp 9-31.

Esping-Andersen, G. (1999) *Social foundations of postindustrial economies*, Oxford: Oxford University Press.

Esping-Andersen, G. (1990) *The three worlds of welfare capitalism*, Cambridge: Polity Press.

Eurostat (1997) *The European Community Household Panel: Data quality, Doc PAN 90/97* (draft), European Commission.

Eurostat (1999) *The effect of attrition on structure of the sample, Doc PAN 119/99*, European Commission.

Ferrera, M. (1996) 'The "Southern model" of welfare in social Europe', *Journal of European Social Policy*, vol 6, no 1, pp 17-37.

Finch, J. (1989) *Family obligations and social change*, Cambridge: Polity Press.

Glendinning, C. and Millar, J. (1992) 'It all really starts in the family: gender divisions and poverty', in C. Glendinning and J. Millar (eds) *Women and poverty in Britain: The 1990s*, Hemel Hempstead: Harvester Wheatsheaf, pp 3-10.

Hobson, B. (1994) 'Solo mothers, social policy regimes and the logics of gender', in D. Sainsbury (ed) *Gendering welfare states*, London: Sage Publications, pp 170-87.

Jacobs, T., Bauwens, A., Speltincx, E. and Lantican, L. (2000) *Gezinsontbinding in Vlaanderen, Boek 1: Persoonlijke relaties in beweging*, Antwerpen: Universiteit Antwerpen (UIA).

Leibfried, S. (1991) *Towards a European welfare state? On integrating poverty regimes in the European Community*, Bremen: Zentrum für Sozialpolitik.

Lewis, J. and Ostner, I. (1992) 'Gender and the evolution of European social policies', Paper presented at the CES Workshop on 'Emergent Supranational Social Policy: The EC's Social Dimension in Comparative Perspective', Centre for European Studies, Harvard University, 15-17 November 1991.

Maître, B. and Nolan, B. (1999a) 'The distribution of income and relative income poverty in the European Community Household Panel', *Chapter for the European Panel Analysis Group* (www.iser.essex.ac.uk/epag/).

Maître, B. and Nolan, B. (1999b) 'Income mobility in the European Household Panel Survey', *Chapter for the European Panel Analysis Group* (www.iser.essex.ac.uk/epag/).

Millar, J. (1988) 'The costs of marital breakdown', in R. Walker and G. Parker (eds) *Money matters. Income, wealth and financial welfare*, London: Sage Publications, pp 99-114.

O'Connor, J.S. (1993) 'Gender, class and citizenship in the comparative analysis of welfare state regimes: theoretical and methodological issues', British Journal of Sociology, vol 44, no 3, pp 501-18.

O'Connor, J.S. (1996) 'From women in the welfare state to gendering welfare state regimes', *Current Sociology*, vol 44, no 2, pp 1-130.

OECD (Organisation for Economic Co-operation and Development) (2001) *OECD Employment Outlook*, Paris: OECD.

Orloff, A.S. (1993) 'Gender and the social rights of citizenship: the comparative analysis of gender relations and the welfare state', *American Sociological Review*, vol 58, June, pp 303-28.

Orloff, A.S. (1996) 'Gender in the welfare state', *Annual Review of Sociology*, vol 22, pp 51-78.

Ostner, I. (1993) 'Slow motion: women, work and the family in Germany', in J. Lewis (1993) *Women and social policies in Europe. Work, family and the state*, Aldershot: Edward Elgar, pp 92-115.

Ruspini, E. (1998) 'Women and poverty dynamics: the case of Germany and Great Britain', *Journal of European Social Policy*, vol 8, no 4, pp 291-316.

Ruspini, E. (1999a) 'Longitudinal research and the analysis of social change', *Quality and Quantity*, vol 33, no 3, pp 219-27.

Ruspini, E. (1999b) 'The contribution of longitudinal research to the study of women's poverty', *Quality and Quantity*, vol 33, no 3, pp 323-38.

Ruspini, E. (2000) 'Poverty and the gendered distribution of resources within households', *Issue of Radical Statistics on Money and Finance*, vol 75, Autumn, pp 25-37.

Sainsbury, D. (1994) 'Women's and men's social rights: gendering dimensions of welfare states', in D. Sainsbury (ed) *Gendering welfare states*, London: Sage Publications, pp 150-69.

Saraceno, C. (1994) 'The ambivalent familism of the Italian welfare state', *Social Politics*, vol 1, pp 60-82.

Siaroff, A. (1994) 'Work, welfare and gender equality: a new typology', in D. Sainsbury (ed) *Gendering welfare states*, London: Sage Publications, pp 82-100.

Van Dam, R. and Van den Bosch, K. (1997) *Hoeveel armen zijn er in België? Resultaten van diverse studies*, Antwerpen: Centrum voor Sociaal Beleid, Universiteit Antwerpen (UFSIA).

SIX

Women's incomes over a synthetic lifetime

Heather Joshi and Hugh Davies

Introduction

Longitudinal data illustrate the unfolding of the life course, but they seldom give a complete account of real lifetimes. Where they do it is mainly of historic interest. Prospectively, there is more interest prospectively in the long-term, that is, lifetime consequences of developments in early and mid-life. This chapter presents some results of a simulation model of earnings, income and pensions over the lifetime of illustrative British individuals, built upon both longitudinal and cross-sectional evidence. The model started as an exploration of the long-term impact of childbearing on women's lifetime earnings, but it has since been elaborated to illustrate, among other things, gender differences over a hypothetical lifetime, in pay, earnings and net income; the role of the family and the state in redistributing income over time, and the different lifetime experiences of people with different initial levels of earning power. As the latter are very striking, and affect differentials by motherhood and by gender dramatically, they are paid special attention in this overview of findings.

Wherever income varies over the life course, a one-period snapshot of a person's income may not be very informative. For example, it would not necessarily be correct to infer that someone observed at one point with no earnings would necessarily never have earned in the past, or would remain in that state in the future. Likewise people who are employed at one point may not always be employed at another. The longitudinal perspective, unlike cross-sections, can show the proportions of a history devoted to various states, and the sequences among them. It can also relate the history of labour force activity to events in other domains, such as partnership and childrearing.

In the case of women, family-related fluctuations in earnings over the lifecycle increase the need to take a long-term perspective. This can show the influences of childbearing on earnings and income, and draw out the labour market and income consequences of different marital histories for women's finances. By looking over the whole life course it is possible to show how far taxes, benefits and pensions smooth women's incomes over lifetimes. Especially where there are gender differences in earnings, it is relevant to investigate how the family itself may redistribute lifetime income towards women, and to put gender differences in earnings in this long-term perspective.

This chapter presents some of the findings of an exercise, the intention of which was to get an impression of earnings and incomes over a hypothetical lifetime for British women. These results are synthesised using a range of assumptions about education, fertility, partnership and pension arrangements. The data, which forms the basis of the analyses reported, is drawn from the British Household Panel Study (BHPS) (see the Appendix to this chapter for details).

Childbearing and childrearing may affect British women's incomes throughout their lives. Mothers may take time away from paid work in order to look after their children, especially when they are very young. This is particularly important in Britain where subsidised day care facilities have been relatively rare (Meyer et al, 1999). British mothers may also take part-time employment to accommodate their responsibilities. Although common in Britain, part-time jobs are often at lower hourly wages than full-time jobs (Blossfeld and Hakim, 1997; Joshi et al, 1999; Rake, 2000). Loss of labour-market experience may affect wages later on, so that a woman who has taken time out to have children may never catch up with the wage rate she would have earned with a continuous employment history. To the extent that pensions are deferred earnings, the income costs of childrearing will stretch into old age. Mainly because of childrearing, women's incomes at any moment in time have traditionally borne a more complicated relationship to their lifetime incomes than do men's. Women's incomes over the life course can also include transfers from the state or the family, which may, in part, offset the original income penalties of their reproductive role.

Why it is necessary to invent longitudinal data

There is no empirical data source which tracks the incomes of individuals over their whole lifetime. Collecting complete lifetime histories would require waiting for many years, by which time the information from the early years would be rather out of date. Tracking the lifecycle path of income therefore requires modelling, as well as description. Here we use a simulation model to construct earnings and incomes of hypothetical, stylised individuals. We use a combination of cross-sectional and longitudinal data on life histories that are still in progress to build complete but artificial life histories following their course in a 'time warp'.

This concept is similar to the commonly used estimate of life expectancy. Life expectancy at birth is not a prediction of how long today's babies will live, given the prospects for medical advance (or ecological catastrophe) during the course of their actual lifetimes. Rather, it is an estimate of how long they would live if they faced the risks of dying that apply today at each age. In the case of lifetime incomes, we generate a stream of income based upon observations of a contemporary relationship between wages and accumulated work experience, and for women, a contemporary relationship between employment participation, family building and earning power. Accumulated employment experience feeds into earning power, which feeds back into the prediction of employment in subsequent years. Further details of the method and supporting data are given in the appendix to this chapter.

Background: the British labour market in the 1990s

The archetypal 'Mrs Typical' we described using 1980-based data (Joshi et al, 1996) stayed at home while her children were yet to reach schooling age, and consequently loses half her earnings after childbearing. Since 1980, however, there has been a spectacular increase in the proportion of British mothers of children under five with paid work (rising from less than one third at the start of the 1980s to over one half in the mid-1990s). Life history data from two cohort studies (Macran et al, 1996) suggest that the median gap in employment after childbearing fell from 5.5 years for women born in 1946 (mostly having children in the 1970s) to 2.2 years for women born in 1958 (entering motherhood mostly in the 1980s). This involved increasing numbers of women who were using improved maternity leave to sustain employment continuity throughout childbearing. The proportion of women who had been employed during pregnancy and were actually in work nine months after the birth was 25% in 1979, 45% in 1988 and 68% in 1996 (Callender et al, 1997). The proportion of mothers employed full-time has risen since the mid-1980s, notably through those following continuous careers. The rise in maternal employment was concentrated among the better educated (see also Chapter Four). Although public provision of day care in Britain remains low by international standards, the use of privately purchased childcare has grown rapidly during the 1990s (Finlayson et al, 1996).

The qualification level of British women has continued to improve relative to that of men. For example in the period 1995-96, 23% of female school leavers had at least two A-levels compared to 20% of males (Rake, 2000, Chapter 2). The relative rates of pay for identically qualified and experienced men and women have also improved. The gender premium among full-time employees was 19% (of women's pay) in 1980, and 9% in 1994 (evaluated for married persons in 1980 and all partnered in 1994. However, the penalty of part-time employment increased. In the same samples, the full-time premium on hourly pay amounted to 11% in 1980 and 22% in 1994 (Wright and Ermisch, 1991; Ermisch and Wright, 1992; Davies et al, 1998; Rake, 2000, appendix 1). The benefit of increasing employment experience in full-time work has risen a little in women's wages. These changes tend to widen the pay gap among women, part of the process of increasing wage dispersion in a less regulated labour market (Dex et al, 1996; Hills, 1996). Men's earnings have also become more dispersed and uncertain, though their wives' labour force participation seems to have become less affected by husbands' income. Many of these developments would tend to reduce the extent to which British mothers stay away from the labour market while they raise children, while they would have increased the cash penalties of not earning, particularly not earning full-time.

The new simulations presented in this chapter explore how far, and for whom, the picture and prospects have changed.

Cross-national perspectives

Evidence from other countries suggests that the experience of Mrs Typical in Britain was neither universal nor immutable (Joshi and Davies, 1992; Davies and Joshi, 1994; Dankmeyer, 1996; see also Chapter Four in this volume). This evidence reflects cross-national similarities and differences in labour market, and welfare state institutions (discussed, for example, in Sainsbury, 1999). Britain resembled (West) Germany and the Netherlands, with a long break common in mothers' employment while children were under school age, often followed by part-time employment once they were at school. Sweden provided a greater contrast, where part-time employment, on relatively favourable terms, was typical from the early pre-school years. In the case of France, it proved difficult to construct a 'typical' scenario since mothers' employment histories tended to polarise those with near continuous full-time employment and those where there was a very long break, as noted by Dex et al (1993) when studying actual retrospective histories. By the 1990s the British picture, however, had become somewhat more like the French.

Plan of the chapter

Our exercise presents generated lifetime earnings and incomes, including pension, after state taxes and transfers, and allows for pooling of income in marriage, for a series of hypothetical women. These women are reasonably standard examples, set at three possible levels of education or skill, with similarly qualified husbands, and with up to four children, or none at all. We have also explored further variant biographies, reported elsewhere (for details, see Rake, 2000; Davies and Joshi, 2000). These include moving the age of first birth, mixing the educational levels of partners, exposing them to divorce and remarriage, or to prolonged episodes of unemployment in late middle age or early retirement. In general there tend to be cash gains to postponing motherhood, but the implications of marital break-up are less straightforward. They depend on a number of assumptions about post-divorce employment and income transfers. In this chapter we review the results for gross earnings of the standard scenarios by education-related level of earning power, and then at the net income profile of one of them. We generate hypothetical individuals at levels of earning power, schematically labelled 'skill', without intending to suggest that qualification, skill and remuneration are identical in reality. Neither should the increase in earning power with level of education be interpreted as only a pay-off to gaining qualifications. It also encapsulates other advantages in family background generally present among those who get degrees, and generally absent among those who remain unqualified (Bynner et al, 2000). Think of our 'skill' levels as three social strata. The lowest level of earning power we set is at that expected for a person with no formal qualifications likely to be doing a 'low-skill' job such as shop assistant. The highest level of skill is equated with degree level qualifications; a typical occupation might be in teaching. The middle level of skill, or educational attainment, is set at a moderate level of school leaving qualifications, ('O' level or GCSE in England), required for a secretarial occupation, for example. The penultimate section compares across these three levels of educational attainment, as the implications of motherhood and gender are manifest in very different ways. The conclusion summarises the results and recognises that earnings are only one side of the coin.

Results

Gross earnings

In the 1990s 'time warp', the low-skilled woman still had an attachment to the labour force once she became a mother, but was still likely to have a long break in employment. In our simulations, following a first birth at 23 she would take nine years out of employment if she had two children, or 17 if she had four children. When she resumed employment, it was part-time; if she had four children, she would never resume full-time employment, but if she had two she would have a spell of full-time employment from age 40. Some of this reflects contemporary longitudinal data, but the longer-term outlook is generated by the model as well as contemporary data on older ages. This low labour force attachment of the unskilled had also been simulated and observed in Britain in the 1980s, and among the unskilled in France. Figure 6.1 illustrates the simulated earnings of a woman without children (solid line) and those of mothers. The difference between the solid line and the mothers' trajectories represents earnings forgone due to childrearing. In this case, they amount to about half lifetime earnings after motherhood, much as they did for both low- and mid-skilled women in the 1980-based simulations. The gap between the top two lines

Figure 6.1: Gross lifetime earnings – low-skilled couple

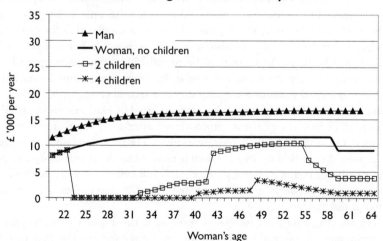

Figure 6.2: Gross lifetime earnings – mid-skilled couple

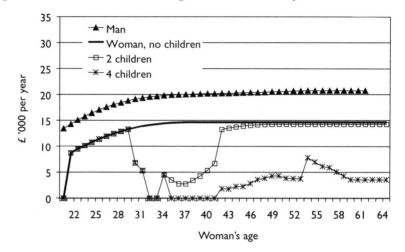

represents the difference between the earnings expected of a husband and the earnings of a wife without children. This assumes that both are fully employed, with the man on, typically, longer hours, and at higher rates of pay for his equal education. The lifetime earnings gap between the man and woman without children is 27% of the man's earnings, of which 8% in this case is due to unequal pay (Rake, 2000, Table 3.5). Because of the unequal hours, the earnings gap is not simply the direct result of pay discrimination, but an outcome of the mutually reinforcing interplay of the gender division of labour in the home and unequal treatment in the labour market. If the low-skilled couple have children, the simulation assumes a fairly high division of domestic labour, with implications for the wife's financial dependence on the man.

The mid-skilled woman, married to a similarly qualified man, was assumed to delay childbearing until she was 28 (the average age at first birth by the late 1990s). If her childbirth came much earlier, her earnings profile and proportion of earnings lost to motherhood, would be much the same as for Mrs Low, or indeed her predecessor, Mrs Typical. However, as simulated in the central case (depicted in Figure 6.2), her history is quite different. In her first year of Mrs Mid's motherhood she appears to be in full-time employment, probably on maternity leave; in the second two years she drops to part-time hours, but she does not leave the labour force until she has a second child. Such a pattern also appears in the real employment histories reported by Harkness (2000) in BHPS data. She resumes part-time employment after a break of only two years, unless she decides to have more children. Thus, in this family, the loss of earnings due to bearing two children is reduced to about one quarter of post-motherhood earnings, although it remains substantial for four children. The earnings gap between husband and wife is also 27% (but in this case 13% is due to pay differences).

In the high-skilled case (see Figure 6.3), the mother's interruption of employment is minimal – only one year part-time for two children, five years

Figure 6.3: Gross lifetime earnings – high-skilled couple

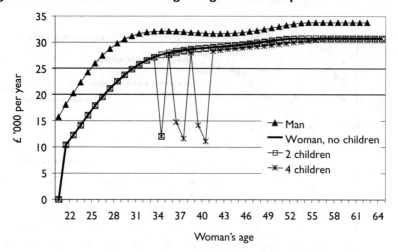

with four children. Mothers' earnings are close to those of the childless, and there is very little earnings cost to motherhood (which is likely to be facilitated by the purchase of childcare). There is also relatively little difference between the earnings of men and women (11% for the childless couple) since pay rates converge (7% of men's pay) and the hours gap is (by assumption) smaller. The graduate woman is less likely to be dependent on her husband's earnings, whether or not she has children.

Net income

These earnings profiles were transformed into net income profiles on the basis of tax, benefit, pension contribution and simulated pension (see Appendix to this chapter). In this way, both incomes can be monitored up until both partners have died. This is assumed to happen when the woman is 81, after five years of widowhood, given age differences at marriages and sex (but not class) differences in longevity.

The results are illustrated for a mid-skilled couple with two children (Figure 6.4). The shapes of the net income profiles for men and women are roughly similar to the gross earnings trajectories, though modified by tax and benefits, which raise mothers' incomes above zero when they have no earnings. This is illustrated on the right hand side of Figure 6.4. The man's net income in retirement is hardly reduced from his previous income, given our assumption that he has been continuously contributing to a good pension scheme. His wife, by contrast, is assumed to accumulate only modest pension rights over and above her basic state pension, the State Earnings Related Pension Scheme (SERPS). Differences in earnings with children are reflected in differences in earnings related pension. Basic pension puts a floor under these pension costs of motherhood. For the last five years of her life the woman benefits from the survivor's pension which she inherits from her husband's pension. It is unlikely,

Figure 6.4: Net income over the lifetime – mid-skilled couple

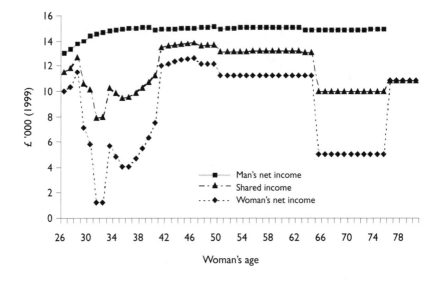

however, that she will have to wait until her husband dies to share in his income. If the couple pools their incomes and shares equally, the trajectory of pooled income can be illustrated using triangles in Figure 6.4. We describe the net gain to the partner with lower income from pooling as 'the family transfer' and the woman's net income including such an assumed transfer as 'the woman's portion'. Pooled income dips during the early years of childbearing, and falls off during the years of their joint retirement, but in neither case is the drop in joint income as sharp as the woman's. The family transfer, if it is made, compensates women for their low and interrupted earnings, but demonstrates women's dependence on marriage where there is a traditional division of labour, or a greater gender gap in earnings.

Differentials by earning power

We now summarise the total lifetime income after marriage for couples at low and high levels of earning power, as well as the middle hypothetical case illustrated in Figure 6.4. Figure 6.5 shows the total lifetime net income of each partner according to number of children. The lines for Mr and Mrs High are roughly parallel, but those for Mrs Mid and Mrs Low fall away from their husbands' the more children they have. The differences are expressed as percentages in Figure 6.6. This illustrates clearly that Mr and Mrs Low, should they have four children, have the biggest relative gap, though their incomes are relatively close if they have no children (reflecting partly the pension of the low-skilled man and the low taxation of the low-skilled woman). The shortfall below 100% between the childless mid-skilled husband and wife is larger (36%) than for the low-skilled (24%), although the ratios of lifetime gross earnings are the same at the two earnings levels. This is because the mid-skilled woman pays relatively

Figure 6.5: Net lifetime incomes, husbands and wives, from marriage, according to number of children

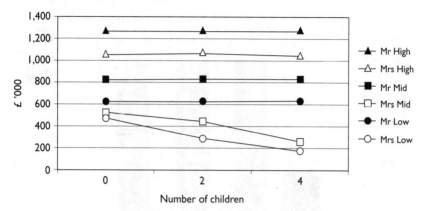

more tax than the low-skilled woman, and her husband is assumed to receive a more generous occupational pension than the SERPS allocated to Mrs Mid and both Mr and Mrs Low. By introducing children to these equations, the ranking reverses, since Mrs Mid is not assumed to cut her employment as much as Mrs Low. Perhaps the most striking feature of Figure 6.6 is the relative closeness of the income, as well as the earnings, of the graduate spouses, regardless of the number of children they have. Gender differences have narrowed most at the top of the labour market. Our study warns readers to be careful about making generalisations concerning the achievements of gender equality policies from the experience of perhaps the most visible educational group to that of people in general.

Figure 6.6: Ratio of wife's to husband's net lifetime income

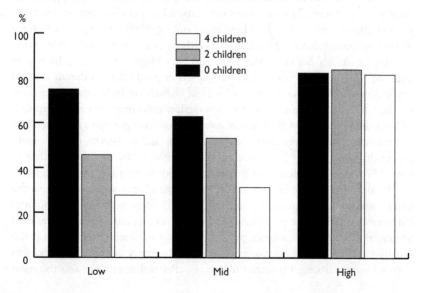

Figure 6.7: Gross lifetime earnings – women in educationally matched couples

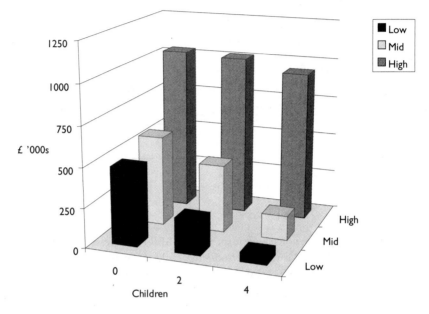

The theme of this work is the diversity of British women's experience of income over their lifetimes. Our project generated illustrative earnings and income biographies, which range considerably over the number and timing of children, and somewhat over marital history. All of these differences pale in comparison to the differences between women at our three education levels. Figure 6.7 shows the levels of total earnings in marriage, whereas Table 6.1 reports the relative difference between the high, mid and low cases, given the number of children. The graduates earn around one million pounds over the years of their marriage, but Mrs Low totals only £59,000 during her marriage if she has four children. In other words, there is a sixteen-fold gap in post-marriage earnings between Mrs Low and Mrs High if they each have four children. As shown by Table 6.1, the gap arises partly from different rates of pay, different lifetime hours of employment (which are induced in the model by the different rates of pay), and an interaction reflecting the greater number of hours being paid at higher rates of pay. All three components are particularly important for mothers of four, comparing high- and mid-levels of skill. Here the graduate earns over five times as much (519%) as the mid-skill mother of four: 157% due to higher rates of pay (at the lower number of hours), 141% due to more hours of paid work (at the lower rate of pay), and 221% due to the extra hours being paid more. By contrast, the 14% difference in lifetime incomes between the childless wives of low- and mid-level earning power is more than accounted for by a 20% average pay difference (the offsetting terms reflect the fact that the lower-earning woman is assumed to marry younger and hence to have a longer earning life within marriage). Pay differences are also the most

Table 6.1: How Mrs Low and Mrs High differ from Mrs Mid in lifetime earnings, by number of children, as % of Mrs Mid's lifetime earnings

	Number of children		
	0	2	4
Mid-Low difference			
Total	14	50	61
Different pay	20	28	24
Different hours	−7	29	49
Interaction	1	−8	−12
High-Mid difference			
Total	82	138	519
Different pay	98	111	157
Different hours	−8	13	141
Interaction	−8	14	221
Baseline level			
Mrs Mid			
Total (£000)	566	426	152

Note: The totals cover a different number of years, as they start from different marriage ages. Allowing for this would increase the contrast. Couples are equally matched educationally.

important component of the bigger difference between mid- and high-skilled childless women. For mothers, differences in the length of employment are also a factor in the 'class' differences.

Whatever their source, differences in earning power are magnified by the different strategies by which each woman combines motherhood and paid work. The woman with low-earning power provides her own childcare until her children go to school. The high-earner probably pays for someone else to help. However much the childcare expenditures of the high-earners may be (for example, an average of £10,000 per year for 15 years), this comes nowhere near bridging the £900,000 gap between these two extreme cases. The constraints of motherhood used to be a force for equalisation among the incomes of British mothers (Harkness et al, 1996). The outlook for the 1990s and onwards is polarisation rather than levelling.

Educational differentials in women's net income

Table 6.2 compares the three levels of earning power in terms of net income, in similar fashion to Table 6.1. The 'woman's portion' is defined as her income earnings net of taxes, plus benefits and including the presumed transfer within the family, assumed to be set at half the difference between the husband's and the wife's income after taxes and benefits. (There is, however, no adjustment for net of childcare expenses.) The differences between educational classes are shown in terms of sums of money received during the marriage rather than as

Table 6.2: Wife's portion of net lifetime income: differences from Mrs Mid (£000s)

	Number of children		
	0	2	4
Mid-Low difference			
Total	126	179	141
Labour market	89	219	99
State	−38	−54	−28
Family	75	13	70
High-Mid difference			
Total	491	539	620
Labour market	762	890	1,109
State	−226	−256	−303
Family	−45	−94	−186
Baseline level			
Mrs Mid			
Total	675	638	545
Labour market	591	446	161
State	−67	−2	85
Family	152	194	299

Notes: Couples are equally matched educationally. Lifetime from wedding. Labour market incomes include earnings related pension.

percentages of the baseline, as in Table 6.1. This is to facilitate comparison of the three main sources of the woman's portion: labour market, state and family. The labour market element reflects gross earnings plus any earnings related pension net of the associated contributions.

Let us first consider the baseline figures. Allowing for a within-family transfer, Mrs Mid has a lifetime 'portion' of £675,000 with no children, £638,000 with two and £545,000 with four children (that is, net own income plus presumed transfer). The labour market component is greatest where there are two children or less, but it falls with increased family size, and at four children the family transfer is the biggest element, at £299,000 over the lifetime. With four children, the contribution of the state becomes positive, as benefits exceed taxes. The differences in terms of the woman's portion between the baseline and the low-skill are shown in the top panel. The total gaps (£126,000, £179,000 and £141,000, respectively) increase between low- and mid-skills. The differences are greater here than in the labour market component, since the mid-skilled wives are assumed to get more in family transfer, though they also pay more tax than the low-skilled women. Between mid- and high-skill cases (middle panel) the differences are much greater (£491,000, £539,000 and £620,000, respectively), increasing with family size, and less than the labour market component.

The highly-skilled woman receives more earnings related pension, as well as earnings, but this is offset by less family transfer and more taxes (revealed by the substantial negative terms in the middle panel for net income from the state).

The gap between having no children and four children in terms of gross earnings has been cut from £414,000 in the baseline case in Table 6.1 to £130,000 in Table 6.2. It has also been cut by about £300,000 for the low paid case. This is due to taxes, benefits and the family transfer. The smaller earnings gap between the graduate woman with no children and four children is even smaller in net income terms.

As the baseline panel of Table 6.2 shows, Mrs Mid makes a net contribution to the state, over her lifetime, of £67,000 if she has no children; if she has four children, she receives more in state benefits than she pays in taxes; and with two children she more or less breaks even. Mrs Low gains more than Mrs Mid from state benefits, and is a net gainer from this source with two, as well as four, children. She can be said to be the most dependent on the state over the long term. Mrs High, by contrast, makes the biggest net contribution in taxes, with a net contribution to the state of around a quarter of a million pounds over her lifetime, whatever the number of children. In the baseline case, the family transfer assumed to be received rises from £152,000 with no children to £299,000 with four. Mrs Low receives absolutely less from this source (her husband is less well paid), but it is the source of income which drops less from the baseline than the labour market earnings (that is, the fourth row of Table 6.2 is smaller than the second). At £181,000 for a mother of two and £229,000 for a mother of four (combining the fourth row of Table 6.2 with the bottom row), it is an important source of income (39% and 57% of Mrs Low's lifetime 'portion' respectively). Mrs High is assumed to 'receive' much less family transfer than the rest (around £100,000 for each number of children). The graduates are thus more financially independent of their husbands. Total incomes at each skill level (reconstructed by adding the difference in the first two panels of Table 6.2 to the baseline) show that extremes in the wife's portion of lifetime net income, for a mother of four, range from £404,000 (Mrs Low) to £1,165,000 (Mrs High). These calculations understate the 'class' differences between the women, insofar as they take no account of the fact that Mrs High might be expected to live for four years longer than Mrs Low.

Conclusion

The gap between men's and women's earnings, which we have projected over their lifetimes, is not intended to be simply an account of gender discrimination, although it can be misinterpreted as such. Rather, it is an account of the interplay of several features of the gender order, albeit synthetic. The synthetic couples all face some degree of unequal pay by gender, and they all observe some gender division of labour. The excess male earnings in relation to a childless wife partly reflect the assumed (but realistic) differences in paid hours. However, these are reinforced by the pay gap. In two out of three of the childless lifetime earnings gaps we constructed, this is the largest component.

The gender gap is smallest for women of high-earning power, in both its components. This may or may not represent the shape of things to come for the other groups. Rather, it would require further convergence towards equal pay, as well as (another) revolution in expectations for it to seem realistic to build model families with the fathers sharing in employment disruption. Even then, however, the developments might not be uniform across the social spectrum.

It still seems relevant to contemplate a stylised world in which mothers alone make adjustments to their labour force careers. This study warns against making generalisations about mothers: we have shown that it makes a lot of difference how much earning power a woman has. Gender, class and motherhood operate together to produce diverse outcomes.

In our model, education reduces the earnings consequences of motherhood and financial dependence on marriage. For a lifetime lived under these 1990s conditions, low-skilled women are still highly dependent on a male earner. If they become lone mothers, either outside marriage or after it, the low-skilled are particularly dependent on the state. Increased education and accompanying deferral of childbearing appears a good individual strategy but may not be achievable by everyone. There may also be limits to the extent that good quality subsidised childcare can be developed. The low-skilled would benefit especially from improving the terms of part-time employment. More family-friendly employment practices might change the earning profiles we have simulated for all of the mothers – and fathers.

Women's earnings forgone through motherhood are in these cases enlarged by low (rather than high) female earning power. One should be cautious, however, about concluding that income 'loss' should necessarily be prevented, without also thinking of the reproductive work entailed. The raising of lifetime income by avoiding forgone earnings is not a woman's only objective. There are, as Beveridge (1942) put it, 'other duties', in the unpaid sphere, which are normally expected to be on a woman's agenda. Time withdrawn from the labour market, and its long-term costs have their positive side in the reproductive work that it permits. The work of rearing the next generation remains as valuable as when Beveridge and Rathbone (1917) pointed it out. We are now seeing a divide among British women where the less economically advantaged still provide all their own childcare within the domestic economy, while the highly paid, who forgo few earnings, use the services of the market to help them take care of their children. On the one side are women who cannot afford market childcare, and on the other are those who cannot afford *not* to use it. Among upcoming generations, some have gained unprecedented earning power through educational advance, and strategies to protect it are also being proposed (see the chapter by Gustafsson, Kenjoh and Wetzels in this volume). The work of the poorly paid and the unpaid deserves our attention still.

Acknowledgements

The work reported here has been developed over a number of years, but the latest behavioural parameters were estimated on funding by the Leverhulme Trust 'Living Arrangements and Livelihoods over the Life Cycle' (grant F/353/ G), with the help of Romana Peronaci. The construction of income variables was done as part of a project *Women's Incomes over a Lifetime*, funded by the Women's Unit of the Cabinet Office (Rake, 2000). Randa Alami assisted us at this stage. Katherine Rake and other members of the Women's Unit collaborated on the production of the detailed report on which this chapter draws.

Appendix on methods

This simulation model has been developed from previous work (Joshi, 1990; Davies and Joshi, 1995; Joshi et al, 1996). This was based on data collected in 1980 by the *Women and Employment Survey* (Martin and Roberts, 1984). The simulated lifetimes took place in a time warp where the participation, hours and pay parameters observed in 1980 were frozen in perpetuity. Our work has focussed on bringing this story up-to-date. We used evidence from the BHPS up to 1994 to generate a formula for hourly wages, for men in full-time jobs, and women in full-time and part-time jobs separately. Women's probabilities of participation, in full-time, part-time or no employment were estimated from a cross-section of women of all ages in the 1994 BHPS. The threefold outcome was estimated in a (multinomial logit) model, controlling the presence and age of children, details of marital status, other socio-demographic factors and imputed earning power (see Table A6.1). Imputed earning power is the wage that a woman of her education and employment experience, whether actually working or not, would command according to the wage equation (Table A6.2). Longitudinal evidence, from previous waves and the retrospective employment histories, is brought in via the construction of the employment history variables in the wage formula.

The simulation proceeds by specifying illustrative individuals of various levels of education and family building histories. We do not attempt to mimic a whole population. The illustrative women are assigned to an employment state (or none) in each year up to age 65, according to whether or not their predicted chances of any employment exceed those of not being employed. If employed they are assigned to full-time or part-time employment according to which probability is greater. Full-timers are attributed standard work hours, and part-timers are set to work a number of hours in proportion to their relative probabilities of full- and part-time work. The earnings of those in work are obtained by multiplying these hours by the wages implied by the formula in Table A6.2. The incomes for men, who appear in the model as the women's husbands, are generated more straightforwardly, by assuming a normally continuous full-time employment history and applying the wage predicted by the formula in Table A6.3. The marital and childbearing scenarios stipulated

Table A6.1: Female employment participation: multinomial logit estimates

	Part-time		Full-time	
	coeff	z	coeff	z
Partnered (D)	1.098	4.762	0.303	1.288
Square of age -45, if partnered[a]	−0.351	−1.926	−1.023	−5.160
Square of age -45, not partnered[a]	0.127	0.518	−0.888	−3.139
Presence of child under 16 (D)	−1.737	−5.477	−3.107	−9.192
Presence of dependent child 16-18 (D)	0.964	0.951	1.897	1.858
Age of youngest child[b]				
if under 5	0.245	3.356	0.003	0.036
if 5, but under 11	0.120	2.171	0.343	5.167
if 11, but under 16	0.061	0.621	0.124	1.164
if 16-18	−2.873	−1.807	−2.389	−1.666
Number of other pre-school children	0.123	0.471	−1.449	−3.164
Number of grown-up children[c]	−0.023	−0.359	−0.228	−3.224
Log of full-time wage (imputed)	1.343	6.395	3.764	15.713
Has mortgage (D)	0.595	4.080	0.769	4.974
Partner unemployed (D)	−1.411	−4.213	−1.023	−2.773
Partner not working, other reason	−1.434	−5.332	−1.044	−3.805
Woman's non-labour income, if unpartnered[d]	−0.030	−1.110	−0.161	−4.954
Woman's non-labour income, if partnered[d]	−0.152	−4.324	−0.254	−5.850
Partner's net income[d]	−0.005	−1.111	−0.017	−2.960
London (D)	−0.522	−2.266	−0.950	−4.025
Constant	−2.119	−6.261	−3.646	−9.984
N	2,221			
chi^2 (38)	1,306.81			
Log Likelihood	−1,707.41			
Pseudo R^2	0.2768			

Notes:

Partnered = married or co-habiting

(D) indicates dummy variable.

[a] Measured as square of (Years-45)/10.

[b] Linear spline function- coefficients shown are marginal effects.

[c] Whether or not co-resident.

[d] Pounds per week/10.

Source: BHPS wave 4, 1994, and estimates of imputed wage based also on wave 2.

Women 18-59, excluding cases with missing data

for the illustrative individuals reflect the later family formation of the more educated. Net income and pensions, for individuals and couples, were generated within the model on the basis of tax, pension and benefit rules mostly applying around 1999. Money values are expressed at 1999 prices.

Table A6.2: Women's wages: selection adjusted regressions

Dependent variable: log of hourly wage

	Part-time		Full-time	
	coefficient	t	coefficient	t
Employment experience				
If low- or mid-skill level				
Linear	0.135	3.797	1.185	4.981
Quadratic			–6.196	–2.526
Cubic			1.422	1.518
Quartic			–0.130	–1.109
If high-skill level				
Linear	0.111	2.009	1.767	6.443
Quadratic			–11.629	–4.056
Cubic			3.422	3.089
Quartic			–0.369	–2.690
Time out of employment	–0.031	–0.934	–0.135	–4.320
Education level (D)				
Degree	0.780	8.401	0.680	5.900
Other higher/further education	0.381	4.862	0.294	2.545
A-levels	0.251	3.581	0.338	6.695
O-levels	0.177	3.698	0.230	5.456
CSE	0.066	1.065	0.151	2.890
Other	0.421	2.248	0.192	1.421
London (D)	0.216	3.398	0.223	6.264
Lambda	–0.120	–3.041	0.039	1.221
Constant	1.244	20.266	0.752	9.119
N		596		1027
F (17, 1009)		15.110		51.230
R-squared (R^2)		0.222		0.463
Standard error of regression		0.410		0.367

Notes:

(D) indicates dummy variable.

Omitted categories: no educational qualifications, living outside London.

Lambda is a sample-selectivity correction term, derived from a reduced-form multinomial logit participation function which includes age and family composition variables.

Powers of years of experience are measured as follows:

Linear: years x 10^{-1}

Quadratic: years^2 x 10^{-3}

Cubic: years^3 x 10^{-4}

Quartic: years^4 x 10^{-5}

Similarly for years out of employment.

Source: BHPS wave 4, 1994, and estimates of employment experience based also on Wave 2.

Women 18-59, excluding cases with missing data

Table A6.3: Men's wages: selection adjusted regressions

Dependent variable: log of male hourly wage

	coeffient	t
Employment experience		
If low- or mid-skill level		
Linear	1.232	6.243
Quadratic	−6.003	−3.592
Cubic	1.299	2.483
Quartic	−0.104	−1.912
If high-skill level		
Linear	1.912	7.336
Quadratic	−12.528	−5.621
Cubic	3.462	4.781
Quartic	−0.340	−4.314
Time out of employment	−0.408	−5.922
Education level (D)		
Degree	0.727	6.054
Other higher/further education	0.363	2.969
A-levels	0.390	9.391
O-levels	0.287	7.444
CSE	0.236	4.135
Other	0.091	1.435
London (D)	0.162	4.657
Constant	0.753	10.018
N 1,570		
F (16, 1553)	64.170	
R-squared (R^2)	0.398	
Standard error	0.410	

Notes:

(D) indicates dummy variable.

Powers of years of experience are measured as follows:

Linear: years $\times$ 10^{-1}

Quadratic: years^2 $\times$ 10^{-3}

Cubic: years^3 $\times$ 10^{-4}

Quartic: years^4 $\times$ 10^{-5}

Similarly for years out of employment.

Source: BHPS Wave 4, 1994, and estimates of employment experience based also on Wave 2.

Men 18-64, excluding cases with missing data

The pension scheme attributed to a simulated person includes the flat rate basic state pension: a contributory scheme which includes some credit for Home Responsibility in years when there is no contribution because of child (or dependant) care. A second pension, related to earnings comes either from State Earnings Related Pension Scheme (SERPS) or from the employer, an 'occupational scheme'. This will tend to be the preferred form of provision where the employer can offer the better terms. We have assumed that graduates, male and female, and men of mid-skill have an occupational pension, based on their final salary and years of service. The low-paid men and women, and women of mid-skill are assumed to rely on SERPS.

The model also generates other income flows on the basis of contemporary tax and benefit rules. Mothers are assumed to receive Child Benefit while their children are dependent, and men and women are assumed to pay all taxes due. If they are entitled to in-work benefits such as Working Families' Tax Credit and Child Care Tax Credits, the model included this in the calculation of net income. It can also attribute a means-tested out-of-work benefit where appropriate, but the need does not arise in the relatively fully employed scenarios considered here. The model does not attempt a full replication of the British benefit system. There are no benefits for disability, for example, and maternity benefits, public and private, are only schematically represented by the unrealistic assumption that all maternity leave is on full pay. Full details of the method and the large set of assumptions adopted can be found in our report to the Women's Unit, appendices and chapter 3 (Rake, 2000).

References

Beveridge, W. (1942) *Social insurance and allied services*, Cmnd 6404, London: HMSO.

Blossfeld, H.-P. and Hakim, C. (eds) (1997) *Between equalisation and marginalisation: Part-time working women in Europe and the United States*, Oxford: Oxford University Press.

Bynner, J., Joshi, H.E. and Tsatsas, M. (2000) *Obstacles and opportunities: Evidence from two British birth cohort studies*, London: The Smith Institute.

Callender, C., Millward, N., Lissenburgh, S. and Forth, J. (1977) *Maternity rights and benefits in Britain*, Social Security Research Report 67, London: HMSO.

Dankmeyer, B. (1996) 'Long-run opportunity cost of children according to education of the mother in the Netherlands', *Journal of Population Economics*, vol 9, no 3, pp 349-61.

Davies, H.B. and Joshi, H.E. (1994) 'The forgone earnings of Europe's mothers', in O. Ekert-Jaffé (ed) *Levels of life and families*, Paris: Editions INED, pp 102-34.

Davies, H.B. and Joshi, H.E. (1995) 'Social and family security in the redress of unequal opportunities', in J. Humphries and J. Rubery (eds) *The economics of equal opportunities*, Manchester: EOC, pp 313-44.

Davies, H.B., Peronaci, R. and Joshi, H.E. (1998) *The gender wage gap and partnership*, Discussion Paper in Economics 6/98, Department of Economics, Birkbeck College, London.

Davies, H.B. and Joshi, H.E. (2000) 'The distribution of the costs of childbearing in Britain', in K. Vleminckx and T.M. Smeeding (eds) *Child well-being, child poverty and child policy in modern nations: What do we know?*, Bristol: The Policy Press, pp 299-319.

Dex, S., Joshi, H.E. and Macran, S. (1996) 'A widening gulf among Britain's mothers', *Oxford Review of Economic Policy*, vol 12, no 1, pp 65-75.

Dex, S., Walters, P. and Alden, D. (1993) *French and British mothers at work*, Basingstoke: Macmillan.

Ermisch, J.F. and Wright, R.E. (1992) 'Differential returns to human capital in full-time and part-time employment', in N. Folbre, B. Bergmann, B. Agarwal and M. Floro (eds) *Women's work in the world economy*, London: Macmillan, pp 195-212.

Finlayson, L.R., Ford, R. and Marsh, A. (1996) 'Paying more for childcare', *Labour Market Trends*, July, pp 296-303.

Harkness, S. (2000) *Analysis of BHPS for BBC Panorama*, Typescript, University of Sussex.

Harkness, S., Machin, S. and Waldfogel, J. (1996) 'Women's pay and family incomes in Britain, 1979-91', in J. Hills (ed) *New inequalities: The changing distribution of income and wealth in the United Kingdom*, Cambridge: Cambridge University Press, pp 158-80.

Hills, J. (ed) (1996) *New inequalities: The changing distribution of income and wealth in the United Kingdom*, Cambridge: Cambridge University Press.

Joshi, H.E. (1990) 'The opportunity cost of childbearing: an approach to estimation using British data', *Population Studies*, vol 44, no 1, pp 41-60.

Joshi, H.E. and Davies, H.B. (1992) 'Daycare in Europe and mothers' foregone earnings', *International Labour Review*, vol 131, no 6, pp 561-79.

Joshi, H.E., Davies, H.B and Land, H. (1996) *The tale of Mrs Typical*, London: Family Policy Studies Centre.

Joshi, H.E., Paci, P. and Waldfogel, J. (1999) 'The wages of motherhood: better or worse?', *Cambridge Journal of Economics*, vol 23, no 5, pp 543-64.

Macran, S., Joshi, H.E. and Dex, S. (1996) 'Employment after childbearing: a survival analysis', *Work, Employment and Society*, vol 10, no 2, pp 273-96.

Meyer, M.K., Gornick, J.C. and Ross, K.E. (1999) 'Public childcare, parental leave and employment', in D. Sainsbury (ed) *Gender and welfare state regimes*, Oxford: Oxford University Press, pp 117-46.

Rake, K. (ed) (2000) *Women's incomes over the lifetime*, A Report to the Women's Unit, Cabinet Office, London: The Stationery Office.

Rathbone, E. (1917) 'The remuneration of women's services', *Economic Journal* (reprinted in *Population and Development Review*, 1999, vol 25, no 1, pp 145-58).

Sainsbury, D. (ed) (1999) *Gender and welfare state regimes*, Oxford: Oxford University Press.

Wright, R.E. and Ermisch, J.F. (1991) 'Gender discrimination in the British labour market: a reassessment', *Economic Journal*, vol 101, no 406, pp 508-22.

SEVEN

Fixed-term contracts and unemployment at the beginning of the employment career in Germany: does gender matter?

Karin Kurz

Introduction

The risks of precarious work (such as fixed-term and part-time employment) and unemployment have been on the rise in recent years in most OECD countries, although to different degrees depending on the national macroeconomic and institutional contexts (see, for example, Standing, 1997; OECD, 1998). Many studies indicate that these risks differ by educational and occupational class (for example, OECD, 1998; Bernardi, 2000; Kurz and Steinhage, 2001). The question of how the growth in precarious positions relates to gender inequalities is, however, less well studied (Smith and Gottfried, 1998). Of course, it is well known that one form of precarious employment – part-time work – is the domain of women in most countries (Blossfeld and Hakim, 1997). In contrast, it is less clear whether the risks of other forms of precarious work (for example, of fixed-term contracts) and unemployment are also gender biased.

In this chapter we will study to what extent women and men in the West and East of Germany[1] are affected by fixed-term contracts and the risk of unemployment at the beginning of their career. The focus on employment entrants allows us to observe how gender inequalities might develop from the start of the employment career. At this stage, family work is not yet important to most people. Thus, if gender differences can be found, these cannot be attributed directly to different family obligations of women and men. Furthermore, to study employees at the beginning of their career seems particularly suited since, in the German context of a closed employment system, precarious employment is mainly introduced to new employees (Blossfeld, 2000).

Besides the focus on outcomes in terms of gender inequality, we also investigate whether the risk of being in precarious employment or unemployment is stratified by education, vocational training, occupational class, ethnic origin and region (East versus West Germany), and how these factors interact with gender issues. More generally, we want to know whether precarious jobs and unemployment become more or less likely for all labour market entrants – that is, 'individualised', or whether certain groups are more affected than others by these risks (Beck, 1986; Bernardi, 2000).

For our analyses we use data of the German Socio-Economic Panel (GSOEP), including three parts of the sample: native West Germans, East Germans and migrants living in West Germany[2]. We study all persons who first began employment between 1985 and 1998[3] and focus, first, on the risk of starting on a fixed-term contract and, second, on the risk of experiencing a subsequent period of unemployment.

Why a longitudinal design?

We have chosen a longitudinal design of analysis for two reasons. First, it allows us to observe how gender inequalities emerge in the course of an employment career. In principle at least, we are able to determine at which points in a phased process inequalities arise between men and women. For the sake of simplicity, we concentrate on two steps in the employment career – entrance into employment, and possible unemployment thereafter. Secondly, we are able to investigate, by means of a longitudinal perspective, how early experiences in the life course affect later ones. In other words, we are able to see how inequalities might be deepened or reduced over the life course through earlier experiences. For example, we might observe that early insecurities in the career (starting with a fixed-term position) might affect the likelihood of subsequent insecurity (becoming unemployed).

Structure

We sketch the national macroeconomic and institutional context, since they affect the specific forms of precarious positions and their quantitative importance. We then discuss types and dimensions of precarious positions. Next, we develop hypotheses on what groups of labour market entrants are most likely to be affected by fixed-term contracts and unemployment. Having described data and methods, we then present our empirical results. We conclude with a summary and discussion of our findings.

The German context

The macroeconomic conditions for labour market entrance

Three phases of macroeconomic conditions can be distinguished from the mid-1980s to the end of the 1990s, although our observation of East Germany begins in 1991, the year of German reunification. At the beginning of the 1980s the unemployment rates in West Germany, including those for young people, started to rise (see Table 7.1). At the same time, the demand for apprenticeships exceeded supply (Winkelmann, 1996). Youth unemployment reached a high of 9.1% in 1983, having been as low as 3.2% in 1980. In the second half of the 1980s total unemployment rates began to fall, and at the end of the 1980s and the beginning of the 1990s West Germany experienced a short economic boom, caused mainly by German reunification and the opening up of new markets. In 1991 West German youth unemployment was once more very low at 4.5%; and the apprenticeship supply well exceeded the demand. From around 1993 total and youth unemployment rates began to rise again; reaching a high of 11.0% and 9.2%, respectively, in West Germany in 1997. The total unemployment rates in East Germany were (starting with the reunification in 1991) considerably higher in each year than in the western part of the country (for example, 19.5% in 1997). In contrast, in the first years after reunification the East German youth unemployment rates were only somewhat higher than those in the West. However, with unemployment rates of individuals aged 25 or less, it is clear that East Germans have a higher risk of unemployment. For example, in 1998, 17% of East Germans in this age group were unemployed, compared to 10.4% of West Germans.

Up to 1993, West German women always had a higher unemployment rate than men. In following years, however, the rates were about the same (with the women's rate, in fact, being slightly lower in all years, with the exception of 1994). This contrasts to the situation in East Germany, where women's unemployment rates were always considerably higher than men's. Only in recent years has the difference reduced somewhat.

In sum, we can identify three phases: difficult labour market prospects from the beginning to the end of the 1980s; an upward trend at the end of the 1980s until the beginning of the 1990s; and again more difficult prospects in the 1990s. Furthermore, we find clear differences between the two parts of the country, with the total East German unemployment rate being notably higher than the West German one. In addition, while there are practically no gender differences in West Germany, the unemployment rate for women is considerably higher than the rate for men in East Germany.

Type of economy

Germany has been classified as a flexibly coordinated economy (Mayer, 1997; Soskice, 1999). At the core of employment in such economies are long-term cooperative relationships based on trust. Various institutions work as a framework of incentives and constraints that help to create and maintain such relationships (Soskice, 1999). First among them is the vocational training system (see Blossfeld and Stockmann, 1999, for an overview). Apprentices are intensively trained over two to three years, and job rotation is part of the training process (Maurice et al, 1986). These features foster functional flexibility as well as employment relationships governed by mutual cooperation and trust (Marsden, 1995). Secondly, workers' councils help to keep up cooperative relationships between employer and employees by being involved in a wide range of decisions within the firm. Thirdly, wages are set by collective bargaining agreements between unions and employers' organisations. This wage-setting mechanism keeps conflicts largely away from the company level. About 84% of all German

Table 7.1: Unemployment trends in West and East Germany

	West	East	West Germany Men	West Germany Women	East Germany Men	East Germany Women	West Foreign workers	West < age 20 (< age 25)	East < age 20 (< age 25)
1980	3.8		3.0	5.2			5.0	3.2	
1981	5.5		4.5	6.9			8.2	4.9	
1982	7.5		6.8	8.6			11.9	7.7	
1983	9.1		8.4	10.1			14.7	9.1	
1984	9.1		8.5	10.2			14.0	7.9	
1985	9.3		8.6	10.4			13.9	8.1	
1986	9.0		8.0	10.5			13.7	7.4	
1987	8.9		8.0	10.2			14.3	6.6	
1988	8.7		7.8	10.0			14.4	6.1	
1989	7.9		6.9	9.4			12.2		
1990	7.2		6.3	8.4			10.9	5.0	
1991	6.3	10.3	5.8	7.0	8.5	12.3	10.7	4.5	
1992	6.6	14.8	6.2	7.2	10.5	19.6	12.2	5.0 (5.8)	
1993	8.2	15.8	8.0	8.4	11.0	21.0	15.1	6.4 (7.5)	7.1 (12.8)
1994	9.2	16.0	9.2	9.2	10.9	21.5	16.2	7.3 (8.6)	6.7 (13.2)
1995	9.3	14.9	9.3	9.2	10.7	19.3	16.6	8.0 (8.8)	7.4 (12.3)
1996	10.1	16.7	10.4	9.9	13.7	19.9	18.9	9.0 (10.3)	9.0 (13.8)
1997	11.0	19.5	11.2	10.7	16.6	22.5	20.4	9.2 (11.1)	10.9 (16.2)
1998	10.5	19.5	10.6	10.3	17.4	21.8	19.6	8.7 (10.4)	10.8 (17.0)
1999	9.9	19.0	9.9	9.8	17.1	20.9	18.4	7.9 (9.1)	10.2 (15.8)
2000	8.7	18.8	8.8	8.5	17.7	19.9	16.4	5.9 (7.7)	10.1 (16.6)

Source: Statistisches Bundesamt, Zeitreihen, http://www.statistik-bund.de

employees are covered by collective agreements (Bispinck, 1997). They are reached by negotiations between specific industrial unions and the employers' associations for each region. These regional tariff agreements – called *Flächentarifverträge* – are binding for all employers who are members of the employers' association[4]. All three institutional features – the apprenticeship system, workers' councils and collective bargaining – help to strengthen a work environment of cooperative exchange and trust. In addition, all workers with permanent full-time or part-time jobs (of about 15 or more hours per week) are protected by dismissal procedures that require an advanced notice of at least six weeks on the basis of specific reasons before an employee can be fired. In addition, the workers' council must be heard in all matters regarding lay-offs, a regulation that makes hasty dismissals unlikely.

Deregulation of the labour market since the 1980s

In the face of economic problems and continuously high unemployment since the early 1980s, the highly regulated and cooperative institutional setting in Germany has come under attack. Deregulation of the labour market has been a heavily debated issue in German politics for many years. However, neither the current social democratic/Green government nor the former conservative government have introduced major measures of deregulation. The two most important changes so far have been opening clauses of collective agreements (*Öffnungsklauseln*), and changes of dismissal protection.

Opening clauses mean that the regional tariff agreements admit exceptions on the firm level, which means, in practice, a firm-specific reduction of wages[5]. Opening clauses, therefore, contribute to a diversification of wage levels, but do not concern the employment contracts themselves. Rather, the latter have been affected by changes in the dismissal protection. The most important step to deregulating the employment contract came with the Employment Promotion Act (*Beschäftigungsförderungsgesetz*) introduced in 1985 which made it easier for employers to use fixed-term contracts. Since contracts terminate at a specific date, they circumvent dismissal protection. Before 1985 such contracts were possible only under certain specific conditions, but with this Act employers gained freedom to conclude fixed-term contracts of up to 18 months with new employees and former apprentices[6]. The original legislation was first limited to the year 1990, but was extended several times thereafter. Since January 1996 the law has allowed for fixed-term contracts of up to two years. In January 2001 the Employment Promotion Act was substituted by the Part-Time and Fixed-Term Contract Act, which allows fixed-term contracts of up to two years to newly hired employees without having to give specific reasons for them. In contrast to the private sector, fixed-term contracts in the public sector can be provided only when such reasons are given. Nevertheless, there is a long tradition of this, and they are still more common in the public, rather than private, sector.

The prevalence of fixed-term positions has slightly increased in Germany. The German micro-census of 1991 reported that 7.5% of all employees had fixed-term contracts, rising to 9% in 1999. With a figure of 21% in 1991, temporary contracts were most prevalent among employees aged 30 years or less. Due to employment creation measures (*Arbeits-beschaffungs maßnahmen*) that provide fixed-term positions for formerly unemployed persons, fixed-term contracts are also more prevalent in East Germany. Women appear to be more likely to receive a temporary contract than men (Bielenski et al, 1994; Kim and Kurz, 2001).

Dimensions of insecurity and types of precarious positions

We distinguish between four dimensions of insecurity that may characterise a precarious (insecure) employment position:

- Insecurity in terms of permanency of position. This applies particularly to jobs with a fixed-term contract.
- Insecurity in terms of the social security arrangements (compared to what is typically offered to full-time positions). In Germany, these arrangements cover unemployment, health and old age insurance.
- Insecurity in terms of earnings level. Jobs that do not allow for economic independence are precarious in this sense.
- Insecurity in terms of working hours. This concerns flexi-time jobs where it is mainly up to the employer when and how many hours a person works.

Given the national institutional context there are differences in the precariousness of certain positions. This is obvious with respect to part-time work. In some countries (for example, in the US and, until the 1997 EU Directive on part-time working, the UK) part-time employees do not enjoy the same fringe benefits as full-time employees. This is only partially true for Germany where part-time jobs of about 15 hours or more are included in the social security system, and enjoy the same dismissal protection as full-time jobs. However, most part-time jobs are precarious in the sense that they do not allow for economic independence. Furthermore, part-time employees are less likely to receive advanced vocational training and to be upwardly mobile (Handl, 1988; Blossfeld, 1989; Becker, 1991; Mayer, 1991). Of course, this does not preclude the possibility that a part-time position (and the resulting economic dependency) is chosen voluntarily. As in many other countries, part-time work often permits women to balance paid work and their commitments in the family more easily than full-time work (Blossfeld and Hakim, 1997). In general, part-time jobs (working any number of hours) are not very common for labour market entrants in Germany, but rather for students and women with children.

By focusing on employees at the beginning of their career the important dimensions of insecurity are (a) the permanency of the position, and (b) income level. In cases of unemployment these dimensions are more generally referred to as temporal and economic insecurity. Temporal insecurity relates to labour market positions that do not imply (relative) security about future employment developments. Economic insecurity refers to positions that involve comparably low income and might not allow for economic independence. In practice, then, labour market entrants face the prospect of finding a job that is only fixed-term (temporal insecurity), or becoming unemployed (temporal and economic insecurity[7]). Furthermore, should a position be found, the entrants may have to accept low pay (economic insecurity).

Our empirical analyses, as we outlined in our introduction, focus on the first employment position and ask whether this position is fixed-term or permanent. At the same time, our analyses concentrate on the risk of experiencing a subsequent period of unemployment.

We consider it unnecessary to focus on periods of unemployment immediately following schooling since the transition from school to work in Germany is rather smooth, unlike in most other OECD countries (Winkelmann, 1996; Müller et al, 1998; OECD, 1998; Bowers, Sonnet and Bardone, 1998). This has largely been attributed to the specifics of the German vocational training system.

Hypotheses

The risk of unemployment and precarious employment might be rather 'individualised', or it might differ systematically between groups of labour market entrants. Given that labour market success varies with education (or, more generally, human capital) and gender (Blossfeld, 1987; Handl, 1988; Shavit and Müller, 1998), the same might also be expected with regard to precarious work and unemployment. But what is the theoretical link? Breen (1997) offers an interesting account by suggesting that we distinguish between those employees with easily supervised and clearly defined tasks, and those with less specific tasks that cannot be monitored directly. That is, he draws a line between the labour contract common in manual work, and the service relationship common in non-manual qualified work (see also Erikson and Goldthorpe, 1992). In the latter relationship the employer will need to implement certain measures to foster the employee's motivation and commitment (because her/his work cannot be controlled directly). These measures typically include not only higher earnings, but also employment security and fringe benefits. Therefore, employment risks should be clearly structured by class and – to extend Breen's argument – also by education on which the service relationship is based. This means that pre-existing inequalities of resources (and power) will be deepened (Breen, 1997, pp 484-5). Those with fewer marketable resources (who therefore rank low in the hierarchy of earnings) are also expected to face a higher risk of signing a fixed-term contract and of experiencing unemployment.

What part does gender play in this? It seems unlikely that women per se will be the losers, but that their employment risks will depend to a great extent on education and occupational position, as is the case for men. As several studies have shown, educational expansion and development of a large service sector with highly-qualified positions contributed to the improvement of employment and income opportunities for women (Blossfeld, 1995; Walby, 1997). At the same time, the deindustrialisation process, that went hand-in-hand with a large reduction of low-qualified manual jobs and increasing numbers of unemployed persons, affected men more so than women, since women are underrepresented in manual occupations. We argue, therefore, that low-qualified women and women in routine manual and non-manual work are most at risk of fixed-term contracts and unemployment. However, we do not expect that women are predominantly in occupations with high risks of employment insecurity.

Apart from differential risks of low- and highly qualified women some authors hypothesise that a divide might develop between migrant and German-born women (Rommelspacher, 1999; Leitner and Ostner, 2000). They argue that highly educated and employed women contribute to the creation of low-paid precarious service work since they and their partners can afford to pay for reproductive work, partially by offering precarious employment to low-qualified (mainly) migrant women in their own households. That is, some women's success in the labour market is seen as contributing to the polarisation between women.

A central factor regarding women's success in the labour market is how reproductive work is organised within the household. Where the male breadwinner model is still dominant and fostered by a welfare state, such as in West Germany, women with children typically interrupt their career for some time and return to paid work predominantly on a part-time basis (Holst and Schupp, 1993; Blossfeld and Rohwer, 1997; Kurz, 1998). Those who interrupt their employment face the risk of downward mobility when they return to paid work (Brinkmann et al, 1988; Engelbrech, 1989). This is at least partially due to the fact that on return to work women are often willing to accept a less secure, less qualified or less paid part-time position if this position is more compatible with their family work. Hence, employers' interests in flexible employment arrangements and women's search for flexible jobs might coincide and contribute to a situation where we find women more often in precarious jobs than men (Castells, 1997, p 173; Walby, 1997, pp 74-5). However, this is more likely the case for women with children, and not women who have just started their employment career[8]. Besides the direct influence of family obligations on women's employment decisions, employers might anticipate later employment interruptions and therefore be less willing to offer women secure employment positions. We might observe then, that women are more at risk of fixed-term contracts and unemployment than men, even if they share similar qualifications.

To return to non-gender-related factors, we would also expect the risk of precarious employment and unemployment to vary between different labour market entry cohorts (see above, page 135). Considering the observation window from 1984 to 1998, the risk should be lowest for those entering from the end of the 1980s to the beginning of the 1990s. At the same time, given the turbulence of the East German labour market throughout the 1990s, East Germans should generally be more likely to receive fixed-term jobs and to experience unemployment.

Finally, it seems likely that initial insecurity in the first employment position – having a fixed-term contract – should increase the risk of unemployment, because, by definition, such a contract ends at a certain date. Typically, it is terminated when a firm finds itself in circumstances of economic insecurity.

Data and methods

Longitudinal designs are necessary in order to study how gender inequalities, with respect to precarious work and unemployment, develop from the beginning of the employment career. Well-suited to this purpose is the German Socio-Economic Panel (GSOEP). Here we use the first 15 waves of the GSOEP (1984-98), and the samples of West German, migrant[9] and East German households.

Labour market entrants are identified as those individuals who left general education, vocational training or tertiary education between 1984 and 1997, and report to be full- or part-time employed in at least one later wave. We also restrict our sub-sample to individuals aged 35 or less at the time of finding employment, and to those who entered employment within five years of finishing education.

There are some specific features and problems concerning the data. First, we cannot establish with full certainty that what we perceive as initial employment is in fact the subject's first job. The very detailed retrospective information needed to determine this with certainty is not available in the GSOEP. Second, for almost 25% of labour market entrants (according to our definition above) we lack information regarding whether they started their employment with a fixed-term or permanent contract[10]. We had to exclude such cases from our analysis regarding contract type. However, they are included for the analyses on the transition to unemployment, and the missing group is identified with a dummy variable.

In order to estimate the effects of explanatory variables on the chances that initial employment will be based on a fixed-term or permanent contract, we apply a binomial logistic regression model (Aldrich and Nelson, 1984; Agresti, 1990):

$$\log(p{:}q) = a + b_1 X_1 + b_2 X_2 + \dots + b_n X_n$$

or:

$$p{:}q = \exp(a) \times \exp(b_1 X_1) \times \exp(b_2 X_2) \times \dots \times \exp(b_n X_n)$$

where:
log: natural logarithm
p: probability of having a fixed-term contract
$q = 1 - p$: probability of having a permanent contract; a: regression constant
$b_1, .., b_n$: regression coefficients; $X_1 \dots X_n$: explanatory variables (eg gender, educational levels)
$p{:}q$: denotes the chance (odds) of having a fixed-term contract.

A positive value of b_i means that the estimated log-odds increases by b_i when X_i increases by one unit; conversely a negative value of b_i means that the log-odds decreases.

A value of $\exp(b_i)$ greater than 1 denotes that the estimated odds of having a fixed-term contract increases (multiplicatively) by the factor $\exp(b_i)$.

A value of $\exp(b_i)$ less than 1 implies that the odds of having a permanent contract increases by $1/\exp(b_i)$.

We use the monthly employment calendar of the GSOEP to analyse the transition to unemployment. We start to observe individuals when they enter their first employment position, and follow them until they become unemployed for the first time. Individuals who had yet to leave employment at their last interview, and those who changed to education, took parental leave, or another non-employment position are treated as right-censored. For the analysis we apply a phased constant exponential model to estimate the effects of the explanatory variables on the transition rate (Blossfeld and Rohwer, 1995):

$$\log[r_{jk}(t)] = a_m + b_1 X_1 + b_2 X_2 + \ldots + b_n X_n$$

$$r_{jk}(t) = \exp(a_m) \times \exp(b_1 X_1) \times \exp(b_2 X_2) \times \ldots \times \exp(b_n X_n)$$

where:

log: natural logarithm.

$r_{jk}(t)$: transition rate r from origin state j (being employed) to destination k (being unemployed) which can change over time t. The transition rate is the limit of the conditional probability of a change from j to k at time t given that the unit is still at risk for such a change. It can thus approximately be considered as a conditional probability of a transition from j to k in a very small time interval.

a_m: regression constant which is constant not for the whole time axis, but only for each (pre-defined) time period m from $1, 2, \ldots, M$.

$b_1, \ldots, b_n$: regression coefficients.

$X_1 \ldots X_n$: explanatory variables that can be time-constant (for example, gender) or varying over time (for example, occupational class). Correctly, time-varying variables would be written $X_i(t)$.

A positive value of b_i means that the logarithm of the estimated transition rate increases by b_i when X_i increases by one unit; conversely a negative value of b_i means that the logarithm of the transition rate decreases.

A value of $\exp(b_i)$ greater than 1 denotes that the estimated transition rate to unemployment increases (multiplicatively) by the factor $\exp(b_i)$; a value of $\exp(b_i)$ less than 1 implies that the transition rate decreases by the factor $\exp(b_i)$.

Both analyses control: year of entrance to labour market (1985-89, 1990-93, 1994-97/98); ethnic origin (non-German versus German); region (West versus East Germany); working hours (part-time versus full-time); level of education;

class position (Erikson and Goldthorpe, 1992); and sector (private versus public). With respect to educational level, we not only take into account the level of general schooling, but also occupational qualification. In Germany, this is acquired mainly by formalised vocational training through an apprenticeship. As previous studies have shown, having an occupational qualification or, alternatively, having a technical college or university degree, is of prime importance for labour market success (Shavit and Müller, 1998; Brauns, Gangl and Scherer, 1999).

In addition, in the analysis on the transition to unemployment, we include a variable on the type of contract at entry to the labour market. In this analysis, the values for class position, sector and working hours can vary over time. In order to correct for different sampling probabilities of the West German, East German and non-German population, we apply design weights in the logistic regression models and the transition rate models.

Empirical analyses

Type of contract in the first job

The prime concern of this section is the subject's first job after having finished some kind of general or vocational education. We then look at the type of contract, namely fixed-term versus permanent contract (see Table 7.2). According to the GSOEP data women in West Germany seem to have a somewhat lower probability of receiving a fixed-term contract than men (23% versus 28%). Among East Germans and persons with a non-German background, gender differences are negligible. The result for West Germany stands in contrast to our expectations and to those of previous studies which, unlike ours, did not concentrate on individuals at the beginning of their career (Bielenski et al, 1994; Kim and Kurz, 2001).

Education seems to have equal importance in all three samples. Those with compulsory schooling but without any vocational certificate are more likely to receive a fixed-term contract. Contrary to our hypothesis, however, is the fact that this also holds true for those with a technical college or university degree, and those with lower/upper secondary schooling but without occupational qualifications (at least among West Germans). We suspect that the data are picking up training contracts to some extent, which are undistinguishable from other fixed-term contracts within our data[11]. University graduates are often employed in the public sector where initial fixed-term contracts are very common as can be seen further down Table 7.2 (see also Bielenski et al, 1994). Finally, one might suspect that some highly educated persons actually choose fixed-term contracts if these enable them to receive higher incomes than in dependent positions (Schömann et al, 1998).

The data also reveal a clear class structuring: semi- and un-skilled workers and (less pronounced) higher service class employees have a higher likelihood of receiving a fixed-term contract than other groups. In addition, we find that those who face economic insecurity, namely part-time workers, are more at risk of temporal insecurity. Finally, in line with the changes in the macroeconomic situation, West Germans who entered the labour market between 1984 and 1989 or between 1994 and 1998 exhibit higher proportions of fixed-term contracts. For persons of non-German origin we observe an increase for the period 1994 to 1998 only. For East Germans no difference can be detected for the two periods in the 1990s.

In order to study the combined effects of the explanatory variables we conducted logistic regression analyses (see Table 7.3). Our general modelling strategy is as follows: we first estimate a common model for men and women (model 1) and then separate models for the genders (models 1a, 1b, 2a and 2b). The latter models enable us to investigate whether educational qualification and occupational class protect men and women differently from receiving a fixed-term contract. In order to detect whether the gender differences in the effects of education and class are significant we estimated further models not reported in the table for the sake of simplicity[12]. Model 1 presents the results of the common model for men and women. The significant effect for women (-0.34) indicates that, at the beginning of their employment career, women have a significantly lower probability of finding fixed-term employment than men, even when accounting for educational level and other control variables. Models 1a and 1b show the coefficients for the same model, but now estimated separately for men and women. The coefficients for education reveal a similar U-shaped pattern to Table 7.2. Having compulsory education without any occupational qualification increases the odds of receiving a fixed-term contract for men as well as women compared to those with compulsory schooling plus occupational qualification (the reference group). However, the effect is only statistically significant for women (at $\alpha \leq 0.10$). The difference in the effects for men and women is not significant.

Moreover, having a third-level qualification, or lower/upper secondary education without occupational qualification (in the case of men only), makes a fixed-term contract in the first employment position increasingly likely. The effect for female university graduates is stronger than for men: women have a higher risk of starting in a temporary position than men. For example, the estimated probability for West German women who entered employment in the period 1994-98 is about 45%, compared to 37% for the respective group of West German men[13]. Further analyses showed that the difference between men and women is statistically significant in this group (at $\alpha \leq 0.10$). Also significant is the gender difference for secondary education without occupational qualification: men have a higher risk of receiving a fixed-term position than women, with this educational level.

Switching to models 2a and 2b, we observe that, for both sexes, semi- or unskilled manual workers have a higher risk of starting with a temporary contract than skilled manual workers. At the same time, the likelihood of a fixed-term contract is significantly higher for women in this group than for men (the respective coefficients are 1.64 and 0.92). Employment in the service class increases the likelihood of women getting a fixed-term contract (when compared

Table 7.2: Fixed-term contracts at employment entry[a]

	West German	Non-German ethnic origin (West Germany)	East German
Sex:			
Men	28.1% (647)	23.0% (261)	24.8% (157)
Women	22.9% (499)	25.9% (166)	22.6 % (146)
Education:			
Compulsory education without occupational qualification	27.5% (102)	26.1% (134)	42.9% (7)
Compulsory education + occupational qualification (Ref.)	20.9% (302)	23.7% (148)	26.5% (34)
Lower/upper secondary education without occupational qualification	38.1% (134)	22.6% (53)	28.6% (49)
Lower/upper secondary education with occupational qualification	19.2% (375)	19.4% (72)	17.4% (161)
Technical college/university degree	35.2% (233)	35.0% (20)	34.6% (52)
Occupational class:			
Higher service class	27.1% (118)	25.0% (8)	42.1% (19)
Lower service class	22.0% (332)	18.3% (60)	21.3% (94)
Routine non-manual class	23.3% (146)	12.0% (50)	29.4% (34)
Lower routine non-manual class	20.4% (54)	19.1% (21)	7.1% (14)
Qualified manual worker/technician	23.0% (309)	22.9% (118)	13.8% (94)
Un-/semi-skilled manual worker	42.1% (133)	32.1% (159)	43.2% (37)
Sector:			
Private	21.5% (938)	23.7% (388)	20.6% (252)
Public	45.2% (208)	28.2% (39)	39.2% (51)
Working hours:			
Full-time	24.6% (1047)	23.9% (401)	22.9% (288)
Part-time	39.4% (99)	26.9% (26)	40.0% (15)
Labour market entrance cohort:			
1984-1989	25.4% (500)	20.9% (172)	-
1990-1993	21.8% (307)	22.3% (103)	24.2 % (91)
1994-1998	30.1% (339)	29.0% (152)	23.6% (212)

Note: [a] Persons with fixed-term contract as percentage of all employed persons; in brackets number of employed persons.

Source: GSOEP, waves 1984 to 1998

Table 7.3: Type of contract[a] at entry into the labour market (logistic regression)[b]

	Model I Women + Men	Model 1a Women	Model 1b Men	Model 2a Women	Model 2b Men
Constant	1.39**	-1.73**	-1.42**	-2.38**	-1.75**
Employment entry:					
1985-1989	0.26+	0.06	0.42*	0.09	0.50+
1990-1993 (Ref.)					
1994-1998	0.43**	0.37	0.48*	0.56*	0.69**
Gender:					
Female	-0.34**				
Ethnic origin/region:					
German/West (Ref.)					
Non-German/West	-0.10	0.09	-0.21	-0.14	-0.41
German/East	-0.15	-0.12	-0.21	-0.12	-0.24
Education:					
Compulsory education without occupational qualification	0.47*	0.64+	0.39		
Compulsory education with occupational qualification (Ref.)					
Lower/upper secondary education without occupational qualification	0.64**	0.10	0.96**		
Lower/upper secondary education with occupational qualification	-0.10	0.04	-0.18		
Technical college/university degree	0.70**	1.12**	0.48*		
Working hours:					
Full-time (Ref.)					
Part-time				0.19	1.70**
Class position:					
Service class				0.66+	-0.33+
Routine non-manual class				0.49	0.43
Qualified manual worker/technician (Ref.)					
Un-/semi-skilled manual worker				1.64**	0.92**
Sector:					
Private sector (Ref.)					
Public sector				0.68**	1.54**
Log-likelihood	-969.70	-389.21	-572.31	-384.40	-527.41
Number of cases	1757	762	995	762	995

Notes: [a] Categories: fixed-term versus permanent contract (reference category); self-employed persons excluded; [b] The table shows b-coefficients from additive logistic regression models, predicting the log-odds of having a fixed-term versus permanent contract; Significance: ** at $\alpha \leq 0.01$; * at $\alpha \leq 0.05$; + at $\alpha \leq 0.10$.

Source: GSOEP, waves 1984 to 1998

to qualified manual workers), but decreases the likelihood for men. Again, the difference between men and women is significant (with $\alpha \leq 0.01$).

All in all, the results indicate that being in the high-risk groups (college/university degree, service class or un- and semi-skilled manual position) is clearly linked with a higher probability of temporary work for women than for men. Men come out worse only in that rather small group with secondary education but without occupational training.

With respect to the other explanatory variables, models 2a and 2b show that working part-time does not seem to increase the risk of receiving a fixed-term contract for women. The effect for men, on the other hand, is strong and significant (1.70). This should not be overstated, however, since only 47 (4.8%) of the men in our study work part-time in their first job. Starting paid work in the public sector increases the risk of receiving a temporary contract for both sexes, even after other explanatory factors are controlled. In line with our expectations, the coefficients for male and female employees entering the labour market in the period 1994 to 1998 are positive, although the coefficient is significant for women in model 2a, but not 1a. This indicates a higher risk of fixed-term contracts compared to those entering at the beginning of the 1990s. For men the effect is also positive and significant for the second half of the 1980s. Finally, there seem to be no differences between East and West when it comes to fixed-term contracts at the beginning of the employment career. Furthermore, the coefficients for non-Germans are insignificant. It must, however, be taken into account that the number of (weighted) cases is very low for this group (31 and 48 for women and men, respectively).

The risk of unemployment after the first employment position

In this section we ask whether further gender differences in employment insecurity emerge in the course of the employment career. A major risk that employees face is becoming unemployed. To study the likelihood of the transition from the first (uninterrupted) employment position(s) to unemployment we again first estimated a common model for men and women, and then separate models to study whether educational qualification and occupational class have different effects for the genders (see Table 7.4). Furthermore, we tested the difference between these effects for statistical significance based on models not reported in the table[14]. Model 1 clearly shows that, on average, women face a higher risk of unemployment. The transition rate to unemployment was estimated to be about 30% higher for women than for men.

The first important conclusion to be drawn from models 1a and 1b is that starting with a fixed-term contract heightens the risk of unemployment for both sexes. The respective coefficients (0.87 and 0.74) are positive and significant. Thus, being in an insecure position initially, translates into a higher risk of continued insecurity.

The coefficients for educational level indicate that higher education lowers the risk of unemployment for both men and women, although the concrete educational patterns differ. Among women, those having compulsory education and no vocational training certificate are most at risk. All other educational groups seem to have more or less the same prospects of falling into unemployment[15]. In the case of men, those with compulsory schooling (whether with or without an occupational qualification), are most likely to make the transition to unemployment. The least likely are college/university graduates and those with lower/upper secondary schooling with an occupational qualification. In the case of women, the main line of division runs between those with compulsory schooling but without occupational training, and all others. With regard to men, the division lies between compulsory schooling with and without training, and all others. Furthermore, it can be seen by calculating the transition rate (or log-transition rate) for men and women that at all educational levels (except lower/upper secondary schooling without occupational qualification) West German women usually have a higher transition rate to unemployment than West German men. In addition, a common model for men and women with interaction effects for level of education and gender indicated significantly higher transition rates for women at all education levels (except for secondary schooling without occupational qualification).

Models 2a and 2b, by including variables on occupational class and sector (private versus public), rather than educational level, show that, at the top of the occupational hierarchy, men as well as women have the lowest risk of unemployment. In line with our expectations un- and semi-skilled manual workers seem to be most at risk of unemployment, although the coefficient is significant only for men. The respective coefficients are 0.49 for women (not significant) and 0.86 for men (significant at $\alpha \leq 0.01$). At the same time, we cannot detect significant differences in the transition rates of men and women for the different class positions in common models with various interaction effects for class position and gender. This contrasts with the results for education, and might indicate that, at the same educational level, women reach, on average, lower occupational positions than men. However, if women are in the same occupational position as men they are not more at risk of unemployment.

The effects of labour market entrance period differ according to gender. Apparently the transition rates for women increased from the beginning of the 1990s; in contrast, the transition rates for men increased from the mid-1990s, a result more in line with our expectations based on aggregate unemployment rates. Surprisingly, we find an East–West difference in relation to men only. East German men have a significantly higher transition rate to unemployment than their West German colleagues, even when education or class is controlled. Similarly, according to our models, non-German men – but not non-German women – are worse off than their West German colleagues. This observation, however, results in part from the distribution of educational levels and occupations among persons of non-German origin; consequentially the respective coefficient is no longer significant when education and occupation class are controlled in the analyses.

Finally, we observe that working in the public sector does not significantly change the risk of unemployment for either sex. This is in contrast to previous cross-sectional results which did not, however, focus on the early employment career (Kim and Kurz, 2001).

Conclusions

This chapter investigated how young men and women, who entered the German labour market in the 1980s and 1990s have been affected by employment insecurities. It asked whether gender, education and occupational class made a difference.

We argued that the national macroeconomic and institutional context influences the types of precarious positions that become relevant in a country. Unemployment has been high in West Germany since the 1980s, with a short drop at the beginning of the 1990s. In contrast to some other countries (for example, the UK), labour market deregulation has not been far-reaching in Germany. One main deregulatory measure with respect to employment security has been the facilitation of fixed-term jobs introduced in 1985. Given this context we focused on the risk of having a fixed-term contract in the first employment position and, furthermore, on the risk of becoming unemployed having entered the labour market.

In both analyses we find differences between genders on the aggregate level. Surprisingly, women seem somewhat less likely to receive a fixed-term position. In contrast, their unemployment risk is somewhat higher than that of men. The preferable situation for women with respect to fixed-term contracts mainly holds for West, rather than East, German women. With regard to East German women, and women with non-German background, we find no distinction from their male colleagues.

On average, women's lower risk of fixed-term contracts comes about since a large proportion work in middle and lower level non-manual occupations, with average proportions of fixed-term contracts. At the same time, they are underrepresented in unskilled manual work where the risk of fixed-term contracts is high. They are also underrepresented at the top of the occupational hierarchy where fixed-term contracts are again quite frequent. When women are in these positions, however, they seem to be somewhat more likely to receive a fixed-term contract than their male colleagues. This is not due to women's greater likelihood to work in the public sector where fixed-term contracts are particularly common, since our analysis controlled the sector variable. At the same time, it is not fully clear whether working on a fixed-term contract is always a disadvantage for the employee as we assumed in our initial considerations on precarious employment. In particular, highly educated persons, and those working in the service sector, might choose this employment arrangement in order to achieve higher incomes (Schöman et al, 1998). Moreover, the fixed-term positions we capture might to some extent actually be training contracts that enable career advancements for the employee.

As already mentioned, women are clearly worse off than men when it comes to the risk of unemployment. Not surprisingly, higher education or a higher

Table 7.4: Transition to unemployment (phased constant exponential models)

	Model I Women + Men	Model 1a Women	Model 1b Men	Model 2a Women	Model 2b Men
Time since start of first job:					
Up to 12 months	-6.14**	-6.02**	-6.14**	-5.83**	-6.53**
12 to 24 months	-5.58**	-5.39**	-5.63**	-5.01**	-5.92**
24 to 36 months	-6.20**	-6.03**	-6.22**	-5.64**	-6.49**
36 to 48 months	-6.09**	-5.60**	-6.43**	-5.23**	-6.72**
48 and more months	-6.47**	-6.13**	-6.58**	-5.83**	-6.82**
Employment entry:					
1985-89	-0.20	-0.41*	0.01	-0.41*	-0.02
1990-93 (Ref.)					
1994-98	0.16	0.06	0.43+	0.00	0.43+
Gender:					
Female	0.25*				
Ethnic origin/region:					
German/West (Ref.)					
Non-German/West	0.25	-0.18	0.50+	-0.19	0.40
German/East	0.51**	0.21	0.83**	0.19	0.55*
Type of contract (1st job):					
Fixed-term	0.81**	0.87**	0.74**	0.82**	0.68**
Permanent or self-employment (Ref.)					
Missing information:	-0.01	-0.10	0.08	-0.15	0.11
Education:					
Compulsory education without occupational qualification	0.52**	0.89**	0.27		
Compulsory education with occupational qualification (Ref.)					
Lower/upper secondary education without occupational qualification	-0.66*	-0.84+	-0.52		
Lower/upper secondary education with occupational qualification	-0.41**	-0.06	-0.79**		
Technical college/university degree	-0.68**	-0.29	-0.92**		

(continued)

Table 7.4: Transition to unemployment (phased constant exponential models) (continued)

	Model 1 Women + men	Model 1a Women	Model 1b Men	Model 2a Women	Model 2b Men
Working hours:					
Full-time (Ref.)					
Part-time	0.45†	0.35	0.83+	0.23	0.71
Class position:					
Service class				-0.89**	-0.57†
Routine non-manual class				-0.14	0.13
Self-employed				0.24	0.03
Qualified manual worker/technician (Ref.)					
Un-/semi-skilled manual worker				0.49	0.86**
Sector:					
Private sector (Ref.)					
Public sector				-0.35	-0.50
Log-likelihood	-1970.23	-880.01	-1013.31	-870.12	-1004.77
Number of episodes	317	136	181	136	181

Notes:
The table shows b-coefficients from addictive phased constant exponential models. Categories: fixed-term versus permanent contract (reference category); self-employed persons excluded.

Significance **at $\alpha \leq 0.01$; *at $\alpha \leq 0.05$; † at $\alpha \leq 0.10$

Source: GSOEP, waves 1984 to 1998

occupational class position lowers the risk of unemployment for both men and women, although at the same educational level women seem to face a higher unemployment risk than men. That is, education does not shield women to the same extent as men. However, we do not find a similar result for occupational class position. This might indicate that women are less successful in translating their educational level into an adequate occupational position. If they are in the same occupational position, however, they face a similar risk of unemployment as their male colleagues.

With respect to the differentiation of the unemployment risk by region (East/West) and ethnic origin, we find among men, but not among women, that East Germans and persons with non-German origin are worse off than West Germans. Further research is needed to understand the conclusions. More generally, our data were not very well suited to examine potential divisions between migrant and native German women, since we were only able to look at second generation migrants whose parents came to West Germany in the 1960s and early 1970s. For adequate analyses we would also need data on migrant women who arrived more recently in Germany.

All in all, we can summarise that at the beginning of their career, women in East and West Germany are not, in general, disadvantaged with respect to fixed-term positions. They are disadvantaged, however, with respect to the risk of unemployment, even when our analyses control education or occupational class. This is consistent with the view that, when employers need to decide whether to lay off a man or a woman (from the same occupational position) they will tend to choose the woman. Nevertheless, we cannot preclude that our findings will change when we look at more detailed occupational categories. That is, it might well be that for the labour market entrance cohorts we studied, young women were more frequently in occupations that faced generally higher unemployment risks than men. And yet, even when we do not know the exact underlying processes, it is clear from our findings that, for women, disadvantages in the labour market do not begin when they start having a family, but are already present at the very beginning of their employment career.

Notes

[1] East and West Germany is used throughout this chapter to include eastern and western areas before and after reunification.

[2] It would be useful to extend this approach to include further steps of the life course and to study, in particular, the impact of family formation on the employment careers of women (see, for example, Kurz, 1998).

[3] For East Germans we can only cover the period 1991-98.

[4] With more than 90% membership, the degree of employer organisation is exceptionally high in Germany (Fuchs and Schettkat, 2000, p 211).

[5] Some East German firms had difficulty in paying wages already agreed upon in collective negotiations. After conflicts between the union of the metal industry and employers in the East, opening clauses were introduced in East Germany in 1993. They permit wage reductions in firms that are in serious economic difficulties. Since 1997, opening clauses have also applied to the West German metal industry (Fuchs and Schettkat, 2000, p 225).

[6] Fixed-term contracts had never been limited to specific conditions in firms with up to five employees, and for contracts of up to six months (Bielenski et al, 1994, p 2).

[7] Students, whom we have already mentioned, are not included in our analysis, since we focus on the employment career after leaving school. Labour market entrants, on the other hand, faced with difficult employment prospects, might become self-employed, which means in many cases being insecure economically and in terms of future developments. However, since self-employment is quite rare at the very beginning of the employment career, and also relatively heterogeneous in terms of the insecurity involved (Leicht, 2000; Kim and Kurz, 2001), we did not include self-employment in our analysis.

[8] The flexibility argument holds mainly for part-time work, but not for fixed-term contracts, since the latter do not give women any particular advantage when trying to juggle family work and employment.

[9] In this study, migrant is taken to include children of migrants, that is, the second generation (from Turkey, Spain, Italy, Greece, and the former Yugoslavia), whose parents came to West Germany mainly during the 1960s and early 1970s. We include them among those of non-German ethnic origin.

[10] Most panel waves asked about type of contract (fixed-term versus permanent) only if the respondent had started new employment since the last interview. However, if a person continues to work in the firm where she/he received vocational training, and if she/he considered herself/himself as having been employed while being in vocational training, the person will not answer this question.

[11] Such training contracts are not apprenticeships. Rather, these can be distinguished from regular fixed-term contracts in our data, and are treated as an educational phase which typically takes place before the first employment position.

[12] These were common models for men and women with interaction effects between gender and educational qualification or occupational class, respectively. Results of these models are available from the author on request.

[13] The probabilities were calculated from the coefficients in model 1a and 1b. In general $p = 1/(1 + \exp(- (a + b_1 X_1 + ... + b_n X_n)))$.

[14] These were again common models for men and women with interaction effects between gender and educational qualification or occupational class, respectively.

[15] An exception are women who graduated from middle school or gymnasium (lower or higher secondary schooling) and have no occupational training certificate. According to the model, their transition rate to unemployment is significantly lower (with $\alpha \leq$ 0.10) than that of the reference group (compulsory school plus apprenticeship).

References

Agresti, A. (1990) *Categorical Data Analysis*, New York, Chichester, Brisbane: Wiley.

Aldrich, J.H., and Nelson, F.D. (1984) *Linear Probability, Logit, and Probit Models*, Newbury Park, CA: Sage Publications.

Beck, U. (1986) *Risikogesellschaft. Auf dem Weg in eine andere Moderne*, Frankfurt, Main: Suhrkamp.

Becker, R. (1991) 'Berufliche Weiterbildung und Berufsverlauf. Eine Längsschnittuntersuchung von drei Geburtskohorten', *MittAB*, vol 24, no 2, pp 351-64.

Bernardi, F. (2000) *Economic flexibility, class and risk at entry into the labour market: Changing patterns of early careers in Italy*, Globalife Working Paper Series 7, Bielefeld: University of Bielefeld.

Bielenski, H., Kohler, B. and Schreiber-Kittl, M. (1994) *Befristete Beschäftigung und Arbeitsmarkt. Empirische Untersuchung über befristete Arbeitsverträge nach dem Beschäftigungsförderungsgesetz (BeschFG 1985/90)*, München: Bundesministerium für Arbeit und Sozialordnung.

Bispinck, R. (1997) 'Deregulierung, Differenzierung und Dezentralisierung des Flächentarifvertrags. Eine Bestandsaufnahme neuer Entwicklungstendenzen der Tarifpolitik', *WSI-Mitteilungen*, vol 50, no 8, pp 551-61.

Blossfeld, H.-P. (1989) *Kohortendifferenzierung und Karriereprozeb. Eine Längsschnittstudie über die Veränderung der Bildungs- und Berufschancen im Lebenslauf*, Frankfurt, New York, NY: Campus.

Blossfeld, H.-P. (1995) *The new role of women. Family formation in modern societies*, Boulder, CO: Westview Press.

Blossfeld, H.-P. (2000) *Globalisation, social inequality and the role of country-specific institutions. Open research questions in a learning society*, Globalife Working Paper Series 11, Bielefeld: University of Bielefeld.

Blossfeld, H.-P. and Hakim, C. (eds) (1997) *Between equalization and marginalization: Women working part-time in Europe and the United States of America*, New York, NY: Oxford University Press.

Blossfeld, H.-P.and Rohwer, G.(1995) *Techniques of event history modeling. New approaches to causal modeling*, New Jersey, NJ: Lawrence Earlbaum.

Blossfeld, H.-P. and Rohwer, G. (1997) 'Part-time work in West Germany', in Blossfeld, H.-P. and Hakim, C. (eds) (1997) *Between equalization and marginalization:Women working part-time in Europe and the United States of America*, NewYork, NY: Oxford University Press.

Blossfeld, H.-P. and Stockmann, R. (1999) 'The German dual system in comparative perspective', *International Journal of Sociology*, vol 28, no 4, pp 3-28.

Bowers, N., Sonnet, A. and Bardone, L. (1998) *Background report. Giving young people a good start:The experience of OECD countries*, Paris: OECD.

Brauns, H., Gangl, M. and Scherer, S. (1999) *Education and unemployment: Patterns of labour market entry in France, the United Kingdom and West Germany*,Arbeitspapier 6, Mannheimer Zentrum für Europäische Sozialforschung.

Breen, R. (1997) 'Risk, recommodification and stratification', *Sociology*, vol 31, no 3, pp 473-89.

Brinkmann, C., Engelbrech, G. and Hofbauer, H. (1988) 'Berufsverläufe von Frauen', in D. Mertens (ed) 'Konzepte der Arbeitsmarkt- und Berufsforschung', *Beiträge zur Arbeitsmarkt- und Berufsforschung*, vol 70, no 3, pp 724-47.

Castells, M. (1997) *The power of identity*, Oxford: Blackwell.

Engelbrech, G. (1989) 'Erfahrungen von Frauen an der "dritten Schwelle": Schwierigkeiten bei der beruflichen Wiedereingliederung aus der Sicht der Frauen', *MittAB*, vol 22, no 1, pp 100-13.

Erikson, R. and Goldthorpe, J. (1992) *The constant flux. A study of class mobility in industrial societies*, Oxford: Clarendon Press.

Fuchs, S. and Schettkat, R. (2000) *Why deregulate labour markets?* Oxford: Oxford University Press, pp 211-43.

Handl, J. (1988) *Berufschancen und Heiratsmuster von Frauen. Empirische Untersuchungen zu Prozessen sozialer Mobilität*, Frankfurt, New York, NY: Campus.

Holst, E. and Schupp, J. (1993) *Perspektiven der Erwerbsbeteiligung von Frauen im vereinten Deutschland*, Diskussionspapier no 68, Berlin: Deutsches Institut für Wirtschaftsforschung.

Kim, A. and Kurz, K. (2001) *Precarious employment, education and gender. A comparison of Germany and the United Kingdom*, Arbeitspapier 39, Mannheimer Zentrum Für Europäische Sozialforschung.

Kurz, K. (1998) *Das Erwerbsverhalten von Frauen in der intensiven Familienphase. Ein Vergleich zwischen Müttern in der Bundesrepublik Deutschland und in den USA*, Opladen: Leske und Budrich.

Kurz, K. and Steinhage, N. (2001) 'Globaler Wettbewerb und Unsicherheiten beim Einstieg in den Arbeitsmarket: Analysen für Deutschland in den 80er und 90er Jahren', *Berliner Journal für Soziologie*, vol 11, no 4, pp 513-31.

Leicht, R. (2000) 'Die "neuen Selbständigen" arbeiten alleine: Wachstum und Struktur der Solo-Selbständigen in Deutschland', *IGA - Zeitschrift Für Klein-Und Mittelunternehmen*, vol 48, no 2, pp 75-90.

Leitner, S. and Ostner, I. (2000) 'Frauen und Globalisierung. Vernachlässigte Seiten der neuen Arbeitsteilung', *Politik und Zeitgeschichte. Beilage zur Wochenzeitung Das Parlament*, B48, pp 39-46.

Marsden, D. (1995) 'Deregulation or cooperation? The future of Europe's labour markets', *Labour (IIRA)*, vol 49, pp 67-91.

Maurice, M., Sellier, F. and Silvestre, J.-J. (1986) *The social foundations of industrial powers: A comparison of France and Germany*, Cambridge: MIT Press.

Mayer, K.-U. (1991) 'Berufliche Mobilität von Frauen in der Bundesrepublik Deutschland', in K.-U. Mayer, J. Allmendinger and J. Huinink (eds) *Vom Regen in die Traufe: Frauen zwischen Beruf und Familie*, Frankfurt/New York, NY: Campus, pp 57-90.

Mayer, K.-U. (1997) 'Notes on the comparative political economy of life courses', *Comparative Social Research*, vol 16, 203-26.

Müller, W., Steinmann, S. and Ell, R. (1998) 'Education and labour-market entry in Germany', in Y. Shavit and W. Müller (eds) *From school to work. A comparative study of educational qualifications and occupational destinations*, Oxford: Clarendon Press, pp 143-88.

OECD (Organisation for Economic Co-operation and Development) (1998) *Employment outlook*, Paris: OECD.

Rommelspacher, B. (1999) 'Neue Polarisierung und neue Konvergenzen. Das Geschlechterverhältnis im Zeitalter der Globalisierung', in G. Schmidt and R. Trinczek (eds) *Globalisierung. Ökonomische und soziale Herausforderungen am Ende des zwanzigsten Jahrhunderts. Soziale Welt Sonderband* 13, Baden-Baden: Nomos, pp 243-58.

Schömann, K., Rogowski, R. and & Kruppe, T. (1998) *Labour market efficiency in the European union. Employment protection and fixed-term contracts*, London: Routledge.

Shavit, Y. and Müller, W. (eds) (1998) *From school to work. A comparative study of educational qualifications and occupational destinations*, Oxford: Clarendon Press.

Smith, V. and Gottfried, H. (1998) 'Flexibility in work and employment: the impact on women', in B. Geissler, F., Maier and Pfau-Effinger, B. (eds) *'FrauenArbeitsMarkt': Der Beitrag der Frauenforschung zur sozio-ökonomischen Theorieentwicklung*, Berlin: Edition Sigma, pp 95-125.

Soskice, D. (1999) 'Divergent production regimes: coordinated and uncoordinated market economies in the 1980s and 1990s', in H. Kitschelt, P. Lange, G. Marks and J.D. Stephens (eds) *Continuity and change in contemporary capitalism*, Cambridge: Cambridge University Press, pp 101-34.

Standing, G. (1997) 'Globalisation, labour flexibility and insecurity: the era of market regulation', *European Journal of Industrial Relations*, vol 3, no 1, pp 7-37.

Walby, S. (1997) *Gender transformations*, London/New York, NY: Routledge.

Winkelmann, R. (1996) 'Employment prospects and skill acquisition of apprenticeship-trained workers in Germany', *Industrial and Labour Relations Review*, vol 49, no 4, pp 658-72.

EIGHT

Women and self-employment: the case of television production workers in Britain

Shirley Dex and Colin Smith

Introduction

Massive changes have occurred in the contractual status of the British television industry's workforce since the early 1980s. Estimates in the early 1990s (Holly and Woolf, 1995) suggested that 60% of the workforce were self-employed freelance or self-employed owners of small independent production companies. In the 1970s, however, staff were mainly tenured, working in the few large vertically integrated broadcasters.

There has been a large growth in self-employment in Britain since the 1970s. Both women and men have seen an increase in this type of contractual working arrangement, although men to a greater extent than women. There are relatively few studies of the working experiences of the self-employed and even fewer that examine the gender dimension, although women's representation in the television industry has increased over time. The industry provides an interesting context, therefore, from which to view the experience of self-employment and examine gender inequality in the self-employed workforce[1]. One serious problem faced by the self-employed is maintaining employment continuity, an inherently longitudinal concept. Employment continuity is essential to fulfilling regular financial commitments in life, and it underpins the structure and stability of other relationships.

This chapter offers new insights into gender inequality over time as it is reflected in this growing form of employment status in the British economy. It also examines the in- and out-of-work experiences of self-employed workers in the television production industry in Britain in the 1990s. The data are provided by a Television Industry Tracking Study (ITS), initiated by the British Film Institute (British Film Industry, 1995, 1997, 1999), and are discussed later in this chapter. It is important to go beyond cross-sections in mapping inequalities in gender relations, and this chapter examines some of the dynamic elements of employment experiences. The longitudinal nature of these data allows us to examine the problem of maintaining continuity in respondents' employment contracts.

Table 8.1: Changing profile of women's and men's self-employment, Great Britain (1975-98)

| | % of self-employed in total employment | | | | |
	1975	1981	1986	1994	1998
Men					
All	10.9	11.9	14.6	16.9	15.4
With employees	5.1	7.2	5.6	4.4	4.2
Without employees	5.8	4.7	9.0	12.4	11.2
Full-time			13.7	15.2	14.1
Part-time			0.9	1.8	1.4
N thousands	13,276	13,654	13,423	13,577	14,261
Women					
All	3.9	4.5	6.6	6.8	6.9
With employees	1.7	2.9	2.1	1.8	1.6
Without employees	2.2	1.5	4.5	5.0	5.2
Full-time			3.4	3.3	3.4
Part-time			3.2	3.4	3.4
N thousands	8,086	8,818	9,522	10,751	11,253

Source: Labour Force Surveys (Spring)

In the rest of this chapter, we summarise the research on self-employment based mainly on cross-sectional data. We then present further details concerning the context of the changing structure of the television industry. We answer the question 'Why do we need longitudinal data?' The available panel data are then described, and the methods selected for modelling employment continuity. We discuss the findings from modelling these elements of the employment continuity of women and men working in the television industry, and present our conclusions at the end of the chapter.

The growth in self-employment

In 1975, 10.9% of men and 3.9% of women workers were self-employed in Great Britain, compared to 15.4% of men and 6.9% of women in 1998 (Table 8.1). Most of this increase has been in self-employment without employees – 11.2% of employed men and 5.2% of women were self-employed without employees in 1998. These are more like employees in all but contractual status, except with different terms and conditions, less job security, often less training (Rix et al, 1999), and fewer employment rights. The figures for self-employed workers with employees have remained largely static. This high level of growth of self-employed without employees has been unique among OECD countries (Dex and McCulloch, 1995). It is partly attributed to specific policy inducements for self-employment in Britain in the 1980s (OECD, 1991), partly to shifts in the distribution of industries (Campbell and Daly, 1992), and partly to privatisation and restructuring in the public sector and certain industries. Some of the cross-sectional characteristics of the self-employed have been documented as well as their employment status before becoming self-employed (Meager et al, 1994). However, relatively little is known about their conditions of work and the extent to which they are able to maintain employment continuity. Even less is known about how gender issues affect the self-employed in general, and about self-employed women specifically.

The self-employed are more likely to be male; concentrated in the 35-49 year age groups; married. They are also likely to have A-level qualifications; dependent children where they are women; a larger dispersion of earnings (Meager et al, 1994); and with women being more likely to be at the lower end of the earnings spectrum (Table 8.2). Finally, they are likely to be included among certain minority ethnic groups.

Entry into self-employment in the 1980s was from jobs (approximately one half of the self-employed), from unemployment (approximately one third), and from inactivity (approximately one quarter). The size of these statistics varied from year to year through the 1980s, partly through changes in the business cycle. In addition, men were more likely to have entered self-employment from being employees or unemployed, whereas women were more likely to have been employees or inactive[2] (Hakim, 1988; Campbell and Daly, 1992).

Table 8.2: Mean hourly gross pay of men and women by category and age group at wave 2 of BHPS[a]

	16-19	20-29	30-39	40-49	50-59	60-65
Men						
Self-employed						
With employees	n.a	11.02	12.40	7.73	n.a	n.a
Without employees		5.30	9.71	4.42	6.19	(3.46)
Full-time permanent	2.81	6.36	8.91	9.06	8.52	6.57
Part-time permanent	(3.01)	(3.20)	n.a	n.a	(8.40)	(3.16)
Part-time temporary						
Temporary fixed-term	(1.94)	4.87	10.95	7.49	8.17	
Temporary casual	3.81	6.02	(10.91)	(3.10)	(6.26)	(2.30)
Women						
Self-employed						
With employees		(5.56)	(7.54)	(1.80)	(9.23)	
Without employees		(10.18)	3.87	4.01	(5.23)	
Full-time permanent	3.01	6.21	7.43	7.43	6.11	
Part-time permanent	(2.81)	3.36	5.13	4.43	6.11	
Part-time temporary	(2.65)	5.58	5.27	(5.00)		
Temporary fixed-term		(6.72)	8.96	5.78		
Temporary casual	2.50	4.38	4.68	4.21	(6.45)	

Notes:

[a]Imputed earnings values included in data

() statistic based on sample size of less than 20

Source: Dex and McCulloch (1997, Table 5.11)

Survival rates in self-employment have been found to be higher when individuals were previously in employment, and become self-employed in an area in which they had some previous experience (Carter and Cannon, 1988).

The reasons that people become self-employed include a combination of pull and push factors. By far the most cited of these is the attraction of independence and being one's own boss (Hakim, 1988). Smaller percentages are attracted to self-employment because of its challenge, and the freedom to choose when – and for whom – to work. Financial motivation is given much less emphasis than independence, choice and freedom.

The push factors include having been made redundant, being unemployed, having had a series of temporary, short-term jobs and seeking to avoid the insecurity of this position, and being discriminated against (especially for ethnic minorities). Lack of capital appears to be a constraint that prevents some of those who would like to become self-employed from doing so (Blanchflower and Oswald, 1991).

Taylor (1999) documented the durations of spells of self-employment across all types of self-employed worker and all industries, using the British Household Panel Study (BHPS)[3]. Seventy-six per cent of men and 79% of women survived 6 months of self-employment; 59% of men and 63% of women were surviving in self-employment spells up to 12 months. Analyses of the survival of the self-employed have tended to assume they are all owners of enterprises and that personal assets, wealth and liquidity constraints are the relevant variables explaining the length of survival in self-employment (Evans and Leighton, 1989; Cowling et al, 1997a, 1997b; Taylor, 1999). Gender differences have not yet been given much attention.

Changes in the television industry and its workforce

Until the 1980s, the television industry was structured with one vertically integrated public service broadcaster, the BBC, alongside a few integrated and heavily regulated private sector broadcasters (the regional ITV franchises). As a result of regulatory changes, the 1990s saw private sector broadcasters competing first to get the licence (subject to looser regulation), then attaining maximum ratings, and the BBC itself reorganised with internal markets. Programming in the 1990s was produced and supplied by many small private and a few large independent production companies competing with each other to supply the broadcasters (Price Waterhouse PACT, 1995).

In 1982, the new Channel 4, given a brief to commission, or 'publish', programmes but not to make them itself, was the first stimulus to the new independent production sector. This was followed closely by the creation of a market in external suppliers in 1986 as the BBC and ITV were given the target of introducing a 25% quota of independent productions. In 1996, the BBC was further reorganised. Previously divided vertically, that is, directorates for television, radio, and so on, it became divided horizontally, as BBC Broadcast, BBC Resources and BBC Production. The aim of BBC Production was to seek commissions from BBC Broadcast to produce programmes, in competition with other independent companies. However, in 1997, it was agreed that 60% of annual Broadcast expenditure would be guaranteed to go to in-house BBC Production.

Women's position in television has undergone enormous changes, as Antcliff describes (2001). Before the passing of equal opportunities legislation in Britain in the 1970s, there were few women in senior positions at the BBC (Fogarty et al, 1971) and evidence of much discrimination. Women were concentrated in the lower grades of production (as secretaries and production assistants), with little chance of promotion. By the end of the 1970s, policies had been introduced to try and break down the discrimination within the BBC and ITV. In the early 1980s estimates suggested that women constituted 50% of the workforce and the female proportion of producers and directors had increased to 20%. The latest figures from an attempt to carry out a census of television workers in 2000 (as well as other audio-visual industry workers) suggest that women constituted 48% of the 24,102 workers in broadcast television, and 47% of the 11,572 workers in independent companies (Skillset, 2001). Women also constituted approximately 43% of producers.

Prior to the 1980s, the majority of television workers were in salaried long-term jobs, employed by broadcasters. In the 1990s estimates suggested that 50-60% were freelance (Holly and Woolf, 1995). There have been enormous pressures to cut production costs in the 1990s. Independent companies have not been able to afford more than a skeleton staff with specific short-term contracts when their commissions are so uncertain and on extremely tight budgets. However, the broadcasters followed suit in giving large proportions of their workforce freelance contracts. The pressures on budgets grew increasingly through the tendering for licence and franchises, and the advent of Channel 5 as a low budget channel. In this context, many television workers had no choice but to become freelance workers and, were 'pushed by demand' to start out on their new contractual status. Some took the plunge to start up an independent production company, but these were relatively few. Over time, others decided to join them because they perceived positive supply-side 'pull' factors and negative supply-side 'push' factors of the sort described earlier for those entering self-employment. The total number of freelance workers in the television industry is very difficult to calculate. There are some problems in defining their status as freelance or self-employed, as Ancliff (2001) has noted. The 2000 Skillset Census found 40,981 freelance workers across the audio-visual sector, 26% of whom were women. The Census estimated, however, that these figures were likely to be only two thirds of the total freelance workforce, because of the methods used to obtain the respondents (Skillset, 2001). Higher proportions of women were found among the freelance workers in broadcast television (51%), producers (42%) and 'other occupations groups' (64%)[4].

Why longitudinal data?

Employment security differs between employees and those who are self-employed. This means that it may be more difficult to sustain a continuous employment record and the associated income stream as a self-employed worker, than as an employee. Employment security and employment continuity, therefore, are inherently longitudinal concepts.

The experience of employment in television centres around commissions to produce a television programme. For the majority of freelance workers, the project constitutes their contract and their income. In a few cases, it can be a part of a series, in which case contracts extended beyond the single project. Freelance workers are generally paid a fixed fee to join a project production team and a deadline for production of the programme usually applies. The hours worked on a project can vary enormously as can the hourly rate of pay, given that the price is fixed.

For freelance workers, the failure to obtain a contract to do back-to-back projects results in a period out of employment and disruption to income flow. The shorter the project durations the greater the pressure to secure the next contract. This reality is seen in the quotations from the postal questionnaires of some of our survey respondents in response to open-ended invitations to comment or elaborate. They illustrate very clearly why longitudinal data are required to track individuals' experiences to see how their bad experiences may or may not accumulate over time. Also, status at one point in time will not necessarily uncover the severity of the position of some individuals.

> "[Programme X] ... is the first thing I've worked on, let alone edited since the news and has been exhausting but exhilarating project.... Apart from that, no work and no pay. How typical this is for a freelance producer I don't know." (Female freelance editor/producer)

> "I don't think I'll get any work now 'till after Christmas but if there is no work forthcoming in the New Year I will have to seriously consider my position within this industry. Trying to claim social security between short-term contracts is a bureaucratic minefield – sometimes I go without benefit or wages for weeks." (Female freelance researcher)

> "This has proved to be my worst year since becoming an independent, with no income since March and no immediate prospects. I now find it hard to believe that I can survive in the industry." (Female freelance director)

> "We sporadically-employed freelance drongos feel that no one is sympathetic or concerned about the workers at the coal face. After all, we're so easily replaced." (Female Freelance director)

However, for a few, there was plenty of work, and no problems.

> "I have generally speaking never had to worry about/look for work. I continually turn it down because I'd be working 48 hours a day and that wasn't the idea of going freelance." (Female Productions Manager, freelance)

The differences between some of these individuals' work histories would not be apparent if we were relying on cross-sectional data. Rather, it would only become apparent through collecting longitudinal data.

There may also be gender differences in employment continuity, either because women are more likely than men to be freelance workers, or because within the freelance group, women may have more problems than men obtaining the next contract or project, through having fewer contacts or networks. Testing out whether these potential vulnerabilities involve genuine differences can only be judged by following individuals' experiences over time. Experiences of unemployment may turn out to be equally likely among employees as among self-employed freelance workers, or between men and women. However, it is important to make a distinction between 'choice' and 'constraint'. Some individuals may have chosen freelance work in order to gain more flexibility in their work schedule. Others would prefer a staff job but are unable to secure one. However, it is important to know how the quality of life and status of gender groups compares over time, rather than a single (or successive) cross-section. Cross-sectional data gives at least a partial picture, at worst it can distort.

The Television Industry Tracking Survey (ITS) data

We are able to document some of the longitudinal employment experiences of a group of television workers from a panel study collected from 1994 to 1998 (British Film Industry, 1995, 1997, 1999). The data, described in more detail in the Appendix to this volume, were collected from 447 production workers, men and women, in a range of jobs or skills, by sending them nine postal questionnaires at six monthly intervals over a period of five years, 1994-98.

Each questionnaire collected information about a range of current personal characteristics, working conditions and employment status, as well as retrospective past monthly employment status records and projects over the previous six months using pre-coded questions[5]. These questions were available for the quantitative analyses. In addition, some respondents added comments to their questionnaires and wrote considerable amounts about their experiences in response to some open-ended questions or invitations to elaborate. These comments provide some limited qualitative data to enhance the quantitative analyses of the pre-coded data. Attrition (that is, subsequent loss of membership of the panel due to non-contact, refusal to respond, failure to follow-up sample cases for other reasons, death, emigration) occurred over the life of the panel. Of the 447 original respondents at the first contact, 294 were still in the survey at the final contact wave five years later, a response rate of 67% on the initial sample. Analysis showed that there was a disproportionate loss of young people but the final sample remained representative of the original in terms of gender and occupational groups (Dex and Sheppard, 1998[6]).

In the first wave, 47% of the sample were freelance (44% of which were men, and 56% women), and 15% were self-employed owners of independent companies (20% of men and 9% of women). In this sample women were more likely than men to have the more vulnerable freelance status but less likely than men to be self-employed owners. Over the life of this survey, the percentage of freelancers ranged from 34% in May 1996, to 52% in May 1996 and May 1997. At the end of the survey 43% were freelance. The relative percentage of men and women who were freelance remained the same throughout.

Methods for modelling employment continuity

This chapter approaches the measurement of employment continuity in three ways. First we examine continuity through women's and men's records of monthly spells of unemployment over the whole five-year period of our data, to see how individuals move in and out of employment. We compare the frequencies of unemployment and transitions between states in relation to gender and contractual status. Secondly, we examine transitions between freelance staff and unemployment status again by gender. Finally we examine projects to see if their durations vary by gender or by freelance/staff status. These three perspectives on employment continuity give us a rounded picture of its nature and help us to identify the precise source of any gender differences.

Movements in and out of employment

A number of issues are raised by attempting to model the experiences of being employed or out of paid work for men and women. Women are known to be more likely than men to make transitions between employment and inactivity. Perceiving oneself as being unemployed is also known to be more problematic for women than for men (Dex, 1996). For men, unemployment is the obvious alternative to employment, whereas for women there are 'choices' between unemployment and inactivity to consider. This has prompted us to use a binary-choice framework in relation to men (employment/unemployment), and a three-way choice (employment/unemployment/inactivity) for women's states.

There is also the question of whether the same set of determinants are likely to influence men and women, and whether their influence acts to the same degree for both men and women. We adopt the same sets of predictor variables for being in employment for both men and women (see section on explanatory variables, page 170), but carry out separate model estimations to allow for the parameters to vary between genders.

It is also important to allow for the influence of unobserved effects. For example, if men and women differ in risk aversion, or in their networking capabilities and contacts, these may affect their success in maintaining employment continuity, especially as self-employed workers. In this chapter, we limit our consideration to those dimensions of variation noted above, recognising that there may be other important differences we have to ignore for the moment.

We model the likelihood of individual i being employed E in a particular month, t, as a reduced form of the supply side characteristics S_{it-1} of the individual at $t-1$ and the demand characteristics D_t of the labour market at time t:

Prob $(E_{it}) = f(S_{it-1}, D_t, e_{it})$

On the supply side, the individual's potential wage is likely to influence whether or not an individual accepts a job offer, or stays in the current job. This will be determined by personal characteristics, human capital, other income and the type of contract[7]. On the demand side, the wage and the level of excess demand or supply of varying skills will influence the extent of offers, as will the demand for television programmes. The latter may be influenced by business cycle considerations to the extent that advertising revenue affects the level of programme making.

We estimated a reduced form model using first logistic regression, pooling the monthly panel data. Logistic regression is a way of estimating a multivariate model to explain a dependent variable outcome when the dependent variable only takes the values 0 (not present) or 1 (present). In the first model, we used the dichotomous variable, whether individual i is employed (= 1) or unemployed (= 0) in month t. (Our results are reported on pages 172-4).

As well as the set of explanatory variables we have observed for our data set, it is important to consider possible explanations for differences between individuals that we do not have measures for; differences in attitudes to risk, skill in network building, and the reputation of past work. Also, women are usually thought to be more averse to risk-taking than men[8]. We might expect, therefore, to see lower proportions of women among freelance workers. Yet this is not the case, although many of the staff workers in this sample, men and women alike, did display risk aversion[9]. Whether the self-employed were less risk averse is difficult to discern from the data. On the other hand, there is anecdotal evidence suggesting that the factor behind moves into freelancing has been demand-side push rather than supply-side pull.

If these unmeasured effects were correlated with the variable we are trying to explain, they would bias the results for other variables. Our longitudinal data give us repeated data points for the same individuals, and this enables us to correct for these potential unobserved differences between individuals. Random effects models help to control such potential unobserved effects and make sure the estimates of coefficients on other variables are not biased by these errors. The presence of variation between individuals means that the error terms are not independent of each other, as is assumed in estimating a model. Rather, they are linked by the fact that many data points are entered from the same individual. This individual-specific error component needs to be incorporated using the random effects model and estimation procedure. At the same time, this technique allows for unobserved individual variations which would otherwise bias the other coefficients. It does this by, firstly, using a lagged dependent variable and, secondly, by estimating a random effects logit model in STATA, (1999; one-way error component random effects model).

In another model, we estimated a multinomial logit model, also based on the pooled monthly data records. A multinomial logit model is similar to the logit model, but allows the modelling of more than two dependent variable outcomes, in our case three. This was felt to be potentially more appropriate to modelling women's labour market decisions in particular, between the three states, employment, unemployment and inactivity, also given the problems associated with concepts of unemployment for women noted earlier[10]. Out of three possible outcomes, inactivity is the reference category, against which the probabilities of being employed or unemployed are contrasted. There are a set of coefficients reflecting the impact of a given explanatory variable on the log odds of the ith outcome (employed, $i = 1$, unemployed, $i = 2$) and X_t is a vector set of explanatory variables. The dependent variable distinguishes between employed and unemployed as being qualitatively different states, using individuals' self-definitions.

Although we expect a greater risk of unemployment and job discontinuity among freelance than among staff workers, there may be differences between gender groups, and also within groups of freelance and staff workers. It may be the case that freelance workers are prepared to work for lower wages than tenured staff, other things being equal, which would suggest that freelance workers have a greater probability of being employed. In fact, 54% of the sample of freelance workers in this survey (wave 7) said that they had accepted lower pay rates in order to ensure continuous employment[11]. Even so, there was the evidence from some (such as those transcribed in page 164) that there were significant problems with coordination[12].

Status transitions

As well as affecting employment continuity, transitions between employment statuses may also reflect attitudes towards risk. For example, freelance status is especially associated with a higher risk of unemployment. The freelance and tenured staff groups that have emerged might be the result of individuals self-selecting themselves into these two states, according to their attitudes towards risk. This might occur if tenured staff were more risk averse than those who have moved into freelance employment. If this were the case, we would expect to see little movement between these two states.

Our panel data allowed us to examine transitions between states. We estimated a 3-state first order Markov Chain (Markus, 1985). This is a discrete time stochastic process (based on probability) that can be used to describe the probability of moving from one state to another, in a particular time period, conditional on the state of the person at the beginning of the period. Markov models have been developed specifically for the analysis of longitudinal data and are relevant to the categorical and qualitative variables which are so common in social research (Davies and Dale, 1994, p 167). The first order Markov Chain means that the (transition) probability of moving from one state to another only rests on the state one starts from, and not on other factors. Higher order Markov Chains allow the consideration of other factors that might influence the mobility between states over time.

Formally, if X_0, X_1,... are a sequence of random variables taking values in a countable set (called statespace), the process X is a first order Markov Chain if it satisfies:

$$P[X_n = s \mid X_0 = x_0, X_1 = x_1, \ldots, X_{n-1} = x_{n-1}] = P[X_n = s \mid X_{n-1} = x_{n-1}]$$

Using the Markov Chain model allows us to present some of its properties, although these clearly rely on the validity of the assumption that it is a first order Markov Chain. We are able to predict a steady state distribution across our four states based on the estimated transition probabilities. If the change process is accurately described by this constant transition matrix, R, and the process is allowed to run for a large number of time periods, in many cases an equilibrium or steady state will be reached (Markus, 1985). If the state proportions S_t are constant, we can compute the expected proportions at $t+1$, S_{t+1} using matrix multiplication, $S_t \times R = S_{t+1}$ or using eigenvalues. Similarly we can predict the eventual steady state vector distribution across our four categories, of where the process is heading in the future, if transition rates carry on in the same way as at present.

Project durations

For the majority of freelance workers, their 'project' (see page 180) also constitutes their contract of employment. Individuals in our sample were asked at each wave to recall their projects, and their durations over the previous six-month period. These durations are censored data in our panel. Censoring, in our case, means that we did not necessarily observe the end of each project spell. However, it was possible in some cases to recognise projects that spanned more than one wave given the panel data and details recorded. Since the data are censored and incomplete, models of spell-length that allow for this fact must be used.

The project durations were first displayed in survival curves broken down according to whether the worker was freelance or staff. Survival curves plot the proportions of the sample whose projects last each of the successive monthly time landmarks. The process assumes that the final durations of the incomplete spells have the same distribution as the completed spells. In addition a model of the determinants of project durations was estimated which took into account the censored nature of the data. A Cox proportional hazard model was used as the simplest form of model, imposing the least assumptions on the parameters. The hazard rate takes the form:

$$\lambda(t|x) = \lambda_o(t) \exp(\beta X')$$

where t is the observed time spent in the project, $\lambda_o(t)$ is the baseline hazard, and X is a vector of covariates with β the set of parameters to be estimated.

Explanatory variables

The same explanatory variables are included in all model estimations for both genders. They are a mixture of variables that stayed constant over time (for example, qualifications) and variables that changed over the period of data collection, time-varying covariates, as listed in Table 8.3. Since we have pooled the data from each wave, where characteristics varied over time, the values concurrent with the dependent variable data were entered (hence time-varying in these cases). These variables were used to capture both supply- and demand-side influences. Means and standard deviations are supplied in an earlier version of this chapter (Dex and Smith, 2000). Supply-side variables referred to the beginning of the six-month period over which the employment status was later recorded (in retrospect), since respondents were asked to recall their monthly employment status for the preceding six months at each wave. Alternatively, they were time constant values. Potential wages were captured through including qualifications, age, type of occupation variables and a range of personal and other job-related characteristics. We had particular interest in the effects on the likelihood of being employed or unemployed in month t, and of being self-employed in month $t-1$, either as a freelance worker or an independent television company owner.

Some variables that might be expected to explain employment status were used at an earlier stage, but then discarded since they were not significant, such as having a child, number of children, and having a mortgage. Being very highly correlated with marriage, they were therefore included in this sample. The choice was made to keep marital status in the model and omit the other variables. However, we noted that being married, for the vast majority of this group of men and women, also meant having children and a mortgage.

Out of employment experiences

On average, 7% of the sample were out of employment at each cross-sectional wave, although there were fluctuations, ranging from 5% to 9% at each wave over this five year period. Women were more likely than men to be out of employment. Quite a low percentage specifically said they were unemployed at each wave (as opposed to inactive): between 0% and 3.5% for men and between 1% and 6.5% for women. A much higher proportion of individuals experienced being out of employment at least one month in every six-month period when the continuous monthly records were examined. Between 16% and 20% of men, and between 27% and 35% of women had been out of employment at some time over the previous six months. Women experienced, therefore, more unemployment and larger fluctuations in their employment status than men.

In our model of the determinants of being employed in any month (Tables 8.4 and 8.5), we found that being freelance significantly reduced the probability of being employed and increased the probability of being unemployed in any given month, and this effect was larger for men than for women. Men who

Table 8.3: Variables used in the analyses

Self-employed:
Freelance ✓
Independent owner ✓

Type of job:
Producer ✓
Production ✓
Research ✓
Post-production ✓
Camera or lighting ✓
Writers ✓
Manager ✓
Artistic ✓
TV news workers, secretaries, other (reference group)

Personal:
Female
Age in years ✓
Age squared ✓
Married ✓
Divorced ✓

Human capital:
Higher education (current education status)
Formal training in past year ✓
Informal training in past year ✓
Unemployed in past month ✓
Unemployed any month in past year ✓

Workplace:
Work for broadcaster ✓

Contract continuity:
Working on a serial ✓

Demand:
Unemployment level (diary specific levels) ✓

Time trend:
Month number (current) ✓
1 = April 1994 to 48 = April 1998

Other:
BBC reorganisation from November 1996

Key: ✓ indicates time varying values entered

Table 8.4: Model results for main sample women of likelihood of being employed in month

Variable	Logit		Random effects		Multinomial logit			
					Employed		Unemployed	
	coeff	se	coeff	se	coeff	se	coeff	se
Self-employed								
Freelance	-0.744	**(0.302)	-0.623	*(0.355)	-0.794	**(0.275)	-0.065	(0.401)
Independent owner	0.921	(0.562)	1.525	**(0.747)	0.995	**(0.443)	0.167	(0.696)
Human capital								
Higher education	-0.286	(0.208)	-0.229	(0.338)	-0.054	(0.230)	0.279	(0.301)
Formal training	0.541	**(0.177)	0.368	*(0.212)	0.359	*(0.188)	-0.197	(0.251)
Informal training	-0.184	(0.197)	-0.145	(0.240)	-0.514	**(0.18)	-0.375	(0.262)
Unemployed (m)	-3.311	**(0.143)	-2.862	*(0.167)	0.125	(0.381)	3.446	**(0.38)
Unemployed (y)	0.165	(0.273)	0.311	(0.288)	0.124	(0.290)	0.099	(0.403)
Job related								
Broadcaster	0.547	(0.365)	0.637	(0.412)	0.367	(0.307)	-0.174	(0.470)
Producer	0.426	(0.308)	0.208	(0.386)	-0.093	(0.481)	-0.440	(0.558)
Production	0.858	**(0.350)	0.760	*(0.461)	0.003	(0.501)	-0.786	(0.597)
Research	0.707	*(0.414)	0.850	*(0.484)	1.366	*(0.761)	0.726	(0.851)
Post-production	0.322	(0.531)	0.021	(0.756)	-1.266	*(0.648)	-1.568	**(0.80)
Camera/lighting	0.648	(0.492)	0.634	(0.643)	0.917	(0.770)	0.314	(0.893)
Writers	0.342	(0.428)	-0.099	(0.616)	1.878	*(1.120)	1.611	(1.185)
Manager	1.918	**(0.791)	1.524	*(0.859)	-0.840	(0.536)	-2.692	**(0.94)
Artistic	0.520	(0.423)	0.031	(0.636)	0.661	(0.696)	0.259	(0.793)

(continued)

Table 8.4: Model results for main sample women of likelihood of being employed in month (continued)

Variable	Logit		Random effects		Multinomial logit			
					Employed		Unemployed	
	coeff	se	coeff	se	coeff	se	coeff	se
Contract continuity								
Serial	−0.523	*(0.317)	−0.607	(0.381)	0.449	(0.492)	0.923	(0.563)
Demand								
Unemployment	0.027	(0.054)	−0.012	(0.060)	−0.166	(0.138)	−0.326	**(0.17)
Personal								
Age	0.032	(0.050)	0.075	(0.079)	−0.000	(0.062)	−0.026	(0.077)
Age squared	−0.050	(0.050)	−0.085	(0.080)	0.010	(0.063)	0.055	(0.078)
Married	0.278	*(0.160)	0.287	(0.255)	−1.283	**(0.182)	−1.539	**(0.24)
Divorced	0.040	(0.335)	−0.053	(0.532)	−1.353	**(0.338)	−1.438	**(0.453)
Other								
BBC reorganisation	–		–		−0.705	**(0.360)	−1.164	**(0.463)
Constant	2.597	*(1.331)	1.934	(2.016)	5.233	**(1.947)	3.477	(2.429)
Rho,ρ	–	–	0.444	(0.089)	–		–	
Chi-squared (1)	–	**26.65	–	–	–		–	
Log Likelihood	−843.863		−830.538		−1,569.157			
N, sample size	4,080		4,080		4,279			

Notes: Chi-squared value provided for Likelihood Ratio test of rho = 0

** $p<0.05$, * $p<0.10$

Table 8.5: Model results for main sample men of likelihood of being employed in month

Variable	Logit		Random effects	
	coeff	se	coeff	se
Self-employed:				
Freelance	−2.137	**(0.536)	−2.402	**(0.607)
Independent owner	−1.106	*(0.612)	−1.252	*(0.716)
Human capital:				
Higher education	−0.154	(0.182)	−0.383	(0.385)
Formal training	0.105	(0.198)	−0.045	(0.241)
Informal training	0.291	(0.246)	0.223	(0.307)
Unemployed (m)	−4.002	**(0.150)	−3.346	**(0.191)
Unemployed (y)	−0.438	*(0.258)	−0.539	*(0.276)
Workplace:				
Broadcaster	−1.074	*(0.558)	−1.147	*(0.622)
Type of job:				
Producer	−0.862	**(0.381)	−1.307	**(0.637)
Production	−0.071	(0.625)	−0.663	(1.037)
Research	−0.467	(0.657)	−0.834	(0.921)
Post-production	−0.992	**(0.416)	−1.518	*(0.782)
Camera/lighting	−0.456	(0.428)	−0.946	(0.767)
Writers	−1.002	**(0.502)	−1.294	(0.912)
Manager	0.078	(0.502)	−0.065	(0.783)
Artistic	−0.815	(0.530)	−1.330	(0.923)
Contract continuity:				
Serial	−0.024	(0.270)	0.013	(0.319)
Demand:				
Unemployment	−0.026	(0.055)	-0.005	(0.062)
Personal:				
Age	−0.022	(0.053)	0.110	(0.121)
Age Squared	−0.004	(0.047)	−0.105	(0.110)
Married	0.638	**(0.194)	0.364	(0.462)
Divorced	0.341	(0.276)	−0.099	(0.567)
Other:				
BBC reorganisation	−	−	−	−
Constant	7.468	**(1.587)	4.751	*(2.835)
Rho, ρ	−	−	0.588	(0.095)
Chi-squared (1)	−		**44.81	
Log Likelihood	−867.480		−845.075	
N, sample size	6,283		6,283	

Notes: Chi-squared value provided for Likelihood Ratio test of rho = 0

** $p < 0.05$, * $p < 0.10$

were independent owners also had a significantly increased probability of being unemployed. Women who were independent owners, on the other hand, appear to have an increased probability of employment. The random effects models suggested the same relationships, only now that individual-specific effects are allowed for, the sizes of these independent variable coefficients have changed. For men, the negative effect of being freelance or independent owners on employment was much increased. For women the negative effect of being freelance was slightly lower, but the positive effect of being an independent owner increased after allowing for heterogeneity in the random effects models. The gender differential remained the same. The results for the 3-way multinomial choice set were very similar in size to the other results. The diagnostic tests on the random effects model suggested that the random effects estimator better represents the variation in our data, and therefore that unobserved individual-specific heterogeneity was present[13].

The other results were not surprising. Of the personal characteristics, being married led to an increased probability of employment. This supports the view that the pressures of mortgages and children (highly correlated with marriage) add supply-side pressure to maintain continuity in employment and an income stream. Allowing the coefficients of men and women to vary in separate estimations did not produce many differences in the parameters. However, for women, being married was associated with an increased likelihood of being employed in the standard logit model, although the effect became insignificant in the random effects model. Allowing women the choice of inactivity (in the multinomial model) led to the result that being married (or divorced) was associated with a lower likelihood of being employed, compared with being inactive. In the face of pressures of working in television, some of which are described elsewhere (Willis and Dex, 2002), married women may be more likely to choose homemaking. The human capital measure of formal training was significant in increasing the likelihood of employment for women although not for men. Other human capital variables, such as higher education and age, were never significant. Having been unemployed in the last six months was associated with a large reduction in the likelihood of being employed in the current period, although being unemployed in the previous year (two periods ago) did not always affect employment in the current period[14]. Some of the occupation categories were significant: being a male producer, writer or working in post-production were associated with a reduced likelihood of being employed in any month. Being a female production worker, researcher or manager was associated with an increased probability of being employed. Working on a series did not have any significant impact on the likelihood of being employed in any month for women and men.

The business cycle indicator and a calendar time variable were not significant when entered either separately or together in most estimations. In addition, the dummy variable introduced to equal one after 1996 to capture any effects of the internal reorganisation of the BBC suggested there was a reduced probability of employment for women after the reorganisation. Industry members of our Advisory Board suggested that women may have taken time out to have a family in response to the stress and low morale in the BBC, as was also mentioned in anecdotes.

Figure 8.1 displays a number of predicted probabilities of television producers with selected characteristics that show the differences between gender as well as between freelance and staff status.

Staff television producers all had much higher predicted employment rates than freelance workers and women had lower employment rates than men with the same characteristics[15]. The random effects model all reduced the predicted employment rates, very substantially in the case of freelance men. The fact that researchers had lower predicted employment rates than producers is displayed in Figure 8.2, alongside the very large effects on employment rates of having been unemployed in the previous month.

However, where men tended in the logit model to have better employment rates than women in research or production jobs, in the random effects model, this position was reversed. This suggests that the reason why women appear to do worse than men in maintaining employment continuity is related to their unobserved characteristics: fewer networking skills or different attitudes towards careers and the pressures of television are just two possible explanations.

Figure 8.1: Predicted probabilities of producers with given characteristics being employed in month

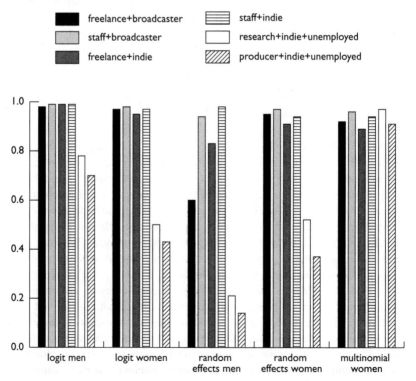

Figure 8.2: Predicted probabilities of freelance worker in independent company being employed in month by type of job and whether unemployed in last month

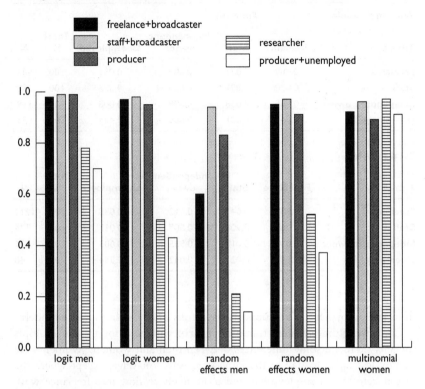

Status transitions

We estimated the six-month transition probabilities for four states (freelance, staff worker, independent owner, and unemployed) using our seven 4 x 4 matrices (Table 8.6). The following general results apply to both genders:

- The majority of freelance and staff workers stayed in the same status between six-monthly waves. Staff workers had a slightly higher probability of remaining in that status wave than did freelance workers of remaining freelance.
- There were small probabilities of moving between freelance and staff contracts each six-month period, although with a slightly higher flow from staff to freelance than in the opposite direction. Those who were unemployed at any wave were most likely to make the transition to freelance status by the next wave, six months later, or else stay out of employment.

There were slight fluctuations, wave-on-wave, in the transition probabilities. The largest concerned moving back into freelance status having been out of work. Clearly freelance status was associated with more spells of unemployment. The probability of making the transition to unemployment was greater from

Table 8.6: Transition probability averages over eight panel waves between different employment status categories for women's and total sample (women plus men)

Women's sample	Time t+1					
Time t	Freelance	Staff	Independent owner	Unemployed	Total %	N
Freelance	0.889	0.051	0.009	0.051	100	587
Staff	0.070	0.897	0.005	0.028	100	358
Independent owner	0.085	0.008	0.899	0.008	100	119
Unemployed	0.545	0.031	0.000	0.424	100	33

Total sample	Time t+1					
Time t	Freelance	Staff	Independent owner	Unemployed	Total %	N
Freelance	0.902	0.047	0.013	0.038	100	1214
Staff	0.068	0.908	0.007	0.017	100	774
Independent owner	0.050	0.012	0.935	0.003	100	321
Unemployed	0.583	0.021	0.042	0.354	100	48

freelance status at the previous wave than from staff status, as was the flow back from unemployment. This supports the results of the earlier logistic models.

Comparing the women's transition matrix with that for the total sample suggests there are some differences between men and women. Women were slightly less likely to stay in the same state wave-on-wave, except where the origin state was unemployment, and more likely to flow into freelance work from being staff workers or owners of independent companies. Women were also less likely than men to move into being an independent owner, irrespective of their origin state. These results could be equally consistent with women being more likely to be pushed into freelance work, or choosing to do freelance work. However, the higher rates of staying in unemployment (stayers) among women suggest that they face something of a disadvantage compared to men in getting back into jobs when they are out of work[16].

The earlier model results suggest that female independent owners are less likely than men to move into unemployment on a month-by-month basis. However, on this six-monthly time horizon, we see a slightly higher probability of women owners becoming unemployed than men owners.

From the initial vectors,

	[Freelance,	**Staff,**	**Independent owner,**	**Unemployed]**
Women's sample				
Initial vector	[0.484,	0.408,	0.100,	0.008]
Steady state	[0.544,	0.293,	0.063,	0.063]
Total sample				
Initial vector	[0.444,	0.411,	0.125,	0.020]
Steady state	[0.504,	0.286,	0.156,	0.038]

we end up with a steady state in which the proportion of freelance workers has increased from 44% to 50% in the total sample. The 6% increase is the same in the women's sample. The proportion of staff workers in the steady state is predicted to decline by 12.5% on the whole sample, slightly more in the women's sample compared with the distribution in 1994. Women are predicted to end up with an even higher percentage in freelance work than men, to be in staff jobs in the same proportions as men, but to be much less represented in independent owner positions and much more represented in unemployment than men.

Whether these are realistic expectations depends on whether the demand and supply-side changes that have been occurring in television over the period of our survey continue in the same way. The figures do give an indication of what might happen if current trends and experiences are rolled forward. Given that the cost pressures are not likely to decline on the demand-side, it seems likely that there may still be some way for the percentage of freelance workers to increase further but presumably not beyond the point at which there are insufficient staff workers left to organise contracts and continuity in companies.

The relatively small flows from staff to freelance status support the idea of difference in risk aversion between these groups. However, on the other hand, there are greater proportions of women (traditionally thought to be more risk averse) in freelance work, with a slightly higher flow for women than men into freelance from tenured staff. This might be taken to suggest that women were more likely to have chosen to work freelance. However, the stated preferences of women (and men) in freelance work go against this interpretation.

Individuals were asked once in this survey, at wave 7, what type of work they preferred. The freelance workers were least likely to indicate that they preferred their current status (only 49%) compared with permanent staff contracts who preferred to be staff (76%) (Table 8.7). There was a strong desire among 37% of the freelance group to have a staff contract.

Women in freelance work were more likely than men to want to change to a staff position, or to do something else. However, women in staff positions (or independent owners) were less likely than men to want to stay in this status and more wanted to work freelance or to do something else. Thus the higher percentage of women than men in freelance work status is not, for the most part, voluntary, although there probably were some women who preferred freelance work, where there was choice.

Table 8.7: Preferences about type of contract (wave 7) (%)

	Current freelance		Current staff		Current owner		All	
	Total	Women	Total	Women	Total	Women	Total	Women
Prefer freelance	48.6	38	10.8	16	10.0	29	28.9	29
Prefer staff	37.0	44	75.5	66	75.0	64	56.3	53
Prefer job outside TV	11.6	7	6.9	8	10.0	0	9.9	8
Other	2.9	10	6.9	10	5.0	7	4.9	10
Total, N	138	86	102	50	40	17	284	154

Project durations

We are interested in whether the self-employed have different lengths of projects compared to staff with permanent contracts. Project length is an important element of freelance work conditions, since it determines their level of uncertainty. It may also affect the amount of concentration they can give to any one project since the search for, or arrangement of, the next employment contract will need to be taking place concurrently if a constant income stream is to be maintained. As one respondent wrote on her questionnaire:

> "My company has a 'convenient' way of employing on short-term contracts. Because mine has rolled I'm told that I'm lucky to have the security and therefore am paid at a lower salary. In fact no security exists – how can it on a one month contract?" (Female in independent company)

Survival estimates of project durations were displayed in an earlier version of this research (Dex and Smith, 2000) for all projects undertaken during the five-year period. The majority of projects were short in duration and there were few visible differences in these curves by gender or by contractual status groups. Half the projects were completed within seven months, and two thirds by one year. Projects done by freelance workers and staff workers were not significantly different in duration; 50% of the projects done by freelance workers were completed in six-and-a-half months, compared to seven months for staff workers. Projects done by men lasted slightly longer than projects done by women, but again the difference at the median was only two weeks (although there were more longer projects for men). In all of these cases, there were variations by wave. These durations are very different from the self-employment spell durations of the BHPS estimated by Taylor (1999), where 4% of men's and 5% of women's spells were completed by six months and 10% of men's and women's spells completed by one year. This is because a television project is not equivalent to a spell of self-employment as measured in other data sets. In general, a 'spell' of self-employment will cover multiple television projects, as long as there is no intervening unemployment.

The results of modelling the determinants of project durations are displayed in Table 8.8[17]. Interestingly, being freelance or an independent owner is not

Table 8.8: Cox-proportional hazard model on duration of projects

Variable	Total Hazard ratio	(SE)	Men Hazard ratio	(SE)	Women Hazard ratio	(SE)
Personal characteristics:						
Female	1.064	(0.062)	–	–		
Age	1.045	(0.023)**	1.032	(0.029)	1.089	(0.043)**
Age squared	0.999	(0.000)*	0.999	(0.000)*	0.999	(0.000)
Married	1.058	(0.065)	1.343	(0.125)**	0.980	(0.092)
Divorced	1.112	(0.105)	1.233	(0.154)	0.676	(0.125)**
Contract:						
Freelance	0.935	(0.097)	1.037	(0.162)	0.805	(0.124)
Independent owner	0.818	(0.103)	1.058	(0.193)	0.475	(0.108)**
Organisation						
Broadcaster	0.967	(0.102)	1.066	(0.170)	0.841	(0.132)
Type of job:						
Producer	0.845	(0.125)	0.999	(0.183)	0.633	(0.162)*
Production	0.982	(0.161)	1.226	(0.315)	0.766	(0.203)
Research	1.169	(0.219)	1.110	(0.291)	1.436	(0.423)
Post-production	1.716	(0.280)**	2.012	(0.393)**	0.846	(0.339)
Camera/lighting	1.676	(0.268)**	1.493	(0.294)**	4.364	(1.334)**
Writer	0.588	(0.143)**	0.058	(0.059)**	0.837	(0.271)
Manager	0.802	(0.132)	0.838	(0.169)	0.577	(0.179)*
Artist	1.004	(0.193)	0.873	(0.216)	0.976	(0.310)
Serial	0.674	(0.091)**	0.591	(0.091)**	0.772	(0.223)
Human capital:						
Higher education	0.937	(0.058)	0.905	(0.073)	0.995	(0.106)
Past unemployment	0.901	(0.074)	0.938	(0.098)	0.946	(0.131)
Past formal training	1.052	(0.059)	1.059	(0.077)	1.065	(0.101)
Past on-the-job training	1.181	(0.075)	1.093	(0.090)	1.331	(0.142)
Period:						
Unemployment rate	1.196	(0.114)	1.107	(0.132)	1.422	(0.231)
BBC reorganisation	1.109	(0.122)	0.986	(0.141)	1.271	(0.227)
N	2416		1514		902	
Log likelihood	–12,666.1		–7,421.5		–3,981.3	

Notes: Significance: * at 90% confidence level; ** at 95% confidence level.

significantly correlated with project duration for men, or in the total sample. Women who are independent owners tend to have significantly shorter project durations than other workers. This may mean that this very small group of women have managed to achieve company ownership because they are prepared to accept short turnaround jobs that their male colleagues may decline. Another perspective on the same results may be that women in this position are not as well connected to the 'right' networks as men, and fail to get the lengthier commissions.

Age was a significant factor influencing project duration for both men and women, with longer projects going to older and more experienced workers. A range of job types and some personal and human capital characteristics had influenced project length, as well as working on a serial which was associated with shorter projects (Table 8.7).

Conclusions

This chapter has examined some of the working experiences of the self-employed women and men in television. Self-employment, as far as employment law and regulation are concerned, is more vulnerable than employee status. However, the increased risks are also associated with higher potential rewards both in terms of pay, but also in terms of satisfaction, autonomy and fulfilment.

By viewing the results of a number of studies, gender differences were found to exist in the experiences of employment continuity in the television industry. Women freelance workers are less likely than men to be unemployed after controlling for other characteristics, but more likely to remain unemployed having become so. Women freelance workers (men also) are disadvantaged compared to other staff workers in this respect and this disadvantage appears to have on-going consequences over time. These findings emphasise the importance of going beyond cross-sectional comparisons of status. Women owners of independent production companies suffer less employment discontinuity than men on a month-by-month basis, although it is higher over a longer time period, but largely because they move into freelance work to a larger extent than men. Men also manage to keep their companies running to a greater extent than women. Women owners clearly avoid some of the discontinuities to their employment record by moving to freelance work. Those who do retain their companies do so by accepting shorter projects than men in an effort to keep their businesses afloat.

The large-scale changes in contractual status in the television industry have affected the workforce in various ways. A large group of workers have clearly suffered a deterioration in their work continuity and in their conditions of work, and possibly in their productivity and creativity as a result. Many of them were continuing to struggle to maintain employment continuity and make a career in television, based on, in some cases, diversifying their income sources (see Dex et al, 1999). Many of the gender differences were related to the demand-side. They were not preferred changes in contractual status, because preferences were expressed for different circumstances. Some women ended up in what appeared more disadvantaged positions than men for these unobserved reasons. We can only speculate here on what these unobserved reasons might be; for example, different attitudes towards risk taking; different attitudes towards combining work and parenting; being excluded from male networks that allocate programme commissions; or having different reputations.

Suffering greater frequencies of unemployment may have damaged their reputations so that their longer-term prospects were worse than those of men. Elaborating and distinguishing the influence and full extent of these potential differences will have to await further study.

The challenges posed by self-employment invigorate some individuals, stimulating them to work their way out of the mundane into the exciting and liberating. These same individuals clearly value the autonomy which, as active agents, they can use to control their own lives and gain flexibility, and which is not on offer in many standard employment contracts. On the other hand some individuals find the uncertainty debilitating, time consuming, costly, unfulfilling and stressful. These ambivalent elements of self-employment were evident in the responses and behaviour of our sample of television production workers. Our analyses of television workers suggest that a greater proportion fall into this second category than the first (BFI, 1999; Dex et al, 1999). With all, there was an overriding commitment to working in television and the creativity it offered. For many, this meant they were prepared to struggle to make a career of it, and put up with employment discontinuity in the short term as well as low income, beyond what employees in other employment contexts would be prepared to endure. These findings cut across gender differences. Indeed, what is striking about television workers who survive in the industry is how similar they are, whether men or women.

Women were more likely than men to be freelance in this sample, and we predict the gap to widen even further. Women may, therefore, be more likely to suffer unemployment spells than men because of their greater likelihood of being freelance, even though freelance men had a higher risk than freelance women of being unemployed. On the basis of the current knowledge about industry population statistics it is not possible to confirm that more women than men are freelance in television, although the statistics certainly allow for this interpretation. Freelance women exhibited a greater preference than men to be in staff rather than freelance positions. In this sense, there are gender disadvantages imposed on many women television workers through the reorganisation of the industry that has made it rely on freelance contract work.

Television workers are an interesting group among the self-employed. As well as being so-called knowledge workers they typically represent the new individual, in an industry singled out to be central to the future health and growth of the British economy (DTI, 1998). Their experiences of self-employment can tell us more about the likelihood of prospects for growth and sustainability in these types of service industries, such as publishing and construction, since these have to rest on sustainability of employment continuity and income streams to maintain the workforce. There are also issues of equality that are on the government agenda. Given that, our findings suggest there are serious issues of sustainability and equality for the industry to face since it has gone over to such a predominance of freelance contract work. Clearly the analysis of the longitudinal experiences of these workers has uncovered some worrying dimensions to their work histories. The impression is that much talent is wasted, and that women suffer this more so than men.

Notes

[1] Variation in the population of self-employed as a whole is controlled in our analyses by virtue of the fact that we are investigating a single industry.

[2] 'Inactivity' includes not working because of long-term sickness, being a housewife, in full-time education, or on a government training scheme.

[3] Taylor's findings are useful since our television industry data do not permit a breakdown by gender, since the sample sizes become small. BHPS data are collected as discrete monthly records of employment status, rather than spells. By treating the recorded status as part of a single spell, we make distinctions between spells when a change in that monthly status occurs.

[4] The 'other occupations' group was by far the largest group covered by the Skillset Census, covering approximately one fifth of the total workforce in audio-visual industries.

[5] The reliability of researching recall may result in some under-reporting of short periods of unemployment (Dex, 1995). However, since we were only asking about periods of unemployment lasting one month or more, we do not consider this a serious obstacle to our analysis.

[6] A refresher sample of 50 young television workers (aged 20-30 years) was added at wave 6. The analysis reports the focus on the main sample.

[7] According to economic theory, an individual's reservation wage (the minimum wage they are prepared to enter the labour market at), entirely determines their decision to work.

[8] There are relatively few studies of gender differences in attitudes towards risk. Commentators tend to point to the lack of women in certain so-called risky occupations, such as stock dealing.

[9] The survey showed that 51% of tenured employees working in the BBC said they had stayed in the same job to avoid uncertainty, a figure that was lower in the sample as a whole.

[10] It was not possible to estimate a similar model for men since there were insufficient cases of inactivity.

[11] Sixty-nine of the 30-50 age bracket accepted lower rates. Also, 32% said they had accepted less skilled jobs in order to secure employment, and 24% had been prepared to put aside ambitions in favour of secure posts.

[12] Many comments in the questionnaires illustrated this dilemma. One 28-year-old film director wrote: "Beginning to get panicky about my next job. There's nothing for

me at X Films coming up so it's back to the beginning." Another freelance researcher in her twenties wrote: "Applied for every long (ie, one year) contract I see in the BBC. Worried now that they think I'll go for anything but I do need the stability."

[13] We carried out a likelihood ratio test, which assesses the relevance of the panel-level variance component in the random effects model. This test compares the pooled logit estimator with the random effects panel estimator. The null hypothesis of the test is that rho = 0, where rho is a function of the panel-level variance; that is, the proportion of the total model variance provided by the random effects variance component. If this quantity equals zero then the panel estimator is the same as the pooled estimator. In such a case, the random effects estimator would be unable to pick up unobserved time-invariant random individual-specific effects above the unobserved effects already accounted for in the pooled estimator error term. The coefficients provided by either model would then be the same. For these regressions, the panel variance was found to be significant by rejecting the null hypothesis of a zero rho.

[14] We were fortunate to be able to include two period lags without loss of data waves, since retrospective information over one year was collected at the first questionnaire, and not just for the previous six months.

[15] The predicted probabilities are derived for a married individual at mean age with higher education and formal training in the previous six-month period.

[16] 'Stayer' means someone whose origin and destination statuses are the same. The 'mover-stayer' terminology is associated with Markov Chain models.

[17] Standard errors were adjusted to allow for the fact that all individuals contributed multiple projects to the data, and were thus repeatedly at risk.

References

Antcliff, V. (2001) 'The impact of casualisation on workers in the UK television industry', Paper presented at the BSA conference, Manchester: Manchester Metropolitan University, April.

Blanchflower, D. and Oswald, A. (1991) *What makes an entrepreneur?*, Institute of Economics and Statistics Discussion Paper, no 125.

British Film Institute (1995) *British Film Institute Television Industry Tracking Study: The First Year: An Interim Report*, London: British Film Institute.

British Film Institute (1997) *British Film Institute Television Industry Tracking Study: Second Interim Report*, London: British Film Institute.

British Film Institute (1999) *British Film Institute Television Industry Tracking Study: Third Interim Report*, London: British Film Institute.

Campbell, M. and Daly, M. (1992) 'Self-employment: Into the 1990s', *Employment Gazette*, vol 100, no 6, pp 269-92.

Carter, S. and Cannon, T. (1988) *Female entrepreneurs: a study of female business owners: Their motivations, experiences and strategies for success*, Employment Department Research Paper no 65.

Cowling, M., Mitchell, P. and Taylor, M.P. (1997a) *Job creation and the self employed: A story of life, wealth and vocational qualifications*, SME Centre Working Paper no 47.

Cowling, M., Mitchell, P. and Taylor, M.P. (1997b) *Entrepreneurial women and men: Two different species?*, SME Centre Working Paper no 49.

Davies, R.B. and Dale, A. (1994) 'Introduction', in A. Dale and R.B. Davies (eds) *Analysing social and political change. A casebook of methods*, London: Sage Publications.

Dex, S. (1995) 'The reliability of recall data: a literature review', *Bulletin de Methodologie Sociologique*, vol 49, pp 58-80.

Dex, S. (1996) 'Women's experience of unemployment', *Economic Affairs*, vol 16, no 2.

Dex, S. and McCulloch, A. (1995) *Flexible employment in Britain: A statistical survey*, Research Discussion Series No 15, Manchester: Equal Opportunities Commission.

Dex, S. and McCulloch, A. (1997) *Flexible employment: The future of Britain's jobs*, Basingstoke: Macmillan.

Dex, S. and Sheppard, E. (1999) *Perceptions of quality in television production*, Judge Institute Research Paper, WP 21/99, Cambridge: University of Cambridge.

Dex, S., Willis, J., Paterson, R. and Sheppard, E. (1999) 'Freelance workers and contract uncertainty: the effects of contractual changes in the television industry', *Work, Employment and Society*, vol 14, no 2, pp 283-305.

Dex, S. and Smith, C. (2000) *The self-employment experiences of the self employed: The case of television production workers*, Judge Institute for Management Studies Research Paper, WP 01/2000, Cambridge: University of Cambridge.

DTI (Department of Trade and Industry) (1998) *Our competitive future: Building the knowledge driven economy*, Government White Paper on Competitiveness, Cm 4176, London: The Stationery Office.

Evans, D.S. and Leighton, L.S. (1989) 'Some empirical aspects of entrepreneurship', *American Economic Review*, vol 79, no 3, pp 519-35.

Fogarty, M., Allen, I. and Walters, P. (1971) *Women in top jobs*, London: Allen and Unwin.

Hakim, C. (1988) 'Self-employment in Britain: a review of recent trends and current issues', *Work Employment and Society*, vol 2, no 4, pp 421-50.

Holly, S. and Woolf, M. (1995) *Employment patterns and training needs*, London: Skillset.

Markus, G.B. (1984) *Analyzing panel data*, London: Sage University Papers, no 18.

Meager, N., Court, G. and Moralee, J. (1994) *Self-employment and the distribution of income*, Report 270, Brighton: Institute of Manpower Studies.

OECD (Organisation for Economic Co-operation and Development) (1991) *Employment Outlook*, Paris: OECD.

Price Waterhouse/PACT (1995) *Production 95: The results of the 1995 Price Waterhouse/PACT survey of UK Independent Production Companies*, London: PACT.

Rix, A., Davies, K., Gaunt, R., Hare, A. and Cobbold, S. (1999) *The training and development of flexible workers*, DfEE, Research Report, no 118.

Sheppard, E. and Dex, S. (1998) 'Analysis of attrition in the longitudinal television industry tracking study', Unpublished Report, London: British Film Institute.

Skillset (2001) *A snapshot in time. Employment Census 2000*, London: Skillset.

STATA Manual (1999) *STATA Reference Manual: Release 6.0*, STATA Press: College Station Texas.

Taylor, M. (1999) 'Survival of the fittest? An analysis of self-employment duration in Britain', *Economic Journal*, vol 109, no 454, pp C140-C155.

Willis, J. and Dex, S. (2002) 'Mothers returning to TV production work in a changing environment', forthcoming in A. Beck (ed) *Cultural work*, London: Routledge Harwood.

NINE

Gender wage differentials in Britain and Japan*

Yayoi Sugihashi and Angela Dale

Introduction

Women still earn less than men. However, a reduction of the gender pay gap has resulted through anti-discrimination legislation, enforcement of 'equal pay for equal work' and 'equal pay for work of equal value', as well as working women's movements, in all industrialised countries over the past few decades.

Japan has the widest gender differences in pay among industrialised countries. Between 1970 and 1999, the gap in men's and women's full-time average monthly earnings has decreased only slowly (Table 9.1). The persistence of these large gender wage differentials has led to submissions from the International Labour Office (ILO) to the Japanese government that the gap should be reduced. Although the gender wage gap has decreased more rapidly in Great Britain, nonetheless it remains substantially higher than countries such as Norway, Sweden, and Australia, where women's full-time hourly earnings are over 90% those of men's.

A noteworthy difference between Britain and Japan is the basis on which pay rates are determined. In Japan, seniority, age and personal appraisals are

Table 9.1: Gender wage differentials in Great Britain and Japan (1970-99), for full-time employees

	1970	1985	1999
Japan	52.7	56.1	62.8
Great Britain	63.0	73.8	81.6

Notes:

Data for Japan are based on gross monthly earnings.

Data for Britain are gross hourly earnings including overtime. For the year 1970, the data relates to men ages 21 and above and women aged 18 and above. For the years 1985 and 1999, it relates to employees on adult rates. All data relates to employees in the survey whose pay for the survey period was not affected by absence.

Sources: Japan: Ministry of Labour (1970, 1985 and 1999); Great Britain: Department of Employment (1970, 1980); ONS (1999)

more important than job content in determining wages. By contrast, in Britain earnings are assumed to be more closely related to the content of the job, although performance related pay is becoming increasingly important (IRS/EOC, 1992).

A number of economic and social theories have been proposed to explain women's lower earnings relative to men. These fall into two main categories: neo-classical theory, and non-neoclassical theory. Neo-classical theories include human capital, non-pecuniary, taste for discrimination, statistical discrimination and the crowding hypothesis. These theories perceive the creation and maintenance of low-paid work as the result of less human capital investment, or innately lower productivity, imperfect competition in the labour market, discrimination by employers, other employees or customers, or the choice of individual workers. On the other hand, theories such as labour market segmentation, patriarchy and the family wage – all of which reject neo-classical theory – make much of the historical viewpoint and attribute the gender pay gap to institutional, social and cultural factors, the process of uneven development of the capitalist economy, or women's position in the family. In general, human capital, labour market segmentation and statistical discrimination theories are those most often applied in the British and Japanese economic and social literature and these are discussed in more detail, with particular respect to comparisons between Britain and Japan.

In addition to these theoretical developments, a great deal of effort has been spent on the statistical measurement of the components of gender wage differences. The most widely used statistical method (the Blinder-Oaxaca decomposition technique[1]) uses multiple regression analysis to measure the extent to which the male/female earnings gap can be explained by productivity-related characteristics included in the analysis. The amount that is not so explained is assumed to reflect discrimination.

In this chapter we set out to compare the earnings differentials between women and men in Britain and Japan, and the reasons for those differences. We review the theoretical explanations for gender pay differences, and we describe the methods used to estimate earnings equations and to decompose the components of the pay gap into different parts. We describe the data sources used for Japan (based on published material) and for Britain (the Labour Force Survey [LFS] and the National Child Development Study [NCDS]).

Ideally, longitudinal data would be used to compare Britain and Japan. However, very little microdata is available for Japan, and therefore analysis of the pay gap is based on published papers that use information about current employment, with retrospective data on length of time in current employment. To construct a model which is as similar as possible to that available for Japan we have used data from the British Labour Force Survey of 1998-99. We decompose the pay gap from British data and compare the results with the Japanese findings. From this we explore the different components of the gender pay gap in Japan and Britain in the light of the institutional, cultural and individual differences between the two countries. Finally, we turn to longitudinal data in order to estimate a fuller model of earnings differences, but in the case of Britain only. This model allows early life influences and parental background to be included and is based on the NCDS – a longitudinal study of all individuals born in Great Britain in one week in March 1958 and aged 33 in 1991 (the most recent date for which we have earnings information). Paci and Joshi (1998) have already explored this issue extensively using the NCDS and the 1946 British Cohort Survey. We shall compare our results, based on rather different models, with theirs, and also with the results from the LFS.

Theoretical background to the analysis

Before turning to our theoretical position, we shall outline the main economic theories on discrimination (Blau and Jusenius, 1976; Kuwahara, 1978; Humphries and Rubery, 1984; Blau and Ferber, 1986; Cain, 1986; Rubery, 1992; England, 1992; Bosworth et al, 1996; Blau, 1998).

Human capital theory offers one of the most important supply-side explanations of gender differences in earnings (Becker, 1975). It argues that workers' productivity corresponds to their past investments in schooling, vocational training and qualifications and experience in the labour market. Therefore, the gender gap in pay is due to the different skills, experience and qualifications that women and men bring to the labour market. Non-pecuniary theory assumes that wages reflect the amenities or disamenities of a job. Gender wage differentials can be explained because women give priority to particular characteristics of jobs such as convenient working hours, proximity to home or safety. They are therefore willing to accept lower wages in exchange for these non-pecuniary amenities.

In contrast, there are several demand-side theories on discrimination. According to Becker's taste theory (1957), an employer who dislikes hiring women will only do so if their pay is low enough to offset the psychological cost of employing them. Alternatively, male workers may refuse to work alongside women, or customers may dislike dealing with women. In all these examples, the 'disutility' of employing women is only overcome by paying them less than men. The crowding hypothesis (Bergman, 1971, 1974) assumes that employers' discrimination against women operates by excluding women from male jobs and thereby creating female jobs and male jobs. The abundant supply of women in female jobs pushes their market wage lower than men's. It thus results in a difference in pay between men and women even if they are equally productive. The theory of monopsonistic discrimination, similarly based on imperfect labour market competition, argues that the less elastic the supply curve of labour, the lower the wage will be. The male–female pay differential is based on the assumption that a firm can have greater monopsony power over women than men, partly because women are more constrained in their employment options due to their additional domestic responsibilities. Statistical discrimination (Phelps, 1972) also operates to produce and maintain gender-based pay differences. As information on an individual worker's performance is too costly for employers to collect, they tend to estimate workers' productivity based on proxy information, for example level of education or gender. If employers believe that women, in aggregate, are less productive than men then they will tend to offer lower wages. Employers' information may or may not be based on well-founded evidence, such as turnover rates or greater variation in productivity between women. The result, however, is that employers may regard it as rational to give preference to men. This, then, is a further explanation of gender wage differentials.

The theories introduced so far fall into neo-classical economics. There are, however, alternative explanations which fall outside these orthodox analyses of the labour market. Labour market segmentation theory (Doeringer and Piore, 1971) argues that labour markets are segmented, with different working conditions in each segment and limited employment transfer between them. Institutionalism sees the gender wage differentials as the consequence of the labour market structure which restricts women to lower paid jobs.

Finally, the family wage theory regards women's lower wage as the result of the differences in men's and women's relationships to the social reproduction system, where men's wages are based on the cost of their own social reproduction and that of their dependants, while women's are based on only part of the cost of their own reproduction. In both Japan and Britain the 'male breadwinner model' has influenced the development of social policy and employment practices (Humphries and Rubery, 1984; Osawa, 1993; Kiso Keizai Kagaku Kenkyusyo, 1995; Crompton, 1999; Gottfried and O'Reilly, 2000). This assumption underpinned the development of social welfare provision in Britain and still has influence through, for example, the joint-assessment of eligibility for benefit. In Britain, during the first half of the 20th century, the male breadwinner model was mainly observed among married middle-class couples, while most working-class women had to work outside the home. In Japan, the male breadwinner model has been evident in employment contracts and in the seniority-based wage system which is available only to male workers. (Recently there has been much debate over whether these systems should be changed [Kinoshita, 1998].) The male breadwinner model is also reflected in the low level of social welfare available in Japan which is still seen as a 'company-centred society'. This is evident where a company may play an important role in sponsoring long-term employment, seniority-based treatment and family allowances for men, especially in large- or middle-sized companies (Goto, 1999; Kinoshita, 1998; Kiso Keizai Kagaku Kenkyusyo, 1995).

In our opinion, each of the economic and social theories discussed above play a role in explaining gender wage differentials. However, our focus is on the earnings of employees in the labour market. Although there is likely to be gender-based discrimination in terms of the educational qualifications obtained, at the point of entry to the labour market and in the jobs available, our analyses of the gender pay differential are based on the assumption that women and men have chosen their educational and occupational trajectories.

Data sources, models and methods

Data sources

Japan

Since access to microdata in Japan is very restricted[2], we have not been able to conduct our own analyses. We have had instead to rely on the work of Nakata (1997), because he uses both wage equations and decomposition and a relatively large set of variables. In addition, there is no nationally representative longitudinal study available for analysis in Japan[3]. Therefore the data source used by Nakata and others working in the field is the Basic Survey on Wage Structure. This is an annual national cross-sectional survey of establishments with more than five workers. The sample size is 72,000 establishments and 1.55 million workers. Workers are sampled within selected establishments. The survey records monthly earnings and the components of earnings, bonuses, full-time or part-time working, sex, education, age, length of service with the current employer, working hours, industry, occupation and region. The Basic Survey on Wage Structure is therefore considered as the key national data source for analysis of wages in Japan.

The British Labour Force Survey (LFS)

The LFS is a survey of households living at private addresses in Britain. In 1992 it adopted a rotating quarterly panel design. Each quarter is made up of five 'waves', each of which contains about 12,000 selected households. The households are interviewed in five successive waves. Data has been used for 1998-99 with response rates of 78-79% in the first wave.

This research requires a dataset large enough to produce accurate estimates. We have therefore used earnings data from every first wave between spring 1998 and spring 1999 - the most recent data available at the time of analysis. Most of the variables used in the wage equation were derived from the same wave and quarter as the data for earnings.

The LFS includes overtime earnings in the measurement of pay. Overtime pay influences the gender pay gap because overtime is paid at a higher rate than the contractual hours of work and the extent of overtime working is much higher for men than for women.

The National Child Development Study (NCDS)

The NCDS holds a wide range of information of relevance to women's employment issues – qualifications, employment status, occupation, earnings, and income and family composition, for example. It also contains retrospective information on marriage, fertility, employment and housing histories. This detailed information enables us to include most of the important determinants for analyses of gender wage differentials, without recourse to proxy variables.

In this respect it is a more extensive data source than that used in most previous studies.

Despite attrition, the survey is generally representative of the 1958 cohort within the population as a whole (Ferri, 1993; Dale and Egerton, 1997; Paci and Joshi, 1998). Nonetheless, it is important to consider the quality of data in relation to our specific research question. This will be discussed for two key variables – earnings and educational qualifications.

In the NCDS, earnings are shown in the form of the usual gross pay of employees, including overtime, commission, bonuses and tips. As we mentioned above, the inclusion of overtime may affect the gender pay gap.

The NCDS has a somewhat higher attrition rate for poorly-educated cohort members than for the better educated, and therefore members still responding in sweep five are more likely to hold higher qualifications. In addition, it is important to remember that the NCDS represents a single cohort, and thus there are cohort effects operating for women in terms of education. In the 1958 cohort, about 13% of the 18-19 age group entered higher education, by comparison with about 33% in the late 1990s. We therefore need to understand the NCDS cohort members as located in an educational context in which the majority of young people expected to leave school and enter the labour market, rather than remain in education after 16 years of age. Higher education was still restricted to an elite minority.

Models

Earnings equations are estimated for both the LFS and NCDS. The model based on the LFS is relatively restricted and includes human capital variables (age and educational qualifications), and employment-related variables (length of time in current job, industrial sector, possible membership of a trade union, as well as region of residence). Variables have been categorised to provide as much comparability as possible with the Japanese study.

In the analysis of the longitudinal data from the NCDS, a much fuller set of supply-side variables is included in the wage equation. This then allows differences in unexplained earnings to be assumed as due to demand-side discrimination (Paci et al, 1995; Paci and Joshi, 1998). Included are:

- Human capital explanations.
  - Those related to background, on the assumption that children acquire cultural capital from their parents and this will differ according to the parents' social class.
  - Those related to qualifications, training and work experience.

This represents the qualities that the employee offers in the labour market (Dale and Egerton, 1997; Paci and Joshi, 1998). In particular, work experience has been confirmed by many studies as an important factor in determining remuneration levels (Mincer and Polacheck, 1974; Zabalza and Arrufat, 1985).

Although one might argue that only human capital variables should be included in wage equations, much work has shown that job-related variables are also important in explaining the gender wage gap. However, in the decompositions of the gender pay gap, job-related variables are assumed to reflect employees' preferences for working in certain sectors and certain occupations. In particular, working in a gender-segregated occupation is regarded as one of the main factors of pay differentials. These variables are treated as exogenous to the employer, that is, they are not affected by the employer's behaviour. They include firm/occupation and working conditions/labour market segmentation.

The model assumes that men and women make choices as to their preferred occupation and where they work. Since different occupations command different levels of pay, for equal amounts of human capital, and the same occupation may be rewarded differently depending upon firm size and whether it is in the public or private sector, then these are important variables to consider.

Variables such as weekend-working or shift-working may offer higher rates of pay to compensate for the unsocial hours that are required. Again, we assume that these are determined by employees' choice rather than labour market discrimination. Thus we assume that women enter 'female' dominated jobs such as nursing not because they are excluded from medicine but because they would rather go into nursing. If women are crowded into 'female' jobs, and this is imposed by the labour market/employers, then discrimination will be underestimated. If, however, supply-side explanatory variables are left out of the model, the explained difference will be too little, and the unexplained – assumed as due to discrimination – will be over-estimated. As Paci and Joshi (1998) point out, the reasons for women being in particular types of jobs may be a combination of demand- and supply-side factors. In addition, variables which record the promotion of an employee should be considered as a component of human capital and the internal labour market.

Finally, we extend the wage equations by including household location. For example, higher wages are paid in the South East of England as a compensation for high living costs, as well as travel-to-work time. Travel to work time is seen as reflecting not only domestic responsibilities, but also the fact that women have a more geographically restricted labour market. The portion of the wage gap unexplained by all of these factors can be assumed to be due to demand-side discrimination. However, the amount of discrimination may be underestimated because of the large number of supply-side variables which are available with this longitudinal study. In addition, some of the variables, such as occupation and promotion, are assumed to be supply-side factors here, although they are also influenced to some extent from the demand-side (Gunderson, 1989; Paci et al, 1995; Paci and Joshi, 1998).

The analysis omits the self-employed, as the determination of pay levels and assumptions regarding discrimination within the labour market cannot be employed in a consistent way to this group. We have also confined our analysis to men and women working full-time. By making this restriction we simplify the interpretation of our results and also provide comparability with Japanese data.

Wage equations and the Blinder-Oaxaca Decomposition Technique

There are two steps to exploring the gender wage differentials and discrimination (Oaxaca, 1973; Gunderson, 1989; ILO, 1993). We estimate separate earning function by sex, and then compute the Blinder-Oaxaca decomposition.

The separate earning equations for men and women can be transformed into the required form for estimating the components of gender wage differentials using the Blinder-Oaxaca decomposition technique. This method divides the difference in pay between women and men into two parts:

- The part of the gender wage gap resulting from the difference in attributes related to productivity between women and men.
- The part of the gender wage gap differentials caused by different remuneration for women and men with the same attributes.

Box 1: The earnings equation

The earnings equation suggests the relationship between the productivity and wage in the following way,

$$w_i^s = \alpha^s + \beta^s x_i^s + u_i^s \tag{1}$$

where i denotes an individual worker, s indicates the individual's sex, w the natural logarithm of his or her wage, a constant term, which would be often regarded as a starting salary. A coefficient (β) is a vector of market returns to each attribute, explanatory variable (x) indicates attributes of a worker such as experience, education and hours, and an error term (u) reflect the random error.

Box 2: The decomposition method

The decomposition equation can be represented thus:

$$\overline{w}_m - \overline{w}_f = (\alpha_m - \alpha_f) + \overline{x}_f(\beta_m - \beta_f) + \beta_m(\overline{x}_m - \overline{x}_f) \tag{2}$$

where subscript m denotes males, f females, a bar ($^-$) represents a mean value.

The left-hand side indicates the wage gap between women and men, on average. It is decomposed into three terms on the right-hand side: (1) the first term is the difference in intercepts between women and men; (2) the second term indicates the difference in market returns between women and men for women's productivity ($\overline{x}_f$); and, (3) the third term shows the difference in the productivity-related characteristics between women and men, assessed on the basis of male market returns (β_m). The first two terms are usually regarded as the unexplained portion of the gender wage gap, namely, 'discrimination', and the third term as the explained component of the wage gap.

Gender differences in endowments, which are regarded as productivity-related characteristics, may reflect discrimination within and outside of the labour market, or women's reaction to discrimination in workplaces (Gunderson, 1989; Sugihashi, 1998). The difference in the number of women and men who are employed as managers serves as an example. Some women voluntarily refuse promotion to the position of manager on the grounds that an administrative post has many responsibilities and requires long work hours. It is reasonable to assume that, in this case, the small number of women managers is due to a *gender difference*. However, some women may be excluded from promotion because they have not been given on-the-job training, or because of unequal treatment in interviews or tests for promotion and so on. In this case the small number of women managers should be regarded as *gender discrimination*. Although a distinction between gender differences and discrimination is often difficult to make, assumptions that differences are due to choice may lead to an underestimation of real discrimination against women.

Sample selection bias

We also need to consider the possibility that women who are in full-time work may have different characteristics from women not so employed. The earnings of women who are in full-time work may be higher than the potential earnings of women who are not in full-time work. If this is the case, the sample of women in full-time work do not represent a random sample of all women and the coefficients for the female wage equations may be biased.

It is possible to correct this selection using a Heckman model (Heckman, 1979), which estimates the probability of employment participation for all women. A correction term is then computed which reflects the probability that a woman with identical characteristics to the sample member is employed. Inclusion of this term in the earnings equation should correct for selection bias. However, the use of this correction is not always straightforward, and depends heavily on the appropriate choice of variables used to model employment participation (Berk, 1983; Robinson, 1986). In this analysis we have conducted a test for selection only with the analysis of longitudinal data in the NCDS. The analysis of Japanese data (see Table 9.5, page 207) did not correct for selection and therefore, in order to maximise comparability, we have not corrected models based on the LFS for Britain.

Wage equations using the LFS

Let us now consider results from wage equations based on the LFS, before looking at the results from a decomposition of the different components of the gender wage gap. The sample and the variables used here have been chosen to provide comparability with Japanese research conducted by Nakata (1997), based on the Basic Survey on Wage Structure – a large, nationally-representative wage survey which is comparable to the LFS. All the variables used in the LFS

Table 9.2: Variables for the Labour Force Survey equations, Britain

Variable	Definition
Wage equations	
Dependent variable	
Log monthly wage	Gross wage per month worked (including overtime)
Explanatory variables	
Age	Age
Squared age	Squared age
Education	Reference category = age when completed full-time education is 16 or less
17-18	Dummy = 1 if age when completed full-time education is 17 or 18
Over 18	Dummy = 1 if age when completed full-time education is over 18 but no degree
Degree	Dummy = 1 if age when completed full-time education is over 18 and hold degree
Years in this job	Years of service with current employer
Squared years in this job	Squared years of service with current employer
Actual working hours	Actual monthly working hours excluding overtime
Number of employees	Dummy = 1 if workplace with more than 50
Industries	Reference category = manufacturing
Mining	Dummy = 1 if industry = mining or quarrying
Construction	Dummy = 1 if industry = construction
Transport	Dummy = 1 if industry = transport, storage and communication
Wholesale	Dummy = 1 if industry = wholesale, retail and motor trade
Finance	Dummy = 1 if industry = financial intermediation
Electricity	Dummy = 1 if industry = electricity gas and motor trade
Service	Dummy = 1 if industry = hotels, restaurants, other community, social and personal
Public	Dummy = 1 if industry = public administration, defence, education, health and social work
Manager	Dummy = 1 if work as manager, foreman or supervisor
Union member	Dummy = 1 if is a union member
South East	Dummy = 1 if work in South East
Participation equations	
Dependent variable	
Full-timer or not	Women in full-time employment =1 Otherwise = 0
Explanatory variables	
Age	Age
Squared age	Squared age
Education	Reference category = age when completed full-time education is 16 or less
17-18	Dummy = 1 if age when completed full-time education is 17 or 18
Over 18	Dummy = 1 if age when completed full-time education is over 18 but no degree
Degree	Dummy = 1 if age when completed full-time education is over 18 and hold degree
Single/divorced	Dummy = 1 if single or divorced
House tenure	Dummy = 1 if household owns house
Kid 4	Dummy = 1 if family has dependent child aged 4 or less
Kid 9	Dummy = 1 if family has dependent child aged between 5 and 9

analysis have been recorded to be as similar as possible to the Japanese research. Table 9.2 shows the variables used in the wage equations and their definition.

Specification of variables

The dependent variable is the log of gross monthly wage including overtime. It is based on gross weekly pay which has been multiplied by 4.33 (52 weeks/ 12 months) to translate into monthly pay. It differs from the Japanese data by the inclusion of overtime pay, although both analyses include number of hours worked during the month.

Educational qualifications have been recorded to give functional comparability with the Japanese analysis. Japanese educational classifications are based on the schooling or duration of schooling, rather than qualifications. The new variables are based on age when full-time education is completed. The lowest level of education is 'full-time education completed at 16 years of age or less', and the next level is 'age 17 or 18 on leaving full-time education'. 'Over 18 without degree' is considered to be similar to graduation from junior colleges and special training schools in Japan, while 'over 18 with degree' is comparable to 'University' in Japan.

Age and years of service with current employer are both included as single years. Squared terms of the two variables are also included because the rate of earnings over age and over years in the job is not linear.

Industries are divided into nine groups which are comparable with Japan. The public sector covers education, health and social work and public administration and defence. The service industry contains hotels and restaurants, and other community, social and personal services activities. Real estate, agriculture, fishing and employment in private households are omitted to retain comparability with the Japanese research. In Britain, most regional variation in earnings is captured by including a dummy variable to represent London and the South East, although the Japanese research uses 11 regions.

See later for an analysis of these variables in relation to the NCDS, as well as a discussion of their rationale.

Results from wage equations

Table 9.3 reports the estimates of the earnings equations for full-time women and men based on the LFS. For women, we give both the uncorrected estimates and the estimates corrected for selectivity bias. However, the decomposition uses only the uncorrected estimates – consistent with the Japanese analysis. All coefficients except union member and construction are significant for men. For women, all variables except construction, electricity and public industry employment are significant at a 5% confidence level.

Educational qualifications. For men and women, education appears as a major determinant of earnings with a particularly high premium on a degree-level qualification.

Age. The positive coefficients for age and the negative coefficients for age

Table 9.3: Log monthly pay: full-time men–women for Great Britain, based on the Labour Force Survey

	Uncorrected				Corrected		Means	
	Men	t-value	Women	t-value	Women	t-value	Men	Women
Log monthly pay							7.32	7.02
Constant	5.1865	110.943	5.1988	87.627	5.4184	82.727		
Age	0.0784	32.804	0.0608	19.693	0.0605	19.263	39.16	37.27
Age squared	−0.0009	−30.172	−0.0007	−18.188	−0.0007	−17.133	1,662.91	1,511.65
Years in this job	0.0147	11.583	0.0154	8.284	0.0142	7.714	8.99	7.25
Squared years in this job	−0.0002	−6.339	−0.0002	−3.572	−0.0002	−3.249	163.18	105.38
17/18	0.1500	15.040	0.1823	16.382	0.1495	12.483	0.19	0.27
Over 18 no degree	0.2515	9.649	0.4036	17.956	0.3339	13.620	0.02	0.04
Over 18 with degree	0.4310	36.608	0.5624	40.976	0.4873	29.456	0.16	0.17
Working hours	0.0009	11.124	0.0011	9.067	0.0011	8.941	162.90	151.80
Manager	0.2370	29.484	0.2120	21.790	0.2107	21.885	0.36	0.34
Size	0.1276	15.523	0.1063	11.093	0.1004	10.557	0.61	0.58
Mining	0.2353	5.604	0.2729	3.122	0.2584	2.983	0.01	0.00
Construction	0.0176	1.301	0.0485	1.289	0.0432	1.161	0.10	0.02
Transportation	−0.0429	−3.336	0.0638	2.725	0.0549	2.366	0.11	0.05
Wholesale	−0.1122	−9.083	−0.1137	−6.732	−0.1163	−6.968	0.13	0.13
Finance	0.1850	9.845	0.1415	7.088	0.1299	6.555	0.05	0.08
Electricity	0.0518	1.601	0.1011	1.923	0.0885	1.697	0.01	0.01
Service industry	−0.2550	−15.152	−0.1753	−9.009	−0.1709	−8.870	0.06	0.08
Public industry	−0.0679	−5.97	−0.0101	−0.733	−0.0115	−0.849	0.19	0.45
Union member	−0.0044	−0.505	0.1130	10.365	0.1126	10.433	0.36	0.37
Working in South East	0.1503	18.355	0.1805	18.193	0.1793	18.259	0.34	0.35
Lambda					−0.1958			
Adj R²	0.3874		0.4376					
n	12663		7385		7366			
F	401.39		288.30					

squared, for men and women, indicate that earnings initially increase with age then decline. However, the larger coefficients for men indicate that earnings increase more sharply than for women and, at older ages, decrease more sharply. These results are also replicated in plots of mean earnings by age (Figure 9.1).

Years of service. As for age, the positive coefficients for years of service with the same employer, and negative coefficients for the square of the terms, indicate that earnings initially increase with years in service and then decline. In Great Britain, we do not expect years of service to correlate strongly with age although, as men on average have longer service than women, any correlation will be greater for men.

Work hours. As expected, longer working hours result in greater monthly earnings. Its positive effect is larger for women than for men.

Size of firm, industry, management and union membership. As expected, employment in a large workplace and holding a management position are both positively correlated with pay, but men get more reward from them than women. For men and women, employment in the service sector and the wholesale sector

Figure 9.1: The age-hourly earnings profile: full-timers in Great Britain (1998-99)

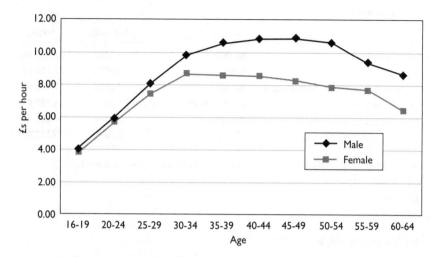

Note: This graph refers to people aged 18-65.

Source: Labour Force Survey (1998-99)

have large negative impacts on earnings, by comparison with manufacturing (the reference category) while mining and the financial sector have significant positive effects. Trade union membership is beneficial for women but not significant for men. (This is an unexpected finding and not replicated in work using a fuller model; Sugihashi, forthcoming.)

South East. Working in the South East, as expected, confers a positive premium to pay for both men and women.

Decomposition of LFS equations

Table 9.4 shows the results from a decomposition of the earnings equations (the method is described in Box 2, page 196). The predicted monthly wage for women is 74.0% of the male wage and the wage gap is therefore 26.0%.

Table 9.4(a) reports the logged and unlogged wages for men [1] and women [2], and the gender wage gap [4] (7.3082-7.0073=0.3009, which is £387.84, or 26.0% of the male monthly wage). Table 9.4(a) also shows estimated log wages and the wage in pounds for decomposed categories of the gender wage gap. The log of non-discriminatory women's wage [3] is 7.2728, and represents the wages that would be paid based on female endowments but using male, rather than female, market returns. This, therefore, represents the amount that women would get paid if they got the same returns as men. On this assumption, women could get £335.89 more per month – the amount of the wage gap due to women being paid less than men for the same qualities or endowments [6].

The gender wage gap is decomposed into the part which results from the

Table 9.4: Decomposition of full-time men–women monthly earnings gap using Labour Force Survey, Great Britain

(a) Decomposition

		log wage	wage
[1] Male hourly wage	**B**m**X**m	7.3082	£1,492.46
[2] Female hourly wage	**B**f**X**f	7.0073	£1,104.63
[3] Non-discriminatory female wage	**B**m**X**f	7.2728	£1,440.52
[4] Gender wage gap	**B**m**X**m-**B**f**X**f	0.3009	£387.84
[5] Wage gap of endowments	**B**m(**X**m-**X**f)	0.0354	£51.94
[6] Wage gap of market return	(**B**m-**B**f)**X**f	0.2655	£335.89

Note: The last column in [1]–[3] is calculated by exponent of log wage. [4]–[5] is drawn by:

[4] = [1]-[2] = [5]+[6]

[5] = [1]-[3]

[6] = [3]-[2]

(b) Decomposition by variables

	Gap of endowments Bm(Xm-Xf)		Gap of market return (Bm-Bf)Xf		Gender wage gap BmXm-BfXf	
	log	%	log	%	log	%
Constant			−0.0124	−1.067	−0.0124	−1.067
Age	0.0146	1.26	0.4170	36.01	0.4317	37.28
Educational qualification	−0.0241	−2.08	−0.0382	−3.29	−0.0623	−5.38
Years in this job	0.0112	0.97	−0.0059	−0.51	0.0054	0.46
Monthly working hours	0.0102	0.88	−0.0258	−2.23	−0.0156	−1.34
Size of the firm	0.0039	0.34	0.0123	1.06	0.0162	1.40
Industry	0.0181	1.56	−0.0357	−3.08	−0.0176	−1.52
Managerial position	0.0035	0.30	0.0085	0.74	0.0120	1.04
Union	0.0001	0.01	−0.0439	−3.79	−0.0438	−3.78
Working in South East	−0.0021	−0.19	−0.0106	−0.91	−0.0127	−1.10
Total (log)	0.0354	3.06	0.2655	22.93	0.3009	25.99

Note: The constant would be changed by choosing a different base for a particular group of dummy variables. Therefore, the amount of market returns of constant and dummy variables would be altered. See Leslie et al (2001).

difference in 'endowments', or productivity-related characteristics (0.0354, or 12% of the total gap) and the part due to the difference in market return for men and women for those characteristics (0.2655, or 88%). The total explained gap (12%) is much less than the total unexplained gap (88%) which accords with earlier research in the UK (Dolton and Kidd, 1994; Harkness, 1996; Dale and Egerton, 1997; Paci and Joshi, 1998).

Table 9.4(b) shows the explained and unexplained portions broken down by the variables used in the wage equations. It also shows the contribution which each variable makes to the total gender wage gap (26.0%). The difference in pay due to the differences in men's and women's endowments is shown in the first column. It comprises only a 3% difference (0.0354 logged pounds). Negative values indicate that women have higher productivity characteristics than men. Thus women's higher education and greater likelihood of working in the South East reduce the wage gap, while men tend to be employed in the higher-paid industries and bring more years of age to the workplace. However, the endowments are not strikingly different for men and women.

The second column shows that part of the gender gap that arises from the different market return of each variable. It also includes the difference in the value on the constant for men and women. This portion is unexplained by an individual's characteristics or endowments and is assumed to be due to discrimination. The gender wage gap caused by this different treatment is 22.9% representing 88% of the total wage gap. A positive sign means that men are better paid than women for the same characteristics, or, that there is labour market discrimination against women. The difference on the constant represents a 'gender' difference that remains after including market returns on endowments. The very small negative value means that, unusually, women are rewarded more than men but that this contributes only a 1% difference in earnings. The biggest impact on the gender wage gap is age. Men are better-paid by £1.52 per month (0.4170 logged pounds) more than women of the same age. Trade union membership, type of industry, educational qualifications, working hours, length of service and working in the South East are all positively rewarded for women and reduce the gender wage gap.

Our estimates indicate that, although education, union membership and working hours are all advantageous to female pay, in total, men gain a much greater return for age than women. Possible explanations for the big effect of age are, firstly, that work experience has not been included and therefore age may reflect years of work experience – found by many researchers to be one of the most important influences on the gender wage gap. However, it may also reflect a substantial lifetime earnings gap between women and men (see Joshi and Davies, Chapter Six, this volume) and thus indicate the penalty that women still pay in the British labour market for being a wife and mother. Thirdly, it may reflect the recent increase in performance related pay and decentralised pay systems in Britain, which may allow personal characteristics to play a larger role in pay determination.

Gender wage differentials in Japan: results from published materials

We begin our discussion of Japanese gender wage differentials with a review of research findings (Yashiro, 1980; Horn-Kawashima, 1985; Higuchi, 1991; Tomita, 1992; Osawa, 1995; Nakata, 1997; Mitani, 1997) and then focus on those of Nakata (1997).

Japan is characterised as a company-centred society that, unlike other developed countries, has a labour market with little regulation by government and little protection from unions. This magnifies Japanese gender inequalities such as men's long working hours and women's concentration in part-time work or domestic work, and leads to large wage differentials between women and men (Osawa, 1993; Kinoshita, 1998). Japan is notorious for having the largest gender wage gap among industrialised countries. Lawsuits against sexual discrimination on the basis of wages have become increasingly frequent in the past decade. At the same time, numerous attempts have been made to analyse gender wage differentials.

Specification of variables

The main hypotheses or theories underlying the Japanese social and economic literature fall into two groups: labour market segmentation, and post-entry human capital differences caused by statistical discrimination. The former assumes that gender wage differentials are the consequence of segmented labour markets where women are confined to low-paid labour markets. The latter assumes that the pay gap results from gender differences in human capital investment by companies. This arises because employers are more likely to exclude women from training on the grounds that they are likely to leave a company earlier than men.

The usual control variables include age, educational qualifications, seniority (the length of service in the same company), number of employees and industry. In addition, a few studies include occupation, region and union membership. The more restricted set of explanatory variables, by comparison with British analyses, is due to the limited amount of information in Japanese surveys.

Results of wage equations

It is generally argued that, in Japan, seniority and age play an important role in the gender pay gap, with age being the more important (Higuchi, 1991; Tomita, 1992; Nakata, 1997). These variables are important because Japanese companies generally have a seniority-based wage system which is available only to male workers. However, for men, they are likely to be highly correlated in Japan.

Like Britain, educational qualifications are also one of the major determinants of wage levels; their effect is found to be greater for women than men by Higuchi (1991) and Nakata (1997), while Tomita (1992) finds the reverse to be true. Qualifications are important in wage determination because they are a key factor for employment in larger companies, and in determining training and promotion. The presence of a labour union in a company is positive for women but negative for men (Nakata, 1997) and reduces female-male wage differentials (Mitani, 1997). Being in a managerial position has a significant positive impact on wages (Nakata, 1997) as does employment in a large firm. Industries are classified as manufacturing, mining, building, transportation, retailing, finance and insurance, electricity, gas and water, and service. The industry with the largest effect for men is finance and insurance, followed by electricity, gas and water. For women, however, it is electricity, gas and water, followed by the service industry. Every industry increases earnings by comparison with manufacturing (Nakata, 1997).

Results of decomposition

There are two opposing views on the main determinants of the gender pay gap in Japan. One is that the gap is mainly explained by women having lower productivity-related characteristics than men. In particular they are younger and have fewer years of service in the same company. Yashiro (1980) argues that three variables, educational qualifications, service in the same company and size of company explained 64% of the Japanese gender pay gap in 1976. According to Tomita (1992), 69% of wage differentials in 1987 were explained by five attributes (educational qualifications, occupations, service in the same company, work experience, and size of company).

The other view is that unequal pay is explained by labour market inequalities rather than gender differences in endowments. Horn-Kawashima (1985) suggests that gender differences in labour market return on endowments (education, age and seniority) is the main cause of the gender pay gap in blue-collar jobs, while for white-collar jobs the productivity-related characteristics are most important. Nakata (1997) finds that 64.2% of the gender wage gap is due to differences in endowments, and 35.8% is attributed to differences in labour market returns. However, he notes the big contribution of age to the gender difference in market returns and argues that most of the gap can be explained by the differences in the way men and women are rewarded for age.

If women had the same endowments as men, the decomposition technique shows that women's full-time average earnings as a proportion of men's would rise from 57% to 82% after controlling on four variables (years in education, the size of company, years in service under the same employer, and age), or 86% after allowing for five variables (years in education, occupation, the size of company, years in service with the same employer, and years since leaving education).

However, we should not overlook the fact that the Japanese employment system, which used to be characterised as employment for life with seniority-based promotion and a seniority-based wage system, discriminates against women in job assignment, promotion and training. It also compels female workers, directly or indirectly, to retire at marriage or at a younger age than men, although some women might be less motivated to continue to work than men (Okuyama, 1993; Working Women's Network, 1997).

Table 9.5 shows the result of the decomposition conducted by Nakata using data from the Basic Survey on Wage Structure for full-time employed men and women in 1993. The female wage is 52.3% of the male wage (the wage gap is 47.7%). This wage gap is decomposed into the part due to the difference in characteristics or endowments of men and women (56.4%) and that part explained by different labour market returns for women and men (43.6%). The portion explained by endowments thus accounts for the majority of the gender wage gap in Japan.

Table 9.5: Decomposition of full-time men–women monthly earnings gap in Japan

(a) Decomposition

		log wage	wage
[1] Male hourly wage	**Bm Xm**	8.1165	¥334,928
[2] Female hourly wage	**Bf Xf**	7.4679	¥175,093
[3] Non-discriminatory female wage	**Bm Xf**	7.7504	¥232,250
[4] Gender wage gap	**Bm Xm-Bf Xf**	0.6486	¥159,835
[5] Wage gap of endowments	**Bm(Xm-Xf)**	0.3661	¥102,678
[6] Wage gap of market return	**(Bm-Bf)Xf**	0.2825	¥57,158

NB. The last column in [1]~[3] is calculated by exponent of log wage. [4]~[5] is drawn by:

[4]=[1]-[2]=[5]+[6]

[5]=[1]-[3]

[6]=[3]-[2]

Source: Nakata (1997, p 187)

(b) Decomposition by variables

	Gap of endowments Bm(Xm-Xf)		Gap of market return (Bm-Bf)Xf		Gender wage gap BmXm-BfXf	
	log	%	log	%	log	%
Constant			-0.5370	-39.51	-0.537	-39.51
Age	0.1581	11.63	0.9545	70.23	1.1126	81.86
Educational qualification	0.0410	3.02	-0.0318	-2.34	0.0092	0.68
Years in this job	0.1083	7.97	-0.0598	-4.40	0.0485	3.57
Monthly working hours	0.0003	0.02	-0.0783	-5.76	-0.078	-5.74
Largest size of firm	0.0078	0.57	0.0199	1.46	0.0277	2.04
Industry	-0.0029	-0.21	-0.0035	-0.26	-0.0064	-0.47
Managerial position	0.0495	3.64	0.0005	0.04	0.0500	3.68
Union	-0.0005	-0.034	-0.0148	-1.09	-0.0153	-1.13
Region	0.0045	0.33	0.0328	2.41	0.0373	2.74
Total (log)	0.3661	26.94	0.2825	20.79	0.6486	47.72

Note: The constant would be changed by choosing a different base for a particular group of dummy variables. Therefore, the amount of market returns of constant and dummy variables would be altered. See Leslie, D., Clark, K. and Drinkwater, S. (2001) "Decomposing Rewards in Earnings Functions" (unpublished).

Sources: Nakata (1997, p 187)

Comparing these results with Britain (Table 9.4), it is evident that the gender wage gap is much bigger in Japan (47.7%) than Britain (26.0%) for full-time earnings. A much larger component of the Japanese gap is explained by differences in characteristics or 'endowments' (56%) by comparison with Britain (12%).

Table 9.5(b) reports the decomposition in which explained and unexplained portions are broken down by each variable and in logged yen (¥). The first column shows the gender gap based on the difference in pay due to the different characteristics of men and women. Age and length of service with a current employer (seniority) are the variables where the gender gap is greatest. The second column indicates the gap due to labour market returns, which is assumed to be labour market discrimination. It is apparent that men are much better rewarded for years of age than women – 70.23% of the gender wage gap due to difference in returns is explained by age.

Looking at the different components of the wage gap (Table 9.5(b)) for Japan, we can see that, as expected, age has the largest impact on the wage gap, increasing the overall difference by 82%. In Britain, age also has the largest effect, although this is much less than in Japan. In both Japan and Britain, women are rewarded slightly better than men for the number of years spent in their current job.

Figure 9.2: Decomposition of female wage in Japan and Britain (male wage = 100%)

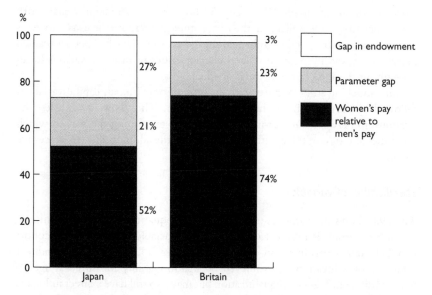

Source: Graph for Japan is based on estimates by Nakata (1997); Graph for Britain is based on our analysis of the LFS (1998/99)

Wage equations using the NCDS

We now move on to report results based on wage equations for full-time women and men using data from the NCDS (a cohort of men and women born in 1958 for whom earning information relates to 1991 when they were aged 33). In this analysis we focus on a full set of factors expected to influence current earnings from employment.

Why longitudinal data?

The ability to fully capture human capital variables is very important for assessing gender differences in earnings and is often not well measured. Using a prospective longitudinal study means that we can use relatively precise and detailed human capital variables that would not otherwise be available. For example, the score on tests at age 11 is more precise than is possible with a retrospective survey because the data do not depend upon recall. Of particular interest, we are able to establish whether family background and parental characteristics continue to have an effect on earnings at age 33, and whether the effect is different for men and women. Thus we are able to establish the effect of influences measured at different points in the individual's life course on outcomes in adulthood.

A longitudinal study also enables us to impute missing data by substituting similar variables from earlier sweeps, if the variables are missing in later sweeps but important for the analysis. Furthermore, the availability of retrospective work history data in NCDS sweep 5 allows us to calculate actual work experience that is not available in the LFS. Although there are the usual problems of recall with retrospective information, most other data has been obtained prospectively, and therefore it reflects characteristics recorded at various stages throughout the life course of the individual.

Our modelling strategy starts with analyses of only human capital variables, followed by current job and household location. This allows us to assess the relationship between each group of variables by examining the way in which the values and sign of the coefficients change by the addition of each successive block.

Specification of variables

Table 9.6 shows the variables used in the wage equations and their definition.

The first group is related to human capital variables. Whether the cohort member's father was in a non-manual occupation is likely to have an indirect influence on education and achieved occupation; ability measured at age 11 has an indirect influence on qualification but may also still have a direct influence on level of pay. Educational qualifications, having received work-related training of more than three days, and length of service with the current employer, are all expected to have a direct impact on a workers' productivity. The last three variables in particular give an employee general and/or firm-specific skills.

Table 9.6: Variables for wage equations: NCDS

Variable	Definition
Dependent variable	
Log hourly wage	Gross wage per hour worked (including overtime)
Explanatory variables	
Human capital	
Non-manual father	Dummy = 1 if father's socio-economic class is non-manual
Ability at age 11	Ability measured in a school test at age 11
Educational qualification	Reference category = no qualifications
Degree	Dummy = 1 if highest educational qualification = university degree
Over 18	Dummy = 1 if highest educational qualification = vocational higher education
A-levels	Dummy = 1 if highest educational qualification level = A-level
O-levels	Dummy = 1 if highest educational qualification level = O-level
Training	Dummy = 1 if ever had any work-related training course since March 1981
Years in this job	Years of service with current employer
Actual work experience	Total number of years in paid work
Current job	
Public sector	Dummy = 1 if work in the public sector
Number of employees	Reference category = establishment with 1-25 employees
Middle-size firm	Dummy = 1 if establishment employs 26-99 people
Large-size firm	Dummy = 1 if establishment employs more than 100
Occupations	Reference category = unskilled occupation
Professionals	Dummy = 1 if job = professionals and senior administrators
Teachers	Dummy = 1 if job = teaching and training (except universities)
Nurses	Dummy = 1 if job = welfare and nursing
Other intermediate	Dummy = 1 if job = other intermediate non-manual occupations
Clerical	Dummy = 1 if job = clerical work
Service and shop	Dummy = 1 if job = routine service or retail, eg shop assistant
Skilled occupations	Dummy = 1 if job = skilled manual, eg hairdresser
Semi-skilled occupations	Dummy = 1 if job = semi-skilled
Hours flexible	Dummy = 1 if employee can vary the time to start and finish working
Non-standard hours work	Dummy = 1 if has to work between 6pm-7am at least once a month
Weekend work	Dummy = 1 if work during weekend at least once a month
Training paid by firm	Dummy = 1 if training has been financed by employer
Promotion	Dummy = 1 if ever promoted while working for current employer
Union member	Dummy = 1 if is a union member
Occupational segregation	Dummy = 1 if percentage of women in occupation is more than 50%
Household location	
South East	Dummy = 1 if live in South East at 1991
Travel-to-work	Reference category = less than 15 minutes
Travel-to-work (15-45min)	Dummy = 1 if spends 15-44 minutes to travel from home to work
Travel to work (45min+)	Dummy = 1 if spends more than 45 minutes to travel to workplace

From the mean values (final column in Tables 9.8 and 9.9) we see that women working full time have a higher ability score at age 11 and are more likely than men to have qualifications. However, they have fewer years with their current employer and fewer years work experience in total.

The second group of variables is related to the cohort member's current job. Although these variables are conventionally regarded as demand-side factors, in order not to overestimate discrimination we are assuming that employees choose these jobs.

The public sector is expected to be more egalitarian in terms of recruitment policy and equal opportunities and also to have a formalised wage determination system. In much of the public sector rates of pay are negotiated at a national level. Women may therefore choose to work in the public sector rather than the private sector as they may expect to get more equitable treatment. The mean values (final column of Tables 9.8 and 9.9) that women are more likely than men to work in the public sector. Large firms or organisations are more likely to have a bureaucratic structure and higher rates of pay than smaller firms. They are also more likely to be unionised.

Occupation is included as it is assumed that women choose their occupation based on a number of factors including the qualifications required, working hours and flexibility. Variables related to working conditions and labour market segmentation are intended to compensate for the job's amenities or disamenities. It includes weekend working, non-standard hours or shift-work, and flexibility of working hours. Although weekend working and shift-working require unsocial hours and may be expected to pay more as compensation, flexibility may be seen as a bonus by many workers, especially women, who may accept lower wages in exchange. Training paid by the firm and promotion could be regarded as a proxy for human capital. However, it is also more likely to be provided in an internal labour market to core workers who are expected to benefit from it through increased productivity. Membership of a trade union is likely to result in higher pay – although pay deals negotiated by the union apply to all the workers covered by the agreement, whether a member of the union or not. An occupation is classified as feminised if more than 50% of employees are female. Feminisation may result from 'crowding' if it is assumed that women are forced into these occupations; alternatively, if women choose a feminised occupation it may be seen as individual preferences.

Finally, household location is designed to capture the better earning prospects in London and the South East, including the additional allowance added by many national employers for the cost of working in London. It also captures the higher living cost in the South East. The amount of time spent travelling from home to the workplace indicates the scope of the labour market within which the individual is willing or able to work and will therefore be influenced by domestic responsibilities. Women with children are often reluctant or unable to travel long distances because of childcare commitments. The presence of child and partner is also thought to affect earnings (Waldfogel, 1997). However, these variables are used in the sample selection equation and are not included in the wage equation.

We begin by discussing the results of the participation equation that models the predictors of working full-time versus not working full-time for women. We then move on to consider the wage equations.

Results from the participation equation

The participation equation includes all the variables in the wage equation except those relating to the current job, and also additional variables which are likely to influence whether or not a woman is in full-time employment. The additional variables include the presence or absence of a partner, having a working partner, the presence of a self-employed partner, the presence of a pre-school child, the presence of a child aged between five and nine, fertility intentions, and home ownership. The results of the probit are presented in Table 9.7. The coefficient of λ – the correction term – in the final wage equation is insignificant. This is a common finding (Zabalza and Arrufat, 1985; Dale and Egerton, 1997; Paci and Joshi, 1998), and suggests that the coefficients in the wage equation are not significantly biased by sample selection for women in full-time employment. Decomposition analysis of earnings, therefore, will be based on the uncorrected estimates.

From the participation equation we see that, as expected, women with qualifications at A-level or higher are significantly more likely to work full-time than those with lower or no qualifications. Receiving at least three days training, years in the current job and total years of work experience all have strong positive effects. For women, these latter two variables are likely to be strong predictors of labour force commitment. As expected, the presence of young children also has strong negative effects.

Results from wage equations

Tables 9.8 and 9.9 present the result of the wage equations for men and women, respectively. Gross log hourly earnings, including overtime, are used as the dependent variable. In the NCDS, earnings are collected only for persons who are currently employed. Women's full-time hourly earnings, in the sample used here, are 85% those of men (=4.77/5.61). This is higher than the figure of 81.6% for full-time employees nationally in 1991. The difference may reflect the fact that the NCDS is a single age cohort and may also reflect some differential attrition. The focus of the analysis here is on those who are currently employed and have sufficient information to enter the wage equations. Columns one to three in Tables 9.8 and 9.9 represent three different models which include, successively, additional blocks of variables. In Table 9.9 the fourth column provides the results for model three corrected for sample selection bias. We discuss each model in turn.

Table 9.7: Variables and result of the NCDS participation equations

(a) Participation equations

Variable	Definition
Dependent variable	
Full-timer or not	Women in full-time employment = 1; otherwise = 0
Explanatory variables	
Non-manual father	Dummy = 1 if father's socio-economic class is non-manual
Ability at age 11	Ability measured in a school test at age 11
Educational qualification	Reference category = no qualifications
Degree	Dummy = 1 if highest educational qualification = university degree
Over 18	Dummy = 1 if highest educational qualification = vocational higher education
A-levels	Dummy = 1 if highest educational qualification level = A-level
O-levels	Dummy = 1 if highest educational qualification level = O-level
Training	Dummy = 1 if ever had any work-related training course since March 1981.
Years in this job	Years of service with current employer
No partner	Dummy = 1 if has no partner
Partner working	Dummy = 1 if a partner is working
Partner self-employed	Dummy = 1 if a partner is self-employed
Fertility	Dummy = 1 if have fertility intention
House tenure	Dummy = 1 if household owns house
Kid 4	Dummy = 1 if family has dependent child aged 4 or less
Kid 9	Dummy = 1 if family has dependent child aged between 5 and 9
South East	Dummy = 1 if live in South East at 1991

(b) Result of participation equation

	Coefficient	t-value
Non-manual father	−0.0681	−1.420
Ability at age 11	−0.0002	−0.115
Degree	0.7431	7.868
Over 18	0.3861	4.618
A-levels	0.3414	3.830
O-levels	0.9340	1.490
Training	0.5342	11.032
Years in this job	0.0889	16.938
No partner	0.3124	2.927
Partner working	0.1540	1.510
Partner self-employed	−0.1989	−1.703
Fertility	−0.0437	−0.959
House tenure	−0.0626	−1.042
Kid 4	−1.4877	−26.840
Kid 9	−0.9644	−16.603
South East	−0.0373	−0.661
Log likelihood	−2,230.129	

Table 9.8: Log hourly pay: full-time men for Great Britain, based on the NCDS

	Human capital		Current job		Home location		Mean of X
	B	t-value	B	t-value	B	t-value	
Constant	1.1464	29.821	1.1228	24.604	1.0675	23.526	
Non-manual father	0.0597	4.758	0.0438	3.528	0.0364	2.988	0.413
Ability at 11	0.0035	7.427	0.0020	4.359	0.0021	4.636	45.012
Degree	0.3757	15.373	0.2781	10.684	0.2749	10.76	0.160
Over 18	0.2275	10.28	0.1454	6.423	0.1520	6.84	0.129
A-level	0.1554	8.278	0.1167	6.241	0.1173	6.397	0.220
O-level	0.0932	5.292	0.0758	4.378	0.0776	4.573	0.254
Training	0.1324	10.175	0.0913	6.907	0.0874	6.745	0.645
Seniority	0.0027	2.491	0.0001	0.114	0.0008	0.722	7.454
Actual work experience	0.0052	2.532	0.0060	3.037	0.0065	3.314	15.153
Public sector			−0.0286	−2.045	−0.0295	−2.154	0.287
Middle-size establishment			0.0879	5.281	0.0777	4.752	0.250
Large-size establishment			0.1557	10.273	0.1401	9.385	0.513
Professionals			0.1003	2.86	0.1033	3.003	0.074
Teachers			0.0876	1.929	0.0983	2.212	0.033
Nurses			0.0626	1.251	0.0824	1.673	0.020
Other intermediate			0.1246	4.303	0.1112	3.91	0.299
Clerical			−0.0324	−0.846	−0.0297	−0.791	0.053
Service and shop			0.0147	0.306	0.0084	0.18	0.021
Skilled occupations			−0.0002	−0.006	0.0038	0.14	0.329
Semi-skilled occupations			−0.1064	−3.474	−0.0934	−3.107	0.122
Hours flexible			0.0571	4.329	0.0505	3.894	0.340
Non-standard hours work			0.0663	5.139	0.0633	5.007	0.663
Weekend-working			−0.0805	−6.34	−0.0658	−5.257	0.561
Training paid by employer			0.0012	0.056	0.0053	0.251	0.084
If you are promoted			0.0417	3.192	0.0384	2.992	0.538
Union member			0.0132	0.996	0.0215	1.651	0.453
Feminised occupations			−0.0462	−2.521	−0.0438	−2.445	0.167
South East					0.1174	8.153	0.197
Travel-to-work (15-45min)					0.0195	1.563	0.445
Travel-to-work (45min+)					0.1055	6.135	0.168
Adj R²	**0.2436**		**0.3323**		**0.3605**		
n	3218		3025		3007		
F	116.12		56.73		57.49		

Table 9.9: Log hourly pay: full-time women for Great Britain, based on the NCDS

	Human capital		Current job		Home location uncorrected		Home location corrected		Mean of X
	B	t-value	B	t-value	B	t-value	B	t-value	
Constant	0.9212	22.584	1.1228	16.412	1.0768	15.969	1.0314	13.931	
Non-manual father	0.0484	2.991	0.0412	2.558	0.0329	2.081	0.0322	2.031	0.418
Ability at age 11	0.0037	5.744	0.0022	3.394	0.0022	3.586	0.0023	3.672	48.644
Degree	0.3471	11.349	0.2440	6.932	0.2263	6.535	0.2382	6.726	0.180
Over 18	0.2207	7.807	0.1976	6.203	0.1954	6.249	0.1975	6.295	0.153
A-level	0.1438	4.825	0.1104	3.589	0.1080	3.566	0.1133	3.717	0.132
O-level	0.0215	0.942	0.0208	0.865	0.0221	0.936	0.0188	0.800	0.353
Training	0.2058	11.990	0.1499	8.403	0.1356	7.720	0.1427	7.688	0.633
Seniority	0.0077	5.006	0.0053	3.038	0.0058	3.437	0.0058	3.404	6.455
Actual work experience	0.0053	2.267	0.0048	2.044	0.0039	1.691	0.0052	2.093	13.752
Public sector			0.0022	0.118	0.0061	0.326	0.0043	0.230	0.437
Middle-size establishment			0.0445	2.119	0.0395	1.913	0.0405	1.976	0.248
Large-size establishment			0.1007	5.369	0.0875	4.730	0.0915	4.972	0.463
Professionals			0.0709	1.043	0.0707	1.063	0.0667	1.014	0.034
Teachers			0.0403	0.672	0.0535	0.909	0.0525	0.902	0.101
Nurses			–0.0785	–1.354	–0.0693	–1.221	–0.0682	–1.214	0.132
Other intermediate			–0.0678	–1.261	–0.0728	–1.383	–0.0689	–1.323	0.223
Clerical			–0.1137	–2.077	–0.1132	–2.111	–0.1157	–2.183	0.288
Service and shop			–0.1594	–2.457	–0.1664	–2.614	–0.1655	–2.634	0.040
Skilled occupations			–0.1492	–2.502	–0.1399	–2.395	–0.1374	–2.372	0.067
Semi-skilled occupations			–0.2466	–4.235	–0.2280	–3.995	–0.2308	–4.08	0.094
Hours flexible			0.0012	0.069	–0.0016	–0.096	0.0014	–0.081	0.325
Non-standard hours work			0.0629	3.539	0.0521	2.976	0.0516	2.960	0.470
Weekend-working			–0.1060	–5.84	–0.0892	–4.968	–0.0920	–5.142	0.353
Training paid by employer			0.0491	1.528	0.0458	1.456	0.0433	1.393	0.064
If you are promoted			0.0543	3.105	0.0568	3.314	0.0538	3.138	0.512
Union member			0.0068	0.378	0.0195	1.093	0.0192	1.085	0.464
Feminised occupations			–0.0620	–3.361	–0.0585	–3.237	–0.0580	–3.126	0.628
South East					0.0779	4.143	0.0776	4.143	0.205
Travel-to-work (15-45min)					0.0493	3.036	0.0522	3.227	0.466
Travel-to-work (45min+)					0.1625	6.659	0.1630	6.734	0.139
Lambda							0.0240	1.358	
Adj R^2	**0.3541**		**0.4277**		**0.4519**				
n	1563		1441		1439		1414		
F	96.17		40.86		40.52				

The effect of human capital variables on wages

Father in non-manual occupation and ability. Having a non-manual father and higher scores on school tests at age 11 have significant positive effects on earnings for both men and women and these variables stay significant in all models.

Educational qualification and work-related training course. Educational qualifications have a strong positive effect on wages, and the coefficients remain significant in all models for men and women (with the exception of O-level qualifications, which are not significant for women), by comparison with the reference group – below O-level qualification or no qualifications. Degree-level qualifications have the greatest impact, followed by vocational higher qualifications. The coefficient on educational qualifications is slightly lower for women than for men, suggesting that men gain more from their qualification than women. There are strong positive associations between having received a training course of at least three days duration and wages; this remains significant in all models for men and women. Women have a considerably higher coefficient than men, suggesting that, holding other variables constant, they get a greater return on a training course than men.

Actual work experience and service with current employer. Years of work experience are positive and significant for men, and just as significant in most models for women. For both men and women earnings increase with the length of time with the current employer (seniority). However, the impact on male wages is smaller and becomes insignificant once job characteristics are included in the model. For women, the coefficient remains significant even after adding job-related variables. This suggests that women may gain more benefit than men from remaining with the same employer. However, men may be more likely to change job in order to improve their level of pay. Unlike other human capital endowments, the coefficient remains almost constant in all models. In other words, this variable is not influenced by other productivity characteristics.

Work experience, measured as the total number of years in paid work, has a larger coefficient than seniority for men but a smaller coefficient for women. This is consistent with the idea that men gain more by changing employer, whereas women gain more by staying with the same employer. Overall, the results show significant rewards for human capital endowments. In particular, educational qualifications and having some training appear as major determinants of earnings.

The effect of job-related variables to wages

The coefficients of the earnings equation including job-related variables are presented in the second column.

Public sector and size of firm. The coefficients for working in the public sector are positive for women in full-time employment, although not significant at a 5% level. For men, working in the public sector has a significant negative effect. Other studies have found the public sector to have a significant positive effect for women. However, the coefficients need to be interpreted in the light of the other variables in the equation. For women and men earnings are significantly higher in larger organisations and many of the public sector organisations in which women work will have over 100 employees – the definition of a large organisation.

Occupation. For women, only professional occupations and teaching have a positive coefficient by comparison with the reference category, unskilled occupations. Among men, only professional and other intermediate occupations have significant positive coefficients. At first sight, these results are unexpected, as the raw data show the expected gradients on earnings for men and women. However, we need to consider the effect of other variables in the model which are strongly related to higher level occupations. These include educational qualifications, training and size of organisation. Similar results are found by Paci and Joshi (1998), with teachers, nurses, other intermediate, service and shop, and skilled occupations all having negative but insignificant effects on the earnings of full-time women, compared with semi-skilled and unskilled occupations.

Flexible working time, shift-working and weekend-work. Flexibility is significantly associated with increased male earnings, while it becomes negative for women after including the household location variables and is insignificant in all models for women. The variable refers to the ability to vary the starting and finishing time of work. This should be seen as an 'amenity' of a job and therefore the negative effects for women may be interpreted as women being willing to accept lower wages for the benefits of flexibility. Generally, in the Britain, the ability to vary working hours is associated with higher-level jobs. By contrast, having to work evenings and nights (non-standard work hours) is generally assumed to deserve some pecuniary reward, and therefore the statistically significant positive coefficient for both sexes can be seen as a compensating differential. Weekend-work is found to have a significant negative coefficient in all models for men and women. This is likely to reflect the fact that many low-paid jobs, for example, hotel catering and retail, require weekend-working.

Training paid by the firm and promotion. As expected, training financed by an employer and promotion with the current employer increase earnings for women and men. However, training paid by an employer is not statistically significant, probably because there are very few in this position (8% of men, 6% women). In contrast, promotion is significant for both groups, which is to be expected as it usually involves a pay increase. These effects are greater for women than men.

Union membership. Union membership is positive for men and women but it is not significant at the 5% level.

Feminised occupation. Working in an occupation which is dominated by women reduces earnings not only for women but also for men. However, the effect of this is greater for women rather than for men.

The effect of household location on wages

The coefficients of the earnings equation allowing for household location and travelling time are shown in the third column, and those corrected for sample selectivity in the fourth column.

Living in London and the South East. As expected living in London and the South East has a positive and significant association for both female and male wages. The South East of England has a higher cost of living than other areas, and this is reflected in the earnings of those who live there.

Travel from home to workplace. There are significant positive associations between the time spent travelling to the workplace and earnings, which are higher for women than for men. In general, women have much shorter travel to work times than men and therefore women who spend a long time getting to work are likely to be in high level and well-paying jobs.

In general there are many similarities between these results and those obtained with the LFS analysis. In both, higher educational qualifications, longer length of service, and working in larger size firms have positive effects on wages for women and men. However, there are differences between men and women in some of the productivity-related characteristics. In the LFS, women get more return than men for educational qualifications, but the reverse appears to be the case in the NCDS.

Decomposition of the NCDS equation

From the mean values in Tables 9.8 and 9.9 (last column) we can see that there are differences between full-time working men and women in the 'endowments' which they bring to the labour market. Women are more likely than men to work in smaller firms, have fewer years work experience and less seniority, are more likely to be in a feminised occupation, and less likely to receive training financed by an employer. However, women are more likely to have higher qualifications and have higher ability at age 11. Assuming that these differences in productivity-related characteristics result from individual choice we use the Blinder-Oaxaca decomposition method to find the portion of the wage gap that is attributable to differences in endowments and the portion regarded as due to labour market discrimination.

Table 9.10(a) shows a gender wage gap [4] of £0.81, or 15%. With no discrimination [3], women's wages rise to 97% of men's. This represents the amount that women would get paid if they got the same returns as men. The gender wage gap can be decomposed into that part due to endowments (20.8% of the total gap), and that due to unequal treatment (79.2% of the total gap). This agrees with earlier research that used the NCDS (Paci et al, 1995; Dale and Egerton, 1997; Paci and Joshi, 1998).

Table 9.10(b) gives the results of a decomposition in which explained and unexplained portions are broken down by the variables used in the full model of the wage equation. The first column shows the gender gap based on endowements. It amounts to 0.0324 logged pounds or 20.8% of the total gap.

Table 9.10: Decomposition of full-time men–women hourly earnings gap using NCDS, Great Britain

(a) Decomposition

		log wage	wage
[1] Male hourly wage	**Bm****Xm**	1.6598	£5.26
[2] Female hourly wage	**Bf****Xf**	1.4933	£4.45
[3] Non-discriminatory female wage	**Bm****Xf**	1.6274	£5.09
[4] Gender wage gap	**Bm****Xm-Bf****Xf**	0.1666	£0.81
[5] Wage gap of endowments	**Bm(Xm-Xf)**	0.0324	£0.17
[6] Wage gap of market return	**(Bm-Bf)Xf**	0.1341	£0.64

Note: The last column in [1]~[3] is calculated by exponent of log wage. [4]~[5] is drawn by:

[4]=[1]-[2]=[5]+[6]

[5]=[1]-[3]

[6]=[3]-[2]

(b) Decomposition by variables

	Gap of endowments Bm(Xm-Xf)	Gap of market return (Bm-Bf)Xf	Gender wage gap BmXm-BfXf	% of gap
Constant	0	−0.0093	−0.0093	−5.6
Non-manual father	−0.0002	0.0015	0.0013	0.8
Ability at age 11	−0.0077	−0.0061	−0.0138	−8.3
Education	−0.0065	0.0230	0.0165	9.9
Training	0.0010	−0.0306	−0.0296	−17.7
Seniority	0.0008	−0.0324	−0.0315	−18.9
Work experience	0.0091	0.0349	0.0440	26.4
Public sector	0.0044	−0.0155	−0.0111	−6.7
Firm size	0.0073	0.0338	0.0411	24.7
Occupation	0.0020	0.1200	0.1220	73.2
Hours flexible	0.0008	0.0169	0.0177	10.6
Non-standard hours work	0.0123	0.0052	0.0175	10.5
Weekend-work	−0.0136	0.0083	−0.0053	−3.2
Training paid by employer	0.0001	−0.0026	−0.0025	−1.5
Promotion	0.0010	−0.0095	−0.0085	−5.1
Union member	−0.0002	0.0009	0.0007	0.4
Feminised job	0.0202	0.0092	0.0294	17.7
South east	−0.0009	0.0081	0.0072	4.3
Travel-to-work	0.0026	−0.0218	−0.0192	−11.5
Total (log)	0.0324	0.1341	0.1666	

Note: The constant would be changed by choosing a different base for a particular group of dummy variables. Therefore, amount of market returns of constant and dummy variables would be altered. See Leslie et al (2001).

As before, negative values indicate women have higher productivity characteristics than men. Thus women are more likely to have a father in non-manual employment, to have higher ability and more educational qualifications and are more likely to be members of a union than men. However, in general there are no great differences between the sexes in terms of these characteristics.

The second column shows the unexplained part of the gender gap which is assumed to be due to discrimination. This includes both the difference on the constant and also the difference in labour market returns. A positive sign means that women are paid less than men for the same productivity-characteristics. Broadly speaking, women have an advantage in labour market return for characteristics related to human capital, such as ability at age 11, training, seniority with current employer, training paid by a firm. In addition, women are better paid than men in the public sector, and have a premium on a longer journey from home to workplace. On the other hand, men get a higher return on education, work experience, size of firm and flexible working hours. The biggest effect in favour of male wages is occupation.

To summarise, we have seen that most of the wage gap is due to different or discriminatory treatment of women rather than the characteristics that they bring to the labour market. However, being in a feminised occupation is the largest component in the explained part of the decomposition, and if there was less occupational segregation we might expect this part of the gap to reduce. Of the unexplained part of the wage gap, the largest is due to occupation and suggests that women are less well paid than men for the same occupation.

Overall, analyses of both the LFS and NCDS find that a similar percentage of the pay gap – 12-19% – is due to productivity-characteristics, and a similar percentage – 81-88% – due to discrimination, although the explanatory variables used in the earnings equations differ in each survey. This suggests that our estimates are fairly robust. However, because the NCDS is a single cohort study we cannot observe the impact of age and, in the LFS, this accounts for the largest amount of the unexplained gender wage gap.

Conclusions

In this chapter we have compared the gender pay gap in Britain and Japan for full-time employees using cross-sectional data and analysed in more detail male-female wage differentials in Britain using longitudinal data from the NCDS.

We have seen that the pay gap in Japan is much larger than in Britain – 48% in comparison with 26%. However, more than half of the Japanese female-male wage differential is explained by differences in individual characteristics rather than the difference in labour market return. By contrast, almost all the gender pay gap in Britain is due to differential rewards between men and women.

In Japan, men in full-time work are, on average, considerably older than women, and this, together with seniority, explains a large part of the difference in the characteristics of male and female workers. In Britain there is a relatively small gender difference in age and years with the current employer. Although, formally, the decomposition assumes that differences in characteristics are due to choice, the age difference between men and women working full-time in Japan is in part due to a system which expects women to leave work on marriage or the birth of a child. Similarly, gender differences with regard to length of service with the current employer are influenced by employment structures which assume that women leave the labour market at marriage or childbirth.

In both countries there is a pay gap of about 22% which is unexplained by productivity characteristics and is mainly due to gender differences in reward for years of age. In Japan the seniority-based system means that there is a high correlation between age and years of service with the current employer. This contrasts with a job-based wage system used in many other developed countries. The data used for the Japanese analyses are for 1993, when Japanese economic performance was strong and seniority-based wage systems were still widely used. Nowadays we may find that age and seniority are less important (Kinoshita, 1998). The LFS data correspond to 1999 and in Britain the use of performance-related pay has been increasing. In Britain, Joshi and Davies (Chapter Six, this volume) show that there is a significant lifetime earnings gap between men and women, particularly among less-qualified women, which is the result of time away from full-time employment during family formation. This may be reflected in the effect of age on the British gender pay gap.

In both Japan and Britain education is a major determinant of earnings for both women and men, although in Britain, unlike Japan, women working full-time are better qualified than men. In Japan, women are more likely than men to take a two-year course at 'junior college' rather than a four-year degree course. In both countries, however, women get higher returns from the labour market for their qualifications. The effect of length of service is similar in both countries, and rewards women slightly more than men. The impact of being in a trade union is positive for women in both countries.

However, these models do not fully capture gender wage discrimination in the two countries. In Japan there is likely to be more serious gender stereotyping or discrimination in the workplace than in Britain. For example most Japanese companies have established job categories, such as management positions, to which women are almost never appointed. Even within the same job category, women tend to be assistants to male workers. Thus to assume that all attributes are due to individual choice is misleading and particularly so for Japan.

From the analysis of British longitudinal data we were able to construct a more detailed model that represented very fully both human capital and workplace effects. Of particular importance, we were able to measure work experience – which brings a significant advantage to men, both in terms of more years of experience and also in the reward for each year worked. Occupation, size of firm and being in a feminised occupation were also important in giving more rewards to men. Again, by assuming that job-related variables – for example, working in a feminised occupation – reflect individual choice or preferences, we are likely to have underestimated gender wage differentials and discrimination.

All the models fail to capture feedback effects which combine supply-side and demand-side effects. As an example of such an effect, Blau and Ferber (1986) suggest that labour market discrimination might discourage women, weaken their motivation, and reinforce the role of the gender division of labour in the family.

Finally, we have not been able to include pre-entry discrimination in our models, for example, in access to educational courses. In Japan most two-year colleges are dominated by women, who earn less than graduates from a four-year university course. However, it is not easy to establish whether women freely choose these shorter courses or whether external labour market factors exert an influence. An additional factor is the big difference in domestic work between men and women in Japan. Men are unlikely to contribute to housework in Japan and this, therefore, is a further factor in deterring women from participation in the labour market.

Our findings suggest some policies that may promote equal pay. Earnings based on personal characteristics (such as age and seniority) may not relate very strongly to ability or achievement, and are likely to lead to pay inequality between women and men. This suggests that the growth in Britain of a merit pay system may, potentially, be subjective. An objective method of wage determination based on the job rather than personal characteristics is more likely to help equal pay between men and women. The importance of occupation and occupational segregation in the gender pay gap suggests that 'equal pay for work of equal value' (comparable worth or pay equity) is more effective than 'equal pay for equal work'. The former requires the same (or substantially similar) work in the same establishment, whereas the latter allows comparisons across dissimilar occupations, usually based on job evaluation procedures. Comparable worth leads to a reduction in the gender pay gap caused by horizontal occupational segregation – female and male jobs at a similar skill level. We have also shown that being in a managerial position also affects the gender wage gap, and it is crucial to reducing vertical occupational segregation. Affirmative action could provide a way forwards: it is designed to compensate for the historical accumulation of inequality, and hence involves actions such as the aggressive hiring of women or giving preference to women when candidates are otherwise equal.

These are some of the possible policies to address male-female wage differentials. However, in order to be effective, policies must be implemented in a way that is appropriate to the different cultural and institutional systems of a particular country.

Notes

* We would like to thank the Centre for Longitudinal Studies, at the Institute of Education, for supplying data for the National Child Development Study (NCDS), and in providing help and documentation. We are also grateful to the many other researchers who have derived variables which we have used. In particular, we acknowledge the use of variables derived by Pierella Paci and Heather Joshi, supplied by CLS. We would also like to thank Jane Elliott, University of Liverpool, for allowing us to use variables derived for an earlier project and for helpful comments. In addition, we acknowledge use of the Labour Force Survey (LFS) and thank the Data Archive at the University of Essex, and MIMAS at the University of Manchester for assistance with access to both the LFS and the NCDS.

[1] This method has no single common name. This chapter follows the ILO use of 'the Blinder-Oaxaca decomposition technique' (ILO, 1993, p 9). However, it has also been termed 'the Oaxaca-Blinder procedure' (Paci and Joshi, 1998, p 29), and 'the Oaxaca decomposition technique' (Wright and Ermisch, 1991, p 519).

[2] The main reason for non-release of national statistical microdata in Japan is to ensure confidentiality. In order to be granted permission to access data, one must endure complicated and time-consuming procedures.

[3] The Ministry of Health, Labour and Welfare has launched a new cohort study, based on those born during one week in January and one week in July 2001. The sample size will be about 50,000 individuals.

References

Becker, G. (1957) *The economics of discrimination* (1st edn) (2nd edn, 1971), Chicago, IL: University of Chicago Press.

Becker, G. (1975) *Human capital: A theoretical and empirical analysis with special reference to education* (2nd edn), New York, NY: Columbia University Press.

Bergman, B.R. (1971) 'The effect on white incomes of discrimination in employment', *Journal of Political Economy*, vol 79, no 2, pp 294-313.

Bergman, B.R. (1974) 'Occupational segregation, wages and profits when employers discriminate by race and sex', *Eastern Economic Journal*, vol 1, nos 2-3, pp 103-10.

Bergman, B.R. (1986) 'Why are women's wages low?', in B.R. Bergman (ed) *The economic emergence of women*, New York, NY: Basic Books, pp 119-45.

Berk, R.A. (1983) 'An introduction to sample selection bias in sociological data', *American Sociological Review*, vol 48, no 3, pp 386-98.

Blau, F.D. (1998) 'The gender pay gap', in I. Persson and C. Jonung (eds) *Women's work and wages*, London: Routledge, pp 15-35.

Blau, F.D. and Jusenius, C.L. (1976) 'Economists' approaches to sex segregation in the labor market: an appraisal', in M. Blaxall and B. Reagan (eds) *Women and the workplace: The occupations of occupational segregation*, London/Chicago, IL: University of Chicago Press, pp 181-99.

Blau, F.D. and Ferber, M.A. (1986) *The economics of women and work*, New Jersey: Prentice Hall Englewood.

Bosworth, D., Dawkins, P. and Stromback, T. (1996) *The economics of the labour market*, Harlow: Longman.

Cain, G.G. (1986) 'The economic analysis of labor market discrimination: a survey', in O. Ashenfelter and R. Layard (eds) *Handbook of Labor Economics*, vol I, Elsevier Science Publishers BV, pp 693-785.

Cain, G.G., Becker, B.E., McLaughlin, C.G. and Schwenk, A.E. (1981) 'The effect of unions on wages in hospitals', *Research in Labor Economics*, vol 4, pp 191-320.

City University, London (1995) *The National Child Development Study: An introduction, its origins and the methods of data collection*, User Support Group, Working Paper 1, London: City University.

Crompton, R. (ed) (1999) *Restructuring gender relations and employment: The decline of the male breadwinner*, Oxford: Oxford University Press.

Dale, A. and Egerton, M. (1997) *Highly educated women: Evidence from the National Child Development Study*, DfEE, RS No 25, London: The Stationery Office.

Department of Employment (1970) *New Earnings Survey*, London: HMSO.

Department of Employment (1980) *New Earnings Survey*, London: HMSO.

Doeringer, P.B and Piore, M.J. (1971) *International labour markets and manpower analysis*, Lexington, MA: Heath.

Dolton, P.J. and Kidd, M.P. (1994) 'Occupational access and wage discrimination', *Oxford Bulletin of Economics and Statistics*, vol 56, no 4, pp 457-74.

Dolton, P.J. and Makepeace, G.H. (1986) 'Sample selection and male-female earnings differentials in the graduate labour market', *Oxford Economic Papers*, vol 38, no 2, pp 317-41.

Elliott, J., Dale, A. and Egerton, M. (2001) 'The influence of qualifications on women's work histories, employment status and earnings at age 33', *European Sociological Review*, vol 17, no 2, pp 145-68.

England, P. (1992) '2 Theories of labor markets', in P. England (ed) *Comparable worth: Theories and evidence*, New York, NY: Alpine de Gruyter, pp 45-124.

Ferri, E. (1993) '1. Introduction', *Life at 33: The fifth follow-up of the National Child Development Study*, London: Children's Bureau and the ESRC, pp 1-15.

Filer, R.K. (1985) 'Male-female wage differentials: the importance of compensating differentials', *Industrial and Labor Relations Review*, vol 38, no 3, pp 426-37.

Freeman, R.B. and Medoff, J.L. (1983) 'The impact of collective bargaining: can the new facts be explained by monopoly unionism?', *Research in Labor Economics*, supplement 2, pp 293-332.

Goto, M. (1999) 'Shin-Fukushi Kokka Senryaku to Josei no Ichi', *Josei Roudou Kenkyu* ['Strategies of the new welfare state and women's position', *The Bulletin of the Society for the Study of Working Women*, vol 35, pp 10-15.

Gottfried, H. and O'Reilly, J. (2000) *The weakness of strong breadwinner models: Part-time work and female labour force participation in Germany and Japan*, Detroit, MI: College of Urban, Labour and Metropolitan Affairs, Wayne State University.

Gunderson, M. (1989) 'Male-female wage differentials and policy responses', *Journal of Economic Literature*, vol 27, no 1, pp 46-72.

Harkness, S. (1996) 'The gender earnings gap: evidence from the UK', *Fiscal Studies*, vol 17, no 2, pp 1-36.

Heckman, J.J. (1979) 'Sample selection bias as a specification error', *Econometrica*, vol 47, no 1, pp 153-61.

Higuchi, Y. (ed) (1991) 'Joshi no Gakureki betsu Syugyo Keireki to Tingin Kozo', *Nihon Keizai to Syugyo Kodo*, ['Women's working career and wage structure by education', *Japanese Economy and Working Behavior*], Tokyo: Toyo Keizai Sinpousya.

Hirsch, B.T and Addison, J.T. (1986) *The economic analysis of unions: New approaches and evidence*, Boston, MA: Allen & Unwin.

Horn-Kawashima, H.Y. (1985) *Joshi Roudo to Rodosijyo Kozo no Bunseki*, [*Analyses of women's work and labour market structures*], Tokyo: Nihon Kezai Hyouronsya.

Humphries, J. and Rubery, J. (1984) 'The reconstitution of the supply side of the labour market: the relative autonomy of social reproduction', *Cambridge Journal of Economics*, vol 8, no 4, pp 331-46.

ILO Bureau of Statistics (1993) *Statistical measurement of gender wage differentials*, Working Paper, Geneva: ILO.

IRS/EOC (1992) *Pay and gender in Britain: 2, Second research report for the Equal Opportunities Commission from Industrial Relations Service*, Redwood Press.

Ishiro, S. (1996) 'Feminisuto Keizaigaku niokeru Danjyo Tingin Kakusa Ron to Pay Equity No.1' *Tokoha Gakuen Tanki Daigaku Kiyou*, ['Theories on wage differentials between men and women and pay equity in "Feminist Economics"', *Journal of Tokoha College*], vol 27, pp 357-69.

Japan Statistics Research Institute (1999) 'Mikuro Toukei Deta no Genjou to Tenbou' ['Present situation and future of micro-data'] , *Bulletin of Japan Statistics Research Institute*, no 25, Tokyo: Japan Statistics Research Institute, Hosei University.

Joshi, H. (1984) *Women's participation in paid work: Further analysis of the women and employment survey*, Research Paper no 45, London: Department of Employment.

Kinoshita, T. (1998) '"Chingin Seido no Tenkan" narumono to Tingin no Kangae Kata (Jo)', *Tingin to Syakai Hosyo*, ['"Switch of wage system" and the way to think of wage (1)', *Wage and Social Security*], no 1224, pp 4-19.

Kiso Keizai Kagaku Kenkyusyo (1995) *Hatasaku josei to kazoku no ima* [*Present situation on working women and family*], Tokyo: Aoki publisher.

Kuwahara, Y. (1978) 'Sabetsu no Keizai bunseki', *Nihon Roudou Kennkyuukai Zasshi*, ['Economic analysis on discrimination', *Journal of Japan Labour Research Committee*], no 235, pp 2-19.

Leslie, D., Clark, K. and Drinkwater, S. (2001) 'Decomposing rewards in earnings functions', Unpublished paper.

Miller, P.W. (1987) 'The wage effect of the occupational segregation of women in Britain', *The Economic Journal*, vol 97, no 388, pp 885-96.

Mincer, J. and Polacheck, S. (1974) 'Family investments in human capital: earnings of women', *Journal of Political Economy*, vol 82, no 2, pp 76-108.

Ministry of Labour (1970) *Basic survey on wage structure*, Tokyo: Centre for Publication, Ministry of Finance.

Ministry of Labour (1985) *Basic survey on wage structure*, Tokyo: Centre for Publication, Ministry of Finance.

Ministry of Labour (1999) *Basic survey on wage structure*, Tokyo: Centre for Publication, Ministry of Finance.

Mitani, N. (1997) 'Josei Koyo to Danjyo Koyo Kikai Kintou Hou', *Kigyou nai Tingin Kouzou to Roudou Shijyo*, ['Women employment and equal employment opportunity legislation', *Wage Structures within Companies and Labour Market*], Tokyo: Keisou Syobou.

Nakagawa, S. (1996) 'Keizaigaku to Jenda: Seibetsu Tingin Kakusaron wo Tegakari ni', *Tingin to Syakai Hosyo*, ['Economics and gender: with a clue of gender wage differentials', *Wage and Social Security*] no 1188, pp 4-16.

Nakata, Y. (1997) 'Nihon niokeru Danjyo Tingin Kakusa no Yoin Bunseki: Doitsu Syokusyu ni tsuku Danjyo Rodousya kan ni Tingin Kakusa ha Sonzai surunoka?' in H. Nakama and T. Suruga (eds) *Koyou Kankou no Henka to Josei Roudou* ['Analyses of wage differentials between men and women in Japan: is there the pay gap between men and women workers in the same occupations?' in *Changes in Employment Traditions and Women Work*], Tokyo: Tokyo Daigaku Syuppann Kai, pp 173-205.

Oaxaca, R. (1973) 'Male-female wage differentials in urban labor markets', *International Economic Review*, vol 14, no 3, pp 693-709.

Office for National Statistics (1999) *New earnings survey*, ONS.

Okuyama, A. (1993) 'Equal pay in Japan', in F. Eyraud, M. Thornton, P.C. McDermott, J. Heikkero, P.K. Koskinen, P. Nikula, C. Pettiti, A. Okuyama, I.P. Asscher-Vonk, R.P Rio, C. McCrudden and J.R. Bellace, *Equal pay protection in industrialised market economies: In search of greater effectiveness*, Geneva: ILO, pp 95-106.

Osawa, M. (1993) *Kigyo Chyushin Syakai wo Koete*, [*Beyond a company centred society: A viewpoint from gender*] Tokyo: Jiji Tsushin.

Osawa, M. (1995) 'The Japanese wage gap re-examined', *Journal of Economics Asia University*, vol 19, no 1, pp 1-25.

Paci, P., Joshi, H. and Makepeace, G.H. (1995) 'Pay gaps facing men and women born in 1958: differences within the labour market', in J. Humphries and J. Rubery (eds) *The economics of equal opportunities*, Manchester: Equal Opportunities Commission, pp 87-111.

Paci, P., Joshi, H., with Makepeace, G.H. and Waldfogel, J. (1998) *Unequal pay for women and men: Evidence from the British Birth Cohort Studies*, Cambridge: MIT press.

Phelps, E.S. (1972) 'The statistical theory of racism and sexism', *American Economic Review*, vol 62, no 4, pp 659-61.

Robinson, P. (1986) 'Women's occupational attainment: the effects of work interruptions, self-selection, and unobserved characteristics', *Social Science Research*, vol 15, no 4, pp 323-46.

Rubery, J. (1978) 'Structured labour markets, worker organization and low pay', *Cambridge Journal of Economics*, vol 2, no 1, pp 17-36.

Rubery, J. (1992) *The economics of equal value*, Manchester: Equal Opportunities Commission.

Sloane, P.J. (1994) 'The gender wage differential and discrimination in the six SCELI local labour markets', in A. MacEwen Scott (ed) *Gender segregation and social change*, Oxford: Oxford University Press, pp 157-204.

Sugihashi, Y. (1998) 'Seibetsu Tingin Kakusa/Sabetsu no Suuryo/Keiryo Bunseki no Kentou: "Roudousya Kousei no Souitsuka Syuhou" To Blinder-Oaxaca Bunkai Syuhou', *Daigakuin Kiyou*, ['Examination on mathematical and econometric methods on gender wage differentials and discrimination: adjusted ratio and the Blinder-Oaxaca decomposition technique', *Journal of Graduate School*], no 41, pp 27-48.

Sugihashi, Y. (forthcoming) 'The gender wage differential and discrimination in Great Britain and Japan', PhD thesis, University of Manchester.

Tomita, Y. (1992) 'Syokusyu wo Koryo shita Danjyo Tingin Kakusa no Bunseki', *Osaka Huritsu Daigaku Keizai Kenkyu*, ['An analysis of wage differentials between men and women with considerations of occupations', *Journal of Economic Studies in Osaka Prefecture University*], vol 37, nos 1 and 2, pp 101-14.

Waldfogel, J. (1997) 'The effect of children on women's wages', *American Sociological Review*, vol 62, no 2, pp 209-17.

Wright, R.E. and Ermisch, J.F. (1991) 'Gender discrimination in the British labour market: a reassessment', *The Economic Journal*, vol 101, no 406, pp 508-22.

WWN (Working Women's Network) (1997) *WWN went to the ILO*, Osaka: Working Women's Network.

Yashiro, N. (1980) 'Dnajyo kan Tingin Sabetsu no Yoinn nitsuite: Sono Gouriteki Kaimei to Taisaku', *Nihon Keizai Kenkyu*, ['On factors of wage discrimination between men and women: its rational solutions and measures', *Research on Japanese Economy*], no 9, pp 17-31.

Zabalza, A. and Arrufat, J.L (1985) 'The extent of sex discrimination in Great Britain', in A. Zabalza and Z. Tzannatos (eds) *Women and equal pay: The effects of legislation on female employment and wages in Britain*, London: Cambridge University Press, pp 70-96.

TEN

Longitudinal analysis and the constitution of the concept of gender

Jane Elliott

Introduction

As the other chapters of this volume have clearly demonstrated, longitudinal analysis provides an invaluable tool for enhancing our understanding of gender differences and inequalities. One of the advantages of longitudinal analysis in examining women's lives is that, for many women, the experience of motherhood necessitates a careful balance between responsibilities for the care of young children and maintaining an attachment to the labour market. Therefore, methodological approaches are required which will allow for an examination of women's transitions between different labour market states and which will also enable an investigation of the long-term consequences of time spent out of the labour market and time spent in part-time work for women's subsequent careers and for gender inequalities later in life. As Joshi and Davies emphasise in Chapter Six, the fluctuations in earnings over the life cycle experienced by many women (and particularly those with children) increases the need to take a long-term perspective. In addition, as Dex and Smith illustrate in Chapter Eight, as certain sectors of the labour market become increasingly characterised as offering temporary and insecure employment, longitudinal data are required in order to examine the different problems that men and women may face in maintaining continuity of employment.

As Ruspini has previously argued, the radically different relationship that many women have with the labour market, compared with men, means that 'women cannot simply be "added in" to existing analyses: instead a different analytic framework is required' (2001, p 102). Longitudinal data and longitudinal approaches to analysis clearly go some way towards providing an appropriate gender-sensitive methodology. However, as this chapter emphasises, it is important that, as the corpus of longitudinal research on women's lives develops and allows for a greater understanding of gender inequalities, we simultaneously develop an awareness of how particular analytic tools and approaches themselves have the potential to shape the way that we think about gender.

True to the spirit of this volume, this chapter aims to illustrate the value of longitudinal data and longitudinal approaches for examining women's lives. In particular, I will focus on the role of part-time work in the context of British women's work histories. However, this chapter has a second and equally important aim. In addition to presenting the results of longitudinal analyses of women's work histories I also want to highlight the need to take a more reflexive approach to the use of quantitative life history data. In particular I will focus on the way in which a great deal of longitudinal research on women's careers has in fact focused on the behaviour of mothers following the birth of their first child. The implications of conflating all women with the subgroup of mothers for reifying the concept of gender will be considered in the context of recent feminist theory, which, as will be discussed in more detail below, has increasingly attempted to problematise the category of women.

The first section of this chapter therefore focuses on conceptualising women's employment. This is divided into two parts. The first part discusses recent research on women's employment behaviour, and highlights the need to understand the role of part-time employment in the dynamic context of women's work histories. The second outlines briefly some of the more theoretical debates about the concept of 'women' within recent feminist writings. The second section of this chapter then reports the results of event history models, based on the analysis of data from the National Child Development Survey (NCDS), that aim to understand the role of part-time work in women's work histories. The final section takes a step back from these substantive analyses to consider how we can use recent feminist theory, which aims to deconstruct the category of women, to inform the way that we conduct and present these types of longitudinal analyses.

Conceptualising women's employment

The fifty years since the end of the Second World War have witnessed important changes in British women's employment behaviour. Whereas before the war almost all women stopped work when they first got married, during the 1950s a rather different pattern of behaviour became established, so that by the end of the decade the majority of women only left the labour market if they became mothers. In 1951, the census revealed that only a quarter of married women aged 15-59 were in paid work. This rose to just over a third in 1961 and had risen to nearly a half by 1971. One of the main reasons cited for this increase in married women's participation in paid employment has been the increase in the availability of part-time work. Part-time jobs have been crucial in enabling British women with children to combine paid-employment and family commitments (see, among others, Myrdal and Klein, 1956; Gallie, 1988; Scheiwe, 1994).

Although high levels of part-time working among women with children are not unique to Britain, the nature of part-time jobs in Britain is distinctive. In contrast, part-time work in Scandinavia is most likely to represent a reduction of hours in a full-time job, while in the Netherlands the growth of part-time jobs has taken place in a strongly regulated institutional context with the same rights and protections as full-time jobs (Pfau-Effinger, 1998; see also Chapter Four in this volume). In Britain part-time jobs tend to have few prospects of promotion and require little by way of educational qualifications and, therefore, a return to part-time work after childbearing typically results in occupational downgrading (Martin and Roberts, 1984; Dex, 1984, 1987).

In Britain during the 1950s and the 1960s, mothers increasingly began to return to part-time work after childbirth, although most mothers still spent many years out of the labour market while their children were young. Over recent decades, this period out of the labour market has grown progressively shorter as mothers return to employment more quickly after the birth of a child (Dex, 1984; Joshi and Hinde, 1993). In 1976, statutory maternity leave was first introduced in Britain, which allowed mothers to take up to 29 weeks leave from work. The proportion of mothers taking maternity leave has risen so that an increasing number of women have maintained a continuous attachment to the labour market during their transition to motherhood (McRae, 1993).

The length of time that mothers spend out of the labour market after the birth of a child has been a major focus for research on women's employment behaviour. For example, in Chapter Four, Gustafsson, Wetzels and Kenjoh relate the time mothers spend out of the labour market caring for young children to the changing policy context in four different European countries between the 1980s and the 1990s. They use the duration of time before a mother's re-entry to the labour market as both a dependent variable and as an independent variable. In other words the length of time spent out of the labour market is partly seen as an outcome of the educational level of women and of the policies on parental leave in each country, but is also used as an indicator of the amount of time women plan to spend out of the labour market. They find that mothers who have apparently planned to spend longer spells looking after children tend to postpone motherhood more than those spending shorter spells caring for children.

Joesch (1994) argues that describing how long women stay at home if they become mothers is important, because the time many women spend away from paid employment taking care of children is an important factor behind gender inequalities in occupational attainment. Women's wages and promotion prospects are lower than those of men with similar qualifications, it has been argued, because women accumulate less experience and lose human capital if they interrupt work during the childbearing years (Mincer and Polachek, 1974; Corcoran and Duncan, 1979; Joshi et al, 1996; Elliott et al, 2001). In Britain, research has emphasised that women who take extended breaks from paid work after childbirth have tended to experience downward mobility when they return to work (Elias and Main, 1982; Stewart and Greenhalgh, 1984; Dex, 1984, 1987), and in particular women who return to part-time work (Martin and Roberts, 1984, p 146). As Dale has argued (1987), when women return to work after childrearing they are in a relatively weak position, both because they are in competition with younger and more recently qualified people, and also because their domestic commitments often limit their working hours and their ability to spend time travelling to work. Although, on the one hand, part-time work can be understood as providing a means by which women can combine paid work and motherhood, Dale argues "the increasing numbers of locally available part-time jobs act as a channel back into a secondary labour market which is able to exploit the domestic situation of these women by paying wage rates at below the supply cost of the labour" (Dale, 1987, p 345).

In addition to paying only relatively low wages, part-time work may also be financially disadvantageous to women in the longer-term. As Ginn and Arber have argued (1998), both the labour market and the welfare state tend to privilege the full-time continuous employment pattern characteristic of middle-class males. This leads to disadvantaged pension provision for those with part-time or interrupted employment. In particular, in countries where earnings-related pensions predominate, such as Germany and UK; it is only by maintaining a relatively continuous employment pattern that women can be sure of a good pension income in later life. As Rowlingson, Whyley and Warren have shown, most women who spend a significant proportion of their working life in part-time employment will accrue at most a meagre company pension by the time that they reach retirement age (Rowlingson et al, 1999).

Understanding women's employment behaviour – why longitudinal data?

The high proportion of British mothers who have part-time jobs clearly raises important questions about the quality of part-time work and its role within women's career histories in Britain. For example, to what extent does part-time work provide a solution for women who want to spend time with their children while maintaining an attachment to the labour market? Are women's long-term career prospects affected if they enter part-time jobs? How easy is it for women to make the transition from part-time to full-time employment? These issues are increasingly being addressed by current empirical research, as will be discussed below. In particular I show that it is important to develop an understanding of the role of part-time work in the dynamic patterns of women's employment behaviour. In other words, the meaning of part-time work can be grasped only in the context of women's work histories. This requires a longitudinal approach to the quantitative analysis of event history data.

The last five years has witnessed an ongoing debate about whether a substantial proportion of women with children freely choose to work in lower-status part-time jobs, or are constrained to take this type of employment due to the lack of publicly-funded childcare and the structure of the labour market[1]. There are a number of respects in which this debate underlines the need for a longitudinal approach to the analysis of women's employment behaviour. For example, as Breugel (1996) has pointed out, the fact that older women continue to work part-time even though they no longer have dependent children cannot, as Hakim (1996) suggests, be simply interpreted to mean that it is women's preferences rather than the lack of childcare which leads them to be in part-time jobs. Indeed the fact that these women continue to work part-time raises interesting questions about both the processes by which women remain in part-time work, and about the employment behaviour of different cohorts of women. In addition, even if we go along with Hakim's use of 'preference theory' to explain why so many women work part-time (and accept that approximately 60% of women freely choose part-time work because they want to work but are not totally committed to a work career), it is still important to understand how this initial choice is likely to constrain subsequent opportunities within the labour market. For example, a married mother with young children who works only a few hours per week and relies on her husband as the primary wage earner needs to know the long-term implications of her decision to work part-time should her husband divorce her and she wants to re-enter full-time employment.

The role of part-time employment in women's work histories

Does part-time work provide 'a bridge' or 'stepping stone' back into full-time employment in women's working lives, or is it better conceptualised as 'a trap' which prevents women from reaching their full potential in the labour market (Tam, 1997)? Without examining the patterns of labour market involvement among individual women over time, however, it is impossible to know whether, for the majority of women, part-time work is indeed a transitional state, or whether women who enter part-time jobs are likely to remain in part-time employment.

Although a great deal of the existing research on women's employment behaviour does not distinguish between part-time and full-time work (Joshi and Hinde, 1993; Joesch, 1994; Gustafsson et al, 1996; Dex et al, 1998), there are a few studies which shed some light on this issue. Blank, on the other hand, does discuss the role of part-time work in women's labour market choices over time (Blank, 1989). She analyses work history data from nearly 4,000 women in the US Panel Study of Income Dynamics for the nine survey years 1976-84. Her results suggest that although spells of part-time work tend to be shorter than periods spent in full-time work or caring for children there is little evidence that women use part-time work as an in-between stage separating non-work and full-time work. Giannelli reports similar findings in the transitions between non-, part-time, and full-time employment for nearly 2000 married women in Germany between 1983 and 1987 (1996). She concludes that part-time work is a state that many women remain in and is not the first step towards full-time employment. The exception to this is that, for foreign women working in West Germany, part-time work is indeed a stepping stone to full-time employment.

In an analysis of data collected as part of the UK Social Change in Economic Life Initiative (SCELI) in the mid-1980s, Tam demonstrates that although the job security of part-time work is similar to that of full-time work, the lack of promotion prospects and the low wage rates associated with part-time employment lend support to segmentation theories of the labour market (Tam, 1997). Tam found that part-time employees in the SCELI survey were less likely than full-time employees to be able to augment their human capital through on-the-job training, and were also less likely to hold managerial or supervisory positions. Previous experience of part-time work was also found to have an adverse effect on current earnings so that longer durations of part-time work experience led to lower wages for women. In addition to looking at the effect of job history variables on current earnings, Tam also used a multinomial logit regression analysis to determine the factors which best predict a woman's current employment status. In particular she examined whether previous experience of working part-time or of being out of the labour market (operationalised as a percentage of working life spent in these two states) had a significant effect on current employment status, once other relevant factors such as formal qualifications and the presence and age of a youngest child had been taken into account. Tam concluded that the labour market structure has a significant effect on women's chances of getting full-time employment, rather than part-time employment, even once these other factors were controlled. She summed up her findings by stating that "more part-time work has an inhibiting effect on the woman's chance of getting full-time rather than part-time work" (Tam, 1997, p 235). In other words she argues that her analyses lend support for a 'job-centred' explanation for women's concentration in part-time employment – part-time work acts as a trap from which women find it difficult to escape into full-time work.

I have outlined Tam's research in some detail here because it shares some important features of the quantitative research that will be reported below. In common with Tam, I would argue that it is important to distinguish part-time and full-time work as separate employment states within women's work histories. I also agree with Tam's criticism that the majority of existing research focuses on women's employment transitions at the birth of a child rather than taking women's whole employment histories into account (Tam, 1997, p 35). However, a major shortcoming with Tam's research is her cross-sectional approach to the analysis of work histories; I argue that it is essential not only to use longitudinal data to understand women's employment behaviour but also fully to exploit the temporal qualities of the data by using event history analyses.

In particular, the problem of analysing this type of longitudinal data using cross-sectional methods is that cross-sectional techniques cannot take account of the fact that previous employment experience is endogenous to the process that is being investigated. In other words, an association between women's previous part-time work experience and current part-time employment status is likely to be a spurious relationship such that both previous and current part-time employment are the result of a separate factor which is not included in the model (Davies, 1994). This is not to argue that results from cross-sectional analyses are necessarily misleading but rather that more appropriate analytic tools should be used to confirm any results. Event history models, and particularly those which include an individual-specific error term, represent a method for analysing longitudinal data that can potentially avoid some of these problems of endogeneity. In the current research, it has therefore been possible to use these methods to address the important question of whether part-time work has a cumulative entrapment effect, so that the longer a woman spends in this type of employment, the more difficult it is for her to make a transition into a full-time job.

Here I briefly describe women's changing employment patterns in the UK over the past fifty years and highlight the growing salience of episodes of part-time employment within these women's work histories. In particular I argue that lengthy spells in part-time employment can potentially exacerbate gender inequalities in a number of different ways. Firstly, part-time jobs tend to be concentrated in the lowest-paid sectors of the economy and this reduces immediate income. Secondly, in the medium term, part-time jobs may have an adverse effect on a woman's ability to re-enter better-paid full-time employment. Thirdly, in the longer term, it reduces her entitlement to pension income. It has been stressed above that cross-sectional methods are not adequate for determining the impact of duration in part-time employment on a woman's possible transition to full-time employment. Longitudinal methods are therefore required to understand the factors which facilitate or prohibit women's transitions between time spent out of the labour market, episodes in part-time employment, and episodes in full-time employment.

At this point it is important to adopt a rather different perspective and to consider the empirical research discussed above in the context of one of the central debates within contemporary feminist theory. This debate asks if it is possible to conceptualise 'women' as a meaningful category, without producing an over-essentialised account of femininity based upon a simple binary division between male and female. As Janet Siltanen has pointed out (1994), it is disappointing how little research, which examines women's behaviour with respect to the labour market and domestic life, has so far taken account of the growing body of work by feminist theorists calling for a deconstruction of the category of women and a reappraisal of the concept of gender as an explanatory tool.

Feminist theory and the problem of the category of 'women'

Empirical research of the kind described above raises an important dilemma for feminists. How is it possible to provide descriptions of the experiences of actual living women without reifying social differences in ways that echo 'essentialist' theories based on the notion of universal differences between men and women? In other words, how is it possible to carry out longitudinal analyses which treat women as a category in order to examine gender inequalities, without obscuring the very real heterogeneities which exist within any large sample of 'women'? This issue of conceptualising the category of 'woman' represents a major problem in contemporary feminist theory (Riley, 1988; Scott, 1988; Marshall, 1994; Crompton, 1999). As Judith Butler argues, 'women' has become "a troublesome term, a site of contest, a cause for anxiety" (1990, p 3). While it is a concept that must be understood as the very basis for feminism as both a philosophical and political project (Riley, 1988), it also reinforces the assumption that, as a group, women have a shared collective identity leading to a shared set of interests. In practice this is clearly not the case.

At first sight in the research reported above, however, the category of 'women' may not appear to be problematic. For empirical researchers whose aim is to investigate the experiences of women, it is a straightforward matter to identify the subjects of their research. Indeed it could be argued that in comparison with categories such as social class or ethnicity, gender is one of the least problematic variables to define. However, difficulties emerge once we try to explain and theorise the differential positions of men and women within the social world. Indeed as Marshall has argued (1994) "Most socialist feminist theory tends towards essentialism based on a historical reification of women's experience and a corresponding reification of 'gender identity'" (1994, p 107).

In defence of empirical research focusing on women's employment patterns, presented above, it could be argued that research such as this does not essentialise women in so far as it does not attempt to produce meta-theoretical explanations of women's disadvantaged position relative to men. Rather such research might be conceptualised as operating at the level of 'middle–range theory' (Layder, 1990). In other words this type of research may be defended by arguing that it provides a useful description of the behaviour of definable groups of women, and that it can be used to test hypotheses about the relative importance of a number of different factors, which influence women's behaviour with respect to the labour market. However, I would suggest that the potential danger of such research in shoring up a problematic conceptualisation of femininity lies in the fact that it almost invariably focuses not on women's employment patterns, but on the behaviour of mothers. And moreover that the distinction between mothers as a specific subgroup and women as a general category is inadequately maintained.

To illustrate this point let us look at the actual phraseology used in empirical research papers. In one of the most methodologically sophisticated analyses of mothers' work histories from the fifth sweep of the NCDS, Dex and her colleagues use the terms 'women' and 'mothers' interchangeably. The concluding section of their paper begins:

> The experiences of mothers in the 1958 generation suggests that women have started to benefit from the equal opportunities provisions enacted in Britain in the 1970s. The age of the youngest child is still the most important determinant of women's participation over the pre-school years, although its impact may well have weakened relative to the influence of the mother's level of qualifications and own wage. (Dex et al, 1998, p 95)

In a paper comparing the labour force transitions of mothers in Germany, Sweden, and Britain, Gustafsson and her colleagues conclude by stating that:

> Our results confirm the polarizing effects found in other studies that career oriented women who are also highly educated delay childbirth and return quicker after giving birth when their maternity leave has expired. (Gustafsson et al, 1996, p 242)

It might be argued that it is stylistically awkward for authors to restrict themselves to referring to the subjects of their research as 'mothers'. However, it is also important to be aware that this constant slippage between the terms 'mother' and 'woman' suggests that the two are synonymous and, in addition, that what crucially defines women in relation to men is their ability to bear children. In rhetorical terms the conflation of mothers and women represents an example of synecdoche, the use of a part to stand in for the whole. As Laurel Richardson has underlined (1991), the use of synecdoche is common in both the practice and the writing of social science. However, it is profoundly unhelpful here. While Dex and her co-authors make it clear that their analyses are restricted to the sub-sample of women within the NCDS who were mothers by the age of 33, the 25% of women who are excluded from their analyses are described by the authors as a 'substantial minority of the cohort' who 'had still not had a first birth by age 33' (1998, p 81). Although it is no more than implicit, the suggestion is that women are all expected to have children, and that the exclusion of some women from the analysis is an unfortunate artefact of the age of the women when the data was collected.

My argument here cautions against the equating of women with mothers, as Annandale and Clarke have done (1996). In their discussion of feminist theory and the sociology of human reproduction, they problematise the way in which reproduction constitutes a central and defining function of being a woman. This may correspond to the reality of some women's experiences, but it is important not to lock women into reproductive roles. In the words of Eisenstein, "women are denied their individuality: all women become the same – mothers – which immediately characterises them as different from men" (1988, p 90).

A similar point, but with reference to more historical material, is well expressed by Denise Riley who cautions that "Because the task of illuminating 'the needs of mothers' starts out with gender at its most decisive and inescapable point – the biological capacity to bear children – there's the danger that it may fall back into a conservative restating and confirming of social-sexual difference as timeless too. This would entail making the needs of mothers into fixed properties of motherhood as a social function" (Riley, 1983, pp 194-5). Riley's work is particularly relevant here because she has emphasised the necessity of using research to understand and articulate the needs of specific groups of women, with respect to childcare, while also recognising that such research runs the risk of portraying an overly essentialised view of women. She suggests that a feminist research agenda should include both the problematising of the category of women alongside illuminating the condition of actual women in a historical context, as a contribution to a more political programme.

The forgoing discussion therefore raises the question of how it is possible to conduct empirical analyses that illuminate gender differences and inequalities without simultaneously reifying the concept of gender. In particular, the challenge is to present the results of a set of longitudinal analyses which examine the role of part-time employment within women's employment histories, without conflating 'women' with 'mothers'. The next section of the chapter discusses the analysis of longitudinal data from the NCDS. The final section of the chapter then highlights the importance of paying attention to recent theoretical work, which aims to deconstruct the category of women, in our analysis and presentation of longitudinal data about women's lives.

Empirical analysis

Data: The National Child Development Survey (NCDS)

The data, which forms the basis of the analyses reported in this chapter is predominantly drawn from the fifth sweep of the NCDS study, which was carried out in 1991 when respondents were 33 years old. A total of 11,407 cohort members were interviewed – 5799 women and 5608 men. This represents a 73% response rate among the population who were eligible to be included in the survey[2]. In addition to the face-to-face interviews carried out in 1991, cohort members were asked to complete a questionnaire entitled 'Your life since 1974'. This collected retrospective event histories of partnerships (marital and cohabiting), childbearing, paid work, periods of unemployment, and housing. For example, in relation to employment, the start and end dates (to the nearest month) of each job are recorded, detailing whether the job was full- or part-time, and whether the individual was an employee or self-employed. The focus in this chapter is on how women combine their working lives with motherhood. Attention is therefore restricted to the women in the sample[3]. The NCDS therefore represents a valuable data source with very detailed life histories available for a relatively large sample of women aged 33 in 1991. In particular the fact that dates are recorded to the nearest month rather than just to the nearest year makes it particularly suited to event history analysis.

Event history analysis: modelling women's work histories

Longitudinal analyses of women's employment behaviour frequently focuses on an analysis of the duration of time spent out of the labour market immediately following the birth of a first child. This approach necessarily restricts the sample to women who are mothers. However, we have already seen why it is important to include all of the women in the sample and to consider a simplified set of different employment transitions that are possible within each woman's work history.

A helpful way of conceptualising the work history data for all of the women in the sample is by means of a state transition matrix. A rather simplified version is given in Table 10.1. The rows represent the starting point, or origin state, of employment: full-time, part-time, or not employed[4]. The columns represent the range of states into which an individual woman might theoretically make a transition. Some elements of the matrix represent transitions which we may consider to be impossible for substantive reasons, or because of the way the data has been conceptualised. These have been denoted by 'X'. For example, since transitions are here defined as occurring between different employment statuses and not between different jobs, we are assuming in this relatively simple transition matrix that it is impossible for a woman to move from an episode of part-time employment directly into another episode of part-time employment.

In summary therefore, Table 10.1 indicates the relative frequency of transitions between three key labour market states, namely full-time work, part-time work, and time spent out of the labour market. An important feature of using the state transition matrix to examine the longitudinal data is that the unit of analysis shifts from the individual women to episodes corresponding to different labour market states. The total sample size of 17,767 in Table 10.1 therefore corresponds to the total number of episodes experienced by the 4746 women with complete work histories in the NCDS survey.

It can immediately be seen from the table that there are relatively few transitions between full-time and part-time work (7.1%), but that transitions from part-time work into full-time work are more common (12.8%). In other words, the majority of transitions are between non-employment and full-time or part-time employment (35% and 42%), or from part-time or full-time employment to non-employment (47% and 67%). This is consistent with our expectation that many women follow a typical employment pattern. That is, full-time employment is interrupted when a woman becomes a mother, an episode will consequently be spent out of the labour market, and the woman will then return to part-time employment. However, it is perhaps surprising that there are relatively few transitions from part-time work back into full-time work (12.8%). As Blank (1989) has argued, if part-time work is understood as a transitional form of involvement in the labour market, which provides a route for women back into full-time work, then we would expect to find a large number of part-time episodes 'sandwiched' between episodes of non-employment and episodes of full-time employment. This would result in a large number of transitions between non-employment and part-time employment and a correspondingly large number of transitions from part-time to full-time employment.

This pattern does not emerge in the transitions displayed in Table 10.1, however. A possible explanation for this is that because the NCDS work histories are right censored at age 33 many women in this sample still have very young children and are therefore not making the expected transition back into full-time employment. In other words, Blank's 'sandwich' is still in the

Table 10.1: State transition matrix based on women's work histories from the NCDS

Origin state	Destination state				
	Full-time work	**Part-time work**	**Not employed**	**Censored episodes**	**Total**
Full-time work	-	518 (7.1%)	4,889 (67%)	1,866	7,293
Part-time work	485 (12.8%)	–	1,767 (47%)	1,522	3,774
Not employed	2,351 (35%)	2,851 (42%)	–	1,498	6,700
Total	2,836	3,369	6,656	4,886	17,767

process of being made – rather, it has the appearance of an open sandwich because women are being observed before they have completed their work histories. This hypothesis can be explored using event history analysis and will be discussed in more detail below.

Using event history analysis to assess the role of part-time employment in women's work histories raises a number of issues. Firstly, the analysis needs to take account of censoring problems (namely that not all women will have returned to employment by age 33). Secondly, there will possibly be duration effects such that the longer a woman is out of paid employment the more difficult it is for her to return. And thirdly, there are likely to be unmeasured differences between individuals affecting their probability of returning to work. These could include the availability of childcare for women who are mothers and the opportunities in the local labour market, as well as variations in individual women's ambitions and motivations to work[5].

Specifying the model

The process of women returning to work has therefore been modelled as a binary recurrent event using specialist software developed at the Centre for Applied Statistics at the University of Lancaster (Barry et al, 1990)[6]. The SABRE program (Software for the Analysis of Binary Recurrent Events) allows the estimation of discrete time event history models while taking account of individual heterogeneity. When modelling women's propensity to return to paid work after a spell out of the labour force, the probability $P(E_{it})$ that individual mother I is in paid employment in month t, given that she is not already in employment, is:

$$P(E_{it} \backslash \square, \square_i ; X_{it}) = \frac{\exp(\square X_{it} + \square_i)}{1 + \exp(\square X_{it} + \square_i)}$$

where $\square$ is a vector of unknown parameters and X_{it} is the set of explanatory variables. The individual-specific error term $\square_i$ is included to take account of the omitted variables due to the potential unobserved variations between women described above. These 'nuisance parameters' cannot be estimated simultaneously with the structural parameters, particularly since there are so many of them. However, the SABRE programme eliminates these error terms. It assumes that the individual error terms are normally distributed. Analysis can then be carried out using a likelihood based on the integrated probabilities:

$$P(E_{it} \backslash \square, \square_i ; X_{it}) = P(E_{it} \backslash \square, \square_i ; X_{it}) f(\square) \, de$$

where $f(\square)$ is the probability density function of the individual error term, also known as the mixing distribution. This integral has to be calculated numerically, however this can be done with high accuracy by Gaussian Quadrature using the SABRE software, since it is univariate. In addition, 'stayers' and 'movers' are allowed for in SABRE by supplementing the quadrature points with masses at each extreme of the mixing distribution.

In order to model the process of women making transitions between full-time and part-time employment, and spells out of the labour market, employment is treated as a recurrent event which can potentially occur in each month of the work history. The unit of analysis therefore becomes the woman-month. The response variable is employment status, with three categories (full-time, part-time, or not in a paid job), indicating the employment status associated with each woman-month. Having constructed a 'discretised' work history for each woman in the NCDS, with valid work history data, a competing risks approach is used to model the work history data (Allison, 1984). As can be seen from Table 10.1 there are a total of six possible transitions that women can make between episodes spent in full-time employment, part-time employment and non-employment. The aim of the analyses reported in this chapter is to focus on the processes by which women return to paid employment after a period out of the labour market. A discrete-time method was therefore used to estimate an event history model for three separate transitions, from 'Not employed' to 'Part-time work'; from 'Part-time work' to 'Full-time work'; and from 'Not employed' to 'Full-time work'. Although several previous authors have focused only on a woman's return to paid employment following the birth of a first child (Even, 1987; Joshi and Hinde, 1993; Gustafsson et al, 1996; Dex et al, 1998; Gustafsson et al, Chapter Four of this volume), the strategy in this chapter is to make maximum use of the work history data by analysing all spells out of the labour market both before and after the birth of any children. Women's work histories have therefore been constructed from the point at which they left full-time education. This approach also clearly includes women who have not become mothers by age 33 (when the data was collected), and indeed who may never become mothers.

There are two sets of covariates, which are included in the models and are summarised in Table 10.2. Firstly, there are time varying covariates such as the presence of a partner in the household, the number of children born to the cohort member, and the age of the youngest child. Secondly, there are fixed covariates such as the cohort member's highest qualification[7].

Duration dependence

In our example, we might expect that time spent in a particular labour market state would have implications for the probability of making a transition into another state. However, a particular advantage of event history modelling is the ability to focus explicitly on duration dependence. Adopting a human capital approach (Mincer and Ofek, 1982), women who are in paid employment over a long period would be expected to accumulate experience and training that increase their career prospects and strengthen their attachment to the labour market. By contrast, women who remain out of the labour market may, over time, lose relevant job-related skills and their probability of making a transition back into the labour market may therefore decline.

Table 10.2: Covariates included in the work history models

Number of children:	
1	One child (reference category)
2	Two children
3+	Three or more children
none	No children at this point in the work history
Aych	Age of the youngest child measured in years
Pregnant	Woman is in the last three months before the birth of her child
Partner	Woman is cohabiting or married
Qualifications	
None	Reference category
Quals(2)	Clerical and other lower than O-levels
Quals(3)	O-levels
Quals(4)	A-levels and other post 16
Quals(5)	Degree or equivalent
AGE	Age of woman measured in years and centred around 28 years.
Duration	Duration in current employment state (measured in years)
Ma wk (PT)	Dummy variable – own mother worked part-time in cohort member's childhood
Ma wk (FT)	Dummy variable – own mother worked full-time in cohort member's childhood
UNEMP	National unemployment rates

A particular advantage of the current research is the ability to distinguish between part-time and full-time employment episodes. As Tam has highlighted (1997), workers in part-time jobs are less likely to receive on-the-job training than those in full-time jobs, and are less likely to hold supervisory positions. It is therefore possible that the length of time spent in part-time work does not have the same implications for the accumulation of human capital as the duration spent in full-time work. As I mentioned earlier, Tam's essentially cross-sectional analyses suggest that the length of time spent in part-time work has an inhibiting effect on a woman's propensity to be in full-time employment, so that part-time work might be understood in some senses as a 'trap' from which women find it difficult to escape into full-time jobs. The purpose of my analyses is to verify these findings using a more appropriate methodology.

Initially very simple models were estimated, which included only main effects and linear continuous variables. More complex models were then estimated which included quadratic terms for continuous variables in the model (that is, which allowed non-linear associations between continuous covariates, such as age or age of youngest child, and the probability of a transition occurring). These more complex models also allowed for significant interaction terms to be included. In this context, interaction terms indicate that the nature of the association between an independent and a dependent variable is contingent upon the level of another variable in the model. For example, if it were the case that qualifications were more salient for the transition probabilities of younger women than for older women then this would be realised in the model through the inclusion of an interaction between age and qualifications. These more complex and inclusive models are reported below.

There are several different methods for selecting a model that accurately and parsimoniously characterises the relationship between a set of explanatory variables and the dependent variable (in this case the hazard rate or, in other words, the probability of a woman making a transition in a particular month). In the current analyses I adopt the likelihood ratio test for comparing nested models. In the next section three models are discussed which were selected because they represented an improvement on the basic models without interaction terms, while also providing a parsimonious description of the observed data. In addition these models have been used to inform the production of graphs demonstrating how the probability of making a particular transition varies over time for groups of women with specific characteristics.

Results of event history modelling: women's transitions into paid employment

Inspection of the parameter estimates in Table 10.3 reveals, firstly, that it is women with one child who have the lowest probability (or hazard) of making a transition into part-time work. The positive parameter estimates for women with no children and women with two, three or more children show that these women are more likely to make the transition from non-employment to part-time employment. As would be expected from previous research, the age of the youngest child in the household also has a significant effect on a woman's propensity of making a transition to part-time employment. The inclusion of the quadratic term, however, suggests that this is not simply a linear relationship. In substantive terms the parameters suggest that the positive association between the age of the youngest child and the probability of a woman returning to work is strong when the child is very young and diminishes as the child gets older. This makes sense given that we expect the needs of a child to change most rapidly during the first few years of life. In addition it can be seen that while being in the third trimester of pregnancy has a strong negative effect on a woman's propensity of making the transition to part-time employment, being in a marital or cohabiting relationship slightly increases the probability of making this transition.

Inspection of the parameter estimates for the qualifications variable suggests that the more highly educated women have a higher probability of making a transition to part-time work. However, inclusion of the interaction between qualifications, and the length of time spent out of the labour market, was also found to significantly improve the basic model. This interaction effect shows a distinctive effect for women with degree-level qualifications. Although women with high-level qualifications have a higher probability of returning to part-time employment than those with lower qualifications, the interaction term suggests that this positive effect of qualifications is attenuated with greater

Table 10.3: Model for transition from non-employment to part-time employment, including quadratic terms and interactions

Parameter	Estimate	se	
Number of children	reference category		
1			
2	0.342	0.054	
3+	0.238	0.083	
none	0.555	0.084	
aych	0.317	0.027	
aych^2	-0.022	0.003	
pregnant	-2.419	0.220	
partner	0.297	0.089	
no quals	reference category		
quals(2)	0.297	0.114	
quals(3)	0.361	0.104	
quals(4)	0.517	0.120	
quals(5)	0.915	0.161	
q2*dur	0.029	0.023	
q3*dur	0.029	0.021	
q4*dur	-0.005	0.028	
q5*dur	-0.175	0.060	
age	0.066	0.0078	
duration	-0.075	0.0182	
ma wk(PT)	0.205	0.0544	
ma wk(FT)	0.178	0.0769	
unemp	-0.034	0.0084	
intercept	-5.208	0.169	
scale	0.644	0.064	
Probability			
end-point 0	0.78113E-01	0.34455E-01	0.72453E-01
end-point 1	0.	FIXED	0.

-2Log Likelihood = 29057.383

Observations = 229906

Cases = 3535

duration spent out of the labour market. In other words, if women with high qualifications spend too long out of the labour market they lose their relative advantage over women with lower qualifications. Indeed the model suggests that after a little over five years out of the labour market, women with degree-level qualifications will have the same probability of re-entering paid employment as women with no qualifications. Although the parameter estimates for the age of the mother and the duration spent out of the labour market are both significant, they are also small in comparison with other covariates in the model (for example, they are much smaller than the estimate connected with the age of the youngest child). The results of this event history analysis therefore confirm existing analyses of British data; namely they suggest that the age of the youngest child and the level of qualifications obtained by a woman have the strongest impact on her propensity of making the transition back into the labour market and in this case specifically back into part-time employment.

It should also be noted that the scale parameter is of a moderate size and is clearly significant. It represents the standard deviation of the distribution of individual error terms that SABRE incorporates in order to take account of unobserved heterogeneities. The fact that the scale parameter is significant indicates that there is a lot of variation in the distribution of individual error terms and it is important, therefore, to include an individual error term or 'random effect' in the model.

As Davies (1991) has highlighted, the problems of interpreting the results of statistical models are often neglected by statistical texts. A set of parameter estimates can be relatively uninformative without further computational work, and this is clearly the case for the type of complex non-linear model presented here. In the current model, for example, the effect of qualifications or duration out of employment on a woman's propensity to return to work can no longer be ascertained by examining a single parameter estimate. The most straightforward method for interpreting polynomial relationships in event history analyses is to plot graphs of the probability of a transition over time. In order to aid the interpretation of the model and to illustrate the interaction between qualifications and the duration of time spent out of paid employment, the parameter estimates were therefore used to calculate the probability of a woman returning to work in the six years following a first birth[8].

Clearly a woman's probability of returning to work will change over time as a function of her age, the age of her youngest child, and the duration she has spent out of the labour market. Figure 10.1 shows how the probability of returning to part-time work changes over time assuming that a woman leaves the labour force when her first child is born and remains out of the labour market for a continuous period (that is, duration out of work = age of youngest child). Of course it is possible to plot an infinite number of curves, each defined by the values of the other variables and the individual-specific error term. For this particular illustration it has been assumed that the woman had her first child when she was 25 years old, that she is living with a partner, that her mother did not work when she was a child, and that the national level of unemployment is constant at 10%. It is important to be clear that these

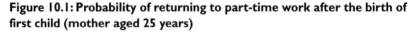

Figure 10.1: Probability of returning to part-time work after the birth of first child (mother aged 25 years)

probabilities do not necessarily apply to a specific individual woman but rather to a hypothetical group of women who share these characteristics. The probability of returning to part-time work is plotted both for women with degree-level qualifications and also for women with no qualifications. The error term was set at its median value taking into account both the estimated proportion of stayers and the standard deviation of the gaussian mixing distribution (given by the scale parameter).

Figure 10.1 clearly shows the effect of the interaction between duration and qualifications on the probability of a woman making a transition back into part-time employment. It can be seen that immediately after the birth of a first child, women with degree-level qualifications have a much higher probability of returning to part-time work than do women with no qualifications. However, as the youngest child gets older, women with no qualifications become progressively more likely to make a transition into part-time work. This effect of the age of the youngest child is effectively reduced for women with degree-level qualifications if they remain out of the labour force continuously because of the relatively high negative effect of duration out of the labour market on their probability of returning to part-time work. The graph emphasises the fact that the probability of returning to part-time employment is actually higher for women with no qualifications than it is for women with degree-level qualifications, if she remains out of the labour market until her child is five years old.

As can be seen by comparing the model for returning to full-time employment in Table 10.4 with the model for returning to part-time employment in Table 10.3, the factors influencing transitions into part-time and full-time employment are indeed rather different, which supports the argument that we should model transitions into these different employment statuses separately. In this model there is a greater contrast between the parameter estimate for women with no children and estimates for women with children, confirming that in Britain, women with children are much less likely to make a transition into full-time employment than women without children. The coefficients for age of youngest child and for being in the third trimester of pregnancy are broadly similar to those in the model for transitions into part-time employment. Once again this suggests that women who are close to giving birth, or who have a very young child are unlikely to make the transition into full-time employment. The negative quadratic term suggests that for the first few years the probability of a woman returning to full-time work increases relatively rapidly as the youngest child gets older but then this effect diminishes. This effect is clearly demonstrated in Figure 10.2, which once again applies the model parameters to an illustrative set of characteristics.

The parameter estimate for cohabiting and married women is negative in this model for transitions to full-time work suggesting that women who are not living with partners are more likely to make a transition into full-time employment. Once again higher levels of qualifications have a positive effect on the probability of transitions into paid employment. But in this model the interaction between duration spent out of employment and qualifications was not significant.

As I mentioned earlier, there are relatively few studies focusing on women's transitions back into paid employment which distinguish between part-time and full-time work. It is therefore interesting to explicitly compare the two models estimated for these separate transitions. However, comparison of the two models is complicated somewhat by the inclusion of interaction terms in the model for transitions to part-time employment. Figure 10.3 therefore illustrates the way in which the probability of returning to part-time work and full-time work varies with the age of the youngest child for women with degree qualifications. It can be seen that, while the hazard or probability of returning to part-time work starts by increasing, as the youngest child gets older, a maximum probability is reached when the child is approximately two-and-a-half years. The probability of returning part-time then gently declines. In contrast the probability of returning to full-time work continues to increase as the youngest child gets older. This suggests that a well qualified woman who is out of the labour market caring for a young child is more likely to return to part-time work while the child is relatively young. However, once the child grows older her probability of returning to full-time work is higher.

Of particular interest to my analysis is whether part-time work acts as a kind of 'bridge' or 'stepping-stone' enabling women to move from a period out of the labour market, back into full-time work, or whether, with increasing durations in part-time work, women are actually less likely to make the transition

Table 10.4: Model for transition from non-employment to full-time employment, including quadratic terms and interactions

Parameter	Estimate	se	
Number of children	reference category		
1			
2	-0.032	0.087	
3+	0.199	0.131	
none	2.879	0.095	
aych	0.439	0.039	
aych^2	-0.016	0.003	
pregnant	-4.131	0.410	
partner	-0.710	0.056	
no qualifications	reference category		
quals(2)	0.293	0.089	
quals(3)	0.558	0.079	
quals(4)	0.875	0.088	
quals(5)	1.189	0.111	
age	-0.056	0.012	
age^2	-0.005	0.002	
dur wk	-0.177	0.015	
ma wk(PT)	0.015	0.056	
ma wk(FT)	0.146	0.077	
unemployment	-0.058	0.013	
intercept	-5.347	0.197	
scale	0.488	0.052	
PROBABILITY			
end-point 0	0.21539E-01	0.12544E-01	0.21085E-01
end-point 1	0.	FIXED	0.

-2Log likelihood =21085.559

Observations = 229906

Cases = 3535

back into full-time work even though their youngest child may be older. If the age of the youngest child is found to be of overriding importance in determining a woman's probability of moving from part-time to full-time employment, then we would expect that subsequent follow-up sweeps of the NCDS would find a rather different pattern of transitions from the state transition matrix displayed in Table 10.1. We would expect that as the cohort, and their children,

Figure 10.2: Probability of returning to full-time work after the birth of first child

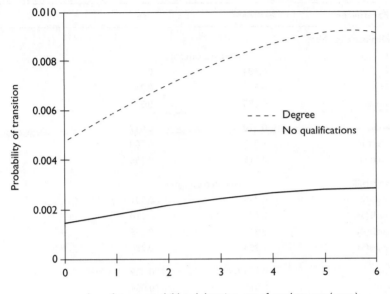

Age of youngest child and duration out of employment (years)

Figure 10.3: Probability of returning to part-time or full-time work after the birth of first child (women with degree qualifications)

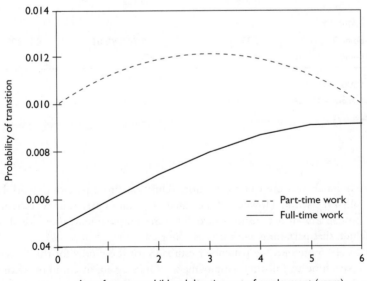

Age of youngest child and duration out of employment (years)

Table 10.5: Model for transition from part-time employment to full-time employment, including quadratic terms and interactions

Parameter	Estimate	se	
Number of children			
I	reference category		
2	0.184	0.171	
3+	0.515	0.243	
none	2.395	0.224	
aych	0.210	0.027	
pregnant	-1.039	0.508	
partner	-0.815	0.156	
no qualifications	reference category		
quals(2)	0.739	0.231	
quals(3)	0.697	0.210	
quals(4)	0.993	0.226	
quals(5)	1.284	0.280	
age	-0.125	0.029	
age^2	-0.010	0.004	
duration	0.049	0.035	
ma wk(PT)	0.028	0.129	
ma wk(FT)	0.132	0.173	
unemployment rate	-0.063	0.033	
int	-6.127	0.492	
scale	0.609	0.157	
PROBABILITY			
end-point 0	0.39661	0.78779E-01	0.28398
end-point I	0.	FIXED	

-2LL= 5572.368

Observations = 104754

Cases = 2375

grow older there would be many more transitions from part-time work back into full-time work. However, if increased duration in part-time work reduces the probability of a transition into full-time employment, then we should conclude that part-time work acts as a 'trap'.

Table 10.5 presents the parameter estimates for the model for the transition from part-time to full-time employment. Once again, in common with the model for transitions from non-employment to full-time employment, none of the interaction terms tested were found to be significant, although including the quadratic term for age of youngest child did improve the fit of the model. What is particularly interesting about this model is that the duration effect is not significant – if anything it is slightly positive. This means that women who spend lengthy episodes in part-time work do not apparently reduce their chances of moving into full-time work. However, as will be discussed below, this does not mean that part-time work is necessarily a 'bridge' back into full-time work for all women.

The model in Table 10.5 is illustrated in Figure 10.4 by applying the parameter estimates to an illustrative set of cases and plotting the way that the probability of making a transition changes with increasing age of youngest child and increasing duration out of the labour market. The most striking feature of this graph is the relatively low overall probability of transitions from part-time to full-time employment compared with the transitions out of non-employment illustrated in Figures 10.1 and 10.2. This is in line with the original state transition matrix displayed as Table 10.1, which showed that women in part-time work are relatively unlikely to move into full-time work. Examination of the parameter estimates in Table 10.5 allows us to move beyond this overall conclusion to determine under which particular set of circumstances women are most likely to make a transition from part-time to full-time work. In this model the relatively high parameter estimate for women with no children is striking. This suggests that part-time work may be acting as a transitional status for this particular group of women, enabling them to move into full-time work. If we look at this coefficient in comparison with the parameter estimate for the age of the youngest child, it suggests that the youngest child in the

Figure 10.4: Probability of making a transition to full-time work from part-time work

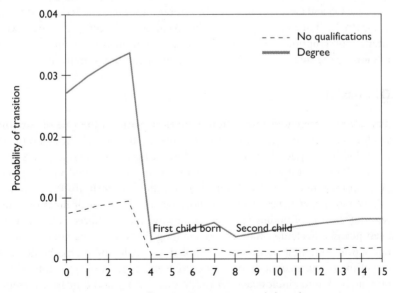

Duration in part-time work (years)

family has to reach at least 11 years of age before a mother has the same probability of moving from part-time work to full-time work, as a woman with no children.

A further feature of this model, which is particularly relevant to the current discussion, is the substantial minority of women who are classified as 'stayers' by the model. This can be seen to be 28.4% in the model including quadratic terms displayed in Table 10.5. These are women who are at the extreme of the mixing distribution. In other words they have some unmeasured attribute (or set of attributes) which makes them unlikely to ever make the transition from part-time into full-time employment. However, it must be emphasised that this attribute will not necessarily be a characteristic of the women; rather it is simply a variable or set of variables that is missing from the model. In other words it could reflect local labour market conditions, which are not captured by the NCDS data, for example.

One of the most interesting findings to emerge from the approach to event history analysis adopted here, then, is that long episodes in part-time work do not appear to reduce women's probabilities of returning to full-time employment. This suggests that the results reported by Tam (1997) may well be misleading. As was suggested above, the negative association, which she finds, between part-time experience and full-time employment may be caused by the endogenous effect of previous employment experience in her cross-sectional model.

It is also interesting to note, however, that in the models discussed above, long durations out of the labour force were significantly associated with a reduced probability of returning to employment. This appeared to be the case for transitions into full-time employment in particular. This result for a cohort of British women born in 1958 is consonant with the findings for women from the US and Germany reported by Drobnic, Blossfeld and Rohwer (Drobnic et al, 1999). They also report that the likelihood of returning to paid work, after an interruption of employment, declines with increasing duration, so that the longer the interruption the lower the prospects of re-employment.

Discussion

This chapter presented results from empirical work on the role of part-time work in British women's employment histories. In particular it demonstrated the value of using longitudinal data and event history techniques that control for unobserved individual heterogeneity. The specific value of using these event history models with an individual specific error term for the current set of analyses is that it has enabled a thorough investigation of duration effects without the risk of finding spurious cumulative inertia effects. It has therefore been possible to demonstrate that while long durations in part-time work do not appear to inhibit transitions into full-time employment, lengthy durations out of the labour market do have a negative effect on a woman's probability of moving back into employment. An additional feature of the analyses presented above is that they have explicitly included both mothers and women who had no children by age 33. As I highlighted above, it is interesting to note that women who have no children and who are in part-time work have a particularly high probability of moving into full-time work, compared to women with children.

In addition to presenting the results of empirical analyses of women's retrospective work histories from the NCDS, this chapter also discussed some of the problems of restricting longitudinal analyses to samples of mothers, and of discussing the results of such analyses as though they are applicable to all women. The danger lies in the implication that femininity, or what it means to be a woman in contemporary society, can be equated with motherhood. As has been discussed above, this slippage between the categories of 'women' and 'mothers' can lead to a conceptualisation of gender and gender differences as emanating from women's biological capacity to bear children and therefore as relatively fixed and immutable. Therefore, I argue that longitudinal analyses that take the birth of a first child as their starting point run the risk of reifying the concept of gender. These reflections on the conflation of women and mothers in a great deal of the recent research on women's labour market behaviour are not intended to denigrate any of the research referenced and discussed here, or to deny the value of the statistical techniques on which such research is based. As I have argued above, the development of event history analysis techniques are important in that they enable us to understand more fully the factors that influence women's careers.

A related issue, which has not been discussed above, is that just as we should not imply that mothers' labour market behaviour can be equated with women's labour market behaviour, we should also avoid the suggestion that results obtained from the analysis of samples of predominantly white women can be applied to all women, for example to minority ethnic women in Britain. The NCDS is not a good source of data on the employment behaviour of minority ethnic women, partly because of the way that the sample has been obtained and maintained. However, analysis of the samples of anonymised records from the 1991 census has demonstrated that minority ethnic women in Britain do have very different patterns of employment and in particular that minority ethnic mothers are much less likely to work part time than white mothers (Dale and Holdsworth, 1998).

To conclude, I argue that it is important to explicitly include women who do not have children in longitudinal analyses, so that we might avoid presenting analyses which implicitly suggest that, in order to understand women's trajectories within the labour market, it is sufficient to examine the employment behaviour of mothers, as well as in the discussion of those analyses. This has the additional merit of avoiding the danger of selection biases which can be shown to distort the coefficients in statistical models (Berk, 1983). In addition, by analysing data from specific cohorts of women, and highlighting the limited applicability of the findings, it is possible to present analyses which are clearly situated in a specific geographic and historical context and do not make claims for the timeless nature of the gendered division of labour and the resultant gender inequalities in the labour market. It is in this way that we can move towards a better understanding of gender inequalities within society without reifying gender in a way that potentially contributes to the perpetuation of those inequalities.

Notes

[1] Hakim (1996); Breugel (1996); Ginn et al (1996); Crompton and Harris (1998, 1999); Proctor and Padfield (1999); Walsh (1999); Hakim (2001).

[2] Analysis of the response bias for this sweep confirms that, although certain groups are under-represented within the sample (most notably those from minority ethnic groups and those with origins in the lowest social classes), overall representation was achieved (Shepherd, 1993).

[3] Once incomplete work histories are excluded, the sample of women is reduced from 5,799 to 5,205.

[4] This division is clearly an over-simplification, since women who are 'not employed' may also categorise themselves as 'out of the labour market, looking after children' or as 'unemployed (actively seeking work)'.

[5] Innumerable variables are, inevitably, omitted from any analysis. It is essential to include these unobserved heterogeneities in the model – omitting them (mis-measured, mis-specified, or not observed) may lead to misleading results and serious effects on the other parameter estimates (Davies and Pickles, 1985; Davies and Dale, 1994; Ruspini, 2002: forthcoming).

[6] In this context a recurrent event refers to an event that can potentially occur more than once in an individual's work history, such as the from non-employment to part-time employment. In contrast, the birth of a first child can occur only once in a lifetime, and is not therefore a recurrent event.

[7] Ideally, qualifications would be included in the model as a time varying covariate. However, the NCDS questionnaire, 'Your life since 1974', instructs respondents to record only jobs that commenced after the end of full-time education. In addition, the 'Not in a job' section of the life history, which records spells out of the labour market in education, contains a substantial amount of missing data. The quality of the data therefore dictated that qualifications be treated as an exogenous variable.

[8] The probability of making a transition was calculated using the fact that $p = \exp(b)$ $[1 + \exp(b)]$, where $B = b_1 x_1 + b_2 x_2 \ldots + b_n x_n + c$, so that x_1 to x_n represent the covariates in the model, and b_1 to b_n represent the corresponding parameter estimates.

References

Allison, P.D. (1984) *Event history analysis: Regression for longitudinal event data*, Berverly Hills, CA: Sage Publications.

Annandale, E. and Clark, J. (1996) 'What is gender? Feminist theory and the sociology of human reproduction', *Sociology of Health and Illness*, vol 18, no 1, pp 17-44.

Barry, J., Francis, B. and Davies, R.B. (1990) *SABRE: Software for the Analysis of Binary Recurrent Events – A guide for users*, Lancaster: Centre for Applied Statistics, University of Lancaster.

Berk, R.A. (1983) 'An introduction to sample selection bias in sociological data', *American Sociological Review*, vol 48, no 3, pp 386-98.

Blank, R.M. (1989) 'The role of part-time work in women's labor market choices over time', *Americal Economic Association Papers and Proceedings*, vol 79, no 2, pp 295-99.

Breugel, I. (1996) 'Whose myths are they anyway? A comment', *British Journal of Sociology*, vol 47, no 1, pp 175-7.

Butler, J. (1990) *Gender trouble: Feminism and the subversion of identity*, London: Routledge.

Corcoran, M. and Duncan, G. (1979) 'Work history, labor force attachment, and earnings differences between the races and sexes', *Journal of Human Resources*, vol 14, no 1, pp 3-20.

Crompton, R. (1999) 'The decline of the male breadwinner: explanations and Interpretations', in R. Crompton (ed) *Restructuring gender relations and employment: The decline of the male breadwinner*, Oxford: Oxford University Press, pp 1-25.

Crompton, R. and Harris, F. (1998) 'Explaining women's employment patterns: "Orientations to work" revisited', *British Journal of Sociology*, vol 49, no 1, pp 118-36.

Crompton, R. and Harris, F. (1999) 'Employment, careers, and families: the significance of choice and constraint in women's lives', in R. Crompton (ed) *Restructuring gender relations and employment: The decline of the male breadwinner*, Oxford: Oxford University Press, pp 128-49.

Dale, A. (1987) 'Occupational inequality, gender and life cycle', *Work, Employment and Society*, vol 1, no 3, pp 326-51.

Dale, A. and Holdsworth, C. (1998) 'Why don't minority ethnic women in Britain work part-time?' in J. O'Reilly and C. Fagan (eds) *Part time prospects: An international comparison of part time work in Europe, North America and the Pacific Rim*, London: Routledge, pp 77-95.

Davies, R.B. (1991) 'The analysis of housing and migration careers', in J. Stillwell and P. Congdon (eds) *Modelling migration: Macro and micro perspectives*, London: Belhaven Press, pp 207-27.

Davies, R.B. (1994) 'Statistical modelling for survey analysis', *Journal of the Market Research Society*, vol 35, no 3, pp 235-47.

Davies, R.B. and Dale, A. (1994) 'Introduction', in A. Dale and R.B. Davies (eds) *Analysing social and political change. A casebook of methods*, London: Sage Publications, pp 1-19.

Davies, R.B. and Pickles, A.R. (1985) 'Longitudinal versus cross-sectional methods for behavioural research: a first round knockout', *Environment and Planning A*, 17, pp 1315-29.

Dex, S. (1984) *Women's work histories: An analysis of the Women and Employment Survey*, Research paper no 46, London: Department of Employment.

Dex, S. (1987) *Women's occupational mobility*, London: Macmillan.

Dex, S., Joshi, H., Macran, S. and McCulloch, A. (1998) 'Women's employment transitions around child bearing', *Oxford Bulletin of Economics and Statistics*, vol 60, no 1, pp 79-97.

Drobnic, S., Blossfeld, H.-P. and Rohwer, G. (1999) 'Dynamics of women's employment patterns over the family life course: a comparison of the United States and Germany', *Journal of Marriage and the Family*, vol 61, no 1, pp 133-46.

Eisenstein, Z. (1988) *The female body and the law*, San Francisco, CA: University of California Press.

Elias, P. and Main, B. (1982) *Women's working lives: Evidence from the National Training Survey*, Warwick: Institute for Employment Research, University of Warwick.

Elliott, J., Dale, A. and Egerton, M. (2001) 'The influence of qualifications on women's work histories, employment status and earnings at age 33', *European Sociological Review*, vol 17, no 2, pp 145-68.

Even, W.E. (1987) 'Career interruptions following childbirth', *Journal of Labor Economics*, vol 5, no 2, pp 255-77.

Gallie, D. (ed) (1988) *Employment in Britain*, Oxford: Blackwell.

Gianelli, G.C. (1996) 'Women's transitions in the labour market: a competing risks analysis on German panel data', *Journal of Population Economics*, vol 9, no 3, pp 287-300.

Ginn, J. and Arber, S. (1998) 'How does part-time work lead to low pension income', in J. O'Reilly and C. Fagan (eds) *Part-time prospects: An international comparison of part-time work in Europe, North America and the Pacific Rim*, London: Routledge, pp 156-74.

Ginn, J., Arber, S., Brannen, J., Dale, A., Dex, S., Elias, P., Moss, P., Pahl, J., Roberts, C. and Rubery, J. (1996) 'Feminist fallacies: a reply to Hakim on women's employment', *British Journal of Sociology*, vol 47, no 1, pp 167-77.

Gustafsson, S.S., Wetzels, C.M.M.P., Vlasblom, J.D. and Dex, S. (1996) 'Women's labour force transitions in connection with childbirth: a panel data comparison between Germany, Sweden, and Great Britain', *Journal of Population Economics*, vol 9, no 3, pp 223-46.

Hakim, C. (1996) 'The sexual division of labour and women's heterogeneity', *British Journal of Sociology*, vol 47, no 1, pp 178-88.

Hakim, C. (2001) *Work-lifestyle choices in the 21st century: Preference theory*, Oxford: Oxford University Press.

Joesch, J.M. (1994) 'Paid leave and the timing of women's employment before and after birth', *Journal of Marriage and the Family*, vol 56, no 2, pp 429-40.

Joshi, H. and Hinde, P.R.A. (1993) 'Employment after childbearing in post-war Britain: cohort study evidence on contrasts within and across generations', *European Sociological Review*, vol 9, no 3, pp 203-27.

Joshi, H., Paci, P. and Waldfogel, J. (1996) *The wages of motherhood: Better or worse?*, Welfare State Programme/122, STICERD, London: London School of Economics and Political Science.

Layder, D. (1990) *The realist image in social science*, Basingstoke: Macmillan.

Marshall, B.L. (1994) *Engendering modernity*, Cambridge: Polity Press.

Martin, J. and Roberts, C. (1984) *Women and employment: A lifetime perspective*, London: HMSO.

McRae, S. (1993) 'Returning to work after childbirth: opportunities and inequalities', *European Sociological Review*, vol 9, no 2, pp 125-38.

Mincer, J. and Ofek, H. (1982) 'Interrupted work careers: depreciation and restoration of human capital', *Journal of Human Resources*, vol 17, no 1, pp 3-24.

Mincer, J. and Polachek, S. (1974) 'Family investment in human capital: earnings of women', *Journal of Political Economy*, vol 82, no 2, pp S76-S108.

Myrdal, A. and Klein, V. (1956) *Women's two roles*, London: Routledge and Kegan Paul.

Pfau-Effinger, B. (1998) 'Culture or structure as explanations for differences in part time work in Germany, Finland and the Netherlands', in J. O'Reilly and C. Fagan (eds) *Part time prospects: An international comparison of part time work in Europe, North America and the Pacific Rim*, London: Routledge, pp 177-98.

Proctor, I. and Padfield, M. (1999) 'Work orientations and women's work: a critique of Hakim's theory of the heterogeneity of women', *Gender, Work and Organization*, vol 6, no 3, pp 152-62.

Richardson, L. (1990) *Writing strategies: reaching diverse audiences*, Beverly Hills, CA: Sage Publications.

Riley, D. (1983) *War in the nursery*, London: Virago.

Riley, D. (1988) *'Am I that name?' Feminism and the category of women in history*, London: Macmillan.

Rowlingson, K., Whyley, C. and Warren, T. (1999) *Wealth in Britain. A life-cycle perspective*, London: PSI.

Ruspini, E. (2001) 'The study of women's deprivation: how to reveal the gender dimension of poverty', *International Journal of Social Research Methodology*, vol 4, no 2, pp 101-18.

Ruspini, E. (2002: forthcoming) *Introduction to longitudinal research*, London: Routledge.

Scott, J.W. (1988) *Gender and the politics of history*, New York, NY: Columbia University Press.

Scheiwe, K. (1994) 'Labour market, welfare state and family institutions: the links to mothers' poverty risks. A comparison between Belgium, Germany and the United Kingdom', *Journal of European Social Policy*, vol 4, no 3, pp 201-24.

Shepherd, P. (1993) 'Appendix 1: Analysis of response bias', in *Life at 33: The fifth follow-up of the National Child Development Study*, London: National Children's Bureau, pp 184-88.

Siltanen, J. (1994) *Locating gender: Occupational segregation, wages and domestic responsibilities*, London: University College London Press.

Stewart, M.B. and Greenhalgh, C.A. (1984) 'Work history patterns and the occupational attainment of women', *The Economic Journal*, vol 94, no 3, pp 493-519.

Tam, M. (1997) *Part-time employment: A bridge or a trap?*, Aldershot: Avebury.

Walsh, J. (1999) 'Myths and counter-myths: an analysis of part-time female employees and their orientations to work and working hours', *Work, Employment and Society*, vol 13, no 2, pp 179-204.

Part III:
Data sources

ELEVEN

Concluding comments

Elisabetta Ruspini and Angela Dale

The chapters in this book have used a dynamic perspective to move forwards our understanding of how women's lives are evolving and in what direction, and how the gender dimension of the system of social inequality is changing. They have also linked the micro- and the macro-elements of such changes in a comparative perspective.

Social change has dramatically altered women's lives in a number of closely linked ways, such as:

- The effects of increasing education on postponement of maternity and family formation processes, and the role of education in influencing labour market participation (Gustafsson, Kenjoh and Wetzels, Chapter Four).
- The long-term impact of childbearing on women's lifetime earnings (Joshi and Davies, Chapter Six).
- The consequences of relationship dissolution for women (Dewilde, Chapter Five).
- Gender differences in the impact of precarious employment on young people, and its association with unemployment (Kurz, Chapter Seven).
- The effect of changes in employment, and in particular the large growth in self-employment, on women's lives. Self-employment, as far as employment law and regulation are concerned, is indeed more vulnerable than employee status (Dex and Smith, Chapter Eight).
- The relationship between human capital and social capital on participation in the labour market, and on the gender wage gap (Sugihashi and Dale, Chapter Nine).

It is important that the study of the individual life course should not ignore the broader context in which it is embedded. In this volume the authors have discussed the role of macro-change (for example, equal opportunities policies, extending higher education, and redistribution policies), and its impact on women in terms of gender inequalities. For example, Gustafsson, Kenjoh and Wetzels looked at the role of education in influencing the timing of motherhood – differences between countries became apparent that suggest that there are institutional factors that mediate this influence. As Mayer and Tuma state (1990, p 3), "the life course is shaped by, among other things, cultural beliefs about the individual biography, institutionalised sequences of roles and positions, legal age restrictions and decisions of individual actors".

The empirical results sustain our initial position: *that women are probably the most important actors of social change.* They have seen their patterns of life and expectations change more fundamentally than those of men. Moreover, their risk of poverty has diversified since the patterns of social exclusion have multiplied.

Crucially, longitudinal data provide the essential empirical basis and tools for understanding the relationship between individuals' (women's and men's) behaviour and social change. The chapters presented here use very different longitudinal data sources: household panel studies, retrospective interviews, cohort studies, retrospective life history data, to name but a few. As Leisering and Walker observe (1999, p 266), social life is intrinsically dynamic; in studying social life, then, dynamic methods of enquiry are naturally superior to the static approaches that have dominated research thus far. In particular, we have seen the value of household panel surveys (see the chapters by Gustafsson, Kenjoh and Wetzels; Joshi and Davies; Kurz) and especially of the European Community Household Panel (Dewilde) which provides comparable data across member states of the EU. In some countries, such as Italy and Spain, this is the only source of panel data that is readily available. Indeed, longitudinal studies in Europe have been developing at two different paces, as the very high costs of such studies has made it difficult for less well-off countries to launch them. It is no coincidence that the countries of northern Europe (Germany, Sweden, Holland, Belgium, UK) adopted dynamic approaches to the study of social phenomena long before those in southern Europe, where there is still a severe lack of dynamic data available and no tradition of serious, in-depth, longitudinal research (Ruspini, 2002: forthcoming).

The importance of longitudinal data as both a national resource and a resource for comparative analysis cannot be over-emphasised. However, there is much room for improvement even in existing longitudinal research, in order to increase their value by allowing a truly gender sensitive research approach. The challenge facing longitudinal research now is how the gender dimension of change, that is, the consequences of social change on women's (and men's) life courses and the role of women and men as actors of change, is to be analysed and understood. This also means there is an urgent need for the organisational practice of social research to make more use of longitudinal data and to bring a gender-sensitive perspective into diachronic analysis.

In what follows we make some recommendations for increasing and improving the role of longitudinal data in researching changes in women's (and men's) lives and life courses. Change, as we have already seen, is above all a highly complex process, involving many factors. Some aspects of change are seen as systematic and predictable, and others as random or coincidental. Within this context, a key issue is to highlight how women (in comparison to men) are conceptualised in longitudinal studies, and how deep longitudinal research can dig into women's life courses. We must also attempt to understand whether gender inequality is effectively investigated within longitudinal studies, and/or whether it has the potential to be investigated in the first place. The final aim is to go beyond the 'indirect gender indicator' model, that is, derived from the difference between total population and male population, and replace it with a research approach that is able, in a dynamic perspective, to highlight important aspects of women's roles, and the ways in which these are changing.

First, research on women needs to be contextualised with information on other actors within the private domestic sphere and, also, outside households. Previous research has shown that there is likely to be extreme inequality between husband and wife and deprivation on the part of the wife and children. Much work has also shown the extent to which women adapt their lives to combine employment with family care. First, women 'go without' more often than men: some women are denied access to resources, while others voluntarily go without in to increase that available for their partners and children (see, among others, Graham, 1987; Brannen and Wilson, 1987; Ruspini 2001). Moreover, as Payne suggested (1991), some resources are apparently bought jointly, but consumption is not shared equally: the family car, heating for the home, hot water. Most wives used their income to buy things for the family, or added their earnings to the housekeeping money (day-to-day living expenses, food, cleaning materials). Women's pay is typically spent on household necessities and only rarely, and in smaller amounts, on women's own needs (Brannen, 1987). Thus, women and men often hold different views over necessary expenditure and the ways in which money can be saved (Charles and Kerr, 1987; Graham, 1987; Wilson 1987), and this pattern of consumption in low-income households makes women's task of making ends meet more difficult. This means that surveys need to ensure that information is collected about all relevant actors – which may require questions about the flows of time and economic resources that lie beyond the walls of the household. Furthermore, detailed information about family composition and change, the division of tasks/duties inside the household, and the shape and variations of networks of informal exchange are desperately needed.

In addition, another relevant issue concerns the need to analyse the process of gender role developments, the inter-generational transmission of gender-role stereotypes and biases and the transformations of these stereotypes. These biases, for example, relate to the acceptance of domestic responsibilities and 'moral obligations' towards family needs or the limitation of occupational aspirations. This could successfully be done by collecting longitudinal information on men, women and children, both prospectively and retrospectively, and, also, by analysing the socio-economic situation of the parents and/or grandparents of the respondents. Such an approach might allow us to perceive the extent to which the gender division of duties and the processes of dependence are transmitted from generation to generation. Through differential reinforcements learned first in the home and then reinforced by other adults (such as teachers, school experience, the child's peers, and television viewing), boys and girls are taught to do 'boy and girl things', to pursue 'gender appropriate' school and academic subjects and to aspire to occupations that fit their own gender (see, among others, Eccles et al, 1990; Sigelman and Shaffer, 1995; Helwig, 1998). Assigning household tasks by gender leads children to link certain types of occupational aspirations to a particular gender.

Another interesting issue is the development of a child's 'economic world', and the exploration of gender differences from childhood to teenage in economic socialisation. Empirical evidence suggests that there are strong differences between boys and girls in money socialisation processes. Different familial experiences promote in children feelings of independence, or of fear, autonomy or dependency, and feelings of expertise or shame around financial matters. For example, recent research in Italy showed that young girls tend to be less interested in economic issues, and slightly more concerned about 'not wasting money on useless things' compared with boys.

Differences between men and women increase with age (Rinaldi, 2001). If both mothers and fathers contribute to the gender stereotyping of their children, fathers have been found to reinforce gender stereotypes more often than mothers (Witt, 1997). It also seems that children whose mothers work outside the home are not as traditional in gender role orientation as children whose mothers are not economically active (Weinraub et al, 1988). Thus, social change, and the role played by women within these changes, is contributing to the modification of gender-role stereotypes. However, we should keep in mind that a period of time needs to pass before intergenerational analyses are feasible, since a consistent number of waves is necessary in order to allow in-depth, long-term analyses to be carried out.

It is also important that topics and questions are compiled in a way that is gender-sensitive. A crucial methodological challenge for gender-sensitive research is how to open the family 'black box' in order to understand the extent to which social exclusion processes and poverty are masked, and to analyse the factors underlying a system of inequality that hinges upon gender differences. This can be done through increased availability of variables which specifically aim to depict the three processes involved in the acquisition and expenditure of resources within the family: (1) the entry of resources into the household; (2) how resources are allocated and controlled; (3) and how resources are expended (Daly, 1992). For example, the provision of questions in the British Household Panel Survey concerning the allocation of resources within the household has provided researchers with an essential and additional tool that supports a gender-sensitive basis for measuring poverty and for comparing gender inequalities within the household.

A second methodological challenge is to analyse the connection between the concepts of dependence and unpaid work and, at the same time, to measure progress toward gender equality in economic autonomy. What is the meaning of 'economic autonomy'? Do we have adequate data for developing statistical indicators and conducting the necessary analysis? Future research must try to answer these questions, and in the process draw attention to aspects of the distribution of caring tasks and unpaid work, of exposure to constraints that inhibit one's ability to make use of opportunities for training and continuing education, and exposure to occupational discrimination and health hazards (Statistics Canada, 2000).

An important argument has been made by a number of commentators (Joshi et al, 1995; Millar, 2000). They propose that the issue of placing individuals within the household and perceiving their contribution to the resources of that household, as well as their dependence on those resources, lies in the examination of sources (not just levels) of income. Another topic relates to the conceptualisation of employment and unemployment where differences in cultural expectations require a gender-sensitive line of inquiry. For example, occupational class analyses should use classifications which more adequately reflect meaningful distinctions between women's occupations and the need to consider both a woman's domestic roles and her structural position (Arber, 1990).

The inclusion of topics relevant to the analysis of gender differences will not only encourage the greater use of these important resources, but will also open them up to a much broader range of researchers. This raises the issue of the accessibility of these analytical tools – it is important that longitudinal data do not come to be seen as too difficult to use by the average social scientist, especially those without a strong statistical background. Chapters in this volume, such as that by Dewilde (Five), have shown the value of relatively simple descriptive, gender-sensitive analyses in a comparative perspective. With comparative longitudinal analysis, in particular, simple, accessible techniques of data analyses are an essential first step in the research process. Elliott (Ten) also demonstrates that a relatively simple analysis can offer considerable insights into women's life courses. This issue is of growing importance, since longitudinal comparative datasets, both ex ante and ex post (such as the European Community Household Panel [ECHP], the Panel Comparability Project [PACO] or the Consortium of Household Panels for European Socio-economic Research [CHER]), are now available for analysis by academics[1].

Finally, as Dex and Elliott demonstrate (Eight and Ten, respectively), a gender-sensitive research approach should combine the 'qualitative' and 'quantitative' dimensions. Quantitative research and qualitative research are often depicted as mutually exclusive models of the social process. While quantitative research is typically associated with the processes of enumerative induction, standardisation, extrapolation and generalisability, the qualitative paradigm places great emphasis on social life as an interlocking series of events. This emphasis can be seen as a response to the qualitative researcher's concern to reflect the reality of everyday life which takes the form of a stream of interconnecting events. Thus, there is an implicit longitudinal element built into much qualitative research: the general image that the qualitative researcher conveys about the social order is one of interconnection and dynamism (Bryman, 1988, pp 65-6). This is why gender sensitive research is well established among qualitative researchers (among others, Finch and Mason, 1993; Mason, 1996), and why feminist research privileges experiential knowledge, reflexivity, the affective components of research, that is, 'qualitative' methods of investigation. Some feminists have argued that quantitative methods are associated with male-dominated assumptions and bias – the positivist approaches, namely surveys, have rendered women (and their perspectives) invisible (Oakley, 1981; Graham, 1983; Brannen, 1992).

It is now important that insights from the 'qualitative' tradition are used to inform the analysis of longitudinal datasets. There are two aspects to this. First, the 'qualitative' theoretical paradigm, being inherently longitudinal, should help to enrich the empirical evidence from quantitative longitudinal analyses. For example, Elliott problematises the meaning of her data and how it is used in the analysis, an approach which contrasts with some survey analysts who take the data as 'given' and do not go beyond the purely statistical evidence. Secondly, longitudinal analysis would benefit from a combination of data sources, such as enriching existing data collection techniques with the ones used in biographical analyses (life history, study of life courses and life events). It is true, however, that longitudinal surveys often combine both extensive (quantitative) and intensive (qualitative) approaches. For example, panel data often include relevant retrospective information, so that the respondents have continuous records in key fields from the beginning of their lives. This makes it possible to develop an analytical prospective of individual life courses, constituting one of the most important developments that has taken place in the area of official statistics in the last two decades.

Thus, new methods of inquiry and new tools are required in order to help understand not only such fast and radical social change, but also the dynamic nature of women's and men's lives and the shifts taking place in the role of social institutions. This should encourage a move towards richer and more sensitive methods of (longitudinal) data gathering and the development of techniques that permit dynamic interpretation of the gender dimension of social change.

Note

[1] The PACO has built up an archive of longitudinal data that can be compared at the supra-national level, since it is drawn from various European and non-European household panel studies, currently underway in Great Britain [UK?], Germany, France-Lorraine, Luxembourg, Poland, Hungary, and the US. It covers about 150 variables which are comparable due to a process of transformation which has created identical names, labels and methods, and has thus been able to create a common data structure. (For further details, see http://www.ceps.lu/paco/pacopres.htm.)

CHER aims to develop and enhance a comparative database for longitudinal household studies by harmonising and integrating micro-datasets from a large variety of independent national panels and from the European Community Household Panel. (For further details, visit the website at http://www.kub.nl/~fsw_2/asz/tisser/research/Cher.htm.)

References

Arber, S. (1990) 'Opening the black box: understanding inequalities in women's health', in P. Abbott and G. Payne (eds) *New directions in the sociology of health*, Brighton: Falmer Press, pp 37-56.

Brannen, J. (1987) *Taking maternity leave: The employment decisions of women with young children*, London: Thomas Coram Research Unit.

Brannen, J. (1992) 'Combining qualitative and quantitative approaches: an overview', in J. Brannen (ed) *Mixing methods: Qualitative and quantitative research*, Aldershot: Avebury, pp 3-37.

Brannen, J. and Wilson, C. (1987) 'Introduction', in J. Brannen and C. Wilson (eds) *Give and take in families. Studies in resource distribution*, London: Allen & Unwin, pp 1-17.

Bryman, A. (1988) *Quantity and quality in social research*, London and New York, NY: Routledge.

Charles, N. and Kerr, M. (1987) 'Just the way it is: gender and age differences in family food consumption', in J. Brannen and G. Wilson (eds) *Give and take in families*, London: Allen & Unwin, pp 155-74.

Daly, M. (1992) 'Europe's poor women? Gender in research on poverty', *European Sociological Review*, vol 8, no 1, pp 1-12.

Eccles, J.S., Jacobs, J.E. and Harold, R.D. (1990) 'Gender role stereotypes, expectancy effects, and parents' socialization of gender differences', *Journal of Social Issues*, vol 46, no 2, pp 183-201.

Finch, J. and Mason, J. (1993) *Negotiating family responsibilities*, London: Routledge.

Graham, H. (1983) 'Do her answers fit his questions? Women and the survey method', in E. Gamarnikow, D. Morgan, J. Purvis and D. Taylorson, (eds) *The public and the private*, London: Heinemann, pp 132-47.

Graham, H. (1987) 'Women's poverty and caring', in C. Glendinning and J. Millar (eds) *Women and poverty in Britain*, Hemel Hempstead: Harvester Wheatsheaf.

Helwig, A.A. (1998) 'Gender-role stereotyping: testing theory with a longitudinal sample', *Sex Roles: A Journal of Research*, March.

Hills, J. (1993) *The future of welfare. A guide to the debate*, York: Joseph Rowntree Foundation.

Leisering, L. and Walker, R. (1999) 'Making the future: from dynamics to policy agendas', in L. Leisering and R. Walker (eds) *The dynamics of modern society*, Bristol: The Policy Press, pp 265-85.

Joshi H., Dale A., Ward, C. and Davies, H. (1995) *Dependence and independence in the finances of women aged 33*, London: Family Policy Study Centre.

Mason, J. (1996) *Qualitative researching*, London: Sage Publications.

Mayer, K.U. and Tuma, B.N. (1990) 'Life course research and event history analysys: an overview', in K.U. Mayer and N.B. Tuma (eds) *Event history analysis in life course research*, Madison, WI: University of Wisconsin Press, pp 3-20.

Millar, J. (2000) 'Genere, povertà e esclusione sociale', in F. Bimbi and E. Ruspini (eds) *Povertà delle donne e trasformazione dei rapporti di genere. Inchiesta*, vol 128, aprile-giugno, pp 9-13.

Oakley, A. (1981) 'Interviewing women: a contradiction in terms?' in H. Roberts (ed) *Doing feminist research*, London: Routledge and Kegan Paul, pp 30-62.

Olsen, R. (1996) 'Young carers: challenging the facts and politics of research into children and caring', *Disability and Society*, vol 11, no 1, pp 41-54.

Pahl, J. (1989) *Money and marriage*, London: Macmillan.

Payne, S. (1991) *Women, health and poverty: An introduction*, Hemel Hempstead: Harvester Wheatsheaf.

Payne, S. (2001) 'Malattia e ruoli femminili: la relazione tra dipendenza economica, responsabilità di cura e povertà', in C. Facchini and E. Ruspini (eds) *Salute e disuguaglianze. Genere, condizioni sociali e corso di vita, Collana Transizioni e Politiche pubbliche*, Milan: Franco Angeli.

Rinaldi, E. (2001) 'Economic socialisation tracks and gender differences. A research on Italian children and teenagers', Paper presented at the International Conference 'Family Forms and the Young Generation in Europe', University of Milano-Bicocca, Milan, Italy, 20-22 September.

Ruspini, E. (2001) 'The study of women's deprivation: how to reveal the gender dimension of poverty', *International Journal of Social Research Methodology: Theory and Practice*, vol 4, no 2, pp 101-18.

Ruspini, E. (2002: forthcoming) *Introduction to longitudinal research*, London: Routledge.

Sigelman, C.K. and Shaffer, D.R. (1995) *Life-span human development* (2nd edn), Pacific Grove, CA: Brooks & Cole.

Statistics Canada (2000) *National priority gender issues and the statistics needed for the implementation and evaluation of policies and programs, with special focus on gender sensitive indicators and broader gender equality indices – The case of Canada*, Working Paper 9, Conference of European Statisticians, Orvieto (Italy) 11-13 October.

Weinraub, M., Jaeger, E. and Hoffman, L.W. (1988) 'Predicting infant outcomes in families of employed and non-employed mothers', *Early Childhood Research Quarterly*, vol 3, pp 361-78.

Wilson, G. (1987) 'Money: pattern of responsibility and irresponsibility', in J. Brannen and C. Wilson (eds) *Give and take in families: Studies in resource distribution*, London: Allen & Unwin, pp 136-54.

Witt, S.D. (1997) 'Parental influence on children's socialization to gender roles', *Adolescence*, vol 32, no 126, pp 253-9.

Appendix: Description and characteristics of longitudinal data sets used in this book

Elisabetta Ruspini

This appendix offers the reader a brief overview of the (longitudinal) datasets used in the book. For more detailed information the reader should consult the books and web pages which deal extensively with the characteristics of the datasets.

British Household Panel Survey (BHPS)

The BHPS was launched in 1991. It is being carried out by the Institute for Social and Economic Research (ISER), incorporating the ESRC Research Centre on Micro-Social Change at the University of Essex. The main objective of the survey is to further the understanding of social and economic change at the individual and household level in Britain, and to identify, model and forecast such changes, their causes and their consequences, in relation to a range of socio-economic variables.

It was designed as an annual survey of each adult member (aged 16 or older) of a nationally representative sample of more than 5,000 households, involving a total of approximately 10,000 individual interviews. The same individuals were re-interviewed in successive waves and, if they had split-off from their original households, all adult members of their new households were also interviewed. Children joined the sample once they reached the age of 16 (there is also a special survey of 11- to 15-year-old household members in waves 4 and 5). That is, the sample for the subsequent waves consisted of all adults in all households containing at least one member who was resident in a household interviewed at wave 1, regardless of whether that individual had been interviewed in wave 1. Thus, with a few exceptions, an attempt has been made to interview all those individuals in responding households who had refused to participate at wave 1, or for any reason had been unable to take part. In addition, a number of households where no contact had been made in wave 1 were approached for interview in wave 2 after confirmation that no household moves had taken place between waves.

The data collected covers a vast range of themes which are important for the social sciences: family composition; income; participation in the labour market; living conditions; education; health; use of Social Services; division of responsibilities within the family; the economic strategies and choices of the family nucleus; and, residential mobility. The questionnaire also asks for

Interviewed households and individual respondents by country[a] in BHPS (Wave 1 to Wave 7)

	England		Scotland		Wales		Total GB	
	Households	Households	Households	Households	Households	Households	Households	Households
1991	4,699	8,774	531	957	281	533	5,511	10,264
1992	4,457	8,406	508	927	260	510	5,225	9,843
1993	4,466	8,215	498	894	268	491	5,232	9,600
1994	4,365	8,099	489	873	273	509	5,127	9,841
1995	4,288	7,915	475	843	270	491	5,033	9,249
1996	4,342	8,134	452	823	269	480	5,063	9,437
1997	4,297	8,064	451	821	276	486	5,024	9,371

[a] Includes respondents with full individual interview or proxy interview

Source: http://www.iser.essex.ac.uk/bhps/rwsum.php

information about any changes that may have taken place within the nucleus since the last annual interview, in addition to retrospective information about the work, family and matrimonial histories of the subjects involved.

The research group which conducts the BHPS has recently created a file, the Work-Life History Project, which puts together prospective and retrospective data (gathered during the Wave 2) concerning the employment conditions and the work histories of those interviewed. This has made it possible to trace and reconstruct the occupational biographies of interviewees from the moment they entered the labour market up to the time of the most recent wave. More precisely, the Work-Life History Project is based on all sources of employment-status and occupational information in the BHPS. These files combine information concerning:

- the inter-wave job history (all waves)
- the main file for current individual status (all waves)
- retrospective occupational history (wave 3)
- retrospective employment-status history (wave 2)

The BHPS data are deposited in the UK Data Archive within 12 months of the completion of fieldwork. Between the end of fieldwork and the deposit date, the ISER carries out a full programme of data cleaning, missing value imputation and weighting. Data from release nine of the BHPS is now available from the Data Archive, incorporating the core data collected at each wave so far. In order to obtain access to BHPS data, potential users have to sign a form agreeing to respect the confidentiality of the data they obtain. The data are supplied free of charge – only the costs of any materials involved (photocopies, diskettes, etc) must be paid for.

- http://www.irc.essex.ac.uk/bhps/

European Community Household Panel (ECHP)

The ECHP is a source of community and regional level statistical information. Its objective is to supply the European Commission with an instrument for observing and monitoring the standard of living of the population in the member states of the EU during the process of convergence towards a monetary and political union. It presents comparable micro-level (households/persons) data on income, living conditions, housing, health and work in the EU. Although the questionnaire was designed centrally at Eurostat, in close consultation with each member state, it allowed enough flexibility to be able to adapt it to national specifications. Thus, the ECHP forms the most closely coordinated component of the European system of social surveys.

The study was launched in 1994, and is conducted in annual waves. It is based on a probability sample drawn from the EC member states, proportional to the size of each state's population. In the first wave (1994) a sample of some 61,000 nationally representative households – that is, approximately 130,000 adults aged 16 and over – were interviewed in the then 12 member states. Austria (in 1995) and Finland (in 1996) have since joined the project, with Sweden remaining the only exception. In wave 2, the EU-13 samples totalled some 60,000 households and 129,000 adults. The 1994-99 waves have been

Sample size and changes in the achieved sample size in ECHP[a]

Country	Wave 1 Number of households interviewed	Wave 2 Number of households interviewed	Wave 2 Achieved sample households interviewed
Belgium	4,189	4,012	3,748
Denmark	3,482	3,225	2,956
France	7,344	6,722	6,542
Germany	5,054	4,687	na
Greece	5,523	5,219	4,923
Ireland	4,048	3,548	3,179
Italy	7,115	7,128	na
Luxembourg	1,011	962	na
Netherlands	5,187	5,110	na
Portugal	4,881	4,916	4,955
Spain	7,206	6,521	6,277
UK	5,779	4,548	3,420
Austria		3,382	3,279
TOTAL (EU 12)	60,819	56,634	
TOTAL (EU 13)		60,016	

[a] In two countries (Italy and Portugal) the wave 2 achieved sample size exceeds the wave 1 sample: the formation of new sample households (split-off) exceeds the non-response in these countries. In most cases, wave 3 sample corresponds to 90-100 percent of the wave 2 sample, with the exceptions of Ireland and the UK.

Source: Eurostat (1997)

completed and the 2000 wave is in progress, although, so far, only the first three waves are available for research purposes.

The longitudinal panel design of the ECHP makes it possible to follow-up and interview the same private households and persons over several consecutive years. The members of the initial sample are studied throughout all the cycles of the survey, while new members can join the household, and any leavers are monitored if there is a change of residence within the EU. New household members are interviewed, as long as they belong to a household containing at least one sample person.

The ECHP started in 1991, when Eurostat – the Statistical Office of the European Communities – set up a Task Force on Household Incomes in order to respond to the strong need for information on household and individual income. The Task Force was mandated to assess, together with EU member states, the income data in registers and in existing national household surveys, and to check whether the available data could be satisfactorily harmonised ex-post. After the failure of this 'output approach', the decision was taken to launch a specific EU survey (the ECHP), to adopt an input-oriented approach rather than strictly try to harmonise existing outputs. ECHP data are collected by 'National Data Collection Units' (NDU), either National Statistical Institutes (NSI) or research centres depending on the country. Dissemination of the database is restricted at Eurostat's discretion.

In order to meet the increasing demand for ECHP-based statistics, and for having direct access to the data, Eurostat decided to develop, together with NDU, a set of rules allowing for easier direct access to 'anonymised' ECHP micro-data. In November 1997, Eurostat proposed to create a user-friendly and widely documented longitudinal users' database (UDB) that would meet various 'objective anonymisation criteria'. Only official requests for consultation are entertained and access is only permitted after payment of a sum which varies according to the category of each user (Marlier, 1999, see Chapter Three).

- http://www-rcade.dur.ac.uk/echp/
- http://www-rcade.dur.ac.uk/archive/3_echp2.htm

It is worth mentioning that there are EU funds available for researchers to visit ISER at Essex and CEPS/INSTEAD in Luxembourg to use UDB data. To visit ISER, one of the leading players in analysing the ECHP, and the UK NDU, researchers should send their application to the European Centre for Analysis in the Social Sciences (ECASS), an interdisciplinary research centre at the University of Essex within the ISER. ECASS is a centre for comparative and longitudinal data analysis, which conducts and facilitates the empirical study of social and economic change by integrating longitudinal and cross-national European datasets, providing the support services required for their analyses, and acting as the host for major substantive research programmes. ECASS visitors can collaborate with ISER researchers on its analysis. Researchers interested in UDB data could also visit CEPS/INSTEAD in Luxembourg through the bursaries offered by Integrated Research Infrastructure in the Social Sciences at CEPS/INSTEAD (IRISS-C/I). IRISS offers access to the facilities and resources of the institute.

- http://www.iser.essex.ac.uk/ecass/
- http://www.ceps.lu/iriss/iriss.htm

German Socio-Economic Panel (GSOEP)

The GSOEP is a wide-ranging representative longitudinal study of private households in Germany. In 1984, 5,921 households containing 12,290 people participated in the 'GSOEP West'. One thousand four hundred of these were headed by non-Germans – they constituted a separate sample of the immigrant component in the West German population, which immigrated in the 1960s and early 1970s. As early as June 1990, in other words, before currency, economic and social union, the survey was extended to include the territory of the former East Germany, where 2,179 households with 4,453 people were surveyed as the 'GSOEP East' sample. In 1994/95 a new immigrant sample was introduced.

The 1998 wave of the data includes 4,285 households with 8,145 people (GSOEP West), and 1,816 households with 3,730 people (GSOEP East). In 1998 (for the first time in 15 years) the GSOEP was extended by a supplementary

---

The GSOEP (as of 1995) contains data on four different subsamples. Each of these was drawn in a different multi-step random sampling process

A   *'West-German' residents: started in 1984*
- *n*=4,528 or 4,298 households[a]
- Head of household is either German or of another nationality than those in Sample B

B   *'Foreigners': started in 1984*
- *n*=1,393 or 1,326 households[a]
- Head of household is either Turkish, Italian, Spanish, Greek, or Yugoslavian

C   *'East-Germans': started in 1990*
- *n*=2,179 or 2,071 households[a]
- Head of household at the time of the survey was a citizen of the GDR

D   *'Immigrants'[b]: started in 1994/95 in two different subsamples*
- 1994: Subsample D1 with *n*=236 households
- 1995: Subsample D2 with *n*=295 households
- total in 1995 *n*=522 households (D1 and D2)
- At least one household member has moved from abroad to Germany after 1984

---

[a] The first number relates to the full 100% version, the second relates to the 95% public use version of the GSOEP data.

[b] This sample is not yet included in the 95% public use version.

Source: Frick (1998)

---

sample of 1,957 people in 1,079 households, in order to ensure stability of the case numbers; permit analysis of panel effects and survey non-response.

Thus, there are five subsamples:

- A and B (started in 1984) cover West Germany (prior to reunification).
- B (started in 1984) was deliberately intended to over-sample each of five nationalities of immigrants (Turkish, Greek, Yugoslavian, Spanish and Italian).
- C (started in 1990) represents the former East Germany.
- D (started in 1994/95) includes people living in private households in the western states of Germany in 1994 or 1995, and containing at least one household member who has moved to Germany from abroad after 1984.
- E (started in 1998) is a random, 'refreshment' sample covering all existing subsamples.

Once a year all members of the household aged 16 or older are questioned. Respondents who move continue to take part in the study as long as the move is within West Germany (prior to reunification this did not include East Germany).

The data supply information about both objective and subjective living conditions, the process of change in various areas of life, and about the links between these areas and the changes themselves. Indeed, the GSOEP covers a wide range of subjects including: household composition; occupational and family biographies; employment and professional mobility; earnings; health and personal satisfaction. In addition, the survey modules cover other topics such as social security, education and training, allocation of time, family, and social services.

The GSOEP was founded as a project of the Special Research Area 3 'Microanalytical Basis of Social Politics' at the universities of Frankfurt (Main) and Mannheim. It is independently funded through the Deutsche Forschungsgemeinschaft (DFG), or German National Science Foundation, and located at the German Institute for Economic Research (DIW) in Berlin. In cooperation with the DIW, the Center for Policy Research at Syracuse University has prepared an English language public use version of the GSOEP, representing a 95% sample of the original data for use by the international research community. The public use file of the GSOEP with anonymous micro-data is provided free of charge to universities and research centres. However, the use of the data is subjected to special regulations. In order to get the GSOEP data, the potential user first has to sign a data transfer contract with the DIW. Once the contract has been signed, the user will receive the data. GSOEP data are disseminated in several formats, such as SAS, STATA, SPSS, ASCII and TDA, all on CD-ROM. Training workshops for GSOEP users are held annually in Germany and abroad.

- http://www.diw.de/english/sop/index.html
- http://www.diw.de/english/sop/uebersicht/

Household Market and Non-Market Activities (HUS)

The Swedish HUS project began in 1980. In 1984 the first main survey was carried out, a comprehensive interview survey that was followed by smaller surveys in 1986, 1988, 1991, 1993, 1996 and 1998. Refresher samples were also added to the panel in 1986, 1993, 1996 and 1998. Data cover many topics, the most important being:

- labour market experiences
- earnings
- socio-economic background
- childcare
- wealth

- current employment
- schooling
- housing
- incomes and taxes
- time-use

Event history data are available for labour market events, household changes, childcare and housing.

The 1984 survey was based on a random sample of about 2,600 households. This sample excluded people aged 75 or older, those who lived in institutions or abroad, and those who did not speak Swedish well enough to be interviewed. In households with two spouses both spouses were interviewed. In some households a third adult was also interviewed. Until 1998 data from all first-time respondents were collected in face-to-face interviews using [paper and pencil?] questionnaires. Since 1998, however, all data from panel members have been collected in computer-assisted telephone interviews (CATI).

In 1986, the 1984 sample was interviewed once more. This time a telephone interview was conducted to obtain information on changes in family composition, housing, employment, wages and childcare. As a complement to the panel, a new supplementary sample of households was interviewed. The supplement consisted partly of the members of the 1984 households who were over 18 or who had moved in with someone included in the 1984 sample, and partly of a new random sample of some 800 households. The individuals included in the supplement were asked very similar questions to the 1984 personal interview.

The 1988 survey was considerably smaller than the previous ones. It was addressed only to participants in the 1986 survey, and consisted of a self-enumerated questionnaire with a non-respondent follow-up by telephone.

In 1991, another self-enumerated questionnaire was administered to the panel. An attempt was also made to include the new household members who had moved into sample households since 1986, as well as the young people who had turned 18 after the 1986 survey.

With respect to its design and content, the 1993 survey was an updated version of the 1986 survey. It was made up of four parts: (1) the panel survey, which was addressed mainly to respondents in the 1991 survey, with some additions; (2) the supplementary survey, which focused on a new random sample of individuals; (3) the non-response survey, which encompassed respondents who had participated in at least one of the earlier surveys but had since dropped

Effective HUS sample size (net of non-response) by wave and sample

Wave	Sample	Number of individuals
1984		2,619
1986	Panel	1,949
1986	Refresher	1,014
1988	Panel	2,297
1991	Panel	2,052
1993	Panel	1,811
1993	Refresher	1,643
1993	Non-response	733
1996	Panel	2,963
1996	Refresher	276
1998	Panel	2,347
1998	Refresher	1,565

Source: http://www.isr.umich.edu/src/psid/inventory_table_links/swedish_overview.do.htm

out; and (4) the time-use survey, which included the same sample of respondents as those in the panel, and supplementary surveys (Klevmarken and Olovsson, 1993; Flood et al, 1997). Time-use interviews were conducted in 1984 and in 1993.

HUS data can only be used for academic research, and are only available in anonymous form. Each user must sign a contract stipulating that data will only be used for research and that the user will not publish or otherwise make public data for single individuals or households, or try to identify the respondents. A general description of the HUS surveys, code-books, test dataset, and instructions as to getting access to data are available at:

• http://www.handels.gu.se/econ/econometrics/hus/husin.htm

Datasets are distributed as zip-files attached to an email message, or on diskettes by regular mail. HUS data can also be obtained from Swedish Social Science Data Service (SSD), Göteborg University (*http://www.ssd.gu.se*). Data and code-books are then distributed on CD. Normally HUS data are distributed as SAS-files. The latest files distributed from the SSD are in a more general format (ASIDE), readable by all computers.

The details of the surveys have been documented in a set of code-books. Interviewing is in Swedish and there is a Swedish code-book for each wave and sample, available as Word-files. Translations into English are currently available. For the period 1984-93 there are also printed code-books in English. All data files and documentation can be obtained at a service charge of approximately 500 USD.

• http://cent.hgus.gu.se/econ/econometrics/hus/husin.htm
• http://cent.hgus.gu.se/econ/econometrics/hus/order/husorder.htm
• http://www.ssd.gu.se/enghome.html

Labour Force Survey (LFS)

The LFS surveys households living at private addresses in the UK. It has been collected since 1973 under a Regulation derived from the Treaty of Rome. The LFS aims to provide information on the UK labour market for international comparisons, but also contains detailed questions of national interest. It is carried out by the Social Survey Division of the Office for National Statistics in Great Britain, and by the Central Survey Unit of the Department of Finance and Personnel in Northern Ireland, on behalf of the Department of Economic Development. The LFS was conducted biennially from 1973 to 1983 (in Great Britain and Northern Ireland), and annually from 1984 to 1991 for Great Britain, and from 1984 till 1994 for Northern Ireland. The Quarterly Labour Force Survey (QLFS), designed on a rotating quarterly panel, has been conducted since the spring of 1992 for Britain, and from the winter of 1994/95 for Northern Ireland. Every quarter is made up of five 'waves', each of which contains about 12,000 selected households. The households are interviewed in five successive waves. Accordingly, at any one time, each quarter will contain one wave receiving the first interview, one wave the second interview, and so on, until the fifth interview. Since it is a panel study, the response rates decrease from the first interview to the next. Households which refuse further participation are not revisited at the next quarter. Nonetheless the response rates are quite high in the first wave (78-79% for 1998-99).

The LFS collects data on all members of the household, allowing us to analyse at both/either the individual and/or household level. Each adult in the household (aged 16 or over) is asked detailed information regarding economic activity, main job, secondary job, unemployment, under-employment, benefit entitlement, education and training, health and income. The rich information in the LFS enables researchers to investigate a wide range of labour market issues. Its large sample size enables smaller specific subgroups to be examined. Furthermore, the panel element also allows research into short-term change.

- http://www.mimas.ac.uk/surveys/lfs/
- http://www.mimas.ac.uk/surveys/qlfs/

National Child Development Study (NCDS)

The NCDS is a longitudinal birth cohort study of those living in Britain who were born in the week 3-9 March 1958. To date, there have been six sweeps to trace all members of the birth cohort in order to monitor their physical, educational and social development: NCDS1 in 1965 (at age 7); NCDS2 in 1969 (at age 11); NCDS3 in 1974 (at age 16); NCDS4 in 1981 (at age 23); and NCDS5 in 1991 (at age 33). In addition contact was made in 1978 with the schools they had attended. A sixth sweep was conducted in 1999. The initial sample size was 17,414, although the number of participants in NCDS5 (1991) was 11,400. Attempts have been made to augment the sample to include additional information and also new immigrants to Britain who were born in the relevant week in 1958. Immigrants were identified from school registers and added to the sample at age 11 and 16. A number of specialised follow-up studies have also been carried out, such as that revealing respiratory illness symptoms in the 1981 and 1991 surveys.

The NCDS is used for a wide range of research, including medical/health research. The data covers a long period of time, and includes a wide range of questions and physical information, such as weight and height. The aim of the study is to improve understanding of the factors affecting human development over the whole lifespan. The NCDS also supports much relevant information in investigating women's employment issues – qualifications, employment, occupation, earnings and income, and family composition. Also it contains retrospective information on marriage, fertility, employment and housing histories.

The study was initially sponsored by the National Birthday Trust Fund; follow-up studies have been undertaken by the National Children's Bureau and the Social Statistics Research Unit, City University (now known as the Centre for Longitudinal Studies (CLS) and based at the Institute of Education, University of London). Sponsorship for the 1981 and 1991 surveys came from Government departments and ESRC and, for 1991, the US National Institute for Child Health and Development. The data are publicly available through the UK Data Archive at the University of Essex, and on-line at MIMAS (Manchester InforMation and Associated Services) and are well documented for secondary analysis.

- http://www.cls.ioe.ac.uk/Ncds/nintro.htm
- http://www.cls.ioe.ac.uk/Ncds/narchive.htm
- http://www.mimas.ac.uk/surveys/ncds/
- http://www.mimas.ac.uk/surveys/ncds/ncds_info.html

Organisatie voor Strategisch Arbeidsmarktonderzoek (OSA)

The OSA has conducted the biennial OSA Labour Supply Panel every two years since 1985 to collect data about the (potential) labour force in the Netherlands. The Supply Panel targets persons aged between 16 and 65, who are not pursuing daytime education. It is aimed at finding out about respondents' employment situation, and about their behaviour on the labour market. Also, information is collected about aspects that may be expected to influence subjects' decisions to participate in the labour market.

The sample is selected from the total number of households in the Netherlands. Subsequently, all members of the households in the sample that can be regarded as (potential) members of the labour force are interviewed. To guarantee continuity, households that have been involved in previous surveys are eligible for participation in subsequent waves. In order to limit the decrease in the

Number of cases in the OSA Labour Supply Panel

Questionnaire	1985	1986	1988	1990	1992	1994	1996	1998
Participation	4,020	4,115	4,464	4,438	4,536	4,538	4,563	4,780
Year								
1985	4,020	2,755	1,974	1,432	1,072	904	661	505
1986		1,360	1.201	751	584	407	346	263
1988			1,469	988	711	560	438	329
1990				1,267	890	678	476	332
1992					1,279	869	578	388
1994						1,119	754	500
1996							1,310	867
1998								1,596

Source: http://osa.kub.nl/osa_eng/datasets/e6_2_1.html

overall response rate, respondents who are unwilling or unable to take part in future surveys are replaced by new respondents, selected on the basis of characteristics of non-responding households.

Questions relate to:

- personal characteristics, such as gender, date of birth, or country of birth
- social background: information about the respondent's parents
- educational background: level and specialisation (5 digit SOI), period education was followed, date of diploma
- attitudes towards employment

- familial characteristics: marital status, number of children
- sources of income other than employment
- employment background: date, type of and reason for change of job, and, until the sixth wave, type of and reason for every change of job, number of hours of employment per week (if employed), and income

Moreover, respondents who are currently employed answer questions related to their current job, while respondents who are looking for a job are asked questions which aim to investigate topics such as: length of time unemployed; job-searching behaviour, amount of effort/frequency; opportunities for finding work; desired and expected salary; type of occupation being applied for.

The OSA Labour Supply database is available for secondary analysis. However, there are a number of access conditions; information can be obtained directly from OSA.

- http://osa.kub.nl/osa_eng/datasets/e6_2_1.html

Television Industry Tracking Study (ITS)

The British Film Institute began the ITS, a longitudinal panel study, in 1994 to examine the impact of structural changes in the television industry on individual production workers. The research was funded initially by the Hoso Bunka Foundation and Skillset. The later stages of the project were supported by a grant from the Economic and Social Research Council to the Judge Institute of Management Studies at the University of Cambridge, and the British Film Institute.

Data were collected by means of a postal questionnaire at six-monthly intervals between 1994 and 1998. Questionnaires were sent to 533 individuals aged between 21 and 65 who were employed in all sectors of the television industry. A response rate of 81% was achieved at the first wave, resulting in 436 cases, 56% of whom were men and 44% women. The sample was drawn primarily from lists of creative workers supplied by broadcasters, the Producers Alliance in Film and Television (PACT), British Film Institute contacts and a self-selected sample from an earlier project entitled 'A Day in the Life of Television'. Respondents were employed in a range of occupations including producer, director, managerial and executive posts, production support, writer, journalist and technical posts. While not a random sample, the generated panel was regarded by the British Film Institute as representative of the range of occupations and employment statuses in the UK television industry.

The data contains demographic details and career histories. A set of core questions collected information about employment status, occupation and recent projects at each wave, while questions relating to creativity and production issues were included once or at later intervals. The rate of attrition was particularly high among young people and in response a new panel of 50 people aged between 21 and 30 was recruited in November 1996.

Women and Employment Survey (WES)

The WES was commissioned by the Department of Employment and carried out jointly by the Office for Population Censuses and Surveys (OPCS) and the Department of Employment. The fieldwork took place in 1980 and was carried out by the Social Survey Division, OPCS. The survey covered a nationally representative probability sample of 5,588 women in Great Britain aged 16-59, and the husbands of 799 of the married women. The response rate to the main survey was 83%. Interviewers carried out short screening interviews at a sample of 9,944 addresses in order to identify women within the eligible age range who were then approached for the full interview.

The main aims of the survey were to establish what factors determine whether or not women are in paid work and to identify the degree to which domestic factors and the sexual division of labour shape women's lifetime labour market involvement. In addition, it aimed to collect full information about the work that women do, their pay and conditions of employment, as well as the way they behave in the labour market when they leave jobs or look for work. The study also set out to determine the importance of work to women and their job priorities.

An important and innovative feature of the survey was the collection of detailed work histories covering the whole of women's working lives since leaving full-time education, and detailed histories of other vital events, such as the births of children, which were likely to have consequences for women's labour market behaviour. Major topics covered by WES are:

- current economic activity
- childcare arrangements
- education and training
- reasons for not working
- work and life histories
- general attitudes to employment and gender roles

- details of current job
- attitudes to work
- future employment plans
- job search activities
- details of husbands' work and attitudes;
- financial circumstances
(Martin and Roberts, 1984a, 1984b)

- http://qb.soc.surrey.ac.uk/surveys/wes/wesintro.htm

References

Flood, L., Klevmarken, A. and Olovsson, P. (1997) *Household market and non-market activities (HUS), Survey Description*, vol III, Uppsala: Department of Economics, Uppsala University.

Klevmarken, A. and Olovsson, P. (1993) *Household market and non-market activities (HUS), Procedures and Codes 1984–1991*, Stockholm: Industrial Institute for Economic and Social Research.

Marlier, E. (1999) *The EC Household Panel Newsletter*, Statistics in Focus, Population and Social Conditions, Theme 3, no 2, Luxembourg: Eurostat.

Martin, J. and Roberts, C. (1984a) *Women and employment: A lifetime perspective*, London: HMSO.

Martin, J. and Roberts, C. (1984b) *Women and employment: technical report*, London: OPCS.

Index

Page references for boxes, figures and tables are in *italics*; those for notes are followed by n